AfroAsian Encounters

AfroAsian Encounters

Culture, History, Politics

EDITED BY

Heike Raphael-Hernandez and Shannon Steen

*with Foreword by Vijay Prashad and
Afterword by Gary Okihiro*

New York University Press

NEW YORK AND LONDON

NEW YORK UNIVERSITY PRESS
New York and London
www.nyupress.org

Library of Congress Cataloging-in-Publication Data
AfroAsian encounters : culture, history, politics / edited by Heike Raphael-
Hernandez and Shannon Steen ; with a foreword by Vijay Prashad and an
afterword by Gary Okihiro.
p. cm.
Includes bibliographical references and index.
ISBN-13: 978-0-8147-7580-6 (cloth : alk. paper)
ISBN-10: 0-8147-7580-2 (cloth : alk. paper)
ISBN-13: 978-0-8147-7581-3 (pbk. : alk. paper)
ISBN-10: 0-8147-7581-0 (pbk. : alk. paper)
1. African Americans—Relations with Asian Americans. 2. African Ameri-
cans—Intellectual life. 3. Asian Americans—Intellectual life. 4. Blacks—
America—Intellectual life. 5. Asians—America Intellectual life. 6.
Ethnicity—America. 7. United States—Race relations. 8. America—Race
relations. 9. United States—Intellectual life. 10. America—Intellectual life.
I. Raphael-Hernandez, Heike. II. Steen, Shannon. III. Title: Afro Asian
encounters.
E185.615.A5935 2006
305.895'073—dc22   2006016122

New York University Press books are printed on acid-free paper,
and their binding materials are chosen for strength and durability.

Manufactured in the United States of America
c 10 9 8 7 6 5 4 3 2 1
p 10 9 8 7 6 5 4 3 2 1

Contents

Acknowledgments

As is always the case, this volume owes a large debt to a wide range of people who showed their genuine interest in the fundamental ideas of *AfroAsian Encounters* and participated with challenging discussions at many different sites and occasions. The inspiration for the project came, for Shannon, from a seminar with Harry Elam, without whom her area of research would never have materialized. Paul Spickard provided the initial impetus for our first panel at CAAR (Colloquium for African American Research) at Winchester, England, in the spring of 2003. We are grateful for the feedback from that audience, as well as that from subsequent audiences at the American Studies Association meeting at Atlanta and the MESEA (Society for Multi-Ethnic Studies: Europe and the Americas) conference at Thessaloniki, Greece, both in 2004. The enthusiasm we encountered in those venues, as well as that at the Afro-Asian Century Conference at Boston University in 2004, convinced us of the need for this anthology.

We have also been the beneficiaries of a series of wonderful editors who saw us through the publishing process. Early in the process, we were supported by Karen Wolny, Graham Hodges, and Deborah Gershenowitz, who gave us the kind of enthusiastic response we needed to get the project off the ground. Emily Park at New York University Press was a terrific champion of the volume and did an amazing amount of work for us, almost invisibly. Denise Sokolowski, the head librarian at the University of Maryland University College in Europe, provided invaluable aid in tracking down elusive materials and citations for us. Deborah Paredez gave us crucial feedback on an early draft of the introduction, for which we are grateful. Yet, we owe our largest debt to our contributors, without whose energy, commitment, and excellent work this volume would not exist.

And, like all writers, we are indebted to those closest to us, who have seen us through the day-to-day neuroses of writing and who have furnished much-needed release from them. We owe to Don, Markus, Jakob, and Jonathan Hernandez and Arun Patel for their patience, love, warmth, humor, and companionship. Our deepest thanks and love to them.

Bandung Is Done
Passages in AfroAsian Epistemology

Vijay Prashad

One evening in early 1955, the African American writer Richard Wright picked up his evening newspaper. He casually glanced over the items but was stopped by one notice. In far off Indonesia, representatives from twenty-nine newly liberated countries in Africa and Asia planned to gather for a conference. Wright rushed to tell his wife, the Communist Ellen Poplar, that he wished to attend the conference and write about it. When Poplar read the article, she exclaimed, "Why, that's the human race," for, indeed, not only did the twenty-nine nations include a vast amount of humanity but also its agenda (disarmament and cooperation) articulated the hopes of the majority. Wright agreed. He wanted to write about it because he knew that writers from the advanced industrial states frequently displaced the actual voices of liberation from the new nations. The journalists spoke of the new nations, often even against them, but they did not give them room to speak themselves. Wright wanted to remedy that: "I know that people are tired of hearing of these hot, muddy faraway places filled with people yelling for freedom. But this is the human race speaking." The book that Wright produced from his trip, *The Color Curtain,* inaugurates our tradition of AfroAsian studies.[1]

Richard Wright was no stranger to the dynamic that would unfold at Bandung. He understood the desire of a people for freedom from his own life and experiences, and he already had contacts with the leaders from the darker nations who would meet at Bandung. Indeed, Wright's political life after he removed himself from the United States in July 1947 intersected frequently with the dynamic of Bandung. In Paris, Wright met the major figures of *negritude,* Aimé Césaire and Leopold Senghor, and the two main political figures of Pan-Africanism, George Padmore and Kwame

Nkrumah. When it had become clear that Nkrumah's political movement would wrest power in Ghana (the Gold Coast), Wright traveled to western Africa, and in the year before Bandung he published his reflections on the possibilities of postcolonialism, tempered by the lure of suppressed traditions (*Black Power: A Record of Reactions in a Land of Pathos*). Wright's own biography intersects partly with that of the Bandung dynamic that developed in the byways of the struggle against colonialism.

At the League against Imperialism meeting in Brussels in 1928, leaders from three continents (Africa, Asia, and South America) had already discussed their discrete ailments and had crafted common dreams. They had heard of each other's struggles and had found that they had come to similar strategic and ideological conclusions. When independence finally dawned in the 1940s and 1950s, the leaders of the various national liberation movements took comfort in the successes of each other. At Bandung, these leaders met and forged an agenda for the international arena in opposition to the "freedom" of advanced capitalism (the First World) and to the "leadership" of the Soviet Union (the Second World). As the Third World, these regimes sought to produce international cooperation for the widest possible development over narrow economic profit and for peace over nuclear confrontation. This energy appealed to Richard Wright.[2]

As the host of the Bandung Conference, Indonesia's President Achmet Sukarno welcomed the delegates and reminded them of the basis for Afro-Asian unity: "We are of many different nations, we are of many different social backgrounds and cultural patterns. Our ways of life are different. Our national characters, or colors or motifs—call it what you will—are different. Our racial stock is different, and even the color of our skin is different." All this is true, but "what does that matter?" What united Africa and Asia, Sukarno noted, was "a common detestation of colonialism in whatever form it appears . . . a common detestation of racialism . . . a common determination to preserve and stabilize peace in the world."[3]

Richard Wright sat in the hall, mesmerized by the proceedings. As he listened to Sukarno, he later wrote, "I began to sense a deep and organic relation here in Bandung between race and religion, *two of the most powerful and irrational forces in human nature.* Sukarno was not evoking these twin demons; he was not trying to create them; he was trying to organize them. . . . The reality of race and religion was there, swollen, sensitive, turbulent."[4] Social traditions and identities had to be worn through, dealt with, reorganized. They could not be ignored or discarded. For Sukarno, and Wright, the foundation of AfroAsian solidarity could not be in these skins, for they had to be the carapace to be outgrown.

The displacement from the Bandung political quake flooded over into political movements within the advanced industrial states, as well as across the formerly colonized world. Examples within the United States of this are abundant: there is the fierce attempt to forge commonality among the Black Panthers, the Red Guard, and the Young Lords, and there is the example of the Third World Women's Alliance (TWWA). These movements identified themselves as the "Third World" in political solidarity with that dynamic of national liberation, whether it emerged from the Bandung currents or the courage of the barefoot Vietnamese and Guinean-Bissau liberation warriors.[5] Yuri Kochiyama, the radical activist, offers the history of AfroAsian connection on this very platform, to learn each other's combined histories to break down "barriers, obstacles and phobias."[6] Bandung provided a major inspiration as well as an epistemological framework for those early scholars and activists who worked both to forge connections across lines of artificial, but historical, race and to study the history of these interactions. In chapbooks and in political journals, in solidarity marches and in the margins of books, these interactions became important for their union in a planetary anticolonialist struggle.[7]

Fifty years have passed since Bandung, and much has changed since then.[8] Freedom's future lay within the project of the national liberation state. With the cannibalization of the state under dictates from the International Monetary Fund (IMF), the national liberation agenda has been largely compromised. Most of the formerly colonized and subjugated nations produced minimally processed raw materials for the world market, and because of the unfair term of trade that would prevail as a result of this historical disadvantage, these countries would always be indebted to their former colonial and now current imperial overlords. To break out of this vise, the new nations needed capital. With few resources, these countries first had to borrow and then went into debt. Into the breech came the IMF, with an agenda not simply to create fiscal stability but to overturn the national liberation and Third World agenda of state construction and to subjugate the darker nations to capitalist globalization. A major consequence of the disembowelment of the state was that "nationalism" itself became transformed. The secular anticolonial Bandung era nationalism fell before the rise of a cruel cultural nationalism that drew on forms of social solidarity provided by either religion, reconstructed racism, or undiluted class power.

AfroAsian solidarity emerged in that Bandung epoch as a political platform both against the cruelty of the past and against colonialism "in its
modern dress."[9] The foundation for that solidarity is now largely eroded,
with Africa and Asia interested in each other's resources and capital, where
the bold pronouncements for a radical reconfiguration of the international political economy has vanished. In this atmosphere, the excavations
of AfroAsian solidarity might be nostalgic, anachronistic, or even aesthetic. My initial impulse a decade ago to write about these interactions
drew largely from nostalgia for a type of political platform that had been
available in an earlier time. I recognize that it was a platform flawed in
many ways, as national liberation itself is suffused with all manner of limitations, but it is certainly true that motion existed then where history
does not seem to move now. In the epoch of structural adjustment, where
struggle against it in the advanced industrial states is episodic, the consideration of AfroAsian interaction might lean toward a nostalgic pessimism.

But nostalgia is a far better entry point into the world of AfroAsian traffic than the process of commodification. From the late 1990s onward, Hollywood has provided a series of products that marry an African American
with an Asian artist—whether *Rush Hour* with Chris Tucker and Jackie
Chan or *Martial Law* with Arsenio Hall and Sammo Hung. This sort of
interaction is premised almost entirely on the colorblind capitalists' desire
to make the most of two ethnic niche markets. When Truth Hurts and
Missie Elliot draw songs and rhythms from Bollywood, their producers do
not necessarily want to make the most of two markets as much as they follow the hip-hop ethos to mine cultural worlds for the phat beat. These links
are made opportunistically or aesthetically, but not politically.

Scholarship on AfroAsian worlds emerged in the late 1970s after the
era of Bandung had ended. It did not take place in departments of area
studies—those that had been set up in the first five decades of the twentieth century to study "areas" of the world such as Africa, East Asia, Near
East, South Asia, and Latin America. The epistemology of these area
studies had its roots in the U.S. strategy during the Cold War to study
these regions of the world for their potential for modernization and for
alliances against the spread of communism.[10] Bewildered by the loss of
their raison d'être at the end of the Cold War, area studies practitioners
hunkered down to do the same sorts of things as they always did: textual
work of the ancient world and international relations of the new. The
field continued to operate with a modernization theory narrative, even as
the political economy of the theory had somewhat disappeared. One

fragment of area studies adopted the idea of transnationalism, or diaspora, to try to locate itself in the new "globalized" framework, although
it did not attempt to articulate its work with that of the Bandung
dynamic. Rather, it attempted to be the mirror of corporate globalization
and to offer marginal liberal criticisms of the post–Cold War international political economy.

Interest in AfroAsian traffic within the United States did not develop in
these area studies programs during the heyday of Bandung. To be fair, the
only English-language nonofficial collection of speeches from the Bandung Conference did come from the precincts of an area studies program; it was edited by the Indonesia specialist George McTuran Kahin, the
associate director of the Southeast Asia program at Cornell University.
Nevertheless, little had been written about the fallout from this conference, and few of the studies that came from the pen of area studies researchers followed the implications of the Bandung dynamic. Area studies
in the United States ignored what could have been a fertile area of investigation—the cultural and political intersections across the artificial geopolitical and academic areas that had come to divide the world.

Instead, the study of AfroAsia within the United States emerged in
ethnic studies programs, either in African American (Black) studies or in
Asian American studies. From the late 1960s to the mid-1990s, however,
the output in ethnic studies was motivated by an epistemology that suffered from similar "area" problems as area studies. To understand why and
how AfroAsian matters entered ethnic studies, it behooves us to trace the
contours of this field of study. Forged in the late 1960s with a social justice
ethos, ethnic studies had become victim to its own epistemology. Early
texts in Black studies and Asian American studies had worked on the terrain of inclusion: the scholarship sought to include the contributions of
the excluded peoples into the narrative of the nation, and it sought to win
its adherents inclusion into the institutions of the state and society as
equal participants. Tremendous feats of scholarship produced high-quality
work that unearthed buried stories. Pioneers created festivals, museums,
textbooks, and other special artifacts to highlight this work, to knock hard
on the doors of the academy and of society to let in the complex stories
that had been written out of it.

The work bore fruit, but not without student revolts across the country
to demand ethnic studies. From the 1968 Third World strike at San Francisco State University to the 1996 hunger strike for ethnic studies at Columbia University, students went at administrations to demand that the

curriculum open itself up to worlds and epistemologies outside the studies authorized by white supremacy. Some student organizations recognized the enormous stakes of what they demanded. At San Francisco State, for instance, the Black Students' Union proposed that the Black studies department be autonomous from the structure of the rest of the departments because, otherwise, it would be prone to incorporation. Their proposal wanted to give the Black studies faculty power over themselves, both in the hiring of faculty and in their firing. They "knew that black studies could not be complacent," wrote Robert Allen in his *Black Awakening in Capitalist America*, "that it must be consciously disruptive, always seeking to expose and cut away those aspects of American society that oppress black people; that it could not be modeled after other departments and accept the constraints imposed on them, because one function of these departments is to socialize students into a racist and oppressive society."[11] The students wanted a department, and they wanted it on revolutionary terms. They wanted to create a department based on a culture of solidarity, in a way similar to what had been envisioned by proponents of women's studies, who argued that "changes in the *content* of the curriculum . . . be correlated with changes in the *form* of instruction," and indeed of the institution.[12]

Power naturally denied these terms. Instead of this autonomous anti-subordination, power adopted a milquetoast version, which we now know as bureaucratic multiculturalism. The university authorities reinterpreted antiracism as the promotion of diversity and shook out any epoch-changing elements as it institutionalized difference. It threw money at students of color to finance our canalized organizations and our various cultural festivals. The content of these festivals would often be highly bourgeois and generally patriarchal and heterosexist. Radical traditions within the world of color would be cast out in favor of traditional social forms that appealed to authority and order. The curriculum began to adopt a pleasant attitude toward the discrete cultural histories of different parts of the world—but, like the older area studies, the new ethnic studies had to operate with the assumption that "European" or "White" culture and history had a separate dynamic than that of the rest of the world. Africa could be taught in schools only if one did not get too obsessive about its contributions to the world, about European colonialism, and about corporate imperialism. Multiculturalism embraced bourgeois cultural diversity as long as white supremacy and corporate power could be set aside and generally left out of any discussion. Colleges would learn to be tolerant of differ-

ences, while social movements would have to forgo any demand for substantial change in the system. Bureaucratic multiculturalism, in the main,
operated entirely within the institutional culture of hierarchy.

Since the university is a crucial institution for the creation and reproduction of culture, and given the role of bureaucratic multiculturalism,
students of color on campus increasingly began to experience the discourse of diversity in upward mobility terms. In 1969, Robert Allen pro-
phetically warned in terms that might be archaic but with a vision that is
meaningful in our context: "The black student is crucial to corporate
America's neocolonial plans. It is the educated and trained blacks who are
slated to become the new managers of the ghetto, the administrators of
the black colony."[13] What Allen wrote then is banal now, for in its 2001
deposition on behalf of affirmative action, a group of Fortune 500 companies made just this point. For them, "today's global marketplace and the
increasing diversity in the American population demand the cross-cultural experience and understanding gained from such an education."[14]
Why must businesses hire a section of managers of color?

> [As the population becomes diverse,] the individuals who run and staff the
> [Fortune 500] businesses must be able to understand, learn from, collabo-
> rate with, and design products and services for clientele and associates from
> diverse racial, ethnic and cultural backgrounds. American multinational
> businesses . . . are especially attuned to this concern because they serve not
> only the increasingly diverse population of the United States, but racially
> and ethnically diverse populations around the world.[15]

The desire for the student of color to become the comprador figure for
global capital is now established.

On college campuses, indeed, this has immense implications for ethnic
studies. The culture of upwardly mobile racialism runs counter to the values of ethnic studies, and yet the epistemology of pluralism in the latter
tends to facilitate the former. Our classes fill up with brave students who
read longingly about the origins of the social movements of identity,
but whose own social location makes those struggles romantically distant.
The students carry an enormous load when they walk into ethnic studies
classes: they are burdened by vast amounts of debt, by the indignity of
everyday prejudice, and by the expectations from a family that is so happy
to see them in college (often as the first generation in college). These pressures drive our students to turn to subjects with a higher rate of return

than antisubordination theory. Often these students are double majors, hard at work in both engineering and ethnic studies. These pressures are complex, and while they move our students toward the logic of inclusion into the system, this dynamic is not always pleasantly accepted. The multicultural academy in our neoliberal world has let down this generation of young students, whose own instincts are not being enabled by these burdens.

What has happened on the college campus is venally replicated at the highest political levels. During the Clinton administration, people of color entered high government offices and the national story learned to incorporate the efforts of our ancestors. But the inclusion had come at a significant price: while a few individuals entered high office, the structures of white supremacy largely remained. The systematic racism against people of color was not altered by the inclusion of a small elect class of color, or by the inclusion of migrants who came with state-produced skills from elsewhere. Indeed, it can be argued that George W. Bush recruited a number of people of color into his cabinet not simply for their skills (for they are skillful people), nor to attract their ethnic constituency, but to ensure that wavering white voters not see him and his circle as the epitome of white supremacy. Outright racism is now illegitimate, so the window dressing allows the racist agenda of Bush to be cloaked for the white suburban voter. This limited inclusion presented all that the system could provide without major social transformation, and the minimal is all that occurred.

The doctrine of pluralist inclusion ran its course by the early 1990s: to document suffering and striving did not necessarily touch on the fundamental elements of subordination, as the symbolic gains of some could be used by power to dissuade any movement demands on the system. It is in this context of the incorporation of multiculturalism that scholars in ethnic studies turned to the interaction between subordinated groups (although this work had been done before in small circles, and without much fanfare). An early approach, by Asian American literary critic Yen Le Espiritu, investigated the phenomenon of "pan-ethnicity," which developed the idea of "racial formations" proposed by sociologists Howard Winant and Michael Omi. These epistemological frameworks proposed that scholars look at "racial" categories as political projects that emerge due to a host of reasons and that are mobilized for a variety of purposes. "Asian American" and "Latino" are very good examples because here we have terms that have little historical resonance and yet take on a life of their own. "Panethnic groups," Espiritu notes, "are products of political and social processes, rather than cultural bonds."[16] The Vietnamese and Burmese might not share much in terms of cultural heritage and practice, but in the United States, Vietnamese Americans and Burmese Americans have a conceptual unity (as having ancestors from "Asia") and an organizational unity (in Asian American groups) that produce them as Asian American. This epistemological move on the part of ethnic studies scholars allowed the idea of "culture" to be seen as political, something refused by mainline multiculturalism. For Espiritu, the concept of pan-ethnicity allows Asian Americans to "contest systems of racism, and inequality in American society . . . in contrast to ethnic particularism or assimilation."[17] The problem and possibility of internal heterogeneity provides the pan-ethnic concept with a combustible charge—no one can rest easy within a category that is always already "un-natural." That instability does not allow the category to become reduced to "culture."

To insist that identity categories are political and not natural-cultural opens many possibilities, but this is not a sufficient exit from the traps set by the ideology of bureaucratic multiculturalism. Self-consciously constructed communities could also operate for inclusion and upward mobility at the cost of others. The most painful example of this is in how Asian Americans frequently mobilize the discourse of the "model minority" to our benefit. In the 1960s, as the U.S. government welcomed highly skilled Asian immigrants into the country (and kept out Asians with fewer technical skills), the media, egged on by elected officials, compared the experiences of Asians to African Americans. The specific context for this comparison was the provision of social welfare schemes for the newly enfranchised populations of color, who had only now been allowed entry into the five-decade-long social wage schemes. Since the Civil Rights Act had made it impossible to block people of color, notably African Americans, from access to the aspects of the welfare state, the media and the politicians began to denigrate them for their use of these services. Asians did not use them, so why should African Americans? The Asian American, like the Jewish American ten years before, had become the "model minority" for those who would deign to access their rights. That Asians had benefited because of state selection (and not natural selection) did not interfere with this racist narrative. To champion Asian America without a well-developed understanding of this scenario would result in a collapse of one's multicultural pride in anti-Black racism. This is why one has to tread carefully in the discourse of bureaucratic multiculturalism. Is it capable of being cognizant of such slippages?

The interrogation of the relations between African Americans and Asian Americans, both seen as political-cultural identities, occurred after two major conflagrations inflamed their communities: the so-called Black-Korean riots of 1991 and 1992 in Crown Heights and Los Angeles. In the aftermath of these very complex phenomena, scholars mined the histories of both Blacks and Koreans (as well as Asian Americans in general) to un-derstand their roots and to see if such confrontations were to be expected. At the same time, spectacularly in 1992 at Lowell High School in San Francisco and in the 1990s fiasco over college admission, debates over entry into school set African American students against Asian American students. This debate over affirmative action on campus provoked discussions in already beleaguered ethnic studies programs: the upwardly mobile ambitions of certain minority groups began to impinge on the values of solidarity that had created ethnic studies. Because AfroAsian traffic came to be interrogated in this vise, it had to disavow the bureaucratic multiculturalism upon which it grew, and it argued feverishly against pluralist inclusion.

Scholars who began to research AfroAsian interaction, and this volume holds a very broad representative sample of their work, demanded that ethnic studies shift its epistemological horizon from pluralist inclusion within a culture of hierarchy to solidarity based on scrupulous attention to the interests of different pan-ethnic formations in the rat race of bureaucratic multiculturalism. Scholars built an archive of interactions at the same time they had to read against the grain of pluralist historical narratives. The work is necessary, and it is on the verge of providing a different epistemological framework than that of pluralist inclusion. What we have before us is a framework in the making, an archive almost ready to be theorized.

Toward the end of his book on Bandung, Richard Wright considered the task ahead for the leadership of the new nations. They had taken power of two-thirds of the world, but Wright worried that "they did not know what to do with it."[18] Such a harsh and overgeneralized verdict came without an engagement with the manifold challenges posed by the social orders where the new nations emerged, and without a sense of the many projects already under way to reorder the former colonial societies. Yet, Wright is correct in one respect, which is that the Bandung meeting simply inaugurated a dynamic of international cooperation against the onslaught of neocolonialism, and in this respect, at Bandung, the powers did not have a carefully honed platform (that would come by the 1961 Belgrade meeting, where they formed the Non-Aligned Movement).

Wright's question was appropriate for the advanced industrial states, however, which, he recognized, had little idea how to deal with the assertion of the darker nations. The European and the U.S. media fulminated against Bandung, and Wright saw that Bandung posed a problem for the region of the world that bore him and now bears with him. The choice for the advanced industrial states is clear: "Either he ["the average white Westerner"] accepts [the freedom of the darker nations] or he will have to seek for ways and means of resubjugating these newly freed hundreds of millions of brown and yellow and black people." If the former, real freedom, is accepted, then the advanced industrial states will also have to accept "a much lower standard of living."[19] There is no other way, for Wright does not go into the latter, the resubjugation.

We live in the resubjugated world, where it is "culture" that does much of the ideological work to justify inequality. Africa is poor because it has something to do with the pathologies of African tradition. Asia is unequal because population growth is a drag on the otherwise genius of Asian scientific development. These are the kinds of cultural arguments that postcolonial theory works against, just as AfroAsian work tries hard to cultivate the epistemological and historical archive of solidarity. The memory of the interactions, now being erased by neoliberal culturalism, has to be unearthed. This will allow us to better analyze the way in which ethnicities are mobilized by power to rub against each other. The only interest served by this conflict is the culture of hierarchy, for the masses of people suffer from these ahistorical generalities. Our task is to reframe conflict into solidarity, to show how conflict is ever present and yet ephemeral if its roots are better understood.

NOTES

Thanks to Heike Raphael-Hernandez for her invitation to participate in this fabulous project, and to her and Shannon Steen for very valuable comments on earlier drafts. I attempted some of these ideas at a roundtable on "Arab/South Asian Americans: Identity and Politics after 9/11" at the Association of Asian American Studies meeting in April 2005. Thanks to Moustafa Bayoumi, Ibrahim Aoude, Sunaina Maira, among others, for a spirited discussion. This short intervention is made possible by Robert Allen's visionary work.

1. Richard Wright, *The Color Curtain: A Report on the Bandung Conference* (Cleveland and New York: World Publishing, 1956), 14–15.

2. I should point out that while solidarity between Asian and African countries marked the early years of Bandung, by the late 1950s, Latin American and Caribbean countries joined in with fervor, led by Cuba, Jamaica, Argentina, and Venezuela. In 1966, Havana hosted the Tricontinental Conference.

3. George M. Kahin, ed., *The Asian-African Conference: Bandung, Indonesia, April 1955* (Ithaca: Cornell University Press, 1956), 43.

4. Wright, *Color Curtain*, 140.

5. Elisabeth B. Armstrong, *The Retreat from Organization: U.S. Feminism Reconceptualized* (Albany: SUNY Press, 2002), 104, and Elisabeth Armstrong and Vijay Prashad, "Solidarity: War Rites and Women's Rights," *New Centennial Review* 5.1 (2005): 213–253.

6. Diane C. Fujino, *Heartbeat of Struggle: The Revolutionary Life of Yuri Kochiyama* (Minneapolis: University of Minnesota Press, 2005), 301.

7. This political and epistemological work has been assembled in such places as Robin D. G. Kelley's and Betsy Esch's "Black Like Mao: Red China and Black Revolution," *Souls* 1.4 (Fall 1999): 6–41, in Fred Ho's edited book *Legacy to Liberation: Politics and Culture of Revolutionary Asian Pacific America* (San Francisco: AK Press, 2000), and in Vijay Prashad, *Everybody Was Kung Fu Fighting: Afro-Asian Connections and the Myth of Cultural Purity* (Boston: Beacon Press, 2001), notably in the final chapter.

8. For a fuller sense of Bandung and the changes, see Vijay Prashad, *Darker Nations: The Rise and Fall of the Third World* (New York: New Press, 2006).

9. As Sukarno put it; see Kahin, *Asian-African Conference*, 44.

10. For a very useful overview, see Bruce Cumings, "Boundary Displacement: Area Studies and International Studies during and after the Cold War," in *Universities and Empire: Money and Politics in the Social Sciences during the Cold War*, ed. Christopher Simpson (New York: New Press, 1998). I have assembled a short history of South Asian studies in Vijay Prashad, "Draft History of 'South Asia' in U.S. Education," *Subcontinental* 2.3 (Fall 2004): n.p.

11. Robert L. Allen, *Black Awakening in Capitalist America: An Analytic History* (New York: Anchor Books, 1970), 261–262.

12. Margaret Ferguson, "Teaching and/as Reproduction," *Yale Journal of Criticism* 1.2 (1988): 219, as quoted in Ellen Rooney, "Discipline and Vanish: Feminism, the Resistance to Theory, and the Politics of Cultural Studies," *differences* 2.3 (1990): 25.

13. Allen, *Black Awakening*, 262.

14. Amicus Curiae Brief by Fortune 500 Firms, May 31, 2001, in *Barbara Grutter v. Lee Bollinger, et al.*, No. 01-1447, United States Court of Appeals for the Sixth Circuit, 4, June 2003, available at http://www.umich.edu/~urel/admissions/legal/gru_amicus/32_internatl.pdf (retrieved 10 March 2005).

15. Ibid., 10.

16. Yen Le Espiritu, *Asian American Panethnicity: Bridging Institutions and Identities* (Philadelphia: Temple University Press, 1992), 13; on Latinos, see Felix Padilla, *Latino Ethnic Consciousness: The Case of Mexican American and Puerto Ricans in Chicago* (Notre Dame: Notre Dame University Press, 1985).

17. Espiritu, *Asian American Panethnicity,* 175.

18. Wright, *Color Curtain,* 207.

19. Ibid., 203–204.

AfroAsian Encounters
Culture, History, Politics

Heike Raphael-Hernandez and Shannon Steen

For a long time, many critics understood W. E. B. Du Bois's famous diagnosis of the twentieth century as plagued by the problem of the color line as a description of white/nonwhite antagonisms. However, in the aftermath of identity movements on the part of a variety of racial and ethnic groups, as well as saddening clashes between them, it has become impossible to construe the twentieth century as riven by a single color line. Instead, we now conceive of the modern world as having been fractured by a network of lines dividing a range of racial and ethnic groups. How else can we comprehend the identity struggles of South Asian visual artists in the Caribbean, the treatment of the Vietnam War by African American novelists, or the absorption of hip-hop by Asian American youth culture?

AfroAsian Encounters addresses an important connection that until recently has received only scant attention: the mutual influence of and relationships between members of the African and Asian diasporas in the Americas. Across the Americas, these two groups have often been thought of as occupying radically incommensurable cultural and political positions. In this collection, we examine AfroAsian interconnections across a variety of cultural, political, and historical contexts in order to examine how the two groups have interacted, and have construed one another, as well as how they have been set in opposition to each other by white systems of racial domination. We build here on the burgeoning interest in AfroAsian cultural histories reflected in a number of venues. From the conferences hosted by Boston University's African American studies department (2002, 2003, 2004), to special editions on AfroAsian studies in *Souls: A Critical Journal of Black Politics, Culture, and Society* (2002) and *positions: East Asia cultures critique* (2003), to the numerous essays and books generated by scholars across a number of disciplines from Gary Okihiro and Vijay Prashad to Claire Jean Kim and Frank Wu, as well as work by contributors we include here, research on black-Asian racial interactions and formations has expanded at a rapid pace during the last decade.[1] We seek to widen the energetic investigations that AfroAsian studies have provided relative to histories of diasporic and racial formations and globalization across a variety of fields, and with this book we hope to offer an important contribution to the ongoing scholarly debate. We have framed our treatment of black-Asian interactions within a neologism—rather, we have altered the typography for the term: AfroAsian. While there have been references to the "Afro-Asian" century and the "Afro-Asian" world, we have decided to drop the hyphen from the term in order to denote a unique, singular set of cultural dynamics that our authors analyze.

This collection constitutes the first interdisciplinary anthology to treat AfroAsian encounters. In keeping with the systems of intellectual inquiry established within African American and Asian American studies, we have gathered here essays that reflect a wide disciplinary range, including literary studies, musicology, history, and performance and visual studies. With this array we follow the recent move in the scholarly academy to allow interdisciplinary analysis to bridge the traditional divides that reflect the specialization of academic knowledge to the detriment of actual cultural and social processes. These essays provide rich, progressive, innovative directions in AfroAsian studies and invigorate the status of current thought on interracial encounters across multiple disciplines. This work does not just present a medley of essays with AfroAsian encounters in the Americas as their only common denominator; rather, we have taken Claire Jean Kim's discussion of "racial triangulation" in Asian American studies as an invitation to further the discourse of AfroAsian encounters. Moving beyond the traditional black/white binary, the essays claim that to understand historical and contemporary AfroAsian encounters, the third, white, signifier, cannot be separated from a discussion as this signifier has informed or influenced AfroAsian binary encounters in the Americas, often without being visibly or literarily present.

Race in the past century and a half has not functioned within national or ethnic boundaries. The cultural and racial groupings examined by our contributors indicate the ways in which these groups do not exist in isolation but within complicated interactions, and they ask us to reevaluate how we define the category "race" itself. Perhaps the most important contribution of AfroAsian studies lies in its potential ability to disrupt the black/white binary that has so persistently characterized race and ethnic studies. Within the last ten years or so, the stability of the term "race" has come under growing scrutiny. Increasingly, race is considered to be not an ontological, coherent category but a dynamic system of affiliation, exclusion, and disavowal that is constantly being reinvented. This sense of "performing" race, of its contingent, assumed nature, has come to be understood in relation to processes of national self-conception, such that "race" is seen as a category produced by the nation itself. As Paul Gilroy, Lisa Lowe, and Etienne Balibar have pointed out in different ways, national and racial boundaries are concomitant; race subtends dominant nationalist discourses—it extends underneath or functions in opposition to definitions of the nation.[2] While the strategic, tactical fluidity of terms like race and nation in this formula are crucial to our understanding of their unstable, changing processes, the logic of opposition that has underwritten this conception of race has also had the unfortunate effect of reinscribing its terms within binary relations and has somewhat perniciously limited our understanding of "race" to dichotomous models largely cast in terms of black and white. To this point, the great intervention in this binary system has been the assertion by postcolonial theorists of an "interstitial" position that occupies the spaces between these oppositions.[3] But this is not our only option.

Scholars in Asian American studies have mounted energetic campaigns to move beyond the conceptual limitations of the racial binary in the last decade or so—we might think here of Claire Jean Kim's above-mentioned discussion of "racial triangulation," Gary Okihiro's question "Is Yellow Black or White?," and Frank Wu's assertion that Asian American identities constitute something "beyond" either. For the most part, this work has demanded that we begin to understand race in terms of a polymorphous, multifaceted, multiply-raced immigration diaspora in combination with the histories of the African slave diaspora. However, race scholars still struggle to produce a flexible model that answers calls to move "beyond the binary." In *AfroAsian Encounters* we contribute to this dialogue around racial formation by moving away from the focus on black-white interactions; moreover, we do so by examining the interactions of two racial groups now set up in opposition to one another within, for example, contemporary U.S. racial systems. We hope that the essays gathered here can intervene in these binary systems—methodologically, in terms of expanding the objects of race studies and, conceptually, through the expansion of the reigning paradigm of race studies away from blackness/antiblackness and whiteness/antiwhiteness schemas.

To understand contemporary U.S. racial systems, we must step more boldly into Europe's past, as Paul Gilroy urges us. He writes:

> We must be prepared to make detours into the imperial and colonial zones where the catastrophic power of race-thinking was first institutionalized and its distinctive anthropologies put to the test, above all, in the civilizing storms of colonial war. . . . That redemptive movement must be able to pass beyond a compensatory acknowledgement of Europe's imperial crimes and the significance of its colonies as places of governmental innovation and experiment. The empires were not simply out there—distant terminal points for trading activity where race consciousness could grow—in the torrid zones of the world at the other end of the colonial chain. Imperial mentalities were brought back home . . . and altered economic, social, and cultural relations. . . . Europe's openness to the colonial worlds it helped to make, might then be employed to challenge fantasies of the newly embattled European region as a culturally bleached or politically fortified space, closed off to further immigration.[4]

With this mindset, Europeans "created" their "New World," and the Americas became their dream, their geographically locatable paradise. That their creation contained problematic cross-cultural and cross-racial encounters from the start was not problematic for white ideology and imagination; the European colonial color hierarchy was designed to regulate such problems.[5] Racial divisions were arranged according to the white/nonwhite binary. In his *Letters from an American Farmer* (1782, 1793) John de Crèvecoeur provided a definition of the only true American "race":

> What, then, is the American, this new man? He is neither a European nor the descendant of a European; hence that strange mixture of blood, which you will find in no other country. I could point out to you a family whose grandfather was an Englishman, whose wife was Dutch, whose son married a French woman, and whose present four sons have now four wives of different nations. *He* is an American, who, leaving behind him all his ancient prejudices and manners, receives new ones from the new mode of life he has embraced . . . and the new rank he holds. . . . Here individuals of all nations are melted into a new race of men. . . . The Americans were once

scattered all over Europe; here they are incorporated into one of the finest systems of population which has ever appeared.[6]

As is quickly apparent, Crèvecoeur's notion of "all nations" includes only all European countries—a generally accepted ideology that is also expressed in the Declaration of Independence's "all men are equal," thus all having the right to pursue happiness. Such a mindset saw no discrepancy between "all men" and African American slavery and Native American genocide. The entrance of the Asian migratory laborer, however, disrupted this ideology. As Ronald Takaki emphasizes, while Asian immigrants "were brought here to serve as an 'internal colony'—nonwhites allowed to enter as 'cheap' migratory laborers and members of a racially subordinated group, not future citizens of American society,"[7] they came as dreamers, too. Asians perceived themselves as eligible for participation in the "New World" if only through hard work. Takaki argues:

> The context of the "modern world-system" and its economic forces only partly explains the Asian migrations to America. While the Asian immigrants did not choose the material circumstances of their times, most of them still made choices regarding the future of their lives. . . . Though driven by "necessity," they were also stirred . . . by "dreams" . . . [and] "hopes."[8]

Not only were they forced to experience racism and discrimination immediately, but also they faced a "triangulated" racial reality: in white perception, they were on the other side of the white/nonwhite spectrum; in their own perception, they did not view themselves as being in "coalition" with black people because they entered the United States as free migrant laborers, not slaves; in black perception, there was indeed no coalition because Asians had opportunities they did not have. This white triangulation forced them to interact—literally and theoretically.

Key to the history of interaction between the two groups is the process by which their intermixing was made possible. The first AfroAsian contact can be traced back to antiquity through the great spice routes that we normally think of as a characteristic of the Greco-Roman cultural world. These routes also provided the conditions for cultural and economic exchange between what we now refer to as Tanzania, Somalia, Egypt, Persia, India, and China, as these empires traded precious commodities such as cinnamon and myrrh (in fact, the archeological record is unclear as to whether the AfroAsian routes preceded the Greco-Roman involvement in the spice trade). Two millennia later, the early- to mid-nineteenth-century abolition of the slave trade produced the context of AfroAsian encounters of modernity. In the wake of the British abolition of the trade in African lives, cheap labor sources were needed to fuel British colonial industries around the globe. Indians were transplanted to southern Africa to build railroads, and Chinese were taken to the Caribbean to work the sugar plantations. A similar economic necessity drove the importation of Asian labor to the United States. As the national debate over slavery grew over the course of the early nineteenth century, and more states (especially western states) were added to the "free soil" roster, the need for cheap labor did not abate. The early development of new states like California happened to coincide with the massive displacement of peoples in Guang-dong province in the wake of the Opium Wars. As John Kuo Wei Tchen has pointed out, prior to the construction of the transcontinental railroad in 1869 it took two to three months to travel overland to San Francisco from Boston or New York, but only two weeks to travel from Canton by clipper ship, creating circumstances that made Chinese immigrants the perfect candidates to step into the labor shortage caused by booming in-dustries in mining, shipping, transportation, and agriculture in Califor-nia.[9] AfroAsian relations, then, are the issue and, potentially, the subver-sion of the European dream of "the new world." Given the extraordinary richness of AfroAsian interactions of modernity, particularly those created within the shadow and against the force of this colonialist history, we have chosen to focus the volume within the period beyond emancipation. The colonial processes that created the Americas made possible the very con-nections our authors investigate.

For these AfroAsian encounters in the Americas, the twentieth century invented another problematic triangulated concept—the "model minor-ity" myth. This construct enabled white society to pit Asian Americans against many other groups, not just African Americans. Yet, for the Afro-Asian mutual perspective of each other and for their encounters, the con-cept has carried additional problems: while Asian Americans have been constructed as model minorities, their economic success heralded as proof of the availability of the American Dream to all, African Americans have continued to be plagued by negative associations and to be systematically excluded from the American political economy.

It would be a mistake to ignore the ways in which racial antagonisms have frequently been aligned along a black-white axis or to elide the histories of African slavery that produced the modern Euro-American economy. So, too, would it be a mistake to ignore the influence of East and South Asia on the making of the modern economic and cultural world. To do so would disregard how South and East Asian labor were key to the maintenance of U.S. and British economies in the wake of abolition, it would overlook the way Asian and African populations were played against one another to produce white supremacy, it would erase the distinct absorption of African versus Asian cultures in a range of national contexts, and it would obliterate the possibility of cross-racial political coalitions, as well as naïvely ignore the conflicts between racial groups. These examples, sketched briefly here, form the basis for several of the essays in this volume.

Regarding Takaki's modern-world system of capitalism and the migrant laborer movement, one might ask why we did not expand our discussion to a more global level and include south Asian labor migration to southern Africa, for example. However, as our focus is the triangulation of AfroAsian encounters in the construction of the Americas, we did not see an inclusion of such otherwise geopolitically highly important discussions necessary for this particular collection. This weight reflects the historical significance of the United States as a primary site of AfroAsian interactions. The North American continent, situated between the geopolitical units of the Black Atlantic and the Asian/Pacific, has seen a uniquely high concentration of AfroAsian cultural interactions.

AfroAsian Encounters addresses a phenomenon that has been culturally active for well over a century. While much contemporary cultural influence between the African and Asian diasporas might be categorized as a result of globalization, our contributors suggest that the mutual imbrication of these two groups constitutes a longer historical phenomenon, with important roots and foundations that warrant examination. This collection traces this history across multiple locations and attempts to trace these interactions, to "catch up," as it were, with the racial dynamics of various national contexts that have been active for over a century now.

AfroAsian Encounters is comprised of a foreword, an afterword, and sixteen essays arranged within four thematic subtopics. Vijay Prashad launches the volume with "Bandung Is Done." His essay frames the volume as a whole with a discussion of "AfroAsian Epistemology," which, he argues, reached its apotheosis in the landmark Bandung Conference of 1955. Sweeping back to the League against Imperialism meeting in Brussels in 1928 and forward to the present, Prashad traces the spirit of cooperation and mutual support around anticolonialist struggles in both Asia and Africa, but he also acknowledges the ways in which the political projects of liberation animated by that spirit have been undermined in the period since Bandung. From the International Monetary Fund's attempt to render newly independent nations dependent on their former colonial masters through the necessity of capital investment, to the commodification and aestheticization of AfroAsian relations in the Hollywood film and American music industries, the political possibilities forged in Bandung have been severely compromised. As a result, Prashad warns, the knowledge project of AfroAsian studies is similarly imperiled. He argues that area studies in U.S. universities were a direct outgrowth of Cold War politics and cautions us that while AfroAsian studies might mimic the form of Bandung, its content runs the risk of simply mirroring the corporate globalization and Cold War exploitation of newly independent countries that the leaders of the Bandung conference wished to inhibit. His essay demands that we reinvest our own epistemological projects with the spirit of independence and expressly anticolonial politics that energized Bandung, a spirit that we hope grounds this volume as well.

With Prashad's caution in mind, we have organized the volume around thematic units that encompass Bandung's sense of struggle. The subsections we describe below capture Bandung's attempt to forge cross-racial political alliances, analyze the tensions that can make those coalitions difficult, and trace the way those alliances are co-opted with monotonous regularity within mainstream cultural venues. We have arranged our subsections to lay out the context of AfroAsian racial positioning within dominant racial regimes throughout North America and the Caribbean in Part I. Investigating the legacy of those racial structures on contemporary AfroAsian connections, the essays of Part II examine the reasons for sometimes conflicted encounters. Part III examines how performance has been used repeatedly as a central medium through which that legacy has been either reinforced or contested. With Part IV, we conclude the volume on a celebratory note; the essays of this section trace how AfroAsian encounters have productively challenged the racial hierarchies dictated by white Euro-American political economies.

The essays in Part I: "Positioning AfroAsian Racial Identities" contextualize the ways in which members of the African and Asian diasporas have been set up against each other within different national ideologies to solidify white privilege. Sanda Mayzaw Lwin begins with an examination of the distinctions between immigration exclusion and internal segregation in the United States at the end of the nineteenth century. In "A Race So Different from Our Own," she analyzes the dissenting opinion of *Plessy v. Ferguson* (1896), in which Chinese immigrants were produced as the eternally-foreign foil to African Americans as part of the argument against segregation in the late nineteenth century. Cynthia Tolentino turns our attention to how early mainstream sociological accounts of African Americans and Asian Americans as blueprint models of "race" were adopted and transformed by Asian American intellectuals. Using the writing of Jade Snow Wong as an example, in "Crossings in Prose" Tolentino argues that Asian American writers "encountered sociological theories that compared 'Negroes' and 'Orientals' as a sanctioned discourse that they could draw on to negotiate racialized and gendered notions of agency and expertise." Following on Tolentino's analysis of sociological accounts of race, Eleanor Ty moves us to Canadian racial discourses and examines the language of "visible minorities" used to categorize different racial groups. She illustrates in "Complicating Racial Binaries" how Canada's official language of race is less dependent on binary systems than that of the United States and as a result "is predicated not only on skin color but on a variety of factors, including accent and linguistic competence, dress, class, and religious affiliation." In doing so, she urges us to consider how AfroAsian racial interactions function outside of an American context. Lourdes López Ropero returns us to the realm of fiction. In her essay "One People, One Nation?" López Ropero analyzes the conception of creolization in Indian Caribbean fiction through the work of Samuel Selvon and Fred D'Aguiar and argues that these writers "refuse to romanticize the Caribbean as a site of unproblematic creolization and foreground the ethnic conflict endemic to creole societies." Samir Dayal closes this section with his "Black-and-Tan Fantasies," in which he traces black and South Asian interracial contact in film to examine racial triangulation in a new way. He argues that "it is not *exclusively* a question of tracking the 'master signifier' of whiteness but of attending to the complexities of the ways in which brownness or blackness or yellowness can also function as the *tertium quid*—the obscured referent or object of desire, the signifier that stitches the triangulation together." Dayal's essay provides a new theoretical framework through which we can read the following chapters on AfroAsian identities.

If the essays of Part I lay out the historical and theoretical context of AfroAsian racial formations, Part II: "Confronting the Color Hierarchy" addresses the contemporary impact of these formations. The essays of this section illustrate the frustrating divisions that often prevent effective Afro-Asian coalitions yet also envision opportune windows for change. In "It Takes Some Time to Learn the Right Words," Heike Raphael-Hernandez discusses possible reasons for the "phenomenon of the missing Vietnam War" in the tremendous explosion of African American novels since the 1970s. In addition, she observes a recently growing interest in Vietnam War–related protagonists in novels published since the late 1990s; with these patterns in mind, she asks why and how these African American writers correct the absence of that conflict from the preceding generation of fiction. Gita Rajan offers *chutney* as a metaphor for the work of black and Indian visual artists in the Caribbean. In her "*Chutney, Métissage,* and Other Mixed Metaphors," she argues that "Asian influences in Caribbean art remained, consciously or unconsciously, on the sidelines" and examines how Indian artists have reinserted that presence into the Afro Caribbean visual arts. Combining the metaphor of *chutney*, or the incorporation of visual symbols both from Indian and African cultural contexts, with Edouard Glissant's notion of *métissage*, Rajan analyzes "a gendered, racialized, and sexualized space that allows for staging identity for . . . Indo Caribbean artists." In "These Are the Breaks," Oliver Wang scrutinizes hip-hop as a site that exposes continuing tensions between black and Asian Americans. Following the career (and recent retirement) of the rising Chinese American hip-hop star Jin, Wang traces the discrimination that Asian American hip-hop musicians face from audiences, critics, and music industry executives. He argues that while "it has become commonplace wisdom and belief that hip-hop culture represents an idealized space for multicultural cooperation and community building," it is also "becoming increasingly clear that the participation of Asian Americans in hip-hop happens within a contested terrain that is inextricably linked to long-standing tensions between Asian and African Americans."

It is striking that so many AfroAsian encounters have been engaged and negotiated through systems of performance. This phenomenon is the focus of Part III, "Performing AfroAsian Identities." These essays do not just address performance in the AfroAsian world but also analyze the different functions of cross-racial impersonation in different contexts. Shannon Steen provides the earliest example of the performative dimensions of AfroAsia in her essay on the swing adaptations of Gilbert and Sullivan's *The Mikado* staged with black casts in the late 1930s. In "Racing American Modernity," she scrutinizes the cultural resonances of black actors' on-stage claims to *be* Japanese and argues that these performances helped white Americans shrug off their anxieties about a Japanese neoimperial threat to U.S. dominance of the Pacific by satirizing Japanese power through minstrelsy tropes. Arguing that the shows deployed "a series of incomplete racial displacements," she illustrates how "conceptions of 'race' are formulated within the relationship between domestic and international racial mappings." In "Black Bodies/Yellow Masks," Deborah Whaley analyzes the use of Asian signifiers by contemporary African American hip-hop artists. "The tactical performance of the 'Oriental,'" she argues, "not only poses a representational dilemma replete with contradictory racial, ethnic, and national signifiers but also opens up questions about the multiple meanings of its precarious usage by black Americans who perform these images." She examines a range of examples, from mainstream music videos, to the 2004 visual arts exhibit *Black Belt* in which artists tried to problematize the use of Asian signifiers, to the 2000 film *Romeo Must Die*. Focusing on the contemporary cinematic world, Mita Banerjee examines in her "The *Rush Hour* of Black/Asian Coalitions" the black/Asian "buddy film," which she dubs the "Hollywood simulacrum of black/Asian coalitions." Locating the roots of the American film industry's fascination with black/Asian dyads in such precedents as Charlie Chan and his black sidekick, Banerjee traces the historical contexts that these films attempt to elide. She moves on to an analysis of the Jackie Chan/ Chris Tucker hit *Rush Hour* to investigate what kinds of racial identities are being "mainstreamed" through movies that feature black/Asian "buddies." Cathy Covell Waegner examines the process of racial impersonation by both black and Asian artists in her essay "Performing Postmodernist Passing." Like Whaley, she takes in a range of objects from mainstream hip-hop videos and parodies of them by contemporary visual artists, to Paul Beatty's novel *Tuff*, which features a black protagonist who takes on an Asian cinematic persona, to Jim Jarmusch's 1999 hit *Ghost Dog*. She uses these artifacts to theorize a new kind of "passing" that carries the potential for "personal empowerment of the cultural self and provides the impulse for new polycultural art forms of the twenty-first century."

Part IV, "Celebrating Unity" begins with Bill Mullen's "Persisting Solidarities," which highlights the history of mutual borrowing between members of the African and Asian diasporas in U.S. literature. Beginning with the outrage expressed by African American literary figures over U.S. postwar foreign policy in Asia, Mullen examines how AfroAsian literary borrowings "present a dialectical and synthetic model of transraciality that abolishes comfortable and discreet categories of 'racial,' 'ethnic,' or even 'disciplinary' modeling." Mullen illuminates the history of AfroAsian writing from W. E. B. Du Bois's engagement with Asian politics to the initiation of Ishmael Reed's *Yardbird* anthologies of the 1970s. Similarly, in his essay "Internationalism and Justice," Greg Robinson examines Paul Robeson's relationship to Asian and Asian American struggle. Robinson traces Robeson's much-vaunted "internationalism"—his attempt to forge cultural links between oppressed peoples across a variety of national, racial, and political contexts—in his performances, beginning with Robeson's 1950 concert at Harlem's AME (African Methodist Episcopal) Zion Church. Starting with Robeson's call to the audience to learn Chinese greetings by way of comparing them to the intonations of African ones, Robinson goes on to point out Robeson's study of China as a site of struggle that could shed light on African struggle, and he illustrates how Robeson modeled these cultural and political links for his audiences throughout his performances. David Stowe moves us to Japan, in "Jazz That Eats Rice," to examine the "unstable ethnic triad" in the career of Japanese jazz artist Toshiko Akiyoshi and the moment in her work in which she "decided to repay jazz by bringing her Japanese heritage to her music." Stowe analyzes two works by Akiyoshi and examines how the composer used classical Japanese instrumentation to integrate into jazz a musical analogy to the blues in order to render it a Japanese form. Fred Ho concludes this section with his essay "Kickin' the White Man's Ass" and returns us to the spirit of Bandung by illustrating how the increasing popularity of Asian martial arts for black and Latino youth in the United States from the late 1960s on was not just a historical accident but part of "the upsurges of the Third World national liberation movements across the planet and in the U.S. oppressed-nationality communities."

We end our volume with a challenging, yet appropriate, invitation to further explorations of AfroAsian encounters. In his afterword, "Toward a Black Pacific," Gary Y. Okihiro returns the volume to the Pacific of Bandung, and he ventures into territory referred to but so far not detailed by AfroAsian scholarship. Claiming that the Pacific is frequently overlooked in considerations of "Asians" and "Asia," and reminding us of its distinctive history, culture, and politics, he reflects on Oceania's islands and inhabitants. He expands on three intersections between Pacific Islanders and African Americans that have created the "Black Pacific": labor, education, and popular culture. It is his wish and ours that the recognition of divergences and intersections that *AfroAsian Encounters* reveals continues to inform our scholarship and our politics.

We recognize that through this organizational principle we have created a narrative for AfroAsian encounters that may be construed by some readers as naïve. We are well aware of and have consciously included essays that analyze the sometimes-contentious character of AfroAsian relationships. However, working in Prashad's vein, we also situate those very real antagonisms within the context of larger systems of racial formation that, while perhaps did not make those conflicts inevitable, unquestionably contributed to them and made them difficult to avoid. We end the volume with the essays "Celebrating Unity" because we believe, moreover, that these conflicts should not delimit the possibility for coalition. The cultural examples gathered in this section provide us with models for how AfroAsian interactions might function *despite* the history of conflict between these groups and commemorate the courage and vision embodied in these examples.

NOTES

1. For a partial bibliography of AfroAsian studies see the following: Fred Ho and Bill V. Mullen, eds., *Afro/Asia: Revolutionary Political and Cultural Connections between African-Americans and Asian-Americans* (Durham: Duke University Press, forthcoming); Bill V. Mullen, *Afro-Orientalism* (Minneapolis: University of Minnesota Press, 2004); Andrew F. Jones and Nikhil Pal Singh, eds., *The Afro-Asian Century,* special issue of *positions: East Asia cultures critique* 11.1 (2003); *Souls: A Critical Journal of Black Politics, Culture, and Society* 4 (2002); Frank H. Wu, *Yellow: Race in America beyond Black and White* (New York: Basic Books, 2002); Claire Jean Kim, "The Racial Triangulation of Asian Americans," in *Asian Americans and Politics: Perspectives, Experiences, Prospects,* ed. Gordon H. Chang (Stanford: Stanford University Press, 2001); Vijay Prashad, *Everybody Was Kung Fu Fighting: Afro-Asian Connections and the Myth of Cultural Purity* (Boston: Beacon Press, 2001); Claire Jean Kim and Taeku Lee, "Interracial Politics: Asian Americans and Other Communities of Color," *Political Science and Politics* 34.3 (September 2001): 631–637; Claire Jean Kim, *Bitter Fruit: The Politics of Black-Korean Conflict in New York City* (New Haven: Yale University Press, 2000); Marc Gallichio, *The African American Encounter with China and Japan: Black Internationalism in Asia, 1895–1945* (Chapel Hill: University of North Carolina Press, 2000); Kwang Chung Kim, ed., *Koreans in the Hood: Conflict with African Americans* (Baltimore: John Hopkins University Press, 1999); Robin D. G. Kelly and Betsy Esch, "Black Like Mao: Red China and Black Revolution," *Souls* 1.4 (Fall 1999): 6–41; Reginald Kearney, *African American Views of the Japanese: Solidarity or Sedition?* (Albany: State University of New York Press, 1998); Gary Okihiro, *Margins and Mainstreams:*

Asians in American History and Culture (Seattle: University of Washington Press, 1994); Yuri Kochiyama, "The Impact of Malcolm X on Asian-American Politics and Activism," in *Blacks, Latinos, and Asians in Urban America: Status and Prospect for Politics and Activism*, ed. James Jennings (Westport, CT: Praeger, 1994); Sumi Cho, "Korean Americans vs. African Americans: Conflict and Construction," in *Reading Rodney King/Reading Urban Uprising*, ed. Robert Gooding-Williams (New York: Routledge, 1993); Lisa Ikemoto, "Traces of the Master Narrative in the Story of African American/Korean American Conflict: How We Constructed 'Los Angeles,'" *Southern California Law Review* 66 (1993): 1581–1598; Sudarshan Kapur, *Raising up a Prophet: The African-American Encounter with Gandhi* (Boston: Beacon Press, 1992).

2. See Paul Gilroy, *"Ain't No Black in the Union Jack"* (Chicago: University of Chicago Press, 1991); Lisa Lowe, *Immigrant Acts: On Asian American Cultural Politics* (Durham: Duke University Press, 1996); Etienne Balibar and Emmanuel Wallerstein, *Race, Nation, Class: Ambiguous Identities* (London: Verso, 1991). As Michael Omi and Howard Winant have argued, however, race should not be seen as epiphenomenal to nation, as merely the external, superficial manifestation of nationhood, but, rather, as a fundamental process through which nations (especially the United States) attempt to render their identities coherent. Michael Omi and Howard Winant, *Racial Formation in the United States: From the 1960s to the 1990s* (New York: Routledge, 1994).

3. See, for example, Homi Bhabha, *The Location of Culture* (New York: Routledge, 1994).

4. Paul Gilroy, "Migrancy, Culture, and a New Map of Europe," in *Blackening Europe: The African American Presence*, ed. Heike Raphael-Hernandez (New York: Routledge, 2004), xx, xii.

5. Frank Shuffelton offers excellent scholarship regarding the establishment of the racial order in the early United States. See, for example, Frank Shuffelton, ed., *A Mixed Race: Ethnicity in Early America* (New York: Oxford University Press, 1993); Frank Shuffelton, "The American Enlightenment and Endless Emancipation," in *Teaching the Literatures of Early America*, ed. Carla Mulford (New York: Modern Language Association of America, 1999), 155–169. We would like to thank Dietmar Schloss for bringing Shuffelton to our attention.

6. J. Hector St. John de Crèvecoeur, *Letters from an American Farmer* (1782, 1793), in *The Heath Anthology of American Literature*, Vol. 1, ed. Paul Lauter et al. (Lexington, MA: D. C. Heath, 1990), 897.

7. Ronald Takaki, *Strangers from a Different Shore: A History of Asian Americans* (New York: Penguin Books, 1989), 31.

8. Ibid.

9. John Kuo Wei Tchen, *New York before Chinatown: Orientalism and the Shaping of American Culture, 1776–1882* (Baltimore: Johns Hopkins University Press, 1999).

Part I

Positioning AfroAsian Racial Identities

Chapter 1

"A Race So Different from Our Own"
Segregation, Exclusion, and the Myth of Mobility

Sanda Mayzaw Lwin

A black man is a person who must ride Jim Crow in Georgia.
—W. E. B. Du Bois, *Dusk of Dawn*

No China Men, no railroad.
—Maxine Hong Kingston, *China Men*

From the late nineteenth century through the mid–twentieth century, two regimes of racialized segregation existed simultaneously on the terrain of U.S. law and culture: Jim Crow and Chinese exclusion. The former traditionally has been perceived as about the "problem" of race relations, while the latter has been perceived as about the "problem" of immigration. This essay examines the invocation of a "Chinese race" in discussions of black-white segregation. In the pages that follow, I focus on two narratives of Jim Crow segregation—the 1896 Supreme Court case *Plessy v. Ferguson* and Charles Chesnutt's 1901 novel, *The Marrow of Tradition,* and question why in each of these texts a figure of a "Chinaman" appears during the height of the era of Chinese exclusion.[1] I argue that the materialization of this phantasmatic figure of the "Chinaman" serves as a convenient repository for fin de siècle anxieties over national identity and, moreover, as a rhetorical foil to make coherent particular narratives of American citizenship. Although both the legal and the literary narratives raise the issue of an Asian presence in the American black-white racial landscape, these texts are rarely read in a context of comparative race relations.[2] I suggest that the *Plessy* case and *The Marrow of Tradition* call for a crucial reassessment of the dialectics of visibility and invisibility that manage black and Asian bodies in U.S. law and culture.

I. Plessy v. Ferguson

Plessy v. Ferguson is a landmark case that is central to understanding the "problem of the color-line" that Du Bois so presciently predicted would be the problem of the twentieth century.[3] Notwithstanding the de jure overturning of segregation laws in *Brown v. Board of Education* (1954), *Plessy* represents a moment of racial crisis that continues to influence American legal discourse to the present day. As legal scholar Kimberlé Crenshaw has succinctly noted, "*Plessy* lives."[4]

On June 7, 1892, Homer Plessy purchased a first-class train ticket in New Orleans, Louisiana. Plessy was "a citizen of the United States and a resident of the state of Louisiana, of mixed descent, in the proportion of seven-eighths Caucasian and one-eighths African blood."[5] The one-drop rule,[6] what Mark Twain once called "the fiction of law and custom,"[7] legally classified Plessy as "black." However, according to contemporary accounts, "the mixture of the colored blood was not discernible in him."[8] After he occupied a vacant seat in a coach designated to accommodate "passengers of the white race," Plessy was ordered by the conductor to move to the coach assigned "for persons not of the white race."[9] Because he refused to comply with this injunction, Plessy was removed from the train, taken to jail, and indicted for sitting in the whites-only car. The Louisiana state supreme court held that Plessy had "criminally violated" state segregation laws, which required "railway companies carrying passengers in their coaches . . . to provide *equal but separate,* accommodations for the white and colored races [and to impose] fines or imprisonment upon passengers insisting on going into a coach or compartment other than the one set aside for the race to which he or she belongs."[10]

Homer Plessy's attorneys appealed this decision all the way to the U.S. Supreme Court, arguing that segregation denied him equal citizenship rights and due process of law. Moreover, they claimed that segregation laws injured their client's reputation, arguing that "the reputation of belonging to the dominant race, in this instance, the white race, is property."[11] Plessy's attorneys defined whiteness as a social privilege, a *reputation* rather than a biological essence. They argued that Plessy was entitled to the social benefits of the status of whiteness through the percentile breakdown of his blood—he was, after all, seven-eighths Caucasian—and through his light appearance: his colored blood was "not discernible." While Plessy's attorneys aimed to expose the contradictions of racial categorization through the claim of whiteness as property, the Court offered a circular counterargument. Only those who "lawfully" qualified for the category of whiteness were eligible to claim a right to the benefits of its reputation—as well as to claim damages against any injury to its reputation. Despite Plessy's outward appearance, Louisiana law deemed that the seemingly negligible fraction of "colored" blood disqualified him from legal recognition as "white." As such, according to the Supreme Court, Plessy could not seek damages for "property" that was never his to begin with. In 1896, the Supreme Court ruled against Plessy by holding seven to one that the "equal but separate" doctrine was indeed constitutional.

The Supreme Court's decision and the lone dissent against segregation by Justice John Marshall Harlan are important cultural texts in late-twentieth-century American studies. Recent critical writings about late-nineteenth- and early-twentieth-century American literature often invoke the *Plessy* case, particularly in conjunction with the work of such authors as W. E. B. Du Bois, Mark Twain, and Charles Chesnutt.[12] The case is also a fundamental part of American legal education. *Plessy* is almost always excerpted in constitutional law textbooks, which as T. Alexander Aleinikoff has noted are "as close as we have to a canon."[13]

In his solitary and passionate dissent that lambasted the majority opinion, Justice John Marshall Harlan famously argued against segregation, claiming: "In the view of the Constitution, in the eye of the law, there is in this country no superior, dominant, ruling class of citizens. There is no caste here. Our Constitution is color-blind, and neither knows nor tolerates classes among citizens. In respect of civil rights, all citizens are equal before the law."[14]

A central—and peculiar—portion of his argument, however, is rarely excerpted. A few lines after his powerful plea for constitutional color blindness, in the full text of his dissent (which law students are rarely asked to read in its entirety), Harlan invokes a third racial category, one that represents neither black nor white. He observes that there exists a third group whose radical alterity prohibited its members not only from becoming U.S. citizens but moreover from entering the very borders of the nation. "There is a race so different from our own," he declared, "that we do not permit those persons belonging to it to become citizens of the United States. Persons belonging to it are, with few exceptions, absolutely excluded from our country. I allude to the Chinese race."[15]

Harlan's peculiar allusion to a third racial group, one "so different" from "black" and "white," was of course also an allusion to the series of race-based immigration acts collectively known as the Chinese exclusion laws (1882–1943).[16] The first of the Chinese Exclusion Acts was passed by Congress in 1882 and held the dubious honor of being the very first race-based immigration act in the United States. The act prohibited Chinese laborers from entering the United States and explicitly denied naturalized citizenship to those Chinese who were already residing there. Renewed consecutively until the repeal acts of the mid–twentieth century, the Chinese Exclusion Acts epitomized the politics of mobility which Chinese laborers were forced to negotiate at the turn of the century.[17]

Harlan invokes the figure of the Chinese in his dissent to provide bodily proof that the Louisiana statute is unjust to "citizens of the black race." Rather than seizing this opening to dislodge the black/white binary, he attempts to resolve the problem of the color line by redrawing it as one between citizens and noncitizens of the United States. He continues:

> But by the statute in question, a Chinaman can ride in the same passenger coach with white citizens of the United States, while citizens of the black race in Louisiana, many of whom, perhaps, risked their lives for the preservation of the Union, who are entitled, by law to participate in the political control of the State and nation, who are not excluded by law or by reason of their race, from public stations of any kind, and who have all the legal rights that belong to white citizens, are yet declared to be criminals, liable to imprisonment if they ride in a public coach occupied by citizens of the white race.[18]

Harlan attempts to expose the hypocrisy of a legal system that granted citizenship rights to African Americans through the Civil War Amendments, allowed them by law, to share in the political control of the nation as citizens, yet criminalized them, also by law, for sharing the same space on a railway car as white citizens. He reminds his colleagues on the bench that many Africans Americans "risked their lives for the preservation of the Union," suggesting that military service—particularly putting one's body on the line for the nation—may have helped African Americans earn the right to legally participate in the U.S. political and legal calculus. He configures both citizenship and membership in the American nation as a right one can earn by proving loyalty to the nation-state. In this way, Harlan suggests that national belonging is organized around a meritocracy that grants citizenship to men who have proved themselves worthy.[19]

Lisa Lowe, writing in the context of the Vietnam war, has argued that "the American soldier, who has in every way submitted to the nation, is the quintessential citizen and therefore the ideal representative of the nation, yet the American of Asian descent remains the symbolic 'alien,' the *metonym* for Asia who by definition cannot be imagined as sharing in America."[20] We might read Harlan's dissent as one early illustration of this problematic.[21] Harlan draws on the notion of the American soldier as the quintessential citizen, yet the image of the African American soldier fighting for the nation is chronologically disjunctive—"citizens of the black race" who fought in the Civil War did so before they were legally citizens. He counters this discrepancy with the image of the Chinese "coolie" who has no legal claim to the nation, a "race so different" he is forbidden from entering the country. That Harlan imagines the "Chinaman" as present within the borders of the nation further underscores its representation as an alien who is trespassing.

The imagined body of the "Chinaman" troubles the order of the color line in a different way from Homer Plessy (who was intentionally chosen to test the separate car laws on the railways because he was "light enough" to pass). Rather than confounding the rigid categories of the "two races" that make up the color line, the *figure* of the "Chinaman" disrupts the notion that there are *only* two races by occupying simultaneously a position of nonblack *and* nonwhite. Moreover, the figure of the Chinaman occupies the space of a noncitizen, perhaps even an illegal alien.[22]

How is it, Harlan seems to ask, that a "Chinaman," a foreigner who is "absolutely excluded from our country" can cross the color line without legal penalty, but a U.S. citizen such as Homer Plessy cannot? Not only does he fall back on the category of "race," but this allusion to the figure of "the Chinaman," as well as to the Chinese Exclusion Acts, unveils a moment where certain dilemmas and discourses about race and racial categorization enter the arena of the national. Harlan makes the Chinaman visible in his text—creating a fictitious Chinaman in effect—by invoking the very laws that render Chinese American bodies *invisible* within the borders of the United States.

II. The Railroad and the Promise of Mobility

It is ironic that Harlan's invocation of the Chinaman—his fictional narrative of a Chinese man boarding a "whites only" car—occurs during the period of Chinese exclusion as well as in the imagined space of the railroad. Chinese laborers were crucial to the completion of the transcontinental railroad and comprised over 90 percent of the railroad's ten thousand workers. While Harlan's dissent justifies the right of African American citizens to claim an America they *earned* through service to the nation in the Civil War, it is striking that he does not argue against the "equal but separate" doctrine by opposing white supremacy.[23] Instead, he chooses to pit the experiences of one racialized minority against another. How might the comparison of the African American citizen to the phantasmatic and foreign Chinaman at once signal and suppress the history of Chinese workers who served the western expansion of the nation through the construction of the transcontinental railroad?

Literary critic Sau-ling Wong has noted that "Chinese American artists . . . have to deal with the peculiar irony of the railroad as an emblem of their past."[24] Simultaneously emblematic of the national myth of boundless mobility, and of national progress and modernity, the railroad also serves as a reminder of Asian American exclusions from access to that mobility. Indeed, while images of movement, adventure, discovery, and travel have long been integral to American national narratives, the trope of the railroad—as a signifier of both mobility and racialized exclusions—have been central in both African American and Asian American writings. For example, the railroad figures in the writings of Charles Chesnutt, Frank Chin, Frederick Douglass, Sui Sin Far, Langston Hughes, Harriet Jacobs, James Weldon Johnson, Maxine Hong Kingston, Booker T. Washington, and Shawn Wong, to name a select few. Embedded in the trope of the railroad are the histories of the flight from slavery, Jim Crow segregation, and Chinese immigrant labor in the United States. I would suggest that the railroad motif presents an important site through which to track the incorporation of African Americans and Asian Americans into American space.

In *Plessy v. Ferguson,* the railroad is the literal setting for Homer Plessy's contestation of Jim Crow laws, as well as the imagined setting for Justice Harlan's fictive Chinaman who ostensibly rides in the "whites only" car. And as we will see in Charles Chesnutt's 1901 novel, *The Marrow of Tradi-*

tion, the railroad functions at the outset of the novel as the backdrop for a similar encounter with the regime of racialized segregation.

Both the *Plessy* case and *The Marrow of Tradition* expose not only injustices of racial segregation but also the hierarchical structure of American citizenship. The Supreme Court's decision in *Plessy* significantly influenced Charles Chesnutt's novels and nonfiction writings. A lawyer and a novelist by profession, Chesnutt often drew on his legal training in his writing. He was in close contact with Albion Tourgée, Plessy's lawyer, who was also a popular novelist of the late nineteenth century. In a speech written sometime between 1908 and 1911, Chesnutt declared that "the opinion in Plessy v. Ferguson [*sic*] is to my mind, as epoch-making as the Dred Scott decision."[25]

The Marrow of Tradition offers a vivid rendering of the interplay between racial exclusion, spatial segregation, and American citizenship.[26] The novel is a fictional account of the 1898 race riot in Wilmington, North Carolina, and was considered by some of its contemporary critics as polemical or political in its portrayal of the issues of racial tension and of white supremacy. The fifth chapter of the novel, "A Journey Southward," opens on a train headed south from Philadelphia to North Carolina.

Two acquaintances, "men of culture . . . accustomed to the society of cultivated people" and "well-dressed," encounter each other by chance on the train.[27] The elder man, Dr. Alvin Burns, is the professor of the younger man, Dr. William Miller, at a prestigious medical college in Philadelphia. At first glance, their conversation, manner of speech, and manner of dress suggest that the two passengers have similar professional and class backgrounds. Chesnutt invites the reader to take a closer look at these two men:

> Looking at these two men with *the American eye,* the difference would perhaps be more striking, or at least the more immediately apparent, for the first was white and the second black, or more correctly speaking, brown; it was even a light brown, but both his swarthy complexion and his curly hair revealed what has been described in the laws of some of our states as a "visible admixture" of African blood.[28]

According to this passage, racial recognition occurs in the field of vision. Chesnutt presents the visual markers that signify or confer racial identity on an individual as legally constituted—the second man is recognized as "black" because he embodies certain physical traits that reflect what the law calls a "visible admixture" of African blood. He gestures to the instability of "blackness" when he explains that Miller is "more correctly speaking brown; it was even a light brown." The differences between these two men are made apparent through the process of "looking at" them and to the "American eye," these differences seem to far outweigh the similarities. Eva Saks identifies one of the "chief tensions of American miscegenation law" as "the power of legal language to construct, criminalize, and appropriate the human body itself."[29] Legal language, as the passage from Chesnutt's novel reveals, merges here with national metaphor in constructing the human body. According to Chesnutt, it is the "American eye" that can recognize that a racial difference exists between these two men as black and white. The rules of racial recognition thus become a national project in which a trained American eye would know how to read these two bodies—how to decode the one man's "light brown" skin color, "swarthy complexion," and "curly hair" as representative of what is legally considered "black." In other words, the American eye sees by the rules of racial recognition.

Chesnutt describes the concept of racial categorization in the United States at the turn of the century as a sort of American idiom. It is through the American eye that one can read the second man as black and the first man as white. It is through the American eye that one knows *how* to look. Internalizing the language of (American) racial recognition means learning how to read or decode bodies, how to translate a certain shade of skin, shape of lip or eye or nose into a legally cognizable entity. It means knowing how to decipher what sociologists Michael Omi and Howard Winant have called the "system of racial meaning."[30] It means knowing how to "race" a person: how to erase "person" and see only "race."

The eye is an instrument of witnessing. It sees evidence. One might presuppose that the eye itself is impartial or that it sees innocently. But the field of vision through which the eye is constituted is racially saturated. Furthermore, the system of racial meaning is plagued with the contradictions of the visible. Bodily markers are unreliable. The exterior is not always a guarantee of the interior; what we see may not always be what we get.

The body of Miller is read as "black" through the recognition of "evidence" in the form of racial cues or markers. What racial cues are necessary for the reading of the other man as "white?" He is described as a "gentleman" and a "fine type of Anglo-Saxon, as the term is used in speaking of our composite white population."[31] That the words "white" and "Anglo-Saxon" can describe him seems merely enough to signify his whiteness. Whiteness is made visible through an absence of a "swarthy complexion" or "curly hair." Dr. Burns's seemingly unmarked body allows for its reading as white.

"The Journey Southward" narrates the legal implications of racialized difference under Jim Crow. The men appear to the reader as social equals until the train crosses the North-South border. When the train moves into Virginia, the two men move out of the sleeping car into a day car governed by the laws of Jim Crow. Upon entering the day car, the train conductor "glances interrogatively at Miller" yet does not immediately evict him from what has become a "whites only" car. After a while, he asks Dr. Burns, "This man is with you?," to which Burns replies, "Certainly. . . . Don't you see that he is?"[32] This exchange represents a willful misunderstanding—the train conductor, seeing the two men in intimate conversation and acting familiarly with each other seems reluctant to evict Miller *because* he is with Burns. He asks an ambiguous question which later, only after another white passenger complains about Miller's presence, he rephrases as "*did I understand you* to say that this man was your servant?" [emphasis added].[33] Burns's indignant response to the second question—"No, indeed! This gentleman is not my servant, nor anybody's servant but is my friend"—disrupts the fragile ruse the conductor has offered the pair. When Burns claims *friendship* as the basis of their relationship, he disrupts the racialized social hierarchy of the postbellum South. Two professional "equals" must be separated.

The encounter on the railroad in *The Marrow of Tradition* dramatizes the irony of a system that claims to be "equal but separate" and demonstrates the rhetorical machinations of the law. In an attempt to bypass the blatant discrimination targeted at his friend, Dr. Burns offers to accompany Dr. Miller into the "colored" car. However, through the "thin disguise of 'equal' accommodations,"[34] the law claims strict impartiality. As the conductor sternly tells Burns, " I warn you, sir . . . that the law will be enforced. The beauty of the system lies in its strict impartiality—it applies to both races alike."[35] The train conductor reasons that the law cannot be considered discriminatory to either race because it applies to *both* races alike. Not only does the equation "equal but separate" rely on the coupling of dissonant terms—the beauty of the system insists on the presence of *two* races to work. Further on in this essay, we will see what happens to "the beauty of the system" when a third race enters the scene.

III. "A Chinaman of the Ordinary Laundry Type"

Literature shows us law's unarticulated possibilities, the moments at which the law might bend. What the legal case does not reveal is the flexibility of the law. Once Miller has been excluded from the "white car" and exiled to (or, included in) the "colored car," he moves from the position of subjected subject to the position of full observer in a subjected car. "Properly" contained within the space of the colored car, he asserts his own authority as a spectator. As he looks out the window of the colored car, he sees two other nonwhites boarding the whites only car: "At the next station a Chinaman, of the ordinary laundry type, boarded the train and took his seat in the white car without objection. At another point a colored nurse found a place with her mistress."[36] Through Miller's eyes, Chesnutt reveals two exceptions to the law of Virginia—the law is surprisingly lenient when a black female servant accompanied by her employer and when a Chinese laborer enter the white car, thus crossing the color line. Observing that the organization of the color line is founded on a notion of racial hierarchy (white supremacy) rather than mere racial *difference,* Miller comments, "White people . . . do not object to the negro as servant—he is welcomed; as an equal, he is repudiated."

It is noteworthy that Chesnutt does not comment any further about the appearance of the Chinese man. Despite the acute awareness of class issues throughout the novel, he makes no comment on the inclusion of what appears to be a Chinese *laborer*—to be specific, a "Chinaman, of the laundry type"—in the whites only car. The Chinaman boards the train and sits in the white car *without objection.* Aside from this acknowledgment, neither Miller nor Chesnutt offers any further response. The Chinaman passes onto the white car—and onto the page of the text without further comment. However, he clearly cannot pass *as* white within the context of American racial categorization. I would suggest that this fleeting appearance of the Chinaman marks a moment of nonrecognition of an Asian presence on the black-white racial landscape. Nonrecognition, as described by legal theorist Neil Gotanda, is a two-part process: the "recognition of racial affiliation followed by the deliberate suppression of racial consideration."[37] Nonrecognition is the decision to adopt color blindness as a legal strategy—or, as Gotanda puts it, it is a *"technique"*—one that assumes the pose of neutrality and objectivity in legal decision-making without any consideration of the material realities of racial subordination.

Why, in these two literary and legal narratives of segregation, does the figure of a Chinaman appear in passing in *The Marrow of Tradition* and as an allusion in *Plessy v. Ferguson*? Harlan's invocation of the specter of the Chinaman establishes the "Chinese race" as radically other. Chesnutt also creates an imaginary Chinaman, whom he describes as of the "ordinary laundry type." That he expects his readers in 1901 to understand this reference, to be able to imagine or visualize this image, suggests that the "Chinaman, of the ordinary laundry type" is already part of the contemporary American racial lexicon. Indeed, the Chinaman was an inextricable part of discourses on race and labor at the turn of the century.

The Chinaman's brief appearance in this literary narrative represents what James Moy has called a "marginal sight." Moy argues that "the notion of Chineseness under the sign of the exotic became familiar to the American spectator long before the sightings of the actual Chinese."[38] Yet, "ordinary" is exactly *not* "exotic"—nor radically different. The repetition of the Chinese as "laundryman" transformed an "exotic" representation into an "ordinary" sight. Through such repetitions, Chinese racial representation had been institutionalized in American culture by the late nineteenth century. The figure of the Chinaman—usually a white actor in yellow face—appeared in dramas, comedies, and opera as exotic spectacles or comic relief. The Chinese were presented as marvels to gawk at in P. T. Barnum's freak shows. The title role of Bret Harte and Mark Twain's 1877 play *Ah Sin* featured a white actor playing "as good and as natural and consistent a Chinaman as he could see in San Francisco."[39] According to Ronald Takaki, after Bret Harte's poem, "The Heathen Chinee," which was widely published in 1870, "the phrase 'heathen Chinee' became a household word in white America."[40] In fact, Harte's poem was cited numerous times during the congressional debates over the Chinese question.[41]

The recognizable image of the "ordinary laundry type" of Chinaman was made visible by what Frantz Fanon has called "a historico-racial schema."[42] Fanon explains that "below this corporeal schema I had sketched a historico-racial schema . . . woven . . . out of a thousand details, anecdotes, stories." Below the Chinaman's imagined corporeal space, written on the body, lay the multitudes of details, anecdotes, and stories made legible by various representations (visual, literary, and legal) of the Chinese in America. Thus this fictive image becomes the repository for a range of cultural representations that have solidified into the stereotype of the Chinaman.

The specter of the Chinaman "of the ordinary laundry type" in Chesnutt's text represents an everyday figure, something common, nothing special. And yet, in *The Marrow of Tradition,* he can board the white car while the character of the gifted black doctor cannot. Harlan's invocation of "a race so different from our own" places the Chinaman as altogether different, uncommon, highly unusual. And yet, in Justice Harlan's fictive account, his Chinaman also can board the white car while an ordinary American citizen such as Homer Plessy cannot. These two fictive renderings pose a paradox: How can the Chinaman be both "ordinary" (*not* exotic) and "so different" (radically other)? This chiasmus—the "ordinary different"—may reveal where the "Chinese" resides and where the "Black" is displaced.

Both Harlan and Chesnutt suggest that the Chinaman enjoys an exceptional sort of mobility within the American racial landscape. One might wonder, however, whether the Chinaman actually was able to enter designated "white" spaces as freely as Harlan and Chesnutt have imagined in their narratives. I would suggest that this imagined narrative of the Chinaman's freedom of mobility effectively obscures the juridical management of physical and geographic mobility placed on Chinese laborers by the Chinese Exclusion Acts and other acts of anti-Asian legislation. The Chinaman serves as a rhetorical foil, a necessary agent to make coherent a particular narrative of American citizenship.

If we consider the peculiar location of the figure of the "Chinaman" in the text of Harlan's dissent and in Chesnutt's novel, we might consider how these two narratives raise important concerns about who is allowed access to national identity and who is allowed access to national space and time. To put it another way, who is allowed to participate in the formation of family and heirs, to property, and to establishing a generational presence on U.S. soil? Both Jim Crow segregation and Chinese exclusion condoned methods of racial subordination that controlled the geographical mobility of nonwhite subjects. These textual moments in the *Plessy* case and *The Marrow of Tradition*, which contain references—however oblique —to Chinese exclusion, mark an important contradiction on the site of American law.

I return in conclusion to the locution "a race so different from our own" that Justice Harlan invokes in his lone dissent against segregation. Harlan creates a phantasmatic image of a "Chinaman" to embody this radical difference between it and "our own" race(s). He appears to extend the concept of "our own" races to include African Americans as members of the nation—as members of a constitutive "we"—in his call for color blindness. Yet in doing so, he invokes a separate racial category that creates another binarism, that of citizen and foreigner. He simultaneously uses the language of inclusion and exclusion—*our* race(s) are *different* from the Chinese race. Harlan sets up the logic of "outsiders within" in his statement, a logic that continues to organize U.S. politics about Asian American subjects through the twenty-first century.

The phrase "our own" is used to signify both whites and blacks—the only two "American" races that qualified for U.S. citizenship at the turn of the twentieth century. However, Harlan (who we may recall was a former slave owner) also may be accounting for African American propinquity through a not-so-oblique citation of slavery—a time in the recent past in American history when the race that was "our own" could be understood not in terms of inclusion but, rather, in terms of ownership, a time when one drop of "African" blood signified a body's "enslaveability," when to belong to this race meant that one's body could be property. This point is made through the body of the Chinese laborer, a body who is triply marked—racially, nationally, and legally—as radically other. "A race so different from our own" unveils the mutual imbrications of segregation and exclusion and ultimately exposes the embedded narratives of Asian American and African American racial formation that exist alongside each other.

NOTES

I am grateful to David Eng, Farhad Karim, Susette Min, Mae Ngai, Teemu Ruskola, and Leti Volpp for their generative comments on earlier versions of this work; to Diana Paulin for valuable reading recommendations; and to Heike Raphael-Hernandez and Shannon Steen for helpful editorial suggestions and great patience.

1. I maintain use of the term "Chinaman" in this essay as it appears in the *Plessy* case and in Charles Chesnutt's literary fiction. In doing so, I seek to flag the currency of the term as a figure and as a popular stereotype in American culture.

2. I focus on the case of the Chinese at this historical juncture to call attention to one important moment of Asian American racial formation alongside an important moment of African American racial formation. The Chinese Exclusion Acts were the first race-based immigration acts and the first of many exclusions to come against immigrants from "Asia." However, I do not mean to suggest that Chinese Americans and Asian Americans are fungible. Rather, I seek to raise the following questions: What was the organizational logic behind the decision to deny immigration to groups from countries of origin within the region understood as "Asia"? How might we consider the series of Asian exclusion orders as a technique of organizing Asian American racial formation?

3. W. E. B. Du Bois, *The Souls of Black Folk* (1903), in W. E. B. Du Bois, *Writings* (New York: Library of America, 1986), 372.

4. Kimberlé Crenshaw, "Color Blindness, History, and the Law," in *The House That Race Built*, ed. Wahneema Lubiano (New York: Pantheon, 1996), 282.

5. *Plessy v. Ferguson*, 163 U.S. at 537 (1896).

6. As Neil Gotanda explains: "American racial classification follows two formal rules: 1) Rule of Recognition: Any person whose Black-African ancestry is visible is Black. 2) Rule of Descent: (a) Any person with a known trace of African ancestry is Black, notwithstanding that person's visual appearance; or, stated differently, (b) the offspring of a Black and a white is Black." Neil Gotanda, "A Critique of 'Our Constitution Is Color-Blind,'" *Stanford Literature Review* 44 (1991): 24. For a book-length study of the one drop of blood rule, see F. James Davis, *Who Is Black? One Nation's Definition* (University Park: Penn State University Press, 1991).

7. Mark Twain, *Pudd'nhead Wilson* (1894) (New York: Penguin Books, 1986), 64.

8. *Plessy v. Ferguson*, 163 U.S. at 537.

9. Ibid.

10. Ibid. at 538.

11. Albion Tourgée, one of Plessy's attorneys, argued in his brief, "Probably most white persons if given a choice, would prefer death to life in the United States as colored persons. Under these conditions, is it possible to conclude that the reputation of being white is not property? Indeed, is it not the most valuable sort of property, being the master key that unlocks the golden door of opportunity?" Brief for Homer Plessy in Error at 9, as quoted in Cheryl Harris, "Whiteness as Property," *Harvard Law Review* 106 (1993): 1748. Harris's article traces the origins of the notion of whiteness as property in American law.

12. See Susan Gillman and Forrest G. Robinson, eds., *Mark Twain's Pudd'nhead Wilson* (Durham: Duke University Press, 1990); Saidiya Hartman, *Scenes of Subjection* (New York: Oxford University Press, 1997); Samira Kawash, *Dislocating the Color Line: Identity, Hybridity, and Singularity in African-American Literature* (Palo Alto: Stanford University Press, 1997); Eric Sundquist, *To Wake the Nations: Race in the Making of American Literature* (Cambridge: Belknap Press, 1993); Priscilla Wald, *Constituting Americans: Cultural Anxiety and Narrative Form* (Durham: Duke University Press, 1995). It is worth noting that the *Plessy* case has become a part of the educational state apparatus—not just in legal curriculum but also, as these works of literary criticism make visible, in the university humanities curriculum.

13. T. Alexander Aleinikoff, "Re-reading Justice Harlan's Dissent in *Plessy v. Ferguson*: Freedom, Antiracism, and Citizenship," *University of Illinois Law Review* 4 (1992): 961–977. For examples of constitutional law textbooks, see Jerome Barron et al., *Constitutional Law: Principles and Policy, Cases and Materials* (Dayton, OH: Lexis Law, 1987), 521; Paul Brest and Sanford Levinson, *Processes of Constitu-

tional Decisionmaking: Cases and Materials (Boston: Little, Brown, 1983), 272–273; Gerald Gunther, *Cases and Materials on Constitutional Law* (New York: Foundation Press, 1991), 647; William Lockhart et al., *Constitutional Law: Cases Comments-Questions* (Washington, D.C.: West Group, 1991), 941; Geoffrey Stone et al., *Constitutional Law* (Boston: Little, Brown, 1991), 489–490.

14. *Plessy v. Ferguson,* 163 U.S. at 539.

15. Ibid. at 561. Anthologized accounts of the case tend to excise Harlan's comments on the "the Chinese race." Legal scholar Gabriel J. Chin has argued that the "great dissenter" was in fact a "faithful opponent of the constitutional rights of Chinese for much of his career on the Court" (168). Indeed, Harlan's allusion to the Chinese in his dissent may not be aberrant but rather emblematic of the Justice's anti-Chinese sentiments. Chin concludes that, ultimately, "Harlan's good result in Plessy was backed by bad reasoning, bad policy, and bad principles. After a hundred years, Harlan's Plessy dissent should be overruled." Gabriel J. Chin, "The Plessy Myth: Justice Harlan and the Chinese Cases," *Iowa Law Review* 82 (1996): 182.

16. The first Chinese Exclusion Act stated that "whereas, in the opinion of the Government of the United States, the coming of Chinese laborers to this country endangers the good order of certain localities . . . : Therefore . . . it shall not be lawful for any Chinese laborer to come, or having come . . . to remain within the United States." Chinese Exclusion Act, ch. 126, 22 Stat. 58, Sec. 1 (1882). Chinese who were not laborers including merchants, students, diplomats, and travelers were allowed to enter and stay. Although individuals of Chinese descent could not naturalize as U.S. citizens, a federal court in California recognized the U.S. citizenship of Chinese born in the United States. See *In re Look Tin Sing,* 21 F. 354 (C.C.D. Cal. 1884). Subsequent legislation was enacted to exclude all Chinese from the United States. Act of July 9, 1884, ch. 220, 23 Stat. 115; Act of May 5, 1892, ch. 60, 27 Stat. 25; Act of April 29, 1902, ch. 641, 32 Stat. 176; Act of April 27, 1904, ch. 1630, 33 Stat. 428. See Sucheng Chang, ed., *Entry Denied: Exclusion and the Chinese Community in America, 1882–1943* (Philadelphia: Temple University Press, 1991); Lucy Salyer, *Laws Harsh as Tigers: Chinese Immigrants and the Shaping of Modern Immigration Law* (Chapel Hill: University of North Carolina Press, 1995); Shirley Hune, "Politics of Chinese Exclusion: Legislative-Executive Conflict 1876–1882," *Amerasia* 9:1 (1982): 5–27.

17. The passage of the 1882 Chinese Exclusion Act has usually signaled the beginning of the "official" era of Chinese exclusion. However, legal scholar Leti Volpp has suggested that we consider the 1875 Page Act law, which explicitly barred the entry of Chinese women who were allegedly being imported as prostitutes, as the initiation of the regime of racialized and gendered exclusion. Through this allegation of prostitution, immigration authorities effectively disallowed the entry of nearly all Chinese women into the United States. After the 1882 Exclusion Act, this prohibition on women was nearly absolute, the wives of merchants being the

one notable exception. Act of Feb. 18, 1875, ch. 80, 18 Stat. 318. See Leti Volpp, "Engendering Culture," paper presented at the annual conference of the Asian American Studies Association, Los Angeles, California, 23 April 2005.

18. *Plessy v. Ferguson*, 163 U.S. at 561.

19. We see here how the politics of citizenship are both racialized and gendered. Military service was only an option for men—white or nonwhite.

20. Lisa Lowe, *Immigrant Acts: On Asian American Cultural Politics* (Durham: Duke University Press, 1996), 6.

21. This problem becomes more pronounced during World War II, when the contradictions between du jure citizenship and de facto membership for Asian American subjects are embodied by the nisei Japanese American soldier. When the Asian American soldier puts his body on the line in defense of the nation, he must literally embody the impossible locale between "quintessential U.S. citizen" and "symbolic alien."

22. Mae Ngai has persuasively argued that the Chinese exclusion laws generated the nation's first illegal aliens, a phenomenon known as "paper sons." Ngai notes that many Chinese laborers "gained entry by posing as persons who were legally admissible, often with fraudulent certificates identifying them as merchants or by claiming to be American citizens by birth or as the China-born sons of U.S. citizens, known formally as derivative citizens." Mae Ngai, *Impossible Subjects: Illegal Aliens and the Making of Modern America* (Princeton: Princeton University Press, 2004), 204.

23. Just before the famous call for color-blind constitutionalism in his dissent, Harlan comments, "The white race deems itself to be the dominant race in this country. And so it is, in prestige, in achievements, in education, in wealth and in power. So, I doubt not, it will continue to be for all time, if it remains true to its great heritage and holds fast to the principles of constitutional liberty." *Plessy v. Ferguson*, 163 U.S. at 559.

24. Sau-ling Cynthia Wong, *Reading Asian American Literature: From Necessity to Extravagance* (Princeton: Princeton University Press, 1993), 151. More recently, David Eng in his *Racial Castration: Managing Masculinity in Asian America* (Durham: Duke University Press, 2001) discusses how Chinese American writers such as Maxine Hong Kingston and Frank Chin have reimagined the "official" photographic records of the completion of the transcontinental railroad to make visible the images of Chinese American laborers that do not appear in dominant national histories.

25. Charles W. Chesnutt, "The Courts and The Negro," in *Plessy v. Ferguson: A Brief History with Documents*, ed. Brook Thomas (Boston: Bedford Books, 1997), 157.

26. Charles Chesnutt, *The Marrow of Tradition* (1901) (New York: Penguin Books, 1993).

27. Ibid., 49.

28. Ibid.; emphases added.

29. Eva Saks, "Representing Miscegenation Law," *Raritan* 8:2 (1988): 39.

30. Michael Omi and Howard Winant, *Racial Formation in the United States* (New York: Routledge, 1986), 63.

31. Chesnutt, *Marrow of Tradition,* 49.

32. Ibid., 52.

33. Ibid., 53.

34. Harlan argues in his dissent, "The thin disguise of 'equal' accommodations for passengers in railroad coaches will not mislead anyone, nor atone for the wrong this day has done." *Plessy v. Ferguson,* 163 U.S. at 562.

35. Chesnutt's formulation echoes Anatole France's well-known observation on "the majestic equality of the French law, which forbids both rich and poor alike from sleeping under the bridges of the Seine." Isaac Balbus has remarked on France's aphorism: "If the law is indifferent to the distinction between rich and poor, it follows that the law will necessarily tend to support and maintain this distinction." Isaac D. Balbus, *The Dialectics of Legal Repression: Black Rebels before the American Criminal Courts* (New York: Russell Sage Foundation, 1973), 5.

36. Chesnutt, *Marrow of Tradition,* 59.

37. According to Gotanda, nonrecognition is composed of three elements: "First, there must be something which is cognizable as a racial characteristic or classification. Second, the characteristic must be recognized. Third, the characteristic must not be considered in a decision. For non-recognition to make sense, it must be possible to recognize something while not including it in making a decision." Gotanda, "Critique of 'Our Constitution Is Color-Blind,'" 17.

38. James Moy, *Marginal Sights: Staging the Chinese in America* (Iowa City: Iowa University Press, 1993), 10.

39. For a historical account of stage representations of the Chinese, see Moy, *Marginal Sights,* in particular chapters 1–3.

40. Ronald Takaki, *Strangers from a Different Shore: A History of Asian Americans* (Boston: Little, Brown, 1989), 104.

41. See Elaine H. Kim, *Asian American Literature: An Introduction to the Writings and Their Social Context* (Philadelphia: Temple University Press, 1982), 14.

42. Frantz Fanon, *Black Skins, White Masks* (New York: Grove Weidenfeld, 1967), 111.

Chapter 2

Crossings in Prose
Jade Snow Wong and the Demand for a New Kind of Expert

Cynthia Tolentino

The "racial uniform," Robert E. Park's 1914 metaphor for the status of the "Oriental," is a strange but somehow familiar image. Used in his theory of racial assimilation, this understudied image is most obviously meant to refer to a biological racial discourse that produces a sense of otherness and limits the life chances of racialized groups.[1] Both African Americans and Asian Americans wear the "racial uniform," he explains, suggesting that it comprises the primary obstacle to an assimilation process modeled on white ethnic groups. At the same time, however, Park argues that only Asian Americans, if given the opportunity by white Americans, possess a cultural capacity to assimilate. Perhaps the familiarity of Park's figure, then, stems from the parallel that it draws between Asian Americans and contemporary conceptions of a model minority.

Yet the "racial uniform" specifically refers to a process by which socio-logical theories of race assign an exemplary status to Asian Americans that is underwritten by denigrating pathologies of African American culture and conceptions of Asian Americans as foreign outsiders.[2] Though it is possible to treat Park's account of the racial uniform as an early example of figurations of Asian Americans as a "model minority" or an illustration of how notions of "otherness" shape sociological theories of race, such readings do not enable us to ask questions about the particular implica-tions of this figure for Asian American and African American racial for-mations.

If Park saw assimilation into the United States mainstream as an in-evitable and natural process for European immigrant groups, he clearly identified "Negroes" and "Orientals" as exceptions to this pattern. Both

Negroes and Orientals, according to Park, are subject to racial prejudice and are therefore unable to complete the final stage of a race relations cycle that would eventually result in their assimilation into an American mainstream.[3] But even as he assigned Negroes and Orientals a common status as aberrations to an American social body, Park implied that only Orientals had cultural advantages that enabled them to advance. Following his comparative and hierarchical logic, Orientals, even as they were perceived to be non-American and the wrong color, could still draw on an exotic culture as an alternative source of self-definition. Park's "racial uniform" thus evokes notions of progress that chart different destinies for Asian Americans and African Americans.

But how were people identified as Orientals interpellated by this relationship of difference and its implications for Asian Americans and African Americans? More than thirty years later, Asian American writers would revise Park's narrative in their literary works, taking up sociological theories of race that refer to cross-racial comparisons between Asian Americans and African Americans in their self-representations. One of my central concerns in this essay is how Asian American writers, including Jade Snow Wong, encountered sociological theories that compared Negroes and Orientals as a sanctioned discourse that they could draw on to negotiate racialized and gendered notions of agency and expertise. Wong did not take up isolated points of racial comparison as much as she specifically engaged the relationship between Negroes and Orientals that Park and other sociologists used to conceptualize racial categories.

The "uniform" aspect of Park's racial uniform brings to mind the way in which this figure is shaped by class dynamics and notions of progress. Conventionally defined as an article of clothing that classifies an individual as part of a distinct profession or class, a uniform implies that membership and official status can be determined through a system of visible, physical markers. How, I ask, did Asian American writers adapt Park's concept to develop ideologies of professionalism and define them as essentially "Asian American"?

My focus here is Jade Snow Wong's autobiography *Fifth Chinese Daughter* (1945), a work deeply concerned with the influence of sociological studies of Negroes and Orientals on Asian American strategies of self-definition and ideologies of professionalism. As I show, writers such as Wong did not interpret the comparisons that sociologists were making between Negroes and Orientals, in solely ideological terms, but offered detailed accounts of the processes by which Asian Americans develop alternative ideas of agency, expertise, and progress. By considering the significance that Asian American and African American writers have historically attributed to sociology in their works, I suggest how such moments offer vital insight into the interracial and cross-disciplinary theories that inform their attempts to negotiate the ways in which they were valued as Orientals in comparison with Negroes.

Let me begin my discussion of *Fifth Chinese Daughter* with a brief plot summary. Set in San Francisco and taking place during the Depression and World War II, the autobiographical novel centers on Jade Snow's education from the ages of five to twenty-four. What unfolds during the course of the book is a narrative in which Jade Snow seems to find her place in relation to her parents, Chinatown business people, and white American elites. Critical to the narrative of Jade Snow's formation, I argue, is her encounter with the discipline of sociology.

In a story that bears a striking resemblance to Richard Wright's description of his encounter with sociological representations of African American life, Wong relates her intellectual awakening in a way that brings sociology's powerful effect into sharp relief. Reflecting on her college courses, she observes: "But if Latin was the easiest course and chemistry the most difficult, sociology was the most stimulating. Jade Snow had chosen it without thought, simply to meet a requirement; but that casual decision completely revolutionized her thinking, shattering her Wong-constructed conception of the order of things."[4] As this passage suggests, studying sociology enables Jade Snow to develop a new perspective and sense of authority that can compete with those that she associates with her family. Wong reinforces this notion by calling attention to sociology's instrumental role in evacuating Jade Snow of her "strangely vague feelings" and instilling a sense of detachment that allows her to break old patterns and challenge her parents in a manner that she favorably compares to "her sociology instructor addressing his freshman class."[5] Wong suggests that what Jade Snow has undergone is not a bland, humanist epiphany but the result of a particular, privileged kind of knowledge production.

Wright's account seems instructive here, for it elucidates a link between sociology and literature that Wong's autobiography pursues, while also showing how sociology might be seen as an entry point to larger questions about racialized agency. The difference is that Wright seems to stake out an explicitly competitive relationship with sociological studies of African American life, claiming that fiction is more adept at exploring the nuances that sociology is not concerned with or does not value. In his famous essay

"How Bigger Was Born," Wright figured the novel as an alternative site, or "laboratory," for exploring the "Negro problem" as the failed assimilation of African Americans into an American mainstream. "Why should I not," he asks, "like a scientist in a laboratory, use my imagination and invent test-tube situations . . . and following the guidance of my own hopes and fears, work out in fictional form an emotional statement and resolution of this problem."[6] Envisioning sociology as both precursor and muse, he seeks to define fiction writing as the ideal mode for questioning science's unique capacity for studying African American communities. Even as he calls attention to sociology's powerful effect, his distant and seemingly objective description of sociology as the "work of men who were studying Negro life" widens the gap between their findings and his own (superior) knowledge production.[7]

Both Wong and Wright suggest that their encounters with sociology are catalysts for new perspectives and self-expression. Yet Wong seems more concerned with elaborating on sociology's analytical methods in order to bring Asian Americans into view. In contrast to Wright, who frames his encounter with sociology as part of his northward migration to Chicago, Wong is introduced to sociology as an academic subject that enables her to consider and write about Chinese Americans as an important part of her college curriculum. Indeed, the novel's interest in exploring the university as a site of Asian American subject formation is made clear by Jade Snow's description of how her "Chinatown stories" offer her validation as a Chinese American woman. Although her parents disparage her research interests as filial disrespect, she finds in her literature course at Mills College that "her grades were consistently higher when she wrote about Chinatown and the people she had known all her life."[8] Tempting as it may be to read the pleasure that Wong finds in writing as a generic discovery of creativity, it is important to note that it refers specifically to writing about her Chinese American family and community. Wong later recounts how fiction writing enables her to improve on sociology's emphasis on objective, "factual reporting" but underscores how it allows her to define "Chinese American" in ways that are different from Park's conception of "Orientals" and also to depict Chinatown as a dynamic space rather than its stereotypical representation as a closed, ethnic enclave. By taking on sociology's representational modes and fascination with Orientals as objects of scientific study, Wong gains access to a scientifically sanctioned language that enables her to showcase her own knowledge production and assume dual roles as researcher and native-informant.

Questions of Agency

Writing provides both Wright and Wong with alternatives to the sociolog-ical narratives that assign limited forms of subjectivity for African Ameri-cans and Asian Americans. For Wright, comparing fiction writing to sci-entific study enables him to parallel an African American writer and soci-ologists studying the "Negro problem," as well as to envision an adversarial relationship between them. To contend with the hypervisibility of Afri-can Americans as objects of scientific study, he directs his energies toward finding ways of unsettling sociology's explanatory authority over African American communities. Wong also seems skeptical of sociology's author-ity, expressing frustration with "some of the so-called scientific reasoning expounded in the sociology class, where heredity and environment were assigned all the responsibility for personal success and failure."[9] To define Asian Americans as knowledge producers rather than passive Oriental objects, Wong points to the ways in which sociology opens up possibili-ties for documenting Asian American self-activity in ways that also lead to public recognition.

Fifth Chinese Daughter repeatedly draws attention to the knowledge that Jade Snow gleans from sociology, as well as to particular aspects of sociology's allure for Asian Americans. Each chapter develops part of a series of transformations that lead to Jade Snow fully assuming the subjec-tivity destined for her—filial daughter, convert to sociology, researcher, Chinese American artist-entrepreneur. Indeed, the novel's interest in situ-ating sociology as a solution to Jade Snow's feelings of dissatisfaction and estrangement seems to answer directly to Henry Yu's observation that Af-rican American intellectuals—including prominent sociologists Charles S. Johnson, E. Franklin Frazier, St. Claire Drake, and Horace Cayton—had already found that sociology equipped them with an authoritative lan-guage for narrating their self-identities and articulating the problems of racial discrimination and marginalization within the United States.[10]

According to Yu, sociological research on the Oriental Problem helped to define Orientals as important objects of study at the same time that it brought about a process by which Orientals could become knowledge pro-ducers. As he explains, sociologists such as Robert Park became interested in studying Orientals in their projects on race relations, which brought about the incorporation of Chinese and Japanese Americans as researchers and a body of scholarship on the Oriental Problem that was produced by whites and Asian Americans. If prevailing views pegged Asians as permanent foreigners, he argues, then sociology provided them with a "power-ful way of naming their own place in American society."[11] *Fifth Chinese Daughter* highlights the instrumental role of academic sociology in defin-ing a process by which Asian Americans could become knowledge pro-ducers of exotic information. As forcefully as Wong's autobiography might seem to argue for a model minority, I believe that it more clearly suggests how the production of Asian American racial identity has to negotiate the history of Negroes and Orientals as intertwined objects of study in acade-mic sociology.

To understand this connection between Asian American racial identity and sociological studies of the Negro and Oriental problems, let me turn to Wong's repetition of the classic scene of a parent telling her child about the "birds and the bees." In her version, Wong suggests that negotiating racial categories in relation to a black/white binary is a rite of passage for Asian Americans. In response to Jade Snow's query about "where babies come from," Mama delivers a narrative of racial evolution: "There are three kinds of babies. When they are nearly done, they are white foreign babies. When they bake a little longer, they become golden Chinese babies. Sometimes they are left in too long, and they become black babies!"[12] Presented in the context of a private, family encounter, Mama's "facts of life" tale revises Park's sociological theory of assimilation, which presents European Americans as the paradigmatic group. In her evolutionary nar-rative, Chinese represent the ideal and whites appear as not quite com-plete, whereas African Americans are depicted as being irreparably dam-aged and off the path of progress that this narrative implies. Wong recov-ers Park's conception of African Americans as extreme aberrations, but she revises the relationship between Asians and whites in order to figure Chinese as more developed, or "evolved," than whites.

This scene also revises conventional ideas about producers of racial knowledge and the contexts in which such knowledge is generated. This scene between Mama and Jade Snow casts a Chinese immigrant as an in-terpreter of racial categories and depicts a different role for second-gener-ation Asian Americans such as Jade Snow, who "turned over this informa-tion in her mind, and concluded that it was quite reasonable."[13] Not only does this scene suggest how Asian American strategies at self-definition both engage and extend racist sociological theories of black, white, and Asian difference, but it also calls attention to the ways in which producing, evaluating, and disseminating knowledge are themselves racialized prac-tices. By calling attention to the pleasure that Jade Snow finds in work that involves research and evaluation, Wong implies that the rise of Asian Americans like herself is made possible by situating Asians as "brokers" of racial difference: active negotiators rather than static models for other racialized groups.

The Rise of Sociology

To explore the possibilities that the field of sociology opened to Asian American writers for negotiating a U.S. society that was conventionally viewed in terms of a black and white dichotomy, I briefly discuss here the ascendance of sociology to the status of official discourse on race, which brought about a cultural concept of race that writers such as Wong could engage in their works. At a time in which urban sociologists were increasingly regarded as the nation's authorities on race, Wong models her protagonist on an urban expert whose authority stems from her first-hand account of traditional practices, community structure, and commerce in San Francisco's Chinatown during the Depression and World War II. Her vision in the novel resembles—and perhaps rivals—that of an urban sociologist, the national expert on race. As Carlo Rotella observes, the new social landscape of the postindustrial metropolis required new forms of intellectual labor to represent the metropolis and its "inner city."[14] Noting the proximity in which fiction writers, scientists, and journalists worked during the 1940s, he points out that this interdisciplinary atmosphere led James Farrell, Richard Wright, and Nelson Algren to join the Chicago novel to disciplines that included sociology.

By the mid-1940s, the field of sociology was the dominant producer of knowledge on race and racism and had assumed an increasingly important role in imagining the trajectory of the nation's future. As numerous critics have observed, one of the markers of sociology's ascendance to the status of official discourse on race was Gunnar Myrdal's influential study *An American Dilemma: The Negro Problem and Modern Democracy* (1944). Sponsored by the Carnegie Corporation, Myrdal's study employed many of Park's former students and elaborated his interracial paradigms. Perhaps a corollary to Park's figure of the racial uniform is Myrdal's argument that African Americans were—in comparison with Chinese and Japanese —"more helplessly imprisoned as a subordinate caste in America, a caste of people deemed to be lacking a cultural past and assumed to be incapable of a cultural future."[15] Figuring Asian Americans as "cultured Orientals," Myrdal defined African Americans as exceptionally pathological and as objects of social reform carried out by white Americans. Although *An American Dilemma* is largely perceived as a black/white study, taking into account the relationship that Myrdal draws between Negroes and Orientals allows us to see how it shapes his overarching theory of racialized agency and progress in the United States. This racist ideology connects Wong to Park and Myrdal but also illustrates how engaging their ideas about "cultured Orientals" (and the implications that this notion carries for white Americans and Negroes) enables her to flesh out a new form of authority.

Scientific Domesticity

As Judy Yung notes, the few Chinese American college graduates with professional degrees found themselves, like black American professionals, confined to menial labor and service-industry jobs in Chinatown and underemployed in general because of racism in the larger labor market.[16] *Fifth Chinese Daughter* comments explicitly on the limited employment possibilities for college-educated Asian Americans, while also indicating that Jade Snow has no problem finding employment as domestic help in white American households. To question the racialization and sexual stereotyping of Asian American women as "permanent foreigners" and "ideal wives," Wong sought to redefine the forms of domestic authority available to Chinese American women.

Domesticity becomes a key factor in Wong's attempts to negotiate a form of agency that engages but is also different from the forms of "cultural agency" that the Chicago School sociologists ascribe to Orientals in their attempts to distinguish them from Negroes. In a scene that registers how domesticity shapes the racialization of Asian American women, Jade Snow describes how her white employers treat her as an inanimate object. In response, she adapts sociological methods to create a vantage point from which she is able to view them as if she were not in a subordinate position. Identifying her employers by "type rather than name," Jade Snow proceeds to describe them as "the horsy family," "the apartment-house family," "the political couple," and "the bridge playing group" and to compare them negatively to the Wong family's "high standards," "Confucian decorum," and "Christian ideals."[17] Composed into a view, sociology helps to make the space of a white American home available for Jade Snow to observe, classify, and define her employers as objects of study. This scene does not suggest that Jade Snow has transcended a racist labor market but that sociology opens up a means of documenting her exclusion and refiguring it as her expert study of the daily rituals and customs of white, middle-class Americans. For Wong, sociology is not so much an academic discipline as an entry point to a privileged discourse that provides her with a new form of agency, enabling her to understand and interpret where she had previously only been the object.

Redefining Agency

Wong describes a shift in ontological status—from object to subject—that is made possible by producing an alternative discourse of race, one that is not limited to binary conceptions of Asian Americans as permanent foreigners or assimilated Asians. To understand how she opens up the problem of Asian American agency, we need to consider how she figures Chinese Americans as transnational subjects. Linking Chinese Americans to global rather than strictly national communities allows her to emphasize their self-activity in a way that frames them as social agents rather than passive subjects.[18]

Describing the wartime restrictions on the flow of Asian and European goods to the United States, she notes the changing practices that Chinese immigrants used to maintain commercial and personal ties to China and how this contributes to her commercial success, for "there was better opportunity for an American potter to sell his wares than ever before."[19] By drawing attention to the global and localized relations that shape Jade Snow's rise as an artist, she suggests how her identities as Asian American female, artist, and entrepreneur take shape through narratives other than assimilation into the U.S. nation.

By showcasing Jade Snow's work as an interpreter of cultural categories, Wong is able to suggest that she is something more than the "cultured Oriental" envisioned in sociological theories. Despite the publicity and financial success that accompanies her chosen career as a potter, Wong suggests that Jade Snow's work is not completely satisfying because only white Americans buy her "Chinese" wares. Describing her pottery as "pretty crude stuff," a Chinatown businessman insists, "Only peasants used that handthrown pottery with the earthy look. . . . Oh, the foreigners here; there are always a few who like to be different, if they can afford it."[20] Contrasting the scornful reactions of her family and Chinatown business owners to her commercial success with elite whites, this scene sets Jade Snow apart, portraying her as an enlightened cosmopolitan artist styled as a Chinese peasant. The attention that Wong devotes to her decision to adopt Shanghai braids rather than the fashionable permanent wave serves to highlight her work in negotiating concepts of ethnicity, particularly their relation to biological or physical characteristics. Hair, as Kobena Mercer reminds us, is a key ethnic signifier, given its adaptability and symbolism within a raced society. More than a biological fact, the act of styling hair becomes "the medium of significant statements about self and society and the codes of value that bind them or don't."[21] Wong's braids are a physical marker, but one that is of her own creation rather than an innate biological trait. Her style choice reflects that she has neither rejected "American" fashion codes nor recovered a "pure" Chinese tradition, but refers instead to her work in revising the criteria for Chinese ethnicity and the practices used to authenticate Chinese culture.

But even when Chinese participate in global processes, Aihwa Ong warns, they continue to be perceived as culturally distinct. Identifying family practices as something inherent in Chinese culture is complicit with ignoring the effects of state discipline and a highly competitive market.[22] Both defenders and critics of Wong have taken up this position, however, framing her autobiographical novel as a struggle of Chinese values in the face of assimilation and as evidence of Wong's successful negotiation of a "middle way." Leslie Bow, for example, has argued that the novel's figuration of culture "rests not so much on cultural convergence as on a similarity between economic ideologies and the tacit acknowledgement that contact with Caucasians can lead to business success."[23] Because Bow assumes that Jade Snow's acceptance by Chinese and Americans rests on a shared identification with capitalism, she does not take into account that her pottery is not perceived as "Chinese" by her family and the Chinatown business community. What this indicates, I argue, is Wong's greater concern with showcasing her work in interpreting ethnicity and cultural practices.

Experts Abroad

Wong's fascination with the figure of a Chinese American female expert offers a new perspective on the demand for ethnic experts during the 1950s Cold War. If there are few moments in which *Fifth Chinese Daughter* explicitly engages arguments about African Americans and Asian Americans, then taking into account the book's broader context and publication history will help to illuminate the larger implications of sociological definitions of "Orientals" and "Negroes" during the early Cold War. As the privileged discourse on race, sociological studies that focused on the Oriental and Negro problems contributed to a dynamic in which African Americans and Asian Americans became critical factors in U.S. government efforts to depict the nation as a model democracy.

Christina Klein cogently notes that the U.S. government drew on and encouraged certain notions of racial and ethnic identity as a means of advancing a Cold War ideology of integration. Ethnic Americans, she explains, were viewed as the ideal "protectors, representors, and explicators of the nation precisely because they were still seen in some way as Navajo, Sicilian, and Chinese, as well as American."[24] Klein's account also implies that the U.S. government was selectively interested in race and ethnicity and recruited individuals from ethnic groups and nations that were seen as compatible with, but not necessarily representative of, U.S. identity and foreign policy.

African American and Chinese American intellectuals, as members of racialized groups located outside the U.S. mainstream, found that their personal narratives were valued as progressive stories of race relations in the United States. By framing their professional accomplishments as typical American experiences, the U.S. government could deflect criticism from other nations that drew attention to the persistence of racism against African Americans and Asian Americans as a way of undermining U.S. claims to global leadership. Significantly, the objective of the State Department tours was not to deny that American racism existed but to suggest that individuals could succeed in the United States, regardless of their race.

As a writer and historical figure, Wong engages and intersects this history. After obtaining the rights to translate *Fifth Chinese Daughter* into numerous Asian languages, the U.S. State Department sent Wong on a four-month lecture tour in 1953 to newly decolonized or U.S.-occupied Asian nations such as Japan, the Philippines, Singapore, Thailand, Burma, India, and Pakistan. Wong was the first Chinese American sent on an official tour overseas, though Asian American writers from nations that were also military allies of the United States had been previously employed in similar capacities by the U.S. government. Filipino writer Bienvenido Santos, for example, was asked by the U.S. Department of Education to give lectures to audiences across the continental United States on the "spirit of Philippine resistance" under Japanese occupation during World War II.[25]

Wong's official tour readily lends itself to comparisons with the State Department tours undertaken by African American artists and intellectuals, including Louis Armstrong and Saunders Redding. Scholarship on the official tours has primarily been concerned with how the tours helped to connect racial segregation in the United States to anticolonial struggles abroad and has tended to focus on the tours undertaken by African Americans.[26] One of the contributions of this body of scholarship has been in pointing out how the tours produced new struggles over African American racial identity and authenticity, particularly in relation to U.S. nationalism. According to Mary Dudziak, the U.S. Information Agency (USIA) sought to engage figures that they saw as "outstanding negro intellectuals" to counter and, in some cases, to denounce more "controversial" visits made by other African Americans figures such as Josephine Baker, who criticized U.S. racist practices during her concerts overseas.[27]

In her autobiography, Wong describes her desire to educate Americans about Chinese culture and support her pottery work—goals that clearly resonate with the larger interests of the U.S. government in having assimilated Asians link their professional goals with racial progress in the United States. Although she clearly reveled in the idea that her autobiography was perceived as a representation of U.S. racial progress, she also suggests that the official tour provided her with new ways of documenting specific issues that confront Asian Americans and producing new understandings of ethnicity and progress that are not confined to sociological theories of assimilation. If the U.S. State Department sought to engage Asian Americans to bridge the gap between racism "at home" and expanding U.S. interests in Asia during the 1940s and 1950s, then Wong takes on this task, but also uses the context of the tour to rethink the implications of Asian American racialization.

While *Fifth Chinese Daughter* brings into relief Wong's attempts to negotiate sociological conceptions of Orientals, this focus is adapted to fit a different historical configuration in her second book *No Chinese Stranger,* published nearly thirty years later. More than an elaboration of her autobiography, *No Chinese Stranger* gives voice to the attempts of Asian Americans such as Wong to reckon with newly globalized notions of the future and of "Asia." Both works center on Wong's efforts to figure herself as a knowledge producer and cultural producer, thus suggesting the inadequacy of viewing her as an assimilated Asian or even as a transnational figure.

When an audience member asks Wong to state her preference for China, America, writing, or pottery, her reply, "I like making pottery in America," draws attention to the difficulty of defining herself in non-binary terms that center on her self-activity and refer to Asian American racialization.[28] The view that Wong offers of this act of self-definition suggests that she depicts herself as a cultural producer instead of as an assimilated Asian, Oriental, or "pure" artist. The emphasis that she places on the fact that her pottery is "made in America" serves to define her as not "naturally" American at the same time that it suggests that her work exemplifies the definition of "American." Though it is possible to interpret the fact that Wong does not use this moment to speak out against U.S. racism and foreign policy as further evidence that she has internalized the ideological goals of the State Department tours, I argue that her statement demands a more complex reading.

If Wong used her encounter with sociology, the prevailing authority on race, as a way to define a Chinese American female as a knowledge producer in *Fifth Chinese Daughter*, then her encounters with audiences abroad help to open up the problem of agency in similar ways. Her second book, *No Chinese Stranger* (1975), centers on her efforts as an Asian American in Asia to develop a network that would also expand her professional contacts as a ceramist. Drawing on notions of kinship and progress to situate Chinese Americans at the helm of the U.S. political turn to Asia in the 1970s, Wong depicts herself as part of a Chinese diaspora that evolved from forced labor in South America followed by migration to Thailand and the Philippines, and that culminates with their descendents as successful investors in China's Special Economic Zones.[29] While Wong envisions a narrative of progress that resonates with the political and economic vision in an emergent Pacific Rim discourse of the 1970s, she also highlights the importance of Asian Americans as knowledge producers in developing conceptions of Asia.

I have suggested that Wong critically engages the ways in which Asian Americans and African Americans have historically been figured as epistemological objects in sociological narratives of assimilation that were part of a privileged discourse on race during and after World War II. Not only does she impress on us how sociological conceptions of "Orientals" and "Negroes" serve as a staging ground for a new notion of agency, but also she defines this new agency in terms of her ability to interpret situations in which she had previously been only the object. In just this way, Wong shows how agency emerges from historical conditions rather than individual will. By bringing into focus the comparative race and cross-disciplinary routes of influence that bring about this form of agency, she offers a new perspective on Asian American knowledge production as an epistemic and material category.

NOTES

1. Robert Park writes, "The Japanese bears in his features a distinctive racial hallmark . . . a racial uniform that classifies him." See Robert E. Park, *Race and Culture* (Glencoe, IL: Free Press, 1950), 208–209.

2. Scholars in Asian American studies have persuasively argued that conceptions of Asian Americans as a model minority can construct Asian Americans as foreign and alien, while also concealing alliances with African Americans. See Gary Okihiro, *Margins and Mainstreams: Asians in American History and Culture* (Seattle: University of Washington Press, 1994); Vijay Prashad, *Everybody Was Kung Fu Fighting: Afro-Asian Connections and the Myth of Cultural Purity* (Boston: Beacon Press, 2001), and Prashad, *The Karma of Brown Folk* (Minneapolis: University of Minnesota Press, 2000); Claire Jean Kim, "Racial Triangulation of Asian Americans," *Politics and Society* 27.1 (March 1999): 105–138.

3. For a more contextualized and detailed account of Park's theory of assimilation, see the discussion of the ethnicity-based paradigm of race in Michael Omi and Howard Winant, *Racial Formation in the United States: From the 1960s to the 1990s* (New York: Routledge, 1994), 14–23.

4. Jade Snow Wong, *Fifth Chinese Daughter* (Seattle: University of Washington Press, 1989), 124.

5. Ibid., 128.

6. Richard Wright, "Introduction: How Bigger Was Born," in Wright, *Native Son* (New York: Harper and Row, 1987), xxi. Originally published 1940.

7. See Wright's foreword in St. Clair Drake and Horace R. Cayton's *Black Metropolis: A Story of Negro Life in a Northern City* (New York: Harper and Row, 1945), xvii. I discuss Wright's relationship with sociological narratives of race at length in an earlier essay. See Cynthia Tolentino, "Sociology's Fictions and Black Subjectivity in Richard Wright's *Native Son*," *Novel: A Forum on Fiction* 33.3 (Summer 2000): 377–405.

8. Wong, *Fifth Chinese Daughter*, 132.

9. Ibid.

10. Henry Yu, *Thinking Orientals: Migration, Contact, and Exoticism in Modern America* (New York: Oxford University Press, 2001).

11. Ibid., 114.

12. Ibid., 24.

13. Ibid.

14. According to Carlo Rotella, the Chicago School's "ecological model" of the city, based on a system of natural successions and group competition, could not account for the development of such fixtures as ethnic enclaves and ghettos in the postindustrial city. Following his lead, this gap led to the decline of the theoretical dominance of the Chicago School in the field of urban sociology during the 1930s and 1940s, even though its postwar studies on topics such as the ghetto and juvenile delinquency continued to be important through the 1960s, when the national spotlight turned once again to the American inner city. Carlo Rotella, *October Cities: The Redevelopment of Urban Literature* (Berkeley: University of California Press, 1998), 50.

15. Gunnar Myrdal, *An American Dilemma: The Negro Problem and Modern American Democracy* (New Brunswick: Transaction Publishers, 1999), 54.

16. Judy Yung, *Unbound Feet: A Social History of Chinese Women in San Francisco* (Berkeley: University of California Press, 1995).

17. Wong, *Fifth Chinese Daughter*, 106.

18. As Mae Ngai observes, scholarship has tended to focus on the productiveness of Orientalist discourse in Western cultures and has helped to establish a dynamic in which the "other" is constructed as an object, not a subject. The problem, she contends, is that this body of work "reproduces, albeit unwittingly, the privileged position of the Western, liberal subject and occludes the role of non-Western peoples as historical subjects in their own right." Mae M. Ngai, "Transnationalism and the Transformation of the 'Other': Response to the Presidential Address," *American Quarterly* 57.1 (2005): 60.

19. Wong, *Fifth Chinese Daughter*, 236.

20. Ibid., 132.

21. Kobena Mercer, *Welcome to the Jungle: New Positions in Black Cultural Studies* (New York: Routledge, 1994), 249.

22. Aihwa Ong, *Flexible Citizenship: The Cultural Logics of Transnationality* (Durham: Duke University Press, 1999), 141.

23. Leslie Bow, "The Illusion of the Middle Way: Liberal Feminism and Biculturalism in Jade Snow Wong's *Fifth Chinese Daughter*," in *Bearing Dreams, Shaping Visions: Asian Pacific American Perspectives*, ed. Linda A. Revilla, Gail M. Nomura, Shawn Wong, and Shirley Hune (Pullman: Washington State University, 1993), 167.

24. Christina Klein, *Cold War Orientalism: Asia in the Middlebrow Imagination* (Berkeley: University of California Press, 2003), 243.

25. Anita Mannur, "Bienvenido Santos," in *Asian American Novelists: A Bio-Bibliographical Critical Source Book*, ed. Emmanuel S. Nelson (Westport, CT: Greenwood Press, 2000), 317–322.

26. For a detailed account of official tours by African American intellectuals and entertainers during the Cold War, see Mary Dudziak, *Cold War Civil Rights* (Princeton: Princeton University Press, 2000), 61–77. Also see Brenda Gayle Plum-

mer, *Rising Wind: Black Americans and U.S. Foreign Affairs, 1935–1960* (Chapel Hill: University of North Carolina Press, 1996), and Penny von Eschen, *Race against Empire: Black Americans and Anticolonialism, 1937–1957* (Ithaca: Cornell University Press, 1997).

27. Dudziak, *Cold War Civil Rights,* 67–77.

28. Jade Snow Wong, *No Chinese Stranger* (New York: Harper and Row, 1975), 97.

29. Ibid., ix.

Chapter 3

Complicating Racial Binaries
Asian Canadians and African Canadians as Visible Minorities

Eleanor Ty

Discussions of "race" today have been strongly influenced by the concepts developed in the United States in the last thirty years. Until recently, the terms "race" and "racism" in America almost always conjure up issues of inequality, differences, and discrimination among black and white people. In their essay, "Does 'Race' Matter?" Robert Miles and Rodolfo D. Torres note that "it is either largely taken for granted or explicitly argued that the concept of racism refers to an ideology and . . . a set of practices, of which 'black' people are the exclusive victim: racism refers to what 'white' people think about and do to 'black' people."[1] Inadequate as this way of thinking is, Miles and Torres observe that this "use of 'race' as an analytical category in the social sciences is a transatlantic phenomenon."[2] Other countries, such as Great Britain, have adopted this binary way of thinking of race as a black and white issue. Historically, however, in Britain, the term "race" was employed in a different way. During the nineteenth and early twentieth centuries, "it was widely believed that the population of Britain was composed of a number of different 'races,'" including the Irish.[3] Race was also employed in discussions about the colonies, referring to people from different "races," such as Caucasians, Africans, Mongoloids, Celts, and so on.

In the United States, racial politics plays out largely in binary terms. In the twentieth century, and up until recently in the twenty-first century, the American media's and culture's tendency to refer to white and black America left native Americans, people from the Middle East, Southeast Asia, South Asia, and Mexico, for example, out of the generalization about races.[4] In his essay, "Is Yellow Black or White?," Gary Okihiro notes the "construct of American society that defines race relations as bipolar—

between black and white—and that locates Asians (and American Indians and Latinos) somewhere along the divide between black and white."[5] Okihiro observes:

> The marginalization of Asians, in fact, within a black and white racial formation, "disciplines" both Africans and Asians and constitutes the essential site of Asian American oppression. By seeing only black and white, the presence and absence of all color, whites render Asians, American Indians, and Latinos invisible, ignoring the gradations and complexities of the full spectrum between the racial poles. At the same time, Asians share with Africans the status and repression of nonwhites—as the Other—and therein lies the debilitating aspect of Asian-African antipathy and the liberating nature of African-Asian unity.[6]

This "disciplining" has worked well, as studies outlining the similarities between African American and Asian American histories and cultures, as Okihiro suggests, have been slow to emerge.[7] In the same way, in Canada, the connections between African Canadian and Asian Canadian communities and movements have only just begun to develop.

"Race" in Canada is positioned somewhere in the middle between the historical view in Britain and the contemporary view in the United States. In Canada, discussions of "race" have been linked to issues of ethnicity from the start. Because of a smaller, less politicized, and less visible "black" population in Canada, the larger presence of South Asians, along with a much more recent spate of immigrants from Eastern European countries, "race" in Canada has not been viewed simply as a black and white binary.[8] Instead, discussions of race and racism refer to discriminatory acts against people who are from the Caribbean and Africa; against South Asians, East Asians, Southeast Asians, and Jews, as well as native peoples; and, at the beginning of the twentieth century, against ethnic minorities such as Italians and Portuguese. Due to the categorization of racial "others" as "visible minorities," and because of Canada's Multiculturalism Act, race in Canada is predicated not only on skin color but on a variety of factors, including accent and linguistic competence, dress, class, and religious affiliation.

Because of Canada's rather unique situation, it is helpful to look at the historical and cultural factors that lead to the understanding of "race" this way. In this essay, I present a brief overview of Canadian cultural policies of the 1970s and 1980s, describe the immigration patterns of Blacks and Asians, and, in particular, look at the use of the term "visible minority" as a way of referring to people of color in Canada. I argue that these factors have delayed the development of specifically African Canadian and Asian Canadian collectives or movements and that they have not paved the way for a strong political coalition between people of color in Canada. In other words, even though the methods of classification and the historical treatment of people of African and Asian descent in Canada have been similar, a number of concurrent government policies have dissuaded cooperation between these and other minority groups. In this essay I look at some reasons that, although African and Asian peoples in Canada as visible minorities have similar experiences, their encounters are still relatively rare. Going beyond scholars who focus on this problem by concentrating on the effect of the Multiculturalism Act in Canada, I explore the connections between this act, the use of the term "visible minorities," and the psychosocial implications of this categorization on racial minorities. Following Michel Foucault, my view is that systems of representation and methods of classification have implications beyond that of organizational principles and utilitarianism. As Ann Laura Stoler notes:

> Taking discursive formations seriously is a way of broaching head on the fact that how we speak and what is unspeakable in written and oral form shape the categories of exclusion and inclusion in which racisms are built. Attention to discursive formations opens to an engagement with the cultural and political rationalities that make certain statements renderable as speech, with what discursive practices produce the conditions of possibility for why statements are taken as adequate truth-claims and not others.[9]

Because the category "visible minorities" encompasses African Canadians, Asian Canadians, and Caribbean Canadians, it has important ramifications for people of color. It shapes the subjectivity of both white and non-white Canadians, and it has a role in the construction of self and other in the national psyche and in the delimitation of citizenship and belonging.

The African diaspora in Canada is at once like and not like that of the African diaspora in America. African Canadian poet, playwright, and critic George Elliott Clarke writes of his own development:

> By the time I published my first book of poetry, Saltwater Spirituals and Deeper Blues, in 1983, I was assuredly "Black Nova Scotian." However, in those days, the adjective "black" was shorthand for "Black American." I knew I was Black Nova Scotian, yes, but I still considered Black America the

Mecca of *true* "blackness," that is to say, of Motown, Malcolm X, and Martin Luther King, Jr, of collard greens and hamhocks, of "projects" and "soul."[10]

Yet, Clarke endeavors to look at African Canadian literature as a separate entity, different from African American literature. He contends that "African Canada is a conglomeration of many cultures, a spectrum of ethnicities."[11] African Canadian writers borrow from "Caribbean and American, but also British, French, and African source cultures to furbish their experiences as a section of the African Diaspora."[12] The phrase "African Canadian," like "Asian Canadian," has only recently been used and is still a contested term. Other black critics, like Rinaldo Walcott, prefer to use the term "black Canadian" rather than "African Canadian." According to Walcott, "It is useful to read black Canadian works within the context of black diasporic discourses. Those who are descendants of Africans (New World Blacks) dispersed by TransAtlantic slavery continue to engage in a complex process of cultural exchange, invention and (re) invention, and the result is cultural creolization."[13] For Walcott, works by Blacks in Canada "are not merely national products, but . . . they occupy the space of the in-between, vacillating between national borders and diasporic desires, ambitions and disappointments."[14] Both Clarke, who stresses a nationalistic sense of belonging, and Walcott, who stresses a transnational diasporic consciousness, agree that the African diaspora in Canada has been and is still evolving, being hybridized and shaped.

Clarke and Walcott represent different kinds of black Canadians in part because of their point of departure. Clarke was born in Nova Scotia, while Walcott was born in Barbados. Demographically, black Canadians born outside of Canada, like Walcott, are becoming a larger group than those born in Canada. According to Will Kymlicka, "The Black community in Canada in the nineteenth century—the descendants of former slaves and Black United Empire Loyalists—was never very large compared with the African-American population in the United States, and it shrank dramatically between 1870 and 1930 as Blacks moved back to the United States."[15] As a result, the largest group of Blacks in Canada today is made up of recent immigrants from the Caribbean. In Montreal, 80 percent of Blacks are from the Caribbean—primarily from Haiti, but also from various British Caribbean islands, particularly Jamaica and Trinidad; descendants of long-settled Blacks form only a small minority, under 20 percent. The same general trend is found in Toronto, although there the largest group is made up of Jamaicans rather than Haitians. The only major Canadian city where the long-settled black population still outnumbers recent Caribbean immigrants is Halifax. Thus the history of slavery and segregation in Canada, while more similar to the U.S. experience than most Canadians realize, is not the source of contemporary race-relations problems. The number of Blacks who experienced these conditions was relatively small, and their descendants are now massively outnumbered by immigrants from the Caribbean or Africa.[16]

There is a similar story and shift in demographics in the case of Asian Canadians. The Asian population in Canada, like that of the black population, was fairly small until the changes to Canadian immigration policy in 1967. Before that, the Immigration Act was based on a "nationality" preference system that favored northern Europeans, immigrants from the United States and Britain. Asians, in particular the Chinese, followed later by the Japanese and Indians, had been recruited to Canada as laborers in the second half of the nineteenth century, but they were restricted from immigrating to Canada in the first half of the twentieth century. Peter Li notes that Chinese immigrants were in British Columbia in 1858, nine years before the Canadian confederation was formed.[17] Similar to the system of contract labor in the United States, the Chinese came to Canada to work as miners in the 1860s and 1870s. Later they worked as laborers building the western section of the Canadian Pacific Railway.[18] The first Japanese came to Canada some ten years after Confederation, but it was not until 1885 that immigration to Canada began in earnest.[19] They were mostly transients, poor and male, who worked in the fishing, farming, and lumbering industries in British Columbia. Like the Chinese, they provided cheap, efficient labor. South Asian immigration to Canada began later, at the start of the twentieth century. In Canada most South Asian immigrants, mainly from the Punjab, worked in the sawmill industry. By 1908 there were around five thousand South Asians.[20]

The influx of foreigners triggered a hostile reaction from the white population during the last two decades of the nineteenth century and continued into the early part of the twentieth century. After the completion of the national railway, the need for cheap labor diminished. A $50 head tax was imposed on the Chinese in 1885, and the amount kept rising until it was $500 by 1903. By 1923, the Chinese Immigration Act virtually halted the entry of all Chinese to the country. For some time in the early part of the twentieth century, the Japanese fared better than the Chinese, as the men were allowed to bring their wives over from Japan. Single men arranged to marry based on a photograph and brought their "picture" brides over to Canada.[21] However, the "gentlemen's agreement" between Canada and Japan ensured that the number of Japanese immigrants to Canada remained fairly small. For South Asians, the Canadian government began in 1908 to limit immigration for people who came by continuous voyage from their native country. Since it was not possible at that time to come from South Asia directly to Canada, the regulation effectively stopped South Asian immigration. In short, like black Canadians, most Asian Canadians arrived only after 1967 when a point system, based on one's education, training, and ability in one of the official languages, came into effect.

The historical discriminations against these groups and the relative lateness of African and Asian immigrants to Canada account in part for the slow development of African and Asian Canadian studies as a field, compared with African and Asian American studies in the United States. As Donald Goellnicht has argued, "for a racial minority literature—. . . in this case a panethnic minority literature united under a sign of 'race': Asian—to emerge with a clear identity there needs to be a strong accompanying and reciprocal national political-social movement focused on identity politics of the politics of difference."[22] Goellnicht notes that besides the relatively small population of Africans and Asians in Canada, these groups did not experience the civil rights era and the Black Power movement the same way as their counterparts in the United States, nor was there an anti-Vietnam movement in Canada in the 1960s.[23] In addition, at this time, "radicalism in Canada was centered primarily on the push for independence for Quebec."[24] Since the late 1960s, one can observe an increasing ethnic diversity in Canadian cities, particularly through the influx of immigrants in the three largest cities in Canada—Toronto, Vancouver, and Montreal.[25] One finds also sizeable immigrant populations in the medium-sized and smaller cities such as Hamilton, Edmonton, Calgary, and Winnipeg.[26] The kind of "political-social movement focused on identity politics of the politics of difference"[27] has become possible in the last ten years. However, to date, literary and cultural encounters between African and Asian diaspora groups—whether it be characters of African origins appearing in Asian Canadian texts or films, or characters of Asian origins in works by black Canadians, or black and Asian Canadian—collaborative efforts at organizing events, conferences, or any other cultural or political activity are still relatively infrequent.

Unlike the identificatory practices of the United States where African Americans and Asian Americans embrace their designated racial grouping because of a history of resistance, solidarity, and self-empowerment from the 1960s, the cultural, political, and historical conditions in Canada have not encouraged Blacks and Asians in Canada to take on the same kind of pan-ethnic Black or pan-ethnic Asian identity. Blacks in Canada tend to still self-identify as Jamaican Canadian, Haitian-born Canadian, Ghanaian, or Ethiopian, while Asians in Canada talk about themselves as Chinese Canadian, Japanese Canadian, Filipino Canadian, Indian, Pakistani, Sri Lankan, Vietnamese, and the like. Compared with the United States, Canada's visible minorities are more recent immigrants, many of them still finding their way in their own communities and within the mixed cultural mosaic of the country.

For example, according to statistics released in 2001, foreign-born residents comprise 43.7 percent of all residents of Toronto, a city that boasts of having the world's highest rate of newcomers. Compared with cities in the United States, the percentage of foreign-born residents in Toronto is considerably higher—30.9 percent foreign-born residents in Los Angeles, and even in a diverse city like New York, only 24.4 percent are foreign-born.[28] It takes time for newcomers to become acculturated to their new community, and time for alliances between them and other minorities to form. These figures do not mean that there has been no history of resistance in Canada. However, the resistance has tended to come mainly from antiracist activists and intellectuals, or from a particular racialized group, like the Japanese Canadians, for example. The National Association of Japanese Canadians (NAJC), formed in 1947, successfully negotiated the historic Redress Settlement on behalf of all Japanese Canadians who suffered injustices at the hands of their own government during and after World War II when they were dispossessed, forcibly relocated, and interned. On September 22, 1988, Prime Minister Brian Mulroney and NAJC President Art Miki signed the redress agreement, acknowledging the wrongs committed against Japanese Canadians.[29]

African Canadians and Asian Canadians, without identifying themselves particularly as belonging to those groups, have initiated and participated in many antiracist events and publications over the last two or three decades. Some of the works that promote equity and social justice for African Canadians and Asian Canadians are done in conjunction with other movements, such as the feminist movement, antipoverty struggles, rights for gays and lesbians, and environmental concerns. African Canadians and Asian Canadians do not tend to separate themselves strictly in their designated groups but work collaboratively with or work on other minority groups, and, in many cases, include issues that pertain to native

Canadians as well. For example, Himani Bannerji's *Returning the Gaze* is a collection of essays by Asian, native, and black women. *Telling It* by the Telling It Book Collective features native, Asian Canadian, and lesbian writers, while *Our Words, Our Revolutions,* edited by G. Sophie Harding includes poems, stories, and essays by black, First Nations, and other women of color in Canada.[30]

In a similar manner, black Canadian Frances Henry has written about the racism experienced by Caribbeans living in Toronto, but her other books discuss the issue of racism in the larger context of Canadian society.[31] Asian Canadian Roxana Ng is known for her work on antiracism in the classroom and has written about being Chinese in Canada, but she has also worked more generally on antiracist education.[32] In the fields of literature and culture, critical work on Black Canadian and Asian Canadian writers, along with work on writers from India, Asia, Africa, and the Caribbean, and on native writers, often appears under the rubric of "postcolonial studies." Unlike the situation in the United States, where Asian American and African American studies are usually distinguished from postcolonial studies,[33] in Canada, "postcolonial literature" includes the study of ethnic and non-ethnic Canadian literatures. *Unhomely States,* a "collection of foundational essays of Canadian postcolonial theory" includes an essay on "A Poetics of Black Space(s)" by Rinaldo Walcott and an essay on reading South Asian Canadian texts by Arun Mukherjee.[34] A sampling of a couple of recent anthologies on "postcolonial" and Canadian literature shows the tendency in Canada to look at what might be called Asian American or African American issues or cultural production through postcolonial approaches and theories.[35]

A number of scholars have attributed the lack of politicization of particular minority groups to Canada's Multiculturalism Act. For them, the Multiculturalism Act promotes only the celebratory aspects of one's culture and does not address contentious political issues. For example, Kogila Moodley argues that Canadian multiculturalism promotes a "festive aura of imagined consensus,"[36] while C. Mullard points out that the model highlights the "three S's": "saris, samosas, and steel bands," in order to diffuse the "three R's: resistance, rebellion, and rejection."[37] Others see Canada's policy of official multiculturalism as a way of managing difference. The policy, called "Multiculturalism within a Bilingual Framework," identified some "eighty different ethnic or cultural groups which could apply for financial support from various ministries, particularly the newly formed Ministry of Multiculturalism, to support programmes for developing and maintaining cultural and linguistic identity."[38] Some have seen it as a means to undercut Quebec's demands for special recognition by bestowing recognition on other cultural groups. Eva Mackey claims, "Multicultural policy extends the state recognition of multiple forms of difference, so as to undercut Québec's more threatening difference."[39] She points out, "By defining and recognising immigrants as 'ethnocultural groups,' the policy provided a means through which cultural difference became politicized, but also politically manageable through the funding of 'cultural programmes,' the main function of the early policy."[40] Peter S. Li remarks that the federal multiculturalism policy "was a calculated political strategy aimed at winning the support of ethnic minorities by promising them cultural equality, and at the same time assuring all Canadians that multiculturalism meant advancing individual freedom without compromising national unity of official language policy."[41]

In contrast to a host of critics who have written against multiculturalism, Will Kymlicka argues:

> There is no evidence to support the claim that multiculturalism is promoting ethnic separateness or impeding immigrant integration. Whether we examine the trends within Canada since 1971 or compare Canada with other countries, the conclusion is the same: the multiculturalism program is working. It is achieving what it set out to do: helping to ensure that those people who wish to express their ethnic identity are respected and accommodated, while simultaneously increasing the ability of immigrants to integrate into the larger society. Along with our fellow multiculturalists in Australia, Canadians do a better job of respecting ethnic diversity while promoting society integration than citizens of any other country.[42]

Approaching the multiculturalism issue from different angles, these scholars do not want to dismantle Canada's policy of diversity as much as demonstrate that federal multiculturalism does not go far enough in promoting opportunities and providing assistance to minority groups. Some scholars, such as Frances Henry and Carol Tator, advocate what they call "radical" or "critical multiculturalism" which "challenges the traditional political and cultural hegemony of the dominant class or group."[43] Going a step further, Peter S. Li points out that the underlying assumptions behind multiculturalism are flawed. He notes that the "pluralist perspective tends to view ethnic cultures as essentially homogeneous and primordial in nature," that it does not allow for "cultural diversities even within the same ethnic group," and that it mainly encourages cultural distinctive-ness in the private rather than the institutional or public lives of ethnic groups.[44] These last points are particularly significant for my purposes because, by promoting cultural diversity, with its assumptions of essential-ism and homogeneity, as noted by Li, federal multiculturalism, in fact, reinforces the separation of ethnic and minority groups and discourages, rather than promotes, a pan-ethnic sensibility.

The encounters between Asians and Blacks in Canada that do take place are theoretically constructed. They occur most often in statistics and lists about minorities. For example, Statistics Canada released a report in June 2004 about hate crimes. According to this report, Jews were the most likely minority group in Canada to be the victim of hate crimes. Of the one thousand cases of hate crimes reported in 2001 and 2002, Jews were the target 25 percent of the time, followed by blacks at 17 percent of the time, Muslims at 11 percent, South Asians at 10 percent, and gays and lesbians at 9 percent.[45] This report is interesting because of its assumptions and defi-nitions of minority groups. In this case, the inclusion of Jews and homo-sexuals as minority groups suggest that race and place of origin are not the only bases for defining minority groups. The report also confirms the point I made at the outset, that "race" and discussions of racial discrimi-nation are more complicated in Canada than those of the black/white binary. Underlying discussions of race are often other factors, such as reli-gious affiliation, sexual orientation, and class.

Originally, the term "visible minorities" was coined by the Canadian government under the liberal leadership of Pierre Trudeau in the 1970s to designate those persons, other than aboriginal peoples, who are non-Caucasian in race or nonwhite in color. Asians belong to this designated group which differentiates racial minorities—Blacks from various parts of Africa; West Indians, Chinese, Japanese, Filipinos, Indians, Pakistanis, Sri Lankans, Koreans, Vietnamese, and so on—from ethnic minorities, such as Italians, Greeks, Ukrainians, Russians, Serbo-Croatians, and so on.[46] This term, aligning Asian Canadians with Blacks, is most often used in government and legal discourses, in studies about employment, immigra-tion, and labor. For example, visible minorities matter in the Employment Equity Act, as in the Canada census, and in literature about multicultural-ism. It has become a widely accepted term, but it was not, initially, a polit-ically motivated nomenclature, unlike a term such as "woman of color," "Asian American," or "African American."[47]

The other frequent site of encounter between Asians and Blacks in

Canada is the census. The newspaper reports and summaries of the 2001 census focus on new immigrants, the percentage of visible minority populations in big cities, and the fact that the Chinese are Canada's largest visible minority group at 3.5 percent of the country's population.[48] Black Canadians are the third largest visible minority group, following South Asians who are the second largest immigrant group to come to Canada in the last decade.[49] What emerges from such newspaper and media reports is the reiteration of the link between racial minorities and the foreign or the other, and the emphasis of racial minorities and their difference from Europeans who are assumed to be the norm.

Asians and Blacks in Canada are caught in the Scylla and Charybdis of categories and naming. The official label "visible minority" marks one as racially different, rendered obvious, vulnerable, non-major. Though the term "visible minority" was created to promote equity and diversity in hiring practices, it has the unintended, or perhaps the surreptitiously intended, effect of rendering all those cultures that are not European in origin marginal, more conspicuously minor against something which is articulated as dominant.[50] Himani Bannerji points out:

> Unlike the radical alternative political-cultural activists, the Canadian state was careful not to directly use the notion of color in the way it designated the newcomers. But color was translated into the language of visibility. The new Canadian social and political subject was appellate "visible minority," stressing both the features of being non-white and therefore visible in a way whites are not, and of being politically minor players.[51]

In the United States, as Okihiro points out, by not being included in the sweeping categories of black and white, Asian Americans, like Latinos, are not named and are therefore invisible and at times rendered inconsequential in government policies and public discourse. Though "visible minority" is not an official term in the United States, categories of black, white, Asian, and Hispanic are still very much predicated on the visible, or what David Palumbo-Liu has described as the "physical sign" of otherness.[52]

In both countries, what generates classification and ordering of things is still predominantly appearance or the scopic drive. Though thinking about races has shifted and changed over time, to a large extent, visibility is still what is used as the basis for discourses about difference. Ruth Frankenberg notes the consequence of this for white people: "While discursively generating and marking a range of cultural and racial Others as different from an apparently stable Western or white self, the Western self is itself produced as *an effect of* the Western discursive production of its Others."[53] The markings on our body have provoked from the dominant culture an array of responses that are predictable and overdetermined. Our appearance—skin color, black hair, nose, eyes—continues to play a large part in determining how others read our identities, and it shapes, in tangible and intangible ways, relations between European North Americans and nonwhites, even in relations between Asian Canadians and Blacks.[54] The concern of mainstream North American culture with surface appearance is a lingering problem that faces Asians, Blacks, and other minority groups today.

A number of critics have noted this obsession with appearance in Canadian culture. In an essay called "Canada's Visible Minorities: Identity and Representation," Anthony Synnott and David Howes similarly note that the term "visible minorities" privileges the visual and foregrounds skin color as "the primary determinant of group identification."[55] For them, there are other kinds of minorities, particularly linguistic minorities and religious minorities, as well as the very old and the very young, which are not covered by the term.[56] They argue that the concept of visible minorities "was not well formulated in the first place, and raises serious questions about the legislation which employs it."[57] Instead of promoting equity, it further entrenches "difference by 'racializing' divisions which . . . have always had more to do with social class and cultural beliefs than with skin colour or 'visibility.'"[58] Other important problems Synnott and Howes outline include the invisibility of such people as light-skinned Arabs or a white Jamaican, and the lumping together of "multicoloured humanity . . . under one rubric."[59] In their essay, they point to a scale of difference between the average income of people of different ethnic origins, noting that not all "visible minorities are equally oppressed, impoverished, marginalized, and victimized by a ubiquitous Canadian racism."[60] According to Synnott and Howes, "Canada does not have a dichotomous racial stratification system with all Whites above, and all non-Whites now recorded as visible minorities, below."[61] Their points about the need to take into account class and economic differences within racial minorities, as well as the way such a term as "visible minority" further racializes people by exaggerating certain physical and phenotypical traits, lead to the last point developed here.

As I argue, the grouping together of Asians and Blacks in Canada as visible minorities has the effect of designating a group of people in the country as unimportant players, or a subnormal group of people against a white group regarded as unmarked or invisible. In terms of a national subjectivity, visible minorities become what Julia Kristeva in *The Powers of Horror* would call the "not-self" or the abject.[62] In order for the self to achieve subjectivity, he or she has to psychically affiliate with the nonvisible majority, rejecting those like himself or herself for those who are deemed to have full subjectivity in the nation. Though the minority subject might feel pride in his or her ethnic origin and celebrate it through multicultural festivals, there is the sociopsychic pressure to affiliate upward and disaffiliate downward in order to have the full privileges and promise of that nation. Disaffiliation occurs not just once but repeatedly for visible minorities. For example, when one racial minority group is stigmatized by the larger community for a particular problem, a member of that group may consciously or unconsciously disaffiliate from his or her community. Recently, for instance, when the Chinese were viewed as the transmitters of the severe acute respiratory syndrome (SARS) virus in Toronto during the winter of 2003, many Chinese people avoided going shopping in Chinatown or the Asian malls in Markham. Some people, Asians included, even refused to sit beside someone on the bus whom they believed to be of Asian origin. The media's association of violence in Toronto with Jamaican youths presents a similar ongoing problem.[63] The negative image of these visible minorities has caused tensions not just between Blacks and the police force but also within the black community. For these reasons, Asians and Blacks are discouraged to form both sociopsychic and political affiliations. Hence, Asian and black diasporic coalitions in communities have not been as developed in Canada as they have been in Great Britain and the United States.

To look at the question of racial identification and coalitions from a different and positive perspective, one could claim that the lack of active coalitions between minorities is a sign that the politics of multiculturalism and diversity are actually functioning relatively well in Canada. Compared with the United States, discriminatory practices based on race in Canada are more muted and less blatant. As Synnott and Howes note, visible minorities in Canada are not equally oppressed. In one of their tables, Synnott and Howes show that the average income for South Asians was higher in 1989 than for those people of French origin.[64] They also note that the Japanese, who form the largest Asian ethnic group born in Canada, fare better than other Asian groups in terms of employment rates and in securing managerial and professional occupations.[65] This is not to say that discrimination and racial prejudice do not exist in Canada; indeed, there is still much antiracist work to be done. Rather, I have tried in this essay to show that racial politics in Canada is layered and complex, involving not just relations between black and whites but also the positioning of ethnic and racialized subjects within government discourse, within economic and social hierarchies; moreover, racial politics depends on the individual's language acquisition and fluency, education and professional skills, and length of residence in Canada. As more and more African and Asian Canadians become aware of and begin to question the privileges and the limitations of occupying the place of the "visible minority" in Canada, as our numbers grow, as people become more accustomed to a shifting rather than a static notion of ethnic identity, productive and cooperative encounters between diverse ethnic groups will rise. Much has changed in the last ten years with the changing demographics and immigrant patterns, especially in the medium to large cities in Canada. Understanding the way we are viewed and the way we came to see ourselves, learning about the experiences and histories that we share with other ethnic groups are steps that lead in the direction of fruitful pan-ethnic coalitional politics.

NOTES

1. Robert Miles and Rodolfo D. Torres, "Does 'Race' Matter? Transatlantic Perspectives on Racism after 'Race Relations,'" in *Race, Identity, and Citizenship: A Reader,* ed. Rodolfo D. Torres, Louis F. Mirón, and Jonathan Xavier Inda (Oxford: Blackwell, 1999), 27.

2. Ibid., 21.

3. Ibid.

4. In the last two decades, black intellectuals like Paul Gilroy have been influential in attempting to move away from the manichaeism of black and white fixed identities in their work. See Paul Gilroy, *There Ain't No Black in the Union Jack* (London: Hutchinson, 1987).

5. Gary Y. Okihiro, "Is Yellow Black or White?" in *Asian Americans: Experiences and Perspectives,* ed. Timothy P. Fong and Larry H. Shinagawa (Upper Saddle River, NJ: Prentice Hall, 2000), 63.

6. Ibid., 75.

7. Only fairly recently have a few studies considered the similarities between African Americans and Asian Americans. See, for example, Anne Anlin Cheng, *The Melancholy of Race: Psychoanalysis, Assimilation, and Hidden Grief* (New York: Oxford University Press, 2000), and King-Kok Cheung, "Don't Tell: Imposed

Silences in *The Color Purple* and *The Woman Warrior,*" *PMLA* 103.2 (1988): 162–174.

8. A number of factors have created differences in the discussion of "race" between Canada and the United States. Enoch Padolsky, for example, points to Canada's dual "*Official Languages Act,* official Canadian multiculturalism, . . . a growing openness to Aboriginal self-government," and the relatively small and new community of Blacks in Canada as compared with the United States. Enoch Padolsky, "Ethnicity and Race: Canadian Minority Writing at a Crossroads," in *Literary Pluralities,* ed. Christl Verduyn (Peterborough: Broadview Press, 1998), 23–24.

9. Ann Laura Stoler, "Reflections on 'Racial Histories and Their Regimes of Truth,'" in *Race Critical Theories: Text and Context,* ed. Philomena Essed and David Theo Goldberg (Oxford: Blackwell, 2002), 419.

10. George Elliott Clarke, *Odysseys Home: Mapping African-Canadian Literature* (Toronto: University of Toronto Press, 2002), 4.

11. Ibid., 14.

12. Ibid., 12.

13. Rinaldo Walcott, *Black Like Who?* (Toronto: Insomniac Press, 1997), xii.

14. Ibid.

15. Will Kymlicka, *Finding Our Way: Rethinking Ethnocultural Relations in Canada* (Toronto: Oxford University Press, 1998), 78.

16. Ibid., 78–79.

17. Peter S. Li, *Chinese in Canada* (Toronto: Oxford University Press, 1998), 3.

18. Ibid., 21.

19. Ken Adachi, *The Enemy That Never Was: A History of Japanese Canadians,* introduction by Timothy Findley, afterword by Roger Daniels (Toronto: McClelland and Steward, 1991), 2, 13. Originally published 1976.

20. Suzanne McMahon, "Overview of South Asian Diaspora," 22 June 1998, available at http://www.lib.berkeley.edu/SSEAL/SouthAsia/overview.html (retrieved 23 June 2004).

21. Adachi, *Enemy That Never Was,* 87.

22. Donald C. Goellnicht, "A Long Labour: The Protracted Birth of Asian Canadian Literature," *Essays on Canadian Writing* 72 (Winter 2000): 3.

23. Ibid., 4, 6.

24. Ibid., 8.

25. Morton Weinfeld and Lori A. Wilkinson, "Immigration, Diversity, and Minority Communities," in *Race and Ethnic Relations in Canada,* ed. Peter S. Li (Don Mills, ON: Oxford University Press, 1999), 70.

26. Ibid.

27. Goellnicht, "Long Labour," 3.

28. Elaine Carey, "City of New Faces," *Toronto Star,* 22 January 2003, A6. This information was based on statistics released by Statistics Canada in 2001.

29. For more information about the work of the NAJC, see their webpage: "Japanese Canadians Then and Now," 2005, available at http://www.najc.ca/index .php (retrieved 28 June 2005).

30. Himani Bannerji, ed., *Returning the Gaze: Essays on Racism, Feminism and Politics* (Toronto: Sister Vision Press, 1993); Telling It Book Collective, *Telling It: Women and Language across Cultures: The Transformation of a Conference* (Vancouver: Press Gang, 1990); Sophie G. Harding, *Our Words, Our Revolutions: Di/Verse Voices of Black Women, First Nations Women, and Women of Colour in Canada* (Toronto: Inanna, 2000).

31. Frances Henry, *Caribbean Diaspora in Toronto: Learning to Live with Racism* (Toronto: University of Toronto Press, 1994); Frances Henry and Carol Tator, with Winston Mattis and Tim Rees, *The Colour of Democracy: Racism in Canadian Society* (Toronto: Harcourt Brace, 1995).

32. Roxana Ng, "Sexism, Racism, Canadian Nationalism," in *Returning the Gaze: Essays on Racism, Feminism and Politics,* ed. Himani Bannerji (Toronto: Sister Vision Press, 1993), 182–196; Roxana Ng, Pat Staton, and Joyce Scane, *Anti-Racism, Feminism, and Critical Approaches to Education* (Westport, CT: Bergin and Garvey, 1995).

33. For more information about postcolonial studies in the United States and its relation to American studies, see Malina Johar Schueller and Edward Watts, eds., *Messy Beginnings: Postcoloniality and Early American Studies* (New Brunswick, NJ: Rutgers University Press, 2003).

34. Rinaldo Walcott's " 'A Tough Geography': Towards a Poetics of Black Space(s) in Canada" (1997) and Arun Mukherjee's "How Shall We Read South Asian Canadian Texts?" (1998) are both reprinted in *Unhomely States: Theorizing English-Canadian Postcolonialism,* ed. Cynthia Sugars (Peterborough: Broadview Press, 2004), 277–288, 249–266. The volume contains seminal essays on Canadian postcolonialism by scholars such as Diana Brydon, Linda Hutcheon, Donna Bennett, Stephen Slemon, Roy Miki, and others.

35. These collections of essays, on multicultural and postcolonial literature demonstrate the way in which Canada's categories of differences are handled. Christl Verduyn's *Literary Pluralities* (Peterborough: Broadview Press, 1998), Laura Moss's anthology *Is Canada Postcolonial? Unsettling Canadian Literature* (Waterloo: Wilfrid Laurier University Press, 2003), and Cynthia Sugar's volume *Home-Work: Postcolonialism, Pedagogy and Canadian Literature* (Ottawa: University of Ottawa Press, 2004) all contain essays on African Canadian and Asian Canadian culture and issues, on European ethnic minorities, native literature, and on non-ethnic or mainstream Canadian culture.

36. Kogila Moodley, as quoted by Eva Mackey, *The House of Difference: Cultural Politics and National Identity in Canada* (Toronto: University of Toronto Press, 2002), 66.

37. Ibid, 67.

38. Ibid., 64.

39. Ibid.

40. Ibid., 65.

41. Peter S. Li, "The Multiculturalism Debate," in *Race and Ethnic Relations in Canada*, ed. Peter S. Li (Toronto: Oxford University Press, 1999), 152.

42. Kymlicka, *Finding Our Way*, 22.

43. Frances Henry and Carol Tator, "State Policy and Practices as Racialized Discourse: Multiculturalism, the Charter, and Employment Equity," in *Race and Ethnic Relations in Canada*, ed. Peter S. Li (Toronto: Oxford University Press, 1999), 98.

44. Li, "Multiculturalism Debate," 165, 166, 167–168.

45. Janice Tibbetts, "Jews Most Often Target of Hate Crimes: StatsCan," *National Post*, 2 June 2004, A9.

46. Enoch Padolsky, referring to a short story by Jewish-Canadian Matt Cohen, notes, "in an earlier Canadian racial terminology, 'visible minority' meant dress and appearance and not just pigmentation." Padolsky, "Ethnicity and Race," 26.

47. Sau-ling Wong has noted that the term "Asian American" "expresses a political conviction and agenda: it is based on the assumption that regardless of individual origin, background, and desire for self-identification, Asian Americans have been subjected to certain collective experiences that must be acknowledged and resisted." Sau-ling Cynthia Wong, *Reading Asian American Literature: From Necessity to Extravagance* (Princeton: Princeton University Press, 1993), 6.

48. Carey, "City of New Faces," A6.

49. "Study: Canada's Visible Minority Population in 2017," *Daily*, 22 March 2005, available at http://www.statcan.ca/Daily/English/050322/d050322b.htm (retrieved 2 July 2005).

50. Smaro Kamboureli makes a similar observation about the ambivalent effect of multiculturalism: "The Multiculturalism Act (also known as Bill C-93) recognizes the cultural diversity that constitutes Canada, but it does so by practicing a sedative politics, a politics that attempts to recognize ethnic differences, but only in a contained fashion, in order to manage them." Smaro Kamboureli, *Scandalous Bodies: Diasporic Literature in English Canada* (Toronto: Oxford University Press, 2000), 82.

51. Himani Bannerji, "The Paradox of Diversity: The Construction of a Multicultural Canada and 'Women of Color,'" *Women's Studies International Forum* 23.5 (2000): 545.

52. David Palumbo-Liu, *Asian/American Historical Crossings of a Racial Frontier* (Stanford: Stanford University Press, 1999), 86. In his chapter on "Race, Nation, Migrancy, and Sex," Palumbo-Liu looks at the willingness of minority individuals to use plastic surgery to transform their features today. The implication is that the body is linked to the psyche: "The morphing of physical form antici-

pates the revision of the psyche within, and the way that transformed body will be viewed by others." Ibid., 95.

53. Ruth Frankenberg, *White Women, Race Matters: The Social Construction of Whiteness* (Minneapolis: University of Minnesota Press, 1993), 17.

54. I have discussed the implications of the bodily features of Asians and their visibility in North America in the introductory chapter of my book, Eleanor Ty, *The Politics of the Visible* (Toronto: University of Toronto Press, 2004).

55. Anthony Synnott and David Howes, "Canada's Visible Minorities: Identity and Representation," in *Resituating Identities: The Politics of Race, Ethnicity, Culture,* ed. Vered Amit-Talai and Caroline Knowles (Peterborough: Broadview Press, 1996), 149.

56. Ibid., 141.

57. Ibid., 138.

58. Ibid.

59. Ibid., 142.

60. Ibid., 144.

61. Ibid.

62. Julia Kristeva, *Powers of Horror: An Essay on Abjection* (New York: Columbia University Press, 1982), chapter 1. David Leiwei Li, *Imagining the Nation: Asian American Literature and Cultural Consent* (Stanford: Stanford University Press, 1998), has also applied Kristeva's notion of the abject to Asian Americans, 6–8. See my discussion of Li's argument and my own use of the term in Ty, *Politics of the Visible,* 26–27.

63. A number of writers have criticized the media and police treatment of Blacks. See, for example, Dionne Brand, *Bread out of Stone: Recollections on Sex, Recognitions, Race, Dreaming and Politics* (Toronto: Vintage Canada, 1998), 120–123, and Walcott, *Black Like Who?,* 118–119.

64. Synnott and Howes, "Canada's Visible Minorities," 144.

65. Ibid., 139–140.

Chapter 4

One People, One Nation?
Creolization and Its Tensions in Trinidadian and Guyanese Fiction

Lourdes López Ropero

In his volume *The Repeating Island,* Antonio Benítez-Rojo provides an illustrative, if not naturalistic, description of how the Caribbean developed:

> Let's be realistic: the Atlantic is the Atlantic because it was once engendered by the copulation of Europe—that insatiable solar bull—with the Caribbean archipelago; the Atlantic is today the Atlantic (the navel of capitalism) because Europe, in its mercantilist laboratory, conceived the project of inseminating the Caribbean womb with the blood of Africa; the Atlantic is today the Atlantic . . . because it was the painfully delivered child of the Caribbean . . . stretched . . . between the *encomienda* of Indians and the slaveholding plantation, between the servitude of the coolie and the discrimination towards the *criollo,* between commercial monopoly and piracy, between the runaway slave settlement and the governor's palace; all Europe pulling on the forceps to help at the birth of the Atlantic: Columbus, Cabral, Cortés, de Soto, Hawkins, Drake.[1]

Historically, the Caribbean archipelago was an arena where Western economic battles were fought by subsequent waves of Europeans. If the archipelago was instrumental in the development of Western capitalism, Western intervention dictated the shape of economic and social change in the Caribbean. More specifically, the establishment of plantation societies accounts for one of the Caribbean's most idiosyncratic features, its complex ethnic makeup. Plantation colonies witnessed a "vast collision of races"—to borrow an expression by Antonio Benítez-Rojo[2]—, the African and the Indian featured prominently among them. This essay ana-

68

lyzes AfroAsian ethnic relations in Samuel Selvon's novels of the Indian peasantry set in colonial Trinidad, *A Brighter Sun* (1952) and *Turn again Tiger* (1958); and Fred D'Aguiar's novels on postcolonial Guyana, *Dear Future* (1996) and *Bethany Bettany* (2003). I trace the discourse of creolization in these works, which the authors uphold as a suitable model of culture and nationality to address the cross-cultural nature of these societies. At the same time, I point at the way these authors refuse to romanticize the Caribbean as a site of unproblematic creolization and foreground the ethnic conflict endemic to creole societies.

The history of the Caribbean is one of displacements and migrations. The Ameridian tribes, the Arawaks and the Caribs, left the South American continent for the Caribbean islands around 5000 BC. These were the peoples that the first European settlers, the Spanish, found on the islands. Other European countries joined in the scramble for the archipelago and, as a result, it was divided into Spanish, French, Dutch, and British territories. In the early seventeenth century, the British established plantation societies and brought Africans to work as slaves. Coolie servitude is linked with the abolition of slavery in the colonies. Antislavery sentiment that had spread throughout Britain during the last quarter of the eighteenth century led to the passing of the Emancipation Act in 1834. Since abolition amounted to the loss of cheap labor, planters implemented two policies in order to maintain profit and ease the transition to a free labor market.[3] Apprenticeship and indentureship were introduced in the post-emancipation period. During the apprenticeship, although working fewer hours and being allowed to work for wages, former slaves were forced to keep working for their masters for a period of six years. Naturally, this policy failed to satisfy emancipated Blacks, who were unwilling to engage in field labor.

Planters then decided to introduce new groups of workers who would compete with the ex-slaves on the labor market and keep wages down. Portuguese from Madeira, Chinese and Indians from the subcontinent— East Indians, nicknamed *coolies*—were brought to the Caribbean islands as indentured servants subject to five-year contracts that they were unable to breach and were lured into renewing. The East Indians, the largest immigrant group, were the ones who eventually replaced Africans in the sugar states. In contrast, unused to heavy agricultural work and taking advantage of their whiteness or near-whiteness, the Portuguese and the Chinese refused to reindenture and turned to the retail trade that they eventually monopolized. Thus, the East Indians became "the new slaves,"[4] confined to the rural. When the practice of reindenture was ended in the 1870s, many East Indians left the plantations to become peasant farmers,[5] which contributed to perpetuating their rural associations. This vast collision of races, therefore, was not natural but engineered in Europe's "mercantilist laboratory,"[6] which has had a profound influence on interethnic relations and social change. Vere Daly argues that "acting on the principle of 'divide and rule' "[7] British planters deliberately encouraged racial disunity and status competition among the different immigrant groups.

The racially heterogeneous societies created by Western powers in the Caribbean have been described as "plural societies," lacking in a "common social will."[8] The situation did not improve after the European withdrawal and the achievement of self-government, which accentuated competition for status. Trinidad and Guyana are two cases in point. Despite having different geographical locations (Trinidad is an island and Guyana a mainland country), these countries share key sociohistorical features. They both have a history of plantation slavery and indenture, which resulted in a similar ethnic composition, Africans and East Indians being the largest groups. They both are encumbered by racial conflict and have created institutions to promote racial harmony, the Centre for Ethnic Studies in Trinidad and the Ethnic Relations Commission in Guyana.

Politics are racially polarized in both islands. Thus, in their march toward self-government, the young democracies went through a brief period of political cooperation between Blacks and Indians, followed by a growing separation across ethnic lines. An infamous example is the split in Guyana's People's Progressive Party, which started out as a multiracial party led by an Indo-Guyanese and an Afro-Guyanese, whose leadership disputes ended the coalition. The slogan *apanjhat,* "support your own race," was then introduced.[9] A brief look at some local newspapers reveals that this ethnopolitical conflict continues today. In Guyana, power sharing is seen as the only solution to alleviate ethnic unrest.[10] In Trinidad, the naming of Arrival Day, originally an Indian celebration, continues to generate controversy. Whereas the African party favors dropping the word "Indian" to commemorate all the groups that came to Trinidad, Indian activists regard this gesture as discriminatory. The 2004 celebration was marked by the same controversy.[11]

In spite of this, the mottoes of Trinidad and Guyana—"Together We Aspire, Together We Achieve" and "One People, One Nation, One Destiny," respectively—attest to the fact that racial harmony was one of the goals that these young independent countries set out to achieve. Moreover, a whole syncretic culture has developed in the Caribbean since plantation societies were established. This development has been termed "creolization," a trademark of the Caribbean cultural experience defined by Martinican theorist Edouard Glissant as "a limitless *métissage*, its elements diffracted and its consequences unforeseeable."[12] Rojo has referred to this limitless *métissage* as a supersyncretism, "arising out of the collision of European, African and Asian components within the Plantation."[13] Creolization differs from *métissage* or hybridity in that the elements forming a creolized cultural expression are no longer identifiable but have blended into something completely new. As Guyanese writer Wilson Harris points out, creolization is "an issue of complex linkages and mixed traditions, transcending *black*, transcending *white* . . . throw[ing] a ceaseless bridge across the chasm of worlds."[14] This paradigm of culture contact is nondirectional and nonhierarchical, transcending ethnic particularisms and "nativist" essentialisms. Glissant places creolization at the centre of his poetics of relation, as opposed to rootedness. A poetics based on rootedness proves inaccurate to describe the sociocultural dynamics of a land which no group can lay exclusive claim to, for its only "native" inhabitants —the Ameridians—were exterminated. Speaking of his "native" island, Glissant claims:

> Indeed, Martinican soil does not belong as a rooted absolute either to the descendants of deported Africans or to the *békés* [whites] or to the Hindus or to the mulattoes. But the consequences of European expansion—extermination of the Pre-Columbians, importation of new populations—is precisely what forms the basis of a new relationship with the land: not the absolute ontological possession regarded as sacred but the complicity of relation.[15]

Creolization amounts to the formation of a complex syncretic culture on "New World" soil, stemming from the new relations that developed there. A creole is someone born in the Caribbean regardless of ethnic affiliation or mixed ethnic background.

Despite its appeal, the notion of creolization is not devoid of problems. Michael Dash warns us that the Caribbean is liable to be turned "into a centre of exemplary creolity."[16] Discussions of creolization should therefore avoid romanticizing the Caribbean and expose the reality of ethnic conflict endemic to creole societies. Besides, nativist claims may encroach into the nonhierarchical discourse of creolization to the detriment of a given ethnic group. In fact, East Indians have complained about the identification of creoleness with blackness as the African component of the culture was incorporated earlier than the Asian one. In 2004, the Letters to the Editor section of the *Stabroek News* featured a heated debate between an Indo-Guyanese and an Afro-Guyanese over this issue. The Afro-Guyanese correspondent claimed that a creole culture is not exclusively Afro-European but contains several elements—European, African, Amerindian, East Indian, Chinese, and others—any of which "may be dominant, marginal or absent . . . at varying times and places,"[17] and by virtue of being born in the Caribbean, East Indians are irreversibly creolized. The Indo-Guyanese respondent, who happened to be an Indian-rights campaigner, protested that creolization had amounted to "an Africanised cultural ethos" with only some fragmented Indian elements in an overwhelmingly African mass.[18] He believed that those Indians who upheld creolization were severing the links with their heritage and contributing to the degeneration of Indian culture in the Caribbean.

Whereas the views on cultural identity of the Afro-Guyanese correspondent strike us as less essentialist than those of the Indo-Guyanese, the former does reveal that it is not difficult for an Afro-Guyanese to slip into the equation "creoleness equals blackness." Thus, in another letter he boasts, "The feminist, nativist, even gay liberation movements are beneficiaries of the models and struggles of *the Africans* in the New World. From liberation theology to movements for ethnic pride and civil rights . . . the pattern of protest and argumentation owe much to *our Creoles*."[19] Such inconsistency, however, partly justifies the East Indian anxiety about creole culture.

From the above, it must be clear that the discourse of creolization coexists with endemic conflicts between Blacks and East Indians in the sociopolitical arena of countries like Trinidad and Guyana. It is the purpose of this essay to show how literary artifacts articulate the complex tension between creolization and ethnic particularism in creole societies. Interestingly, in this regard, one can observe that anthropologists are increasingly turning to fiction for a nonreductionist analysis of creolization. Sylvia Schomburg-Scherff, for example, explains, "I discovered that Caribbean novelists are a special source of knowledge. If we cultural anthropologists want to gain an understanding of the processes of creole identity formation, we cannot neglect the insights Caribbean novelists have to offer."[20] The complex discourse of creolization impregnates the works of Samuel

Selvon and Fred D'Aguiar and mediates their portrayal of AfroAsian relations. In the two sections that follow, I trace this discourse in a selection of
their novels. I highlight the extent to which the generation gap separating
these two authors and the different timeframes of their novels have a bearing on their portrayal of interethnic relations.

Despite being the son of an Indian from Madras and a half-Indian, half-
Scottish daughter of an overseer on a cocoa plantation, Samuel Selvon
grew up "creolized" rather than "Indianized" in the racially mixed streets
of San Fernando, a town in Southern Trinidad.[21] He migrated to London
in 1950, became a writer of the pioneering West Indian Renaissance, and
moved to Canada in the late 1970s, where he died in 1994. Speaking of his
childhood in San Fernando, he wrote:

> She [his mother] spoke fluent English. . . . I never heard my father, who was
> a Madrasee, speak anything but English. . . . In our house, we ate curry once
> a week—the other days it was creole food, souse and black pudding on Sat-
> urday night, and stew beef or chicken and calaloo for Sunday lunch. We
> never observed any religious or cultural ceremonies, nor wore national gar-
> ments. . . . By the time I was in my teens I was a product of my environ-
> ment, as Trinidadian as anyone could claim to be, quite at ease with a
> cosmopolitan attitude, and I had no desire to isolate myself from the mix-
> ture of races that comprised the community.[22]

Creolization became for Selvon a way of belonging to Trinidadian soil.
This process was so effective that he was turned down for a job in the
Indian High Commission of London because he came from Trinidad and
was not an Indian from the subcontinent.[23] His multicultural upbringing
led him to write about Blacks as convincingly as about East Indians, as his
much-acclaimed Moses trilogy[24]—*The Lonely Londoners, Moses Ascending,*
and *Moses Migrating*—has shown.

The plots of his novels reflect Selvon's politics of creolization. In *A
Brighter Sun,* the newlywed East Indian Tiger and Urmilla leave the sugar
state in Chaguanas where they grew up to settle down as free peasants in
Barataria, a suburban town near San Fernando. There they develop a very
close friendship with Joe and Rita Martins, their black neighbors, over-
coming the sectarism and antiblack bias their parents had instilled in
them within the overwhelmingly Indian world of the plantation. In *Turn
again Tiger,* the sequel, the young couple returns to the sugar plantation,

following the invitation of Tiger's father to participate in an experimental crop, only to realize that it was multicultural Barataria that they felt they truly belonged to.

In a key scene of *A Brighter Sun,* the split between Tiger and Urmilla's generation and that of their parents is made clear. Rita and Joe are invited to the party their Indian friends have organized to celebrate the birth of their daughter. The atmosphere becomes strained because the Indian elders disapprove of their children's black friends: " 'Is only nigger friend you makeam since you come?' His *bap* asked. 'Plenty Indian liveam dis side. Is true them is good neighbour, but you must look for Indian friend, like you and your wife. Indian must keep together.' "[25] Urmilla's mother goes so far as to pinch Rita's son for touching the baby: "Nigger boy put he black hand in my *betah* baby face!."[26] Whereas Tiger's and Urmilla's parents perceive the Martins as members of a stigmatized group—Blacks who carry the harmful creolizing influence—the young couple perceives them as individuals they interact with daily, as Urmilla explains: "But, *mai,* these people good to us; we is friends. I does get little things from she [Rita], and sometimes she does borrow little things from me."[27] In general, Urmilla tends to mix more with women like Rita or black-Chinese Berta, avoiding the Indian women who "prattle all the time in sing-song Hindu."[28]

Selvon also dares to foresee the issue of mixed marriages. Through the marriage of Chinese Otto and black-Chinese Berta, a match made by Indian Soylo, the taboo of miscegenation is ironically reversed.

Although Selvon intends to show that his characters are able to interact successfully with each other as individuals, regardless of their ethnic peculiarities, he acknowledges that they may also perceive each other in a biased way when they "become" group members. In this regard, it is important to remember that Selvon's novels on the Indian peasantry are set in colonial Trinidad, a time when group perceptions were deeply entrenched in society. Thus, his narrator admits that in Trinidad "there is a shortcut to identity,"[29] referring to the stereotypes that groups hold of each other. Social psychologists have defined stereotypes as "representations of groups" based on the "accentuation of differences."[30] Far from being mere representations of social reality, stereotypes are political because "in a world of inter-group politics . . . [stereotypes] are carefully-crafted weapons . . . to consolidate advancement."[31] Naturally, stereotyping thrives in situations of intergroup competition, allowing certain groups to enhance their social image by stressing the negative features of another group or providing ideological justification to maintain a given status quo. Caribbean plantation society was a breeding ground for stereotypes, given the status rivalry between the different ethnic groups due to their historical positions. The white plantocracy stereotyped Blacks as savages in order to cast their colonization of the islands as a civilizing mission. Afterward, Blacks were stereotyped as lazy because of their refusal to work on plantations as pseudoslaves. East Indians interiorized those prevailing stereotypes about Blacks soon after their arrival. Blacks, in turn, saw Indians who took the jobs they themselves had refused as being thrifty and backward.

Selvon's characters indeed resort to stereotyped knowledge about each other. When Joe finds out that Rita has lent their bed to Urmilla, who will soon give birth, he invokes the stereotype of Indian thrift: "Dem Indian people does have plenty money hide away. Why Tiger don't buy ah bed for he wife?"[32] Similarly, Boysie, an Indian friend of Tiger's, is incensed when he and Tiger are forced to share a taxi with an old black woman who carries a fish basket. The black woman feels abused by Boysie's complaints throughout the drive and curses him when he leaves the taxi: "Yuh nasty coolie! I smelling of fish, but wat you smelling of?"[33]

Selvon's analysis of AfroAsian relations also includes the Chinese. The Indians and Blacks of Barataria hold the stereotype of the Chinese as hard-working shopkeepers, a trade monopolized by this group. Through his portrayal of Chinese characters, Selvon raises the issue of trade as an ethnicity marker that accentuates the differences between groups. Werner Sollors uses the example of Chinese-American laundry owners to underscore the cultural construction of ethnicity: " 'The Chinese laundryman does not learn his trade in China; there are no laundries in China.' . . . One can hardly explain the prevalence of Chinese-American laundry owners by going back to Chinese history proper."[34] Trade may become an ethnicity marker, but there is nothing essentially ethnic about it. Indeed, there is nothing essentially Chinese about shopkeeping.[35]

Selvon examines the figure of the Chinese shopkeeper to highlight the stifling effects of stereotypes on the individual. Tall Boy, Barataria's Chinese shopkeeper, complains that he is not perceived as "a human being" but just as "the symbol of the shop."[36] He longs to attend the parties that his customers organize because he wants to feel he belongs in the larger creole society. It hurts him that he should be perceived merely as the alcohol provider for the parties, and that nobody should ever think that he might like to join them as well. The fact that he suffers in silence for a long time means that he has internalized the stereotype and resigned himself to the role assigned to him by the stereotype. However, one day he decides to go to one of these parties and, to his surprise, nobody is shocked by his presence. Joe exclaims, "you is a creolised Chinee . . . a born Trinidadian."[37] Through this incident, Selvon is stressing the point that categorical perception is not fixed but context-dependent; outside the shop, the Chinese shopkeeper is perceived simply as Trinidadian. Besides, that the villagers remained undisturbed by Tall Boy's sudden appearance implies that the internalization of stereotypes by those who suffer from them contribute to their persistence. Though Blacks, East Indians, and Chinese may perceive each other as members of ethnic groups in certain contexts, overall they can interact successfully as individuals.

Even though Selvon attempts to resolve ethnic rifts in his novels, he also foregrounds the tensions underlying creole society. The following statement by Joe toward the end of *A Brighter Sun* sounds premonitory: "Yes, Ah hear bout it. Dat [self-government] is wat we fighting for now, but you yuhself know how dis place have so much different people, it go be ah big fight. Is always wite man for wite man, coolie for coolie, nigger for nigger."[38] The character of Mr. Ramroop encapsulates the attitude that Joe denounces, for he mobilized the Indian bloc, promising to fight for "Indian rights" in order to get a seat in the municipal government.[39] It should be noted that though this novel depicts Trinidadian society in the early 1940s when the island was still a colony but the way to independence was being paved, it was published in 1952. By that time it was becoming clear that politics would develop along racial lines in the new democracy since Indian politicians had split from the African party and formed their own party, the People's Democratic Party, during the previous year.[40] Selvon chose not to conceal this problem.

Unlike Selvon, Fred D'Aguiar belongs to the young generation of Caribbean writers. He began his literary career as a poet in the mid-1980s with *Mama Dot* and has combined poetry with the writing of fiction since 1994.

Born in 1962 in London to Guyanese parents, Fred D'Aguiar was raised in Guyana, where he spent his childhood and early youth. Though D'Aguiar was a U.S.-based author teaching at the University of Miami when *Bethany Bettany* was released, Guyana remains the touchstone of his poetry and fiction. Thus, he includes this country in the acknowledgments to his latest novel: "And to Guyana: you keep me dreaming." The word "dream" should be understood here both as inspiration, because Guyana is

at the center of D'Aguiar's poetry and fiction, and as mission, because one
of the characters in this novel protests that the country "remains un-
dreamt" and must be "dreamt into being."[41]

The fact that Selvon and D'Aguiar belong to different generations
accounts for their different treatment of interethnic relations in the novels
that concern this essay. Intending to denaturalize ethnic stereotypes, Selvon uses ethnic labels throughout his novels, echoing their unconscious
absorption into everyday speech in colonial Trinidad and exposing their
functionality in certain contexts. D'Aguiar, however, provides in *Dear
Future* and *Bethany Bettany* a more contemporary picture of Caribbean
society, writing about Guyana's postcolonial condition. He focuses on
characters who are both culturally and biologically creolized, which points
to a higher degree of intermingling and a more fluid social structure in the
postcolonial era. At the same time, D'Aguiar creates an atmosphere of political urgency. The Guyana he portrays is diseased by its past and unable
to handle its independence. He underscores the fact that the manipulation
of ethnic divisions for political purposes has led to the racial polarization
of Guyanese politics. While writing in a nonrealist mode with touches of
allegory and magic realism, D'Aguiar features key political events through
their destructive effects on the domestic life of his characters. Tragedy
befalls the Santos family in *Dear Future* due to their opposition to the ruling party during elections. Through their story, D'Aguiar portrays a fierce
and corrupted struggle for political power, reminiscent of the rivalry between the Afro-Guyanese and the Indo-Guyanese leaders Burnham and
Jaggan. Likewise, *Bethany Bettany* features a quarreling family, the Abrahams, whose fracture can be traced back to the split in the first native-
ruled party of Guyana.

In both novels, D'Aguiar attempts to break the circle of ethnic conflict and to offer a network of social relations based on creolization. The
grandfather of the Santos family, a Portuguese from Madeira, for example,
voices D'Aguiar's identity politics. When the house of an Indian family is
set on fire, he tries to gather a crowd to help find the arsonists. The scene
is described by Red Head, the child narrator of the novel:

> As Grandad began to speak, a strong moon emerged from a bundle of
> clouds. . . . Everyone shone under that moon. The demarcations of white,
> brown and black that were so apparent in daylight were softened by the
> moon to subtle gradations of tone. If people were intent on locating such
> differences they would have to look hard and long in this equalising light.

. . . Grandad spoke of men who'd married women they'd fallen in love with regardless of race and who had been themselves the product of various unions between the races. He pointed to the fact that he was Portuguese, his wife African, one daughter-in-law half Amerindian, another Indian. Let them try and separate us, let them try. . . . Everyone applauded Grandad and shook hands. They divided into groups . . . intent on apprehending the perpetrators.[42]

The Santos patriarch seems to have Guyana's motto, "Together We Aspire, Together We Achieve," in the back of his mind when he lectures the crowd. Earlier, he had already been branded as "coolie lover"[43] for his unprejudiced thinking. In the ethnically polarized election climate, he appeals now to the community for solidarity with the Indian family, reminding them of the creole nature of their society. With this passage, D'Aguiar intends to underscore the arbitrariness of racial categorization; skin complexion is made to appear unimportant, contingent as it is on the fluctuating gradations of light.

In another revealing passage, the patriarch complains that politics in independent Guyana are "skin-deep"—a clear allusion to the prevailing politics of ethnic domination. "What do they know about Africa or India? Anyway I'm from Madeira if they want to be exact,"[44] he goes on to say, referring to the two parties in dispute, the African and the Indian party. Through the old man's voice, D'Aguiar is criticizing the inadequacy of the labels "African" and "Indian" in a culture where both the African and the Indian components are no longer "pure" but creolized. Consequently, India and Africa can only take the role of mythic motherlands rather than of places to return to. Naturally, Singh, the wrestler that the government brings from India to entertain their supporters, wishes to be introduced as "wrestler from India" and not as "an Indian wrestler"[45] to dissociate himself from the creole Indians he meets in Guyana, who do not observe caste and may intermingle with other races. He finds it amusing that the ancestry of his opponent, Bounce Santos, should include "not only African and Indian blood but Portuguese, too."[46] One could see this as D'Aguiar's attempt to criticize the existing labels: besides being inadequate to describe the creole reality, these labels prove to be exclusive, for they fail to include more marginal components such as the Portuguese.

Further evidence of D'Aguiar's concern with creolization is the friendship that develops between Red Head and Sten, the daughter of the Indian family. Usually, D'Aguiar endows his children characters with a privileged insight into the world of adults and turns them into embodiments of union, acting as harmonizing influences in troubled environments.[47] Red Head, of mixed ancestry but with a dark complexion, has several Indian friends like Raj and Sten. The following dialogue between Red Head and Sten as they play in their tree house is worth quoting:

[Red Head] You [Sten] look like a red zebra.
[Sten] You look like a black zebra.
Zebras are black and white.
Then how can I be a red zebra?
Your red skin in these bars of light.
And your black skin in it too.
Our children will be red and black zebras.
What a nice mix-up.[48]

In their innocent dialogue, the children reflect on the arbitrariness of skin complexion, which changes shade as the afternoon light filters through the coconut branches. They project themselves into the future as a mixed couple.

D'Aguiar envisions a more harmonious society with the new generation represented by Sten and Red Head, but he warns that this potential is threatened by the petty conflicts of adults. Violence is unleashed again when Bounce Santos defeats the Indian wrestler sponsored by the government. An angry mob besieges the Santos household, whose men, backed by Sten's father, try to protect their family, and a torch sets the house on fire. The Santos family strand of the plot ends on a tragic note, as smoke creeps under the door where the children are kept, while Sten and Red Head play unconcerned.

The sense of political urgency and racial turmoil is even stronger in *Bethany Bettany,* where Guyana is referred to as a "shared jungle"[49] and a "country of quarrelling people."[50] The Abrahams are a large, locally powerful family, who live in a small village called Boundary, on the edge of the Guyana jungle. This family embodies Guyana racially and politically. The novel's protagonist is Bethany, a member of the Abrahams' youngest generation. Endowed with a privileged mind, like the child protagonist of *Dear Future,* Bethany is despised and mistreated by her aunts and uncles because she takes after her mother, whom the family blames for the suicide of her husband, their kin. For Bethany, her mother resembles an "African princess" with her "onyx" skin.[51] Bethany describes the disappointment of one of her aunts at her dark complexion: "She passes a hand over my hair to ascertain its texture, its coarseness. From the look that plays for an instant around her mouth, as if she tastes tamarind, I must fail some complex indexes of hers defined by the mix of our South Asian, African and European antecedents."[52] The aunt dislikes the fact that Bethany's nappy hair should set off the African component in the family's genetic mixture, which reveals her prejudiced views on Afro-Guyanese people. These allusions to Bethany and his mother's hair type and skin complexion are worth noting, since there is a tendency for D'Aguiar to gloss over the appearance of his characters, who do not appear as distinctively Indo or Afro but mixed, in order to reinforce their creoleness. Yet, D'Aguiar avoids romanticizing creole mixtures. The scrutinizing gesture of Bethany's aunt reveals that some blends are preferred over others.

In the course of a complicated choral narrative with touches of magic realism that defies linearity and forces the reader to piece bits of information together, one learns that the Abrahams are split by their loyalty to different political parties. Reginal Abrahams, the grandfather, and his daughter-in-law, Bethany's mother, represent democratic ideas. The rest of the family blame these ideas for the division of their "big name"[53] and struggle to retain their influence, which is granted by the corrupted government of Boundary. They oppose the short-lived multiracial party the country had launched its new democracy with, which one of the aunts describes as a "coalition government . . . with its many heads on the one glued-together monster body,"[54] to the point that they burn the local school because the headmaster running it supports the coalition and instills subversive ideas in Bethany's head. The headmaster is one of D'Aguiar's spokespersons for racial harmony and democracy in the novel. He believes it is the youth's role to lead the new republic on the road to democracy. He lectures them thus:

> There is the country we see all around us and then there is the country that we dream about and wish to make into a reality. Our country remains undreamt. We live the practical side of it, the side we find ourselves in and tolerate because we lack the dream, the dreamed alternative. The youth, all of you, must dream this country into being.[55]

The burning of the school, run by a headmaster holding democratic views, is tantamount to the burning of the Santos household in *Dear*

Future. The arson motif is used by D'Aguiar to highlight the stifling of the democratic and conciliatory impulse in Guyanese society.

The atmosphere of ethnopolitical turmoil evoked by D'Aguiar in this novel is compounded by the border war raging in the jungle between Guyana and a neighboring country, allegedly Venezuela, over a rich logging area, allegedly the Essequibo region. The border war widens the gap between the two factions of the family, since, whereas most of its members had deserted the war, the head of the household, Bethany's grandfather, chose to stay and fight to regain lost territories, abandoning the family. At the end of the novel, Bethany runs away from the Abrahams household to join her mother and grandfather in the jungle. When she meets her grandfather, whom she had never seen before, he explains to her the need to defend the country from the foreign invasion. "The other side" had sold that region, which was not even theirs but a disputed territory, to a consortium of American logging companies which threaten to turn it into a desert.[56] There is a suggestion that Bethany will stay in the jungle to fight for her country alongside her mother and her grandfather, whereas the rest of the Abrahams continue to support a corrupted local government, undisturbed by the problems of their country. The inclusion of Guyana's border problems in the novel is not gratuitous, since, as it has been argued, the definition of the country's frontiers, unsettled by its complicated colonial history, was one step in its achievement of postcolonial wholeness.[57]

As a conclusion, I would like to pick up the thread of Rojo's metaphorical description of the Caribbean. Once the Caribbean gives birth to the Atlantic, there remains "the febrile wait through the forming of a scar: suppurating, always suppurating."[58] Both Selvon and D'Aguiar bring the legacy of racial slavery and indenture to bear on their examination of ethnic conflict between Blacks and Asians in Trinidadian and Guyanese societies. Such conflicts express themselves in the circulation of stereotypes about ethnic groups, in the reductive perception of creoleness as blackness to the exclusion of other components, and in the political manipulation of ethnic blocs. Writing about and in postcolonial times, D'Aguiar is less optimistic than Selvon about the achievement of wholeness in Caribbean creole societies. The political corruption and *apanjhat* practices that Selvon hints at are rampant in D'Aguiar's novels. His creole families are torn by conflicting views of the Guyanese nation, like the Abrahams, or threatened by the destructive forces within it, like the Santos.

In foregrounding conflict, these writers refuse to romanticize the Caribbean as a site of harmonious creolization and instead explore the complexities of creole identity. At the same time, nonetheless, both authors uphold creolization as essential to the nation-building processes of young Caribbean democracies, showing the extent to which it operates in these societies. Selvon's novels portray healing scenes of interaction among Blacks, East Indians, and Chinese characters. D'Aguiar offers characters that exert harmonizing influences on communities divided across ethnopolitical lines. Moreover, he approaches creolization as an irresistible force within Guyanese society by depicting characters that bear the profound racial mixture of the population in their genes.

At the beginning of the twenty-first century, Trinidadian and Guyanese societies are still in need of a model of nationality and culture that privileges neither the black nor the Indian groups but addresses the creolized nature of the population. Both authors succeed in addressing this need.

NOTES

1. Antonio Benítez-Rojo, *The Repeating Island: The Caribbean and the Postmodern Perspective* (Durham: Duke University Press, 1996), 5.

2. Ibid.

3. T. Vere Daly, *A Short History of the Guyanese People* (London: Macmillan, 1993).

4. Ibid., 189.

5. Ibid., 225.

6. Benítez-Rojo, *Repeating Island*, 5.

7. Daly, *Short History*, 196.

8. Lloyd Braithwaite, "Social Stratification and Cultural Pluralism," in *Peoples and Cultures of the Caribbean: An Anthropological Reader*, ed. Michael Horowitz (New York: Natural History Press, 1971), 97.

9. The party split in 1953, one faction being led by the Indo Cheddi Jagan and the other faction by the Afro Forbes Burnham. This split was formalized in 1957, when Burnham formed the People's National Congress (PNC). Daly, *Short History*, 302–303.

10. Participants of an international conference on political conflict called for "a complete reversal of Guyana's political culture embodied in the concept of power sharing." See "Feel the Other's Pain," *Stabroek News*, 6 February 2004, available at www.stabroeknews.com (retrieved 19 July 2004). In another news item, the leader of the opposition presses the current leader of the People's Progressive Party (PPP), now in power, for shared governance. See "Corbin Withdraws from Dia-

logue," *Stabroek News,* 1 April 2004, available at www.stabroeknews.com (retrieved 19 July 2004).

11. "Beyond Platitudes of Indian Arrival," *Trinidad Guardian,* 31 May 2003, available at www.guardian.co.tt (retrieved 19 July 2004). See also "Racial Undertones Mar Arrival Messages," *TrinidadandTobagoNews.com,* 6 June 2004, available at www.trinidadandtobagonews.com (retrieved 6 August 2004).

12. Edouard Glissant, *Poetics of Relation* (Ann Arbor: University of Michigan Press, 1997), 97.

13. Benítez-Rojo, *Repeating Island,* 12.

14. Wilson Harris, "Creoleness: The Crossroads of a Civilization?" in *Caribbean Creolization: Reflections on the Cultural Dynamics of Language, Literature and Identity,* ed. Kathleen M. Balutansky and Marie-Agnès Souricau (Barbados: University Press of the West Indies, 1998), 5.

15. Glissant, *Poetics of Relation,* 147.

16. Michael Dash, "Psychology, Creolization and Hybridization," in *New National and Post-Colonial Literatures,* ed. Bruce King (Oxford: Clarendon, 1996), 51.

17. "Indians Are Already Deeply Creolised: Mr. Panday Is a Propagandist for a Hindu/Indian Cultural Revival," *Stabroek News,* 13 April 2004, available at www.stabroeknews.com (retrieved 6 August 2004).

18. "Creolization Is Almost Synonymous with an Africanised Cultural Ethos," *Stabroek News,* 27 April 2004, available at www.stabroeknews.com (retrieved 4 August 2004).

19. "We Live in a World of Composite Cultures" *Stabroek News,* 5 May 2004, available at www.stabroeknews.com (retrieved 19 July 2004); emphasis mine.

20. Sylvia Schomburg-Scherff, "Women Versions of Creole Identity in Caribbean Fiction: A Cultural-Anthropological Perspective," in *A Pepper-Pot of Cultures: Aspects of Creolization in the Caribbean,* ed. Gordon Collier and Ulrich Fleischmann (Amsterdam: Rodopi, 2003), 368.

21. Peter Nazareth, "Interview with Sam Selvon," in *Critical Perspectives on Sam Selvon,* ed. Susheila Nasta (Washington: Three Continents Press, 1988), 83.

22. Samuel Selvon, "Three into One Can't Go: East Indian, Trinidadian, Westindian," in *India and the Caribbean,* ed. David Dabydeen and Brinsley Samaroo (London: Hansib, 1987), 14–15.

23. Ibid., 17.

24. See Swift Dickinson, "Sam Selvon's 'Harlequin Costume': *Moses Ascending,* Masquerade, and the Bacchanal of Self-Creolization," *MELUS* 21.3 (1996): 69–106.

25. Samuel Selvon, *A Brighter Sun* (London: Longman, 2002), 47.

26. Ibid.

27. Ibid.

28. Samuel Selvon, *Turn again Tiger* (London: Heinemann, 1979), 78.

29. Selvon, *Brighter Sun,* 50.

30. Craig McGarty, Vincent Yzerbyt, and Russel Spears, "Social, Cultural and

Cognitive Factors in Stereotype Formation," in *Stereotypes as Explanations: The Formation of Meaningful Beliefs about Social Groups,* ed. Craig McGarty, Vincent Yzerbyt, and Russel Spears (Cambridge: Cambridge University Press, 2000), 2–3.

31. Alexander Haslam et al., "From Personal Pictures in the Head to Collective Tools in the World: How Shared Stereotypes Allow Groups to Represent and Change Social Reality," in *Stereotypes as Explanations: The Formation of Meaningful Beliefs about Social Groups,* ed. Craig McGarty, Vincent Yzerbyt, and Russel Spears (Cambridge: Cambridge University Press, 2000), 183.

32. Selvon, *Brighter Sun,* 39.

33. Ibid., 87.

34. Werner Sollors, *The Invention of Ethnicity* (New York: Oxford University Press, 1989), xvi.

35. "The Baker's Story" (1962) by V. S. Naipaul is worth mentioning to illustrate this point further because it presents an extreme example of how stereotype can affect behavior. The black narrator of this story puzzles over the fact that "though Trinidad have every race and every colour, every race have to do special things" (121). Blacks are not accepted in the retail business, especially when it comes to handling food or selling it behind a counter. When he manages to set up his own bakery, having learned the trade from a Chinese family, he realizes that his blackness scares away customers. Therefore, he is forced to put a Chinese man behind the counter, hang "a Chinee calendar with Chinee women and flowers and waterfalls" (122) on the wall, and conceal the fact that it is him who bakes the bread. Only then does he become successful. Through this story, Naipaul exposes the efficacy of the stereotype and, at the same time, denaturalizes it, unmasking the anxieties that underlie it. "The Baker's Story," in *A Flag over the Island* (New York: Penguin, 1969), 111–123.

36. Selvon, *Turn again Tiger,* 14.

37. Ibid., 15.

38. Selvon, *Brighter Sun,* 196.

39. Ibid., 203.

40. Percy Hintzen, *The Costs of Regime Survival: Racial Mobilization, Elite Domination and Control of the State in Guyana and Trinidad* (Cambridge: Cambridge University Press, 1989).

41. Fred D'Aguiar, *Bethany Bettany* (London: Chatto and Windus, 2003), 191.

42. Fred D'Aguiar, *Dear Future* (London: Chatto and Windus, 1996), 48.

43. Ibid.

44. Ibid., 38.

45. Ibid., 72.

46. Ibid., 74.

47. See Joan Hyppolite, "Interview with Fred D'Aguiar," *Anthurium: A Caribbean Studies Journal* 2.1 (2004), available at www//scholar.library.Miami.edu (re-

trieved June 2004); and Gerard Woodward, "A Child of Conflict," *Times Literary Supplement*, 15 July 2003, 22.

48. D'Aguiar, *Dear Future*, 45.
49. D'Aguiar, *Bethany Bettany*, 21.
50. Ibid., 60.
51. Ibid., 36.
52. Ibid., 15
53. Ibid., 226.
54. Ibid., 212.
55. Ibid., 191.
56. Ibid., 293.
57. Daly, *Short History*, 280.
58. Benítez-Rojo, *Repeating Island*, 5.

Chapter 5

Black-and-Tan Fantasies

Interracial Contact between Blacks and
South Asians in Film

Samir Dayal

Discussing the Hollywood biracial buddy films of the 1980s such as *Alien Nation* (1988), Ed Guerrero argues that the sci-fi buddy feature transcodes social tensions and fears about racial mixture as a result of increasing immigration; in doing so, he points beyond the biracial paradigm that often constrains a film's critical reading offered by contemporary scholars.[1] Guerrero writes, "Because its complex imbrication of politicized and racially coded meanings allude to all non-White racial minorities, the film's narrative is allegory for the present wave of Latino, Asian and West Indian immigration to this country, while it also evokes the nation's repressed, historical relationship to Blacks and chattel slavery."[2] As he notes, what makes these films so popular is "their ability to transcode, even into terms of fantasy, social unease over rising racial tensions of a recently pluralized society with an expanding non-White population to accommodate and a shrinking reserve of economic opportunities."[3] Guerrero's claim invites the following questions: How do those non-White populations imagine or fantasize interethnic contact, and how do their nightmares and fantasies complicate the "biracial" paradigm? It is not just that there is a plurality of non-White groups within the multicultural polity of North America. Rather, the question is, what fresh insights emerge on interethnic contact in film if we change our perspective from a two-dimensional view to a three-dimensional one? What interests me is the way in which interracial or interethnic contact is triangulated; for me it is not exclusively a question of tracking the "master signifier" of whiteness but of attending to the complexities of the ways in which brownness or blackness or yellowness can also function as the *tertium quid*—the obscured referent or object of desire, the signifier that stitches the triangulation together. I am interested in the way this third term operates as a spectral third term, structuring what is overtly represented as a binary relation. There is more often than not, although perhaps not always, a third party moving behind the scenes or behind the screen on which interethnic contact is being projected. What is interesting is that sometimes it is not the white man or woman. I am arguing, then, that if there is a structural "three-ness" that characterizes interethnic contact, it is crucial to see that whiteness does not always play the role of the supplementary or constitutive other.[4]

While I agree that the fundamental fantasy of wholeness undergirds the dynamic of racialization, in this essay I look in particular at how the representation of interethnic contact in film—"race" itself being a relational construct—employs fantasy at several levels. Here the racialized fantasy is not just the "fundamental" fantasy. Rather, fantasy here is often to be understood in an everyday sense, as projecting self and other, not in a binary relation but in what I am calling a triangulation. It is not a fantasy of "being" but of being in a social relation to the other that gestures beyond the apparent binary—although I am not claiming that the third is always a strong presence or that it is more significant than the two parties involved in the first instance, and it is not always a relation between white and black people. In films such as *One Flew over the Cuckoo's Nest* (1975), *Indiana Jones and the Temple of Doom* (1984), and *City of Joy* (1992), the primary relation is between whites and red or brown people. Blackness is perhaps not significant here, except as the occluded signifier: after all, in these films, the dominant drive is to affirm the white man as "savior."[5] Yet, my point is that we need to be alert to the spectral presence of the third when it *does* operate as a spectral signifier so that we do not miss the fact that sometimes two parties are in contention precisely because a gesture is being made in relation to a third party, or some message is being encrypted about the second party by way of a cryptic premise about a third. And even if there is a necessary misrecognition or even a scotomization involved in screening off the fundamental fantasy, there can be little question that this more commonplace "fantasy" is powerful and that in this sense social relations among racialized groups have a significant psychological dynamic. If films are "one of the resources through which power is wielded by the classes that benefit from the racial status quo,"[6] I suggest that the very expression of such power exposes the vulnerability of the status quo, as well as its flexibility: for it is not always the black man who is denigrated as the lowest of the low and not always the white man who strives to seem superior to another. On occasion, it is a minority figure who seeks to establish himself or herself as the superior of a person of a different minority group, and this is not just about competition between minorities.

My discussion of AfroAsian or black-brown encounters in contemporary cinema featuring South Asians aims chiefly to offer such a perspective. In each of these black-and-brown interactions, I trace the presence of a third that is screened off in some respects, but which points to the fact that we need to think beyond the binary frame to understand these racialized representations. It is imperative to conceptualize ethnicity as differential, or even, following Jacques Derrida, *différantial,* in the sense that the meaning of each position of the enunciation of ethnic belonging is not known in advance but is deferred into a "sovereign incalculability"[7] in the shifting instantiations of ethnic difference.

The psychic force of race thus does not just tether two parties—us and them—but is haunted by a third, an oppressive or an abject third. This is often glossed over in identity politics. Similarly, what holds ethnic enclaves together is the rhetoric of binaries, and minority group rights claims are often expressed in terms of a competition between and among minority groups. Furthermore, while there has long been, in the black imagination, a *conscious,* strategic knowledge about white people, as bell hooks writes,[8] there has also been a special *unconscious* or spectral presence of whiteness in the way that nonwhites have imagined themselves. This is one of the more pernicious effects of a diffuse racism permeating every aspect of culture. And one could go further and say that spectrality is the very hallmark of racism: the standard against which the other is denigrated (literally and figuratively) is anxiously removed from view, often by the legerdemain of official denial that either race or ethnicity has a role in political or economic determinations such as affirmative action in educational institutions or in the workplace.

Racism indeed takes the form of denial in everyday social intercourse, as when well-meaning white people say that they do not "see color" in friendships or at work. The fact remains that as psychic reality, racism remains entrenched even when it seems to have been erased from the overt discourses of the public sphere. Thus in most Euro-American contexts, whiteness is often reinscribed as a hegemonic standard, simultaneously spectral and obdurately in the position of the Other as it mediates relations between minorities.

Yet, there are situations in which the racial drama is played out in less predictable ways. To understand such staging, we must bring to this familiar model of racism a third dimension that suggests another, third figure operating at a different level. I am proposing an optics of triangulation that would solicit the structural position whiteness occupies but also complicates the narratives of interethnic contact by adding a third dimension. In the first instance, as race theory has it, whiteness functions as the spectral master signifier, or in psychoanalytic language as the phallus of power. This master signifier is often obscured by the very intensity of interethnic contact, even as it functions as a spectral prosthesis, psychologically anchoring and completing the triangulated relationship between brown and black. It plugs the hole in the symbolic fabric of the status quo, obscuring the "real" of racism, to employ a psychoanalytic analogy. According to this analogy, the form of or impediments to one subject's desire for another may in fact have a lot to do with a third party: the mother, the father, a nameless Other whose own enigmatic desire the subject wants somehow to appease or fulfill. As Lacan has it, desire is always the (enigmatic) desire of the Other. The Lacanian Other is the symbolic order itself, a trove of signifiers. But it is also possible to extricate oneself from a Lacanian vocabulary to speak of the order of intersubjectivity where there are others whose desires are sometimes anything but enigmatic and where the other's reality is to be understood in the most immediate, material sense or as a fantasy of a third subject mediating or interfering with a relationship between two other subjects. This is a realist account of race rather than a psychoanalytic account.

It has to be said in this connection that rarely does contemporary South Asian diasporic cinema achieve, much less surpass, such sophisticated realism that engages hybridity in the Deleuzian sense of being multiperspectival and ambivalent—and potentially subversive by opening up "any-spaces-whatever."[9] These are spaces in which agency can emerge in ways not totally determined by the dominant powers. Rarely does it explore psychic interiority in Giorgio Agamben's sense of making possible "whatever" subjective singularities.[10] Such singularity—the "whatever" in Agamben—is admittedly possible only in the utopia that functions as the distant and ever-receding goal of antiracist, postcolonial, and other progressive struggles, where difference is recognized and acknowledged but not enforced to entrench a hierarchy of power. However, that need not make the struggles meaningless, for the journey can transform social relationships, including those among members of racialized groups. Furthermore, in the films I am considering, those "any-spaces-whatever," those singularities sometimes show themselves only momentarily, as it were, despite what seems to be happening at the surface. In looking at diasporic South Asian films, then, we need to be alert to trace moments—evanescent intensities in which fantasies and anxieties of interracial contact leap up, revealing the saturated affect and ideological background of professional, political, or personal contact between brown and black individuals.

Mira Nair's *Mississippi Masala* (1992) is a key cinematic text in this connection. The triangulation of race flashes up painfully in the scene when Demetrius, Mina's black lover, upbraids her father, Jai, for his racist objections to his being with Mina. Jai is a double diasporic from Idi Amin's Uganda, now an immigrant in Mississippi; Demetrius accuses him of "acting *white*" in the United States—in other words, of misrecognizing himself in the racialized economy of U.S. culture. Demetrius seems to be suggesting that, in a psychological calculus, this is a category error—not just a matter of definition or semantics but of behavior, of presentation of self to self. For Jai and other Indians with skin only a shade lighter than Demetrius's black skin, to "act white" is not willful, perverse behavior. It is not as though Indians know that they are "*only acting* white" but that this acting white is a part of the *performative* subjectivity of South Asians like Jai. It stems from a deeper identification with whites: a psychic motor drives the identification. That is the real point of Demetrius's critique.

In this revealing irruption of whiteness as fantasmatic prosthesis, we glimpse the real of racism. The film shows that interracial contact does not necessarily transcend a racism complicated by class and sexual overtones. Indeed, there is an isomorphism between race and sex in the (Lacanian) real, but they are also chained together in actual social or symbolic relations. As Kalpana Seshadri-Crooks argues, "Race should be understood in its particularity as something that is neither totally like sexual difference, which is indeterminate and exceeds language, nor purely symbolical or cultural lie class or ethnicity. Race resembles class in that it is of purely cultural and historical origin, but it is also like sex in that it produces extra-discursive effects."[11] These extradiscursive effects are the real objects of antiracist critique. Throughout the film, sexuality and race are imbricated in a rich intertextuality. In a cameo appearance, the director herself makes a comment that desublimates class from the fantasmatic chromatism that divides browns from blacks. Nair's character says that Mina, dark of skin and short of money, cannot hope to catch a match like Harry Patel, well-off and Westernized, with his Americanized name and bow tie and tux—a wannabe white.

Yet things are not quite so simple, even in the case of Harry: when he takes Mina dancing, it is to a club where there are more blacks than whites or even browns present. Surely, in Mississippi this cannot have been a surprise to Harry. At the critical moment, feeling out of place among the dancing black people and their various pleasures, he tries to pull Mina away from Demetrius, who is dancing close to Mina; she chooses to stay with Demetrius. Unlike Mina, Harry makes no effort all evening at the club to interact with blacks, and his body language suggests his alienation from them. When he leaves, he clearly seems to understand that he has lost both a racial and a romantic contest. In Harry's reaction to this embarrassment and to the whole evening one can read not so much surprise but what David Roediger might call an envy of the pleasure principles of black culture—or, more simply, the brown man's envy of the black man's sexuality, as seen through the desire of the woman he desires. Once again, we see a triangulated structure.[12]

Yet, if Harry is a wannabe white who disdains blacks, what about Mina? She appears much more open to interacting with blacks even as a young girl; in Uganda, Mina had cultivated an extremely deep bond with Okelo, a childhood friend of her father and possibly a rival for the affections of Mina's mother. Mina's bond with Okelo is almost as deep as that with her own father. She certainly seems not to have the stereotypical disdain for blacks that Indians are supposed to have. Clearly, she is the protagonist of the film, and the spectator is supposed to find this openness to black people at every level admirable. Yet, can we assume that the ordinary South Asian or South Asian American spectator will identify with her desire for the black as erotic object? Or is that the pedagogical object of the film itself, to endorse such an object choice or to educate the brown person to be open to erotic attraction to a black person? Does Mira Nair really believe that her film shows that she wants us not to see color at all—that most feeble liberal attitude? And how is the mainstream (white) audience, surely an important target audience for this diasporic film, expected to enter into a triangulated spectatorial relationship (exoticized brown woman, projected as eye candy for mainstream white viewers; black erotic object choice; and white mainstream viewer). However, we are expected to interpret the filmmaker's position on Mina's attitude: the spectral presence of whiteness haunts all the black-brown interactions in such diasporic films, acting as a prosthesis to complete the fantasy.

Across the Brown Atlantic, though in a very different social context, Gurinder Chadha's *Bhaji on the Beach* (1994) offers another landmark example of a complexly triangulated interracial contact. Hashida, a South Asian woman, is pregnant with the child of her black Caribbean boyfriend. Their miscegenating relationship is presented as considerably more distressing to the older generation than to the younger South Asians, who also seem much more tolerant than their counterparts in *Mississippi Masala*. In Chadha's film, however, whiteness shows itself in a lurid, hallucinatory masquerade of brownness. Asha, an older South Asian woman, is courted by a white man who seems sympathetic, unlike the South Asian men. She fantasizes a Bollywood romance with her white admirer in brownface and Indian clothes chasing her around trees. Although clearly the white seducer's role, however innocuous it may seem, requires interpretation, here it is not primarily a question of the white man's perfidy. Rather, the performance testifies to the vectors of the brown woman's desire. She is on the rebound from her failing relationship with a South Asian man, and in her fantasy the white man, though transformed into a romantic hero in a Hindi film's song-and-dance sequence, offers an alternative; the white man appears to her to be more sympathetic, but this is not just a casual episode.

In the film, South Asian men are portrayed as almost universally unsympathetic. Even the black men in the film, such as Hashida's boyfriend and his father, are presented in a much more positive light. Yet if the central theme of this film has to do with the fact that the South Asian women are mistreated by "their" men and that is why they are going to the seaside in exclusively female company for a break from the rigors of having to answer to men, then this central argument is presented by triangulating the black, white, and brown men. Asha's Bollywood fantasy collapses when her would-be white suitor/savior/seducer's brown makeup runs down his face in a rain shower, calling attention to the flimsiness of the fantasy. Yet, Asha's fantasy speaks volumes about her unfulfilled desires as a South Asian woman. In this heavily cathected triangulation of race in Chadha's film, a third agent again functions as spectral prosthesis, completing the minoritarian narrative of interracial contact. For instance, the white man's appearance as a lovable if unreliable rake, like the black man's appearance as a confused but ultimately loyal lover, is intended to shed light by contrasting the brown man's inadequacies or brutishness. When the brown man finally shows up at the beach where the women are vacationing, he reveals himself as utterly despicable and violent—and the climax of the film hardly redeems him.

Such examples of the cinema of the Brown Atlantic are usefully contrasted with films in which it is not whiteness but Asianness or blackness that occupies the position of the spectral Other. What does this mean? In *Specters of Marx,* Derrida speaks of the "helmet effect." The power of the ghost of Hamlet's father comes, as it were, from the fact that he wears a helmet with a visor. The visor is an index of the power to see without being seen. Derrida writes this is the "supreme insignia of power."[13] When the white man—or whiteness, which is not the same thing—enjoys this privilege, whiteness functions as the master signifier. But the visor does not function as a rigid designator for whiteness. Even in many Hollywood films, whiteness is sometimes displaced from its default position of master signifier, and thirdness offers a more adequate category for analysis than a mere binary frame.

In recent years, there is no better example than *The Matrix* (1999), in which a black man, Morpheus, is placed in a position of power as the oracle—or, we could say, the Other. Even though this film once again presents a white messiah, Neo, for a change it is the black man who must reeducate him, welcome him to "the desert of the real"—and is that not the task of the Other, to beckon toward the real? Morpheus's blackness is here a trace that marks the fact that he is able to move beyond "the Matrix": he is explicitly associated with the "real." Vera Hernán and Andrew Gordon remark that *The Matrix* "seems to favor racial and gender diversity through its casting. Morpheus is black, and his crew are both black and white, men and women. . . . The movie . . . implies that the real, human world in which the good guys live is multicultural and multigendered whereas the computer simulation world of the Matrix is dominated by white men."[14] Yet, the issue of diversity is more complex than they suggest. First, Neo's training, both mental and physical, is clearly marked as "Asian" because it is a mishmash of neomystical Zen mind-bending and guy-wired martial arts. Indeed, one could argue that Asianness is even inscribed into Reeves's half-"Asian" eyes. The very multiracial presence of Keanu Reeves as Neo as well as Morpheus, not to mention Tank (an ambiguously black character played by Marcus Chong) and Choi (played by Marc Gray) seem to gesture to an Asian subtext, thus triangulating the interracial contact.

Occasionally, what is crucial is simply that whiteness is displaced from the position of master signifier: no one wears the helmet, as it were. In Spike Lee's *Do the Right Thing* (1989), the primary conflict is between the Italians who own Sal's Pizza and the blacks who predominantly patronize

it. Pino, one of Sal's sons, says, "I'm sick of niggers. . . . They're animals,"
while Sal insulates himself from his black customers by focusing on the
bottom line: money is his anodyne against political reality.[15] The racial
standoff sublimates the differential class positionings of the two groups.
Yet in the film's climax of racial violence the saturated triangulation of
race flashes up on the screen, in what I have called a saturated moment of
intensity, desublimating class again from race by the intrusion of a third
ethnic party, this time a Korean American. When this worthy fears his
store is about to be looted in the racial conflict, he protests, "I no white, I
no white, I black. You me same." Yet, the blacks advisedly reject this attempt to collapse difference. One of the blacks disabuses him: "Same? We
black. Open your eyes, motherfucker." The film insists on a kind of equiv-
alence-in-difference among these communities as a precondition for a
remaking of the multicultural polity. If the black community is devastated
by Radio Rahim's murder, Sal's pizzeria is also razed to the ground, and
the Korean's desire to remain safe behind the façade of "sameness" is revealed as a misrecognition. Doing the right thing means refusing misrecognition of the differential positionings of blackness (and Asianness)
vis-à-vis the hegemonic position of whiteness as the master signifier and
phallus. For my purpose, it is remarkable that the film knocks whiteness
out of its presumptive role as master signifier. It is not because of an unseen white gaze that the African Americans, the Italians, and the Koreans
are thrown into a conflicted triangulation.

In *The Royal Tenenbaums* (2001), blackness again stands in the place of
the mediating Other without quite displacing whiteness. But it is not an
unseen white gaze beneath the visor that structures the interethnic contact
in this film. Here the white man is once again not the all-powerful Other:
the triangulation or race is somewhat more complex than that. The film
presents the curious spectacle of Pagoda, an Indian who stabbed Royal
Tenenbaum in Calcutta, and then, inexplicably, saved him. Grateful for
having been saved in turn by the white man from the black hole of the
former empire, Pagoda remains Royal's only faithful companion. But that
this is a deeply troubled relationship is clearly evident, for the almost
voiceless brown retainer seems to find only one way of registering his frustration, namely stabbing Royal again, only to revert to taking care of him
again, as if the two were bound together in a neocolonial codependency.
The fantasized orientalization of the South Asian Other precisely references a third: in this case a black man, Henry Sherman (Danny Glover),

who now stands in place of the Other without displacing whiteness. This black rival of the white man has usurped Royal's bed, having moved in with his wife. If there is an Other, then it is the black man, for it is against him that the brown man is measured. Here blackness is prosthetically affixed to the minor plot of the neo-orientalizing relationship between Royal and his factotum, Pagoda.

A more explicit triangulation of race could hardly be imagined. Each figure illumines the place of the others. Today it is no longer politically correct to openly denigrate the black man. So here the black man is dandified and thus covertly made ridiculous. Yet, he is not as ridiculous as the brown man, the newly abject figure within the social triangle. In one notable scene, the triangulation of ethnic positionalities is starkly on view. The long-suffering but elegantly restrained black suitor of Royal's separated wife, Henry Sherman, rises up the stairs in bow tie and blue blazer to confront the Asiatic lounging in his room, glorified servants' quarters with the bric-a-brac of orientalia on the walls and on the tables. He accuses Pagoda of being paid by Royal to support him in his lies that go against his own (Henry's) courtship of the white woman. The white man (Royal) does not appear in this scene, but whiteness itself is strongly inscribed in the tense scene. For instance, Henry seems to mimic the white man, produced by the ambition to enjoy the white man's enjoyment (white man's bow tie and jacket, white man's house, white man's wife). And the brown man is similarly produced by a white regime of power as a near-mute servant of the white "sahib" who saved him from his own culture, "the black hole" of Calcutta. For a change, the brown man looks even more ridiculous than the black man. Why? The answer may be that while "multiculti" political correctness has made it improper to denigrate blacks in public discourse, American pop culture still considers it safe to denigrate or exoticize the South Asian. For example, in Stanley Kubrick's *Eyes Wide Shut* (1999) Sanskrit verses are chanted in an orgy scene—provoking a storm of protest against the exoticizing misappropriation.

It is not only the discourses of domestic multiculturalism that license this totemization according to which ethnic categories trade places in a fluid hierarchy. The flows of globalization also affect South Asians' positioning as a model minority, happy to seek approbation and appropriation by whites simultaneously and unable to protest their co-optation in the project of denigrating blacks. In *Mississippi Masala,* Mina's willingness to clean toilets (work that is anathema to aspirational South Asians) takes on a political edge as a refusal of this model minority syndrome, of what Anannya Bhattacharjee calls the habit of "ex-nomination." Bhattacharjee writes:

> As a minority community in a foreign nation, the Indian immigrant bourgeoisie experiences the loss of its power of ex-nomination. Where once it had stood for the no-name universal in the nation of its origin, it now perceives itself (and is perceived) to be in a position defined by difference. It now risks being named. The immigrant bourgeoisie's desire to overcome this condition manifests itself through its grasping for familiar essentials in whose shadows it can regain the power to remain un-named.[16]

Cleaning toilets refuses the anxiety of the South Asian immigrant bourgeoisie of descending into racialized visibility as black, as nonwhite. As Bhattacharjee writes, the Third World immigrant bourgeoisie in the First World "finds itself in a position of subordination to the native bourgeoisie: a position defined partly by the experiences of Western Colonialism and imperialism."[17] For Indian immigrants, "considered to be predominantly highly educated and relatively wealthy," this subordination "is defined more through race/nationality than through class."[18] However, I would suggest, pace Bhattacharjee, that it is as much about class as it is about color, and as much about the desire to be seen as successful as it is about the desire for "ex-nomination." Seshadri-Crooks argues that "the signification of class belonging, so long as it is purely a category of economic discrepancy, can be manipulated by its subjects. But the minute class makes a claim to inheritance through the language of 'stock' and 'blood,' it lapses into 'race,' and this is true for all other categories of group identity."[19]

In another telling moment in the film, one of the Indians tells two black men that they hold the same position in society: "United we stand, divided we fall." In context, however, this turns out to be a hollow and phony gesture of class and racial solidarity. *Do the Right Thing* poses similar questions about the interpellation of Asians within a triangular racialized economy, but there, too, it is clear that class is at least as much a factor as race or nationality in the self-construction of Korean Americans vis-à-vis African Americans.

In addition, Bhattacharjee's approach fails to emphasize the triangulation that intensifies the desire for "ex-nomination." It is precisely in order to distinguish themselves from blacks and to approximate the comfortably ex-nominated whites that Indians often behave as they do. Bhattacharjee's analysis might have been more effective if she had recast the dynamics of ex-nomination in light of the powerful spectral presence of whiteness in this racialized economy of power. Rarely is this complexity captured, however, even in theoretically astute readings of the South Asian presence.

Contemporary South Asian diasporic films even more rarely rise to this level of self- consciousness about the triangulation of race. Often the truth about interracial contact glances out of the fabric of the film only in the most saturated but evanescent moments, as a fragmentary inscription of the real affect and psychological investment that motivate such contact *or its avoidance.* For example, in *American Desi* (2001), Salim mimics black speech, clothing, and style. Does this racial masquerade constitute cultural appropriation, middle-class racial slumming, or emancipation from South Asian racism toward blacks? Can it be all three at once? I would argue that it is not so much black drag as a parody of blackness, and we should see it as both approach and distancing from blackness by a South Asian. Marjorie Garber, in another context, suggests that we look *at* rather than *through* masquerades of race: to see the masquerade for what it is, to be alive to its possible reincorporation and recommodification by culturally hegemonic interests or even by young South Asians themselves as a sign of their own hipness to contemporary hip-hop.[20] Many middle-class youths, both white and brown, adopt black culture chic in their college years, but only until it is time to get serious and get a job.

An analysis of racial triangulation also projects, even etymologically, its deconstruction. With the uncovering of the spectral third term, a new optics—or politics—can emerge, a corollary of which would be a critique of the state and institutions of power. In the Benjaminian flash of saturated intensity there is a spark of a promise for challenging the transcendental signifier of whiteness, a dethronement of the phallic plenitude against which minorities are played off against each other in a semblance of competition for the goods of a multicultural society. Truly liberatory interethnic contact would transform the language of miscegenation *and* preservation of culture.

Perhaps one of the most important questions to ask is whether films in which such contact is portrayed have market appeal—perhaps as reformulated interethnic buddy films. But at the level of the social, the real challenge of interculturalism entails risking the cultural self and individual subjectivity. Risking the self means first recognizing the co-production of social selves, not necessarily in a binary frame. This, in turn, involves defamiliarization of what is most intimate to oneself: dismantling the carapace of race and delaminating cultural stereotype from ethnicity. It means challenging the presumptive colorless "normativity" of whiteness. I do not share Dinesh D'Souza's optimism about how the melting pot will naturally bring about the end of racism.[21] Rather than such a homogenized, McDonaldized dystopia, we might seek to preserve Agamben's singularity as a precondition for heterotopia in which multiple and unpredictable interracial alliances are nurtured, where black-brown alliances need not be haunted by the spectral Other but might invite the other to share the agonistic space of civil society. Heterotopic singularities, then, are what representation can aim for: not setting off minority against minority, forgetting about the spectral presence of whiteness, but seeking to prevent the closure of the space in which social meaning emerges through negotiation of difference.

The question is, what more than entertaining fantasies can this cinema of interracial or interethnic contact offer—and particularly cinema representing South Asians—*even if* it does not rise to the level of a Third Cinema? As Paul Willemen observes, this kind of cinema "was selected as a central concept in 1986, partly to re-pose the question of the relations between the cultural and the political, partly to discuss whether there is indeed a kind of international cinematic tradition which exceeds the limits of both the national-industrial cinemas and those of Euro-American as well as English cultural theorists." It eschewed emotional manipulation, insisted on clarity, avoided prescribing an aesthetic, and condemned the smothering of thought while it disavowed professionalized intellectualism just as it was opposed to colonial and imperialist power.[22] Can it offer a better cognitive or diagnostic representation of the actual conditions faced by the parties involved in interethnic contact, and can it offer a springboard to imagine other ways of seeing that respect singularity—difference as well as shared hopes of a more democratic future? If in this essay I have sought to burden popular cinema featuring interracial contact with the question of whether it can transform social interaction particularly with regard to "race" relations, that is because, unlike the specialized discourses of the scholarly academy, or the sometimes too narrowly targeted screeds of progressive or "radical" groups, films have the potential to break through to a broad audience. For now, there is mostly potential.

NOTES

1. See, for example, Vera Hernán and Andrew Gordon, eds., *Screen Saviors: Hollywood Fictions of Whiteness* (Lanham, MD: Rowman and Littlefield, 2003).

2. Ed Guerrero, "The Black Image in Protective Custody: Hollywood's Biracial Buddy Films of the Eighties," in *Black American Cinema,* ed. Manthia Diawara (New York: Routledge, 1993), 240.

3. Ibid.

4. In an essay on Josephine Baker, I argue that sometimes the black as Other is what phantasmatically completes and confirms subjectivity even for the Euro-American subject. See Samir Dayal, "Blackness as Symptom: Josephine Baker and European Identity," in *Blackening Europe: The African American Presence,* ed. Heike Raphael-Hernandez (New York: Routledge, 2003).

5. Hernán and Gordon, *Screen Saviors,* 40.

6. Ibid., 13.

7. Joan Copjec, *Read My Desire: Lacan against the Historicists* (Cambridge: MIT Press, 1994), 208.

8. bell hooks, "Representing Whiteness in the Black Imagination," in *Displacing Whiteness: Essays in Social and Cultural Criticism,* ed. Ruth Frankenberg (Durham: Duke University Press, 1997), 165.

9. Laura U. Marks, "A Deleuzian Politics of Hybrid Cinema," *Screen* 35.3 (Autumn 1994): 245.

10. Giorgio Agamben, *The Coming Community* (Minneapolis: University of Minnesota Press, 1993), 2.

11. Kalpana Seshadri-Crooks, *Desiring Whiteness: A Lacanian Analysis of Race* (London: Routledge, 2000), 4.

12. David Roediger, *The Wages of Whiteness: Race and the Making of the American Working Class* (New York: Verso, 1991).

13. Jacques Derrida, *Specters of Marx: The State of the Debt, the Work of Mourning, and the New International* (New York: Routledge, 1994), 8.

14. Hernán and Gordon, *Screen Saviors,* 49.

15. See Dennis Sullivan and Fred Boehrer, "Spike Lee's *Do the Right Thing*: Filmmaking in the American Grain," *Contemporary Justice Review* 6.2 (June 2003): 148.

16. Anannya Bhattacharjee, "The Habit of Ex-Nomination: Nation, Woman and the Indian Immigrant Bourgeoisie," *Public Culture* 5.1 (Fall 1992): 19–44, available at http://www.hsph.harvard.edu/grhf/WoC/feminisms/bhattacharjee.html (retrieved 21 November 2004).

17. Ibid.

18. Ibid.

19. Seshadri-Crooks, *Desiring Whiteness,* 4.

20. See Marjorie Garber, *Vested Interests: Cross-dressing and Cultural Anxiety* (New York: Routledge, 1997).

21. Mayer Schiller and Dinesh D'Souza, "Racial Integration or Racial Separation? Two Views," American Enterprise Online, *Deep Politics* (January/February 1996), available at http://www.taemag.com/issues/articleid.16404/article_detail.asp (retrieved 28 June 2005).

22. Paul Willemen, *Looks and Frictions: Essays in Cultural Studies and Film Theory* (Bloomington: Indiana University Press, 1994), 177–180.

Part II

Confronting the Color Hierarchy

Chapter 6

"It Takes Some Time to Learn the Right Words"

The Vietnam War in African American Novels

Heike Raphael-Hernandez

When one thinks of African American involvement in the Vietnam War, the following, probably well-known facts come immediately to mind: African Americans were more than twice as vulnerable to draft-board calls as whites—in 1967, for example, 64 percent of eligible blacks were drafted in comparison with only 31 percent of eligible whites[1]—and blacks were many times more likely to serve in combat units, whereas many white troops were assigned to support duties in the rear. In many combat units, together with Puerto Ricans, Chicanos, and Latino Americans, African Americans constituted more than 50 percent of the group.[2] Of the sixteen thousand people who served on draft boards, blacks constituted less than 2 percent of the total and were not represented at all on draft boards in Alabama, Arkansas, Louisiana, and Mississippi. Therefore, since these minority units did much of the "dirty" work, the death rate percentage was much higher for them than for whites. For example, by 1965 alone African Americans accounted for 25 percent of American combat deaths.[3]

Because of these obvious forms of draft injustice and because of disproportionately high numbers of casualties and permanently disabled veterans, one would assume that the Vietnam War had caused some immediate reflection in the literature by African American authors. One would expect to meet fictitiously the fighting soldiers, the returning dead bodies, the physically disabled and emotionally destroyed veterans, the mothers and wives who contemplate their lost loved ones even many years after the war's end, the "disproportionate numbers of blacks among incarcerated veterans . . . among homeless veterans . . . among jobless veterans,"[4] and the next generation that had to grow up with either a dead or a dysfunctional father. But, to one's surprise, this is not the case at all. Regarding the Vietnam War in African American fiction, one can observe the strange fact that for the longest time, the war seemed not to have existed in the immense explosion of African American literature that has occurred since the 1970s. On the contrary, it is astonishing how silent the literary black community was about the Vietnam War during the war itself and during the decades afterward.

Likewise astonishing is the current growing interest and even a certain intellectual fascination with the war. Starting in the late 1990s, an increasing number of novels focus either on the historical battlefield itself or on the problems of the returned soldier, dead or alive, and his impact on his home society. In addition, we find an expanding body of academic studies dealing with the same issues. One might wonder from where such an interest after a long period of silence has sprung. In this essay, I first discuss possible reasons for that "phenomenon of the missing war" in African American novels, and I then look at those recent novels published since the late 1990s that include Vietnam, comparing their discussion of the legacy of the Vietnam War with similar discussions by their earlier writing peers. My thesis is connected to the complicated positioning of the Vietnam War in general—societal, in popular cultural, and in intellectual discourse—a positioning that tore apart a whole society already during the "hot" years and that still caused rifts as "war legacy" in the decades that followed. I claim that the seeming silence of the older African American writers generation is a logical one, and understandable when connected to the idea that African American writers have often served as intellectual vanguards of their communities, yet any intellectual positioning of the Vietnam War was much more complicated for African Americans than for any other group in the United States as they simultaneously faced the different racist connotations of the war on the one hand and the turmoil of the civil rights movement on the other hand. As I show with Alice Walker's novels, for example, it took writers time to suggest wisely any possible positioning of the war and its legacy for African America.

In 1989 Sandra Wittman compiled a bibliography of Vietnam War novels; from these nearly six hundred novels only six were by African American authors: three were published during the war itself—*Coming Home* by George Davis (1972), *Captain Blackman* by John A. Williams (1972), and *Runner Mack* by Barry Beckham (1972)—and three were part of the Vietnam Renaissance of the late 1980s and early 1990s that produced a substantial number of novels and movies about the Vietnam War by white authors but only three by black authors: *De Mojo Blues* by A. R. Flowers (1985), *Shaw's Nam* by John Carn (1986), and *Fallen Angels* by Walter Dean Myers (1988).[5] When looking at other genres, one does not discover a radically different number. In his 1997 article in *African American Review,* Jeff Loeb supplies a list that in addition to novels includes also poetry collections, interviews, oral history projects, and autobiographies. Loeb lists exactly nineteen books by African Americans.[6] Nineteen is indeed a small number, considering the amount of black people involved in the war. Several scholars have wondered about it, and one of the common explanations is that since a disproportionately large group of black soldiers had received poor education—historian Gerald Gill states that fewer than half had a high school degree,[7] and from the remaining half many did not have any basic college education—they were not the group that would deal with their experiences in books.

But while this answer might apply to the battlefield writing and to Vietnam veterans becoming writers themselves, it is not relevant in connection with the tremendous number of African American authors who have entered the market since the end of the war. What is really astounding is the fact that the war seems not to exist in the immense explosion of African American literature that has occurred since the 1970s. Considering that African American authors during this period dealt in their works with nearly everything that has been connected to contemporary and historical forms of racism and injustice done to the black community, it is strange that the Vietnam War was so rarely addressed. To write about Vietnam, it is not even necessary to have had any battlefield experience because, as it has often been stated, the war also influenced and changed communities at home. Bobby Ann Mason, a white Vietnam fiction author, for example, explains that she had had no prior connection to the war and did not know any veteran personally; simply by being an American, she says, it hit her one day that Vietnam was also part of her community, so "eventually I had to confront the subject."[8] Barry Beckham, one of the above-mentioned few African American authors who wrote a Vietnam novel and a nonveteran himself, supports Mason's point about the "forced" realization: in an interview, he admits that his novel *Runner Mack* is not supposed to be about Vietnam but about baseball; however, "Vietnam was in the background, the landscape, as I was writing from 1970–1971, so I think the military action was something I could not ignore."[9] His statement suggests that Vietnam and the large number of returning black soldiers, dead or alive, cannot have gone by unnoticed by the African American community.

Yet, one wonders where the war is in all these fictitious black communities that were created during the war and during the three following decades. Where are the physically disabled and emotionally destroyed veterans, the grieving mothers and wives, the fatherless children, the incarcerated, homeless, and jobless veterans? Two novels, Alice Walker's *Meridian* (1976) and Toni Cade Bambara's *The Salt Eaters* (1980), even make the 1960s their focus and deal with many aspects of this period in connection to the black community. But Vietnam is not part of their critical discussion. In *The Salt Eaters,* the political spectrum ranges from the civil rights fight to nuclear disarmament, pan-Africanism, ecological and environmental issues, and revolutions in Latin America. Vietnam, however, makes it into the book only on a T-shirt: seven women, the seven political sisters, take a bus to the Clayborne Festival, and the bus driver, a black man, tries to read their T-shirts while driving down the road. He has a hard time with one T-shirt that says GET THE U.S. OUT OF. He is unable to read the last word because the woman is not wearing a bra; although he goes through every possible word asked for in a crossword puzzle, he is not able to think of the last word to GET THE U.S. OUT OF.[10] One can hardly claim that as a serious discussion of the Vietnam War.

In *Meridian,* Vietnam is not critically reflected on, either, although the book carries this possibility: Alice Walker makes her protagonist even state at one time that the 1960s were a "decade marked by death. Violent and inevitable. Funerals became engraved on the brain."[11] Yet, *Meridian*'s long list of people who died during the 1960s includes names such as Medgar Evers, John F. Kennedy, Martin Luther King, Malcolm X, Che Guevara, Robert Kennedy, and Patrice Lamumba,[12] but there is no mention at all of the tremendous dying in Vietnam. Nevertheless, Vietnam is indeed mentioned in the book once: a young preacher who imitates Martin Luther King thunders commands at the different groups in his church. Among them is one Vietnam-related command: "He looked down at the young men in the audience and forbade them to participate in the Vietnam war."[13] However, Walker does not include and does not intend any critical discussion of this statement, for she makes the statement being followed by many other, non-Vietnam related ones; the preacher had one for every particular group:

He told the young women to stop looking for husbands and try to get something useful in their heads. He told the older congregants that they should be ashamed of the way they let their young children fight their battles for them. He told them they were cowardly and pathetic when they sent their small children alone into white neighborhoods to go to school. He abused the black teachers present who did not, he said, work hard enough to teach black youth.[14]

A few books by black writers seem logically connected to the Vietnam War, but their authors do not allow this connection to happen. Gloria Naylor's *Bailey's Cafe* (1992) presents such an example: Naylor depicts one of her protagonists, Miss Maple, a man who wears women's clothes, as a "female" man. To show his otherness, she creates him with many features and traits a "normal" man would not possess; among other things she makes him a Conscientious Objector (CO).[15] Considering that the novel was published in 1992 and Miss Maple is a man in his forties and Naylor's other protagonists in the same novel fit into her logical timeframe, the reader expects Miss Maple to be a CO against the Vietnam War. But Naylor makes him a World War II CO without any further explanation, thus avoiding any possible Vietnam War positioning.

Other novels do mention Vietnam, but in very minimalist ways. Paule Marshall's novel *Daughters,* published in 1991, serves as an example here. Marshall mentions Vietnam in one paragraph as rather a side remark as the paragraph's focus is on another aspect. She makes one of her characters be unable to spend the weekend with his girlfriend as his weekends are often committed to his sister and her three boys whom he supports financially and emotionally since the husband was killed "in the stupid war," which he himself was able to avoid by going to college.[16]

One simply has to ask why the reader encounters such seeming silence about Vietnam in African American fiction. Wallace Terry, an African American journalist who covered the war for *Time* magazine and who is the author of *Bloods,* was asked that question in an interview in 1991. He agreed that this silence is particularly disturbing since blacks were so disproportionately represented in Vietnam, but he, too, had no answer to this troubling question.[17]

One could perhaps argue that one of the reasons was connected to the fact that all the returning soldiers, whether black or nonblack, were facing a historically new dilemma; Maria Bonn notes that "never before had

Americans returned so quietly and so unwelcomed" after the end of a major war since their failure had violated America's sense of mission.[18] However, this phenomenon would be an excuse for the general public for not talking about the war and its resulting influence on American everyday society, yet writers often see their responsibility especially in confronting the public with the unspoken, the denied. American writers of all ethnic groups at all times have seen it as their responsibility to present the public with the myth of American innocence and American righteousness.

Alternatively, it has sometimes been suggested that most of the large group of newly emerged African American authors are women, and women traditionally do not write about war. Even Beckham suggested this answer in his interview; he claimed that "you have to look for a male to write about war. Women writers are just not that interested."[19] While this answer might apply to typical battlefield writing, it does not work with writings that cover society at home: women do indeed deal with the families that are left behind, with the reception of the war at home, with the possible problems and changes that a returning soldier or a dead soldier might bring to his family and his community, and with the problems that the war might cause for future generations long after its end.

So, here is my attempt to answer this question of strange silence: I think that the Vietnam War and the period during which it took place embodied extremely complicated aspects for the African American community that made it much harder for them than for any other group in American society to grapple with the war and later with its legacy. From the start, African America was deeply divided over the issue of protesting or supporting the war, which has to be seen in close linkage with the historically simultaneous civil rights movement. While many public African American figures vehemently protested not only the draft-connected and militarily institutionalized forms of racism but also the deadly irony of forcing soldiers to fight for democracy in another country and denying the same democratic rights to them at home, initially also many African Americans supported the war for various reasons. Many hoped that by actively participating in the war, they would finally win the respect and recognition long overdue to them at home. And even later, when many realized that Vietnam would not help them to gain that hoped-for respect and began to oppose the war, a large part of the black community was still not in favor of openly protesting the war. Many feared that openly criticizing the government would endanger any possible improvements promised to them for their civil rights status; others believed that African America needed all its protesting strength to concentrate on the civil rights struggle, which did not allow any leftover time or energy to deal with other forms of injustice that were not in direct relationship to their own.

To make this dilemma even worse, the war in Southeast Asia meant that, for the first time in history, African Americans participated in racism toward another people of color, thus not being the victim but becoming themselves the oppressor and the racist. And African American writers in their function as intellectual vanguards of their communities at first seemed to have missed not just the words but perhaps even the theoretical frame for placing all these dilemmas—the war itself, the conflict it caused for the American society at large, the linkage of the war to the civil rights movement, racism in all its different forms, the war as war against another people of color, the concept of individual responsibility and personal guilt, and the African American place in all of this—into a meaningful relationship that would make interpretative sense for African America. It seems logical and understandable that African American writers took their time to suggest wisely any possible positioning of the war and its legacy for African America.

To understand this claim, one has to look in detail at these diverse forms of African American protest and nonprotest. Many voices considered both the draft and combat injustices repugnant, and they pointed to the American government's hypocrisy of fighting for democracy (or at least claiming to do so) in a far-away country and of using for that deadly fight African American soldiers who were denied basic democratic rights in their own country. Public figures such as Malcolm X and Martin Luther King often spoke out against this special form of American hypocrisy.[20] King, for example, told his audience during one of his Massey lectures:

> We [are] taking the black young men who ha[ve] been crippled by our society and sending them eight thousand miles away to guarantee liberties in Southeast Asia which they ha[ve] not found in Southwest Georgia and East Harlem. And so we have been repeatedly faced with the cruel irony of watching Negro and white boys on TV screens as they kill and die together for a nation that has been unable to seat them together in the same schools. We watch them in brutal solidarity burning the huts of a poor village, but we realize that they would never live on the same block in Detroit.[21]

Not only famous African American intellectuals like King and Malcolm X saw the hypocrisy of the U.S. government in connection with Vietnam and the black community.[22] In David Loeb Weiss's documentary film *No Vietnamese Ever Called Me Nigger,* many so-called normal people voice their concern about that fact and show that they indeed recognize the connection; many express ideas similar to those of one black woman: "I think the war, I think it's very unfair. Why should the people, American boys, white and black, go to Vietnam to fight when a quarter of the American population can't even vote?"[23] And radical groups such as the Black Panthers and the Student Nonviolent Coordinating Committee (SNCC) spoke out vehemently against what they called the genocide of young black males by the U.S. government.[24] If Vietnam had only implied these different forms of racism experienced by the black community, I assume that postwar African American literature would have dealt more with Vietnam, and any positioning of the African American community would have been possible or at least easier.

Yet, the African American connection to Vietnam is not only determined by experienced injustice and racism and subsequent protest. With the Vietnam War, the position of the oppressed and the oppressor is not that easy to determine because, especially during the first half of the war, many black Americans supported the war in the same way white Americans did. African Americans used the same justification as white people for U.S. imperialism—namely, that the United States had a right to be in Vietnam because they had the duty or a special call to fight the spread of communism. A Gallup poll in early 1966 found that three out of four African Americans still supported the war and the draft.[25] Writer Ralph Ellison himself declared his full support by stating in an interview, "I don't see us withdrawing from the war. We have certain responsibilities to the Vietnamese and the structure of power in the world."[26] According to historian Gerald Gill, "in letters and in comments to journalists, many [African American soldiers] proudly defended their presence in and the American military commitment to South Vietnam."[27] For some African Americans even the high death rate offered some sense of pride; for example, Lieutenant Colonel George Shoffer, one of the highest-ranking blacks in the army in 1968, said, "I feel good about it. Not that I like the bloodshed, but the performance of the Negro in Vietnam tends to offset the fact that the Negro wasn't considered worthy of being a front-line soldier in other wars."[28] In the beginning years of the war, many black soldiers who fought in Vietnam were not draftees at all, but enlistees and career soldiers. Of course, the explanation for that fact is also connected to the racism that African Americans had to experience in American society because many black military personnel and civilians alike viewed the armed forces favorably as an opportunity for black people for social mobility and occupational advancement that was not possible for them in the more racially stratified civilian world.

But even with these occupational aspects in mind, many African American soldiers defended the war like many other white Americans with all the well-known arguments, such as "America has the duty to fight the spread of communism." This attitude, shared by many, is partly understandable because many African Americans felt that it was ill-timed and even disloyal or hypocritical to ask their government for full citizenry rights and simultaneously to criticize the same government for their politics. Concerning this loyalty to the American government and its politics and personal citizenry duty, the University of California conducted a survey of urban African Americans in 1967, and 90 percent indicated a willingness to fight for the United States.[29] Private First Class Reginald Edwards serves as an example for this ambivalent attitude; in an interview he confessed: "What we were hearing was that Vietnamese was killing Americans. I felt that if people were killing Americans, we should fight them. As a black person, there wasn't no problem fightin' the enemy. I knew Americans were prejudiced, were racist and all that, but, basically, I believed in America 'cause I was an American."[30]

From 1967 on, the period of the demands of increased manpower, things changed because many African Americans were draftees. This fact, coupled with the rising Black Power movement in the United States, led to more and more black troops who were opposed to the war and were openly protesting against it. Their protest had several reasons. On the one hand, along the same lines of the antiwar protest back in the United States, they started to doubt the legitimate rights of the U.S. military to be in Southeast Asia, calling it the white man's war—the white man who was hypocritical enough to talk about bringing democracy to an Asian country but was simultaneously using black soldiers for that task and denying them these same democratic rights in their own country. On the other hand, as a result of a rising black consciousness, black soldiers protested against the racism they had to experience in the military itself. That included, for example, protests against the underrepresentation in the officer's corps, against being passed over for promotions, and against being sent by racist commanding officers on patrols or missions that they perceived as overly dangerous or suicidal.

However, even these later years of the Vietnam War did not cause African Americans to stop considering the armed forces a career choice. Contrary to post-Vietnam assumptions of hostility toward the military in the black community,

> African American enlistment in the new "all-volunteer" army rose significantly. In the first postwar year, 1974, African Americans constituted around 16 percent . . . not much different from the prewar 1964 percentage. . . . As the services continued the conversion to an all-volunteer force, the number of African Americans in uniform quickly rose, peaking in 1979, when blacks made up nearly one third of the enlisted strength.[31]

Even during the heavy-draftee times of the second part of the war, African Americans continued to voluntarily enlist and former draftees reenlisted, as a government report showed in 1970.[32]

Closely connected was another form of collective nonprotest: silence. Many African Americans who were involved in the civil rights movement believed that their own fight needed all their undivided attention, so there would simply be no room for any antiwar protest. This aspect already points in the direction of "triangulating" the claim of African Americans participating in a racist war. Many interviewed soldiers in *Bloods* expressed their concern about their stay in Vietnam, not because of any antiwar notions but simply because they believed that as black people they should fight the civil rights war at home. Such an attitude led many blacks to protest Vietnam only in regard to the specific racism African Americans had to experience by the war. In *No Vietnamese Ever Called Me Nigger,* for example, not one voice talks about the racism and the oppression the Vietnamese had to experience, but many interviewees voice their concern about the racism the black community had to face.

Martin Luther King's experience is a good example of how many African Americans approached any black anti-Vietnam war protest. King reported that his antiwar protest was often questioned with "Peace and civil rights don't mix. Aren't you hurting the cause of your people?"[33] His protest was still accepted by his community when he was just protesting the obvious racism of the war toward African Americans. However, when he started to not connect his critique to black topics any more but simply straightforwardly criticized the government for its imperialistic ideas and for their genocide of an Asian people, he got into serious trouble with his peers. A speech like the following was not viewed favorably at all by many black people:

> When I see our country today intervening in what is basically a civil war, mutilating hundreds of thousands of Vietnamese children with napalm, burning villages and rice fields at random, painting the valleys of that small Asian country red with human blood, leaving broken bodies in countless ditches and sending home half-men, mutilated mentally and physically; when I see the unwillingness of our government to create the atmosphere for a negotiated settlement of this awful conflict by halting bombings in the North and agreeing to talk with the Vietcong—and all this in the name of pursuing the goal of peace—I tremble for our world. I do so not only from the dire recall of the nightmares of the wars of yesterday, but also from dreadful realization of possible nuclear destructiveness and tomorrow's even more [disastrous] prospects.[34]

Speeches like this caused the Southern Christian Leadership Conference (SCLC), for example, to vote that, if King were to speak out against the war in Vietnam, he had to do so as a private person but not as the president of SCLC.[35] In their defense, one has to recognize that they were in a tricky situation because President Lyndon Johnson told them in no uncertain terms that if anti-Vietnam War protests like King's and SNCC's under Stokely Carmichael continued, civil rights negotiations would cease.[36]

In addition to all these various aspects of protest, quite a few African American individuals and groups pointed openly to another complicated aspect of Vietnam: U.S. military intervention in Southeast Asia implied not only a fight in ideological terms—capitalism or so-called democracy against communism—but Southeast Asian U.S. involvement carried strong racist connotations. This already partly applied to the U.S. involvement in Japan in World War II as well, and several black intellectuals such as Langston Hughes clearly called the Pacific war a "race war." In Southeast Asia, whether it was Japan, Korea, or Vietnam, soldiers were taught to see the local population as racially inferior. The tragic novelty for Vietnam, however, was that this time black soldiers were "invited" to take a higher place in the colonial color hierarchy and to see Asian people as inferior people with different skin and facial features and different cultures— Buddhists and Animists who "farmed wet rice [and] plowed fields with oxen"[37]—and to develop ideas of racist superiority, ideas that had been reserved for "whites only" before. In her analysis of Vietnam buddy movies, Hazel Carby comments about that tragic novelty of Vietnam for the black community: "It is the history of the desegregation of the United States armed forces and the 'policing' of Southeast Asia that enables the relationship of equality between [men who] become buddies not in a movement for liberation but in a shared experience as oppressors."[38]

In his autobiography, Korean American writer Heinz Insu Fenkl observed that many soldiers, black and white, who were stationed in Korea during the Vietnam War period became "full of hate for Asian people and tense with the fear" of them.[39] And the military not only supported that attitude but also actively promoted it among its troops; soldiers were brainwashed to enable them to commit murder and atrocities without too much sense of guilt. One example of this general, indoctrinated sense of racist superiority can be seen with a Marine who in Fred Turner's study of the Vietnam War, *Echoes of Combat*, confesses that he and his buddies were "disgusted with the Vietnamese" and describes his impressions of the people:

> They dress differently and the women chew betel nut and have these ugly teeth. The kids deal dope all the time and all these things which to us make them look like animals—and they wear filthy clothes and they have all these habits we're not used to, like sleeping on dirt, picking up and spreading out manure with their hands, eating food we wouldn't be seen with, drinking terrible water, not brushing their teeth or washing. I realized the Vietnamese people were the enemy.[40]

Many African American soldiers interviewed by Wallace Terry supply examples of military racist indoctrination; Haywood Kirkland, for instance, reports:

> Right away they told us not to call them Vietnamese. Call everybody gooks, dinks. Then they told us that when you go over in Vietnam, you gonna be face to face with Charlie, the Viet Cong. They were like animals, or something other than human. They ain't have no regard for life. They'd blow up little babies just to kill one GI. They wouldn't allow you to talk about them as if they were people. They told us they're not to be treated with any type of mercy or apprehension. That's what they engraved into you. That killer instinct. Just go away and do destruction. Even the chaplains would turn the

thing around in the Ten Commandments. They'd say, "Thou shall not murder," instead of "Thou shall not kill." Basically, you had a right to kill.[41]

Of course, that does not imply that every black soldier turned into a racist, but in many personal reports African American veterans confess that they had been so brainwashed by the military that they too were buying into the lies of racial superiority.

Black troops must have been aware of the racialized aspect of the war because the North Vietnamese and the Viet Cong themselves made sure that black soldiers knew about it. For example, they sometimes dropped leaflets among U.S. troops with statements like the following: "Black soldiers of America. . . . Our battle is not against the exploited, captive Black Soldiers of America, but against the white imperialist government that threatens the peace of Asia. Lay down your arms. No harm will come to you. We welcome you as Brothers seeking freedom."[42] And Radio Hanoi played messages like "Soul brothers, go home. Whitey raping your mothers and your daughters, burning down your homes. What are you over here for? This is not your war. The war is a trick of the Capitalist empire to get rid of the blacks."[43] And there were stories among the soldiers that the Viet Cong would shoot less at black than at white troops. Whether these stories were true or not does not matter here, as they serve for the awareness of the white/brown/black color hierarchy perspective among the U.S. soldiers.

Protest back at the home front was definitely aware of this racialized aspect—of being second-class citizen at home because of their color and being first-class citizens in Vietnam, fighting against another people of color. Individual protests in this regard such as Muhammad Ali's became famous, but also several African American organizations were very outspoken about this aspect. The Black Panther Party, for example, forbade its members to fight in the "colonial wars of aggression."[44] One branch of the Mississippi Freedom Democratic Party declared, "No one has a right to ask us to risk our lives and kill other colored people in Santo Domingo and Vietnam, so that the white American can get richer."[45] SNCC leaders spoke up repeatedly against a war that embodied the "American pattern of racism," and the Congress of Racial Equality (CORE) resolution in 1965 criticized the Johnson administration for its "immoral policy of racism abroad."[46]

So, how should African American authors then address the role of African America concerning the war and the protest and nonprotest? Protest the racism they themselves had to experience and quietly ignore any possible support or involvement? Or first admit the guilt of support and involvement and then protest the racism African Americans had to endure? Or even address the complicated issues of participating in racist superiority? In his novel, John A. Williams, one of the above-mentioned three authors, did just that already in 1972—describing African American soldiers in Vietnam that tasted racial superiority; he has his Captain Blackman meditating about that new black soldier:

> They'd killed people—old men, women and children—who *might've* been Viet Cong. In other words, killed them because they had the same skin color that was what it amounted to. . . . Who's Gonna Care What Happen to These Dinks Out Here? White soldiers you could understand talking like that, but black soldiers? . . . Black men became like white men; they too raped, murdered and castrated: murdered in the heat of hysteria. Once, wherever the American Army had been, from Guam to Germany, its black soldiers had been its kindest; the stories of those kindnesses were legion. But today. A sickness of laughing and giggling hit everyone. The whites were relieved that blacks at last had joined them, had lost, finally that essential human quality for which they were well known. And his black soldiers had been giggling and murdering because they'd come to know what it felt like to kill without fear of punishment, in broad daylight, challenging the universe to break out of positions in the heavens; had come to know, like whites who'd done most of it in history, just how mothafucking easy it was to kill a colored sonofabitch.[47]

To portray one's own people in such a harsh way might not have felt correct to many other authors. Therefore, it might indeed have been the case that out of certain helplessness, they rather avoided any positioning of the war for the African American community. Only recently, in the late 1990s, African American authors began to address the complex alliance of forced participation in racism and of defining for oneself the borders for individual responsibility. It seems that perhaps Elie Wiesel's words in connection to the Holocaust, "when an event is unspeakable, it takes some time to learn the right words"[48] applies also to this specific silence. Toni Morrison and Alice Walker both initiated this new discourse in their novels published in 1998. They both succeed in using literature for something that Michael Rogin has observed as a typical characteristic of Vietnam literature of the 1990s in general; he sees the move away from the silent, the violent, the psychotic veteran to "the healing returned soldiers and thera-peutic communities," to healing communities.[49] Yet, Morrison, Walker, and the young authors of the twenty-first century all go further: they do not simply allow the returned soldier and the community to heal but ask both to realize the close connection between forced duty and personal re-sponsibility.

Walker especially seems to prove the point that authors needed this time as she had tried to deal with the Vietnam War before in her above-discussed novel, *Meridian.* Her second attempt, *By the Light of My Father's Smile,* displays the maturity of time and distance. This time, one meets a Vietnam veteran, Manuelito, who gets the chance to heal from his spiritual wounds. In a somewhat "Alice-Walker-new-age" fashion, Walker has him die first in desperation about his guilt, only to give him a chance to come back as an angel with unfinished business in Vietnam. In his specific case, his soul can only find peace when he confesses his personal guilt and re-sponsibility to a little Vietnamese girl whose parents he had killed during the war. When another angel tries to ease Manuelito's pain by telling him that in a war setting, a soldier cannot be blamed for crimes committed, Manuelito answers him, "It does not seem to work that way, Señor. It seems we are responsible for everything we do, no matter how the chain of events began."[50]

In *Paradise,* Morrison portrays one of the mothers, Soane, having a hard time dealing with her everyday life and her mental stability even many years after her two sons' deaths in Vietnam. For the longest time, Soane's only answers to cope with the deaths have been bitterness and confusion. Yet, Morrison allows Soane to start a healing process when Soane finally begins to meditate on the complex relationship between rac-ism and personal guilt. Contemplating the death of her two sons, Scout and Easter, Soane realizes how much she, too, was guilty of their deaths by being so naive about Vietnam. Her sons' intention had not been to vol-unteer for Vietnam but to go up north to the big cities and join some rad-ical civil rights movement groups there. Since she had not questioned at all the imperialistic goals of the U.S. government in Vietnam, she had talked them out of their own plans into her Vietnam volunteering plans, thus unintentionally, but still actively, supporting U.S. imperialism: "How proud and happy she was when they enlisted; she had actively encouraged them to do so. Their father had served in the forties. Uncles too."[51] In her naïveté, Sloane indeed had believed that young black men would be safer in Vietnam than in any other American city, "safer in the army than in

Chicago where Easter wanted to go. Safer than Birmingham, than Montgomery, Selma, than Watts. Safer than Money, Mississippi in 1955 and Jackson, Mississippi in 1963. . . . [In Vietnam] her sweet colored boys [would be] unshot, unlynched, unmolested, unimprisoned."[52] But Morrison makes Soane also realize that her naïveté was actually caused by the lifelong personal experience of American racism; because of American racist reality, Soane was indeed right to assume that her black teenage boys would be in true danger in any American place. Soane learns to see and understand the complex connection between racism and personal guilt. By finally admitting personal responsibility and accepting her failure and at the same time recognizing the parts where she has a right to blame America for its racism, Soane is able to find the distance necessary to heal spiritually.

Like Walker, Devorah Major in *Brown Glass Windows* (2002) depicts a Vietnam vet, Ranger, in all his agonizing pain about personal guilt; for example, she has him conversing with his wife:

> "I'm going to have to pay. You can't kill somebody's baby and not pay the price."
> "Ranger, it was a war, for God's sake!"
> "Yeah, I saw it that way at the time, but I am not so sure now."[53]

After repeatedly failing to battle his drug addiction, he allows himself intentionally to be killed in a drive-by shooting. His teenage son, Sketch, cannot cope with his own life as he has been hoping for a father who would indeed do what he always promised—to pick up the pieces of his spiritually broken life and start all over again. After his father's death, Sketch travels to Washington to write on the Vietnam Monument "1989-Ranger E."[54] Yet, it is another Vietnam vet, his stepfather, who finally helps him understand the next generation's responsibility in dealing correctly with the legacy of the war when he forces Sketch to look into a mirror: "You are your father's fucking Vietnam monument. . . . Stand up straight with your poop-butt self. . . . You are the one that keeps it going, not some damn piece of marble."[55]

The unfinished and problematic legacy of the war for the next generation is also the focus of Asha Bandele's *Daughter* (2003) and Marcia King-Gamble's *Jade* (2002). Bandele's Vietnam vet, Bird, often had agonized about the connection between his personal guilt and the government's politics, asking "how this country could send me halfway around the world to kill people who are half my size. People I ain't got no struggle with. People who didn't enslave my ancestors yesterday or patrol or endanger my community today."[56] She allows her character to find that much needed spiritual rest, yet to have him only shortly thereafter getting killed "accidently" by a police officer. Bandele uses an interesting symbolic twist in her legacy plot for her next generation, as Bird's daughter, Aya, has suffered throughout her childhood and early youth from growing up without a father. When she finally is able to pick up her emotional pieces and starts to rearrange her life, she also becomes the fatal victim of white law enforcement "mistakes."

Marcia King-Gamble's Jade is an adopted Amerasian "burnt rice" child in search of her birth mother and father in Vietnam. On her way over to Vietnam, she meets Cameron, who is also searching for some information about his father, missing in action (MIA). Both adults, Jade and Cameron, are very successful professionals in their respective careers, and an outsider would not guess that anything is wrong with their emotional lives. Yet, as King-Gamble depicts them, dealing with missing parts for their war-determined identities is a negative legacy that both are not able to cope with. From the few fragments of information they have about their missing parents, they both initially make the mistake of blaming their parents entirely for any wartime-related action or decision. Jade, for example, freaks out when she learns that her biological mother was a bar girl, meaning prostitute, for GIs—something that for Jade is under no circumstances morally excusable at all with any notion of poverty and war and desperation. After their spiritual quest, however, both learn that the next generation holds responsibilities in their hands even many decades after the war's end—to understand the complex nexus of personal responsibility and government-enforced action that does not give the next generation any right for righteously judging or even condemning the involved ones.

Grace F. Edwards's *The Viaduct* (2004) tells the story of Chance and Marvin, two Vietnam vets in New York. When Marvin's newborn baby daughter is being kidnapped, he can only think that since he had killed children in Vietnam, fate finally punishes him for committing murder. Yet, like the other authors, Edwards throughout the course of the novel allows him to grow in his understanding of personal guilt, and he is finally able to put his agony into the correct perspective.[57]

In his *Bombingham* (2001), Anthony Grooms offers the perhaps most radical confrontation of personal responsibility with blindly following official duty. His protagonist, Walter, grew up in rural Alabama and participated in workshops and civil right marches in Birmingham with Martin Luther King before being drafted. In Vietnam, he considers himself quite a responsible "race man"; yet, his consciousness only connects to the binary black/white position. One event, however, changes his concept and catapults him into many years of spiritual searching for answers. When he shoots an old Vietnamese man for no apparent reason other than that he was Vietnamese, Walter is being haunted by the image that he turned into the same white firefighter who sprayed water at the marchers in Birmingham. Over the years, he contemplates again and again:

> I was cool, when I shot that papa-san. But I was loose. I saw him long before Haywood pointed him out. He was wearing the black pajamas, and he was running away, so I said to myself, I can shoot him, if I want. It would be all right. I couldn't see him, but my heart told me he was an old man. My heart said, so what if he was a VC? He was just an old man. A man tending his crops. A man just strolling along, minding his business, thinking about the blueness of the sky and the warm way the sun lay on the rice. That was when I decided to shoot him. Who was he to enjoy the sun. . . . I wasn't raised this way, and I have been in the civil rights workshops with Reverend King. I know better. What a murderer I have become. I don't feel like a murderer, though I don't feel like anything, but scared. And I think I know how those firemen in Birmingham felt, and I think I know how Mr. William who shot my grandfather felt . . . but no. I don't know because they had never been to a civil rights workshop. They had never heard Reverend King. I have a dream . . .[58]

Walter's spiritual renewal begins when he accepts this "triangulated" black/brown/white position; and, like the other protagonists, he learns to understand the complex nexus of personal responsibility and government-enforced action.

In 1992, Wallace Terry claimed that the African American novel about the Vietnam War and its legacy was still waiting to be written.[59] The novels since the late 1990s present the answer to this void.

NOTES

A shorter version of this essay with a different focus is also part of the collection *The Sixties Revisited: Culture, Society, Politics,* ed. Jürgen Heideking, Jörg Helbig, and Anke Ortlepp (Heidelberg: C. Winter Universitätsverlag, 2001), 287–302.

1. Herbert Shapiro, "The Vietnam War and the American Civil Rights Movement," *Journal of Ethnic Studies* 16.4 (Winter 1989): 136.

2. Gerald Gill, "Black Soldiers' Perspectives on the War," in *The Vietnam Reader,* ed. Walter Capps (New York: Routledge, 1991), 173.

3. Ibid. For further facts, see also James E. Westheider, *Fighting on Two Fronts: African Americans and the Vietnam War* (New York: New York University Press, 1997), chapter 1.

4. Wallace Terry, "It Became an Absolute Crusade," in *Vietnam, We've All Been There: Interviews with American Writers,* ed. Eric James Schroeder (Westport, CT: Praeger, 1992), 69.

5. Sandra Wittman, *Writing about Vietnam: A Bibliography of the Literature of the Vietnam Conflict* (Boston: G. K Hall, 1989).

6. Jeff Loeb, "MIA: African American Autobiography of the Vietnam War," *African American Review* 31.1 (Spring 1997): 105–124.

7. Gill, "Black Soldiers' Perspectives," 173.

8. Bobby Ann Mason, "Eventually I Had to Confront the Subject," in *Vietnam, We've All Been There: Interviews with American Writers,* ed. Eric James Schroeder (Westport, CT: Praeger, 1992), 165.

9. Barry Beckham, Personal interview via e-mail (6 July 1999).

10. Toni Cade Bambara, *The Salt Eaters* (New York: Random House, 1980), 65.

11. Alice Walker, *Meridian* (New York: Pocket Books, 1976), 33.

12. Ibid.

13. Ibid., 195.

14. Ibid., 195–196.

15. Gloria Naylor, *Bailey's Café* (Thorndike: G. K. Hall, 1992).

16. Paule Marshall, *Daughters* (New York: Atheneum, 1991), 92.

17. Terry, "It Became an Absolute Crusade," 62.

18. Maria S. Bonn, "A Different World: The Vietnam Veteran Novel Comes Home," in *Fourteen Landing Zones: Approaches to Vietnam War Literature,* ed. Philip K. Jason (Iowa City: University of Iowa Press, 1991), 2.

19. Beckham, Personal interview.

20. For Malcolm X's examples of public protest, see Westheider, *Fighting on Two Fronts,* 18–19.

21. James Washington, ed., *A Testament of Hope: The Essential Writings and Speeches of Martin Luther King, Jr.* (San Francisco: HarperCollins, 1986), 635.

22. For an excellent compilation of prominent African Americans' public protest, see the following two essays: J. Craig Jenkins, David Jacobs, and Jon Agnone, "Political Opportunities and African-American Protest, 1948–1997," *American Journal of Sociology* 109.2 (September 2003): 277–303; Shapiro, "Vietnam War," 117–141.

23. Beate Karch, *"No Vietnamese Ever Called Me Nigger" (1968): Eine Analyse* (Trier: Wissenschaftlicher Verlag Trier, 1994), 57.

24. For SNCC and Black Panther documents, see Westheider, *Fighting on Two Fronts*, 180, notes 10 and 11.

25. Ibid., 19.

26. Richard Kostelanetz, *Master Minds: Portraits of Contemporary American Artists and Intellectuals* (Toronto: Macmillan, 1969), 55.

27. Gill, "Black Soldiers' Perspectives," 174.

28. Westheider, *Fighting on Two Fronts*, 12.

29. Ibid., 34.

30. Wallace Terry, *Bloods: An Oral History of the Vietnam War by Black Veterans* (New York: Ballantine Books, 1984), 6.

31. Westheider, *Fighting on Two Fronts*, 170.

32. Thomas Gates, *Report of the President's Commission on an All-Volunteer Armed Force* (Washington, D.C.: U.S. Government Printing Office, 1970), 16.

33. Washington, *Testament of Hope*, 634.

34. Ibid., 627.

35. David Lewis, *King: A Biography* (Urbana: University of Illinois Press, 1978), 296.

36. Ibid., 311.

37. Heinz Insu Fenkl, *Memories of My Ghost Brother* (New York: Plume, 1997), 132.

38. Hazel V. Carby, *Race Men* (Cambridge, MA: Harvard University Press, 1998), 183.

39. Fenkl, *Memories of My Ghost Brother*, 131.

40. Fred Turner, *Echoes of Combat: The Vietnam War in American Memory* (New York: Anchor Books, 1996), 23.

41. Terry, *Bloods*, 90.

42. Ibid., 306.

43. Ibid., 39.

44. Westheider, *Fighting on Two Fronts*, 33.

45. Shapiro, "Vietnam War," 119.

46. Ibid., 120, 121. Shapiro's essay in general offers a thorough overview of protest by different African American organizations.

47. John A. Williams, *Captain Blackman* (New York: Thunder's Mouth Press, 1972), 315.

48. Walter Capps, ed., *The Vietnam Reader* (New York: Routledge, 1991), 1.

49. Michael Rogin, "Healing the Vietnam Wound," *American Quarterly* 53.1 (September 1999): 702.

50. Alice Walker, *By the Light of My Father's Smile* (New York: Random House, 1998), 205.

51. Toni Morrison, *Paradise* (New York: Alfred A. Knopf, 1998), 100.

52. Ibid., 101.

53. Devorah Major, *Brown Glass Windows* (Willimantic, CT: Curbstone Press, 2001), 111.

54. Ibid., 174.

55. Ibid., 177.

56. Asha Bandele, *Daughter* (New York: Scribner, 2003), 90.

57. Grace F. Edwards, *The Viaduct* (New York: Random House, 2004).

58. Anthony Grooms, *Bombingham* (New York: One World Ballantine Books, 2004), 299–300.

59. Terry, "It Became an Absolute Crusade," 69.

Chapter 7

Chutney, Métissage, and Other Mixed Metaphors
Reading Indo Caribbean Art in Afro Caribbean Contexts

Gita Rajan

In this essay, I explore the staging of identity by select Caribbean artists of Indian descent as they simultaneously assimilate and resist the influences of Afro Caribbean politics and cultures within their contemporary national contexts.[1] By using the work of situated artists like Bernadette Indira Persaud and Shastri Maharaj, who are from Guyana and Trinidad, and comparing them to doubly diasporic artists like Lucilda Dassardo Cooper and Andrew Cheddie Sookrah, who are from the United States and Canada, I reveal complicated and hybridized representations of identities. My rationale for selecting Indo Caribbean artists from the United States and Canada is simultaneously a matter of gesturing toward one strand of the recent theoretical work emerging from Atlantic studies, which reinscribes the ocean as a spatial continuum as a metaphoric Caribbeanization and acknowledges the migration of an educated class of Caribbeans who have come to the new world of their own volition.

At the risk of simplifying history, it is accurate to say that the presence of Indians in the Caribbean is the result of British colonial impulses to control the African slave revolt of the nineteenth century and maintain optimum labor levels in the sugarcane fields. Consequently, Indians, mostly from the Bihar region, were brought to Jamaica, Trinidad, and Guyana as indentured workers.[2] After almost two centuries of living together in relationality and as a consequence of various multiracial contacts with already hybridized African, Creole, Amerindians, and European peoples, Indo Caribbeans embody the metaphor of *chutney* in their lived realities. In the section below, I explain more fully what *chutney* has come to signify in Indo Caribbean identity politics in the public sphere. I also explain the rationale for using *métissage* as a theoretical term to see how this identity functions in recognizably Afro Caribbean contexts. Then, I interpret select artworks of the four artists to show how the metaphor of *chutney* combined with the concept of *métissage* reveals wonderful instances of Afro-Indo encounters in the Caribbean.

In order to appreciate the creation and reception of Caribbean art made by those of Indian origin, it may be useful to understand the cultural history of Afro Caribbean art and its reception in a global art world. A reason for this brief digression is to show how firmly our perceptions of Caribbean art are entrenched solely in its Afro Caribbean systems of signification. From the perspective of art and art history, strategies of Black resistance efforts provided fertile ground for what has come to be known, over the last century, as Caribbean art. Afro Caribbean art and artists have been anchored in a transcontinental space of a racial and sociocultural continuum of Black resistance originating in the United States, Europe, and Mexico. This framing of an aesthetic of Caribbean art includes representations of anti-imperialist struggles, aspects of the negritude movement, and the coalition-building efforts of African American literary and cultural theorists with African diasporas; it even incorporates modernist modalities that are rooted in nodes of cultural nationalism. This presented a caveat, though; modernism in the hands of Caribbean artists of the early twentieth century was not a mimetic exercise based on European techniques and styles but was an innovative revisioning of resistance to European political and cultural hegemony. As an aside, it is ironic that Africa was made to stand as a monolithic entity in order to facilitate the reading of sociocultural symbols as translatable representations of numerous and distinct nations, peoples, and cultures from the continent.

When modernism was all the rage in major metropolises like Paris and New York, for example, both in the literary and art worlds (and in art markets), Cuban, Puerto Rican, and Haitian artists were credited with combining modernist styles with vocabularies of local nationalisms. One of the earliest standards of measuring the value of Afro Caribbean art was the idea of authenticity as linked to a proximity to the primitive, or what David Boxer, a cultural historian from Jamaica called the "intuitive." This idea of intuitive became firmly entrenched in both creating and receiving Afro Caribbean art, which suggests at once its distance from traditional Western art and a specific reliance on mythical and originary African cultural symbols and religions. While such measures of artistic value may sound pejorative today because of their reliance on stereotypes of racial-ized differences constructed on an ideology of Western supremacy, they have, nonetheless, helped promote Afro Caribbean art and artists over the last century.

But the overall aesthetic undergirding Afro Caribbean art is larger than the sum of its parts. Veerle Poupeye notes in *Caribbean Art*:

> Although anti-colonial nationalism was brewing among the peasantry and working class, it was essentially articulated and spearheaded by the emerg-ing Caribbean intelligentsia. Many of these intellectuals studied in London, Paris, Madrid, or New York. . . . Martiniquan writer and politician Aimé Césaire . . . met the future Senegalese president Léopold Senghor there in the late thirties, an encounter that led to the development of the negritude movement, one of the most influential expressions of black cultural nation-alism.[3]

Afro Caribbean art thus effectively fused high culture with pop cultural morés and brought together transcontinental and cosmopolitan tastes with an indigeneity presumed to be inherent in island cultures and exem-plified by its peoples. This was a signal feature in promoting Afro Carib-bean art within the world of museum aesthetics and Western art markets.[4] In contrast, Asian influences in Caribbean art remained, consciously or unconsciously, on the sidelines.

This is indeed a strange omission because art critics have credited Car-ibbean artists with the ability and propensity to borrow from other sign systems such as Amerindian cultural codes and Mexican muralism, for example. As a case in point, Poupeye is correct in stating that Afro Carib-bean art produced at this moment also exhibited "significant" traces of transcontinental elements because of a "relationship between cultural na-tionalism and the developments in African American culture." She states:

> The migration of West Indians to North American cities contributed to this alliance and provided new channels for intellectual and cultural exchanges. Claude McKay, key literary exponent of the Harlem Renaissance, was a Jamaican, as was Marcus Garvey, the founder of the internationally active United Negro Improvement Association (UNIA). . . . Several important Harlem Renaissance figures traveled to the Caribbean, including the writer and anthropologist Zora Neale Hurston who studied Afro-Caribbean ritual practices in Jamaica and Haiti as a Guggenheim fellow in the late thirties.[5]

In other words, the range and depth of influences shaping Afro Caribbean art of the early twentieth century were indeed disparate. And these combined forces resulted in complicated borrowings from metropole aesthetic conventions, indigenous art and myths, and popular Caribbean culture and religions. This, in effect, resulted in theatrically hybridized representational forms that juxtaposed local, modernist styles against Vaudou and Santería symbols and practices.[6]

In contrast, Sino and Indo Caribbean artists are less well known, and their art is less readily circulated. One of Poupeye's critical insights is useful even though she glosses over art created by peoples of Asian origin (she mentions Bernadette Persaud and provides brief analyses of Wendy Nanan and Isaiah James Boodhoo's work) in her encyclopedic review of Caribbean art, to write:

> Until recently, the Afro-Caribbean components in Caribbean popular culture have received most academic attention. . . . The contributions of other ethnic groups are nonetheless also significant and are now beginning to attract attention. The East Indians of Trinidad and the Guyanas have started claiming their space in national culture and this is reflected in contemporary visual art. The Trinidadian artist Wendy Nanan . . . used popular religion as an ironic token of hope in the . . . very troubled "marriage" of multiracial, multi-cultural Trinidad in her relief construction, "Idyllic Marriage" (1989). It represents La Divina Pastora in a wedding scene with Lord Krishna. La Divina, as she is popularly known, is a wooden statue of a Black Virgin Mary in the town of Siparia in southern Trinidad that is venerated by Hindus and Roman Catholics alike for its purported miraculous powers. As a sacred sculpture of uncertain, probably Hispanic or Amerindian origin, La Divina embodies the syncretism of Creole Caribbean culture. Although the "bride" seems reluctant, her "marriage" to Lord Krishna challenges the perception that the East Indian population of the Caribbean has retained its own culture and does not participate in the creolization process.[7]

Such intrinsic confluences of African, Indian, Hispanic, Amerindian, and Creole cultures with Hindu and Catholic symbols is a distinctive feature of Caribbean life, yet, they remain relatively unexplored in reading Indo (creolized) Caribbean art. Even though people of Indian origin make up a sizeable part of Trinidad, Tobago, and Guyana populations, few writers other than V. S. Naipaul have theorized their historic situatedness, and he is a problematic figure to invoke here.[8] There have been no concerted

local or diasproic efforts made by peoples of Asian origins (Indian specifically) to nurture Indo Caribbean artistic creativity. This oversight is
gradually undergoing a corrective, in literature at least, as now one finds
tangential references to Indo and Sino Caribbean and Creolized Indians
in Patricia Powell's *Pagoda,* Maryse Condé's *Crossing the Mangrove,* and
Shani Mootoo's *Cereus Bloom at Night.*

One can speculate that the reasons for Afro Caribbean art shooting into
prominence lie both in external and internal conditions. External factors
can be partly attributed to the greater emphasis placed on the use of African religious symbolism by local artists as their signature syntax, which
was read as uniquely Caribbean by the developed West and by transnational critics. Another external factor was the active manner in which
major Black intellectuals mapped a cohesive African diaspora and thus
brought Afro Caribbean art into global consciousness and markets. The
internal reasons are contradictory and more damaging. A certain part of
the problem is the deliberate marginalization of Indo Caribbean arts by
local (national) institutions because of class hostilities that are manifested
in racial tensions (Indians are perceived to be thriving merchants and thus
privileged and distanced from Afro Caribbean realities). This omission is
noted most vocally by Guyanese artist, activist, and educator Bernadette
Persaud, whose work I explicate below. But a vital factor in the occlusion
of Indo Caribbean artists from the eyes of the world is because Indians in
India and members of the Indian diaspora in general have had a history of
barely acknowledging the presence of these indentured workers—a problem that is evident even today. Vinay Lal notes how clearly class status
marks the ways in which Caribbeans of Indian descent are perceived and
writes with biting irony:

> One hundred and fifty years ago, a ship carrying 217 Indians set anchor on
> May 30 in Port of Spain, thereby inaugurating a new chapter in the history
> of Trinidad, the Caribbean, and indeed the Indian diaspora [now celebrated
> as Indian Arrival Day].
>
> So unusual a holiday . . . should have received prominent attention in
> Indian newspapers and the media. Had such a holiday been proclaimed in
> the United States, the event would have been celebrated in India as an ac-
> knowledgment, however belated, of the achievements of Indians, and of the
> "arrival" of India upon a world stage as a not inconsiderable economic and
> military power. But, Trinidad, and indeed a greater part of the non-Western
> world, is of little interest to middle-class Indians, and few people in India

are aware that Indians have been settled in Trinidad, Guyana, Surinam, Mauritius, Fiji, Malaysia, and a host of other countries for a much longer period than they have been in the West. There is a worldwide community of Indians, but the world-view of middle-class Indians extends no further than the culture of middle-class America.[9]

What Persaud reads as nationalist (racist) politics and Lal as class prejudice, I would argue, is also a prototypical caste bias that is inherent in social interactions among Indians—both in India and in its diaspora.

Indo Caribbeans thus present a difficult analytical problem because of their layered history and entry into the nation as indentured laborers and their contradictory impulses of racial insularity on the one hand and the reality of interracial marriages with indigenous, Spanish, African, and French peoples (or *douglarization,* a contested marker of racial mixing) on the other. Race was the point of simultaneous desire for contact and of the fear of contagion. Further, culture—both high and popular—became the problematic contact zone wherein such conflicting realities played out. This makes reading Indo Caribbean art (and life) a challenging critical problem. Many of these factors are inextricably bound together in the multicultural, multilinguistic lifestyles today, which, in turn, are manifested in Indo Caribbean artworks in the situated and diasproic artists discussed here. Because of a totally different sociocultural system (albeit hybridized now), theoretical parameters of creolization do not fit our inquiry very well, hence finding vocabularies to analyze Indo Caribbean art becomes a difficult adventure. As a result, Indo Caribbean art has yet to gain acceptance in the public sphere as legitimate cultural representation and read in its own right.

It is here that the word *chutney* proves useful. *Chutney* is a self-anointed term—a Hindi word—it is an integral feature of Indian cuisine. It is a spicy mixture of condiments, fresh herbs, raw vegetables, and unripe fruits; the recipe has hundreds of variations and permutations because each version of a *chutney* changes in content based on the vegetation of the region. While *métissage* signals Afro Caribbean adaptations through language, customs, and culture working primarily from French linguistic conventions, *chutney* in the Indo Caribbean context suggests a similar kind of hybridized, uneasy syncretistic fusion of words, secular and sacred symbols, and folk and popular cultural mythologies gleaned from memories of home and adapted to Caribbean contexts. By the late 1960s, East Indian pop music, dubbed as *"chutney,"* was the most exciting new sound broadcast by a local radio program by the Mohamed brothers called "*Mastaana Bahar*," where Indian film music was combined with folk songs from the Bihar, reggae music, and set to disco dance beats. Connell and Gibson in *Soundtracks* note that this form soon became the most spectacular celebration of East India in the West Indies. By the early 1990s a newer version was created that fused Bollywood music with island sounds and frenetic dance beats and rhythms from soul and calypso music to produce a pulsating musical form called *chutney soca*. This became extremely popular all over the Caribbean and a much anticipated feature of the Trinidadian Carnival celebrations.[10] *Pure Chutney* (1998) is a tongue-in-cheek film made by Sanjeev Chatterjee and narrated by Amitava Kumar that dramatizes the history and lifestyles of Indo Caribbeans who merge social and religious rituals as the remembered legacy of their indentured ancestors from India with Afro Caribbean words and rhythms to create a Caribbean reality. *Chutney in yuh Soca*[11] is still another documentary film that explains the immense popularity of a performative cultural form that combines *Bhojpuri* lyrics (from the Bihar region) with calypso sounds and Bollywood dance styles as a uniquely Indo Caribbean part of the national parade in the pre-Lenten Carnival. Thus, *chutney* captures the complicated, fused sign systems deployed by Indo Caribbeans and is useful now in explaining some of the hybridized iconography and representations of identity in Indo Caribbean art.

Edouard Glissant, speaking of African influences on creolized subjects, says in *Poetics of Relation* that "what took place in the Caribbean, which could be summed up in the word *creolization,* approximates the idea of Relation. . . . It is not merely an encounter, a shock . . . a *métissage*, but a new and original dimension allowing each person to be there and elsewhere, rooted and open, lost in the mountains and free beneath the sea, in harmony and in errantry."[12] Even though Glissant places a higher value on the phenomenon of creolization because he sees it as continuously incorporating other life and cultural signs, the practice of *métissage* which constantly proliferates meaning illustrates better how Afro and Indo Caribbean artists deploy visual syntax in their works. His theory of *métissage* as encoding "a poetics of Relations" serves as an apt metaphor to describe the Caribbean question because of the relational proximity that exists between the different islands and among the various peoples who inhabit this region. Thus, *métissage* not only combines randomly the various lived experiences but also defies notions of racial or cultural purity and singular origin, which then can be productively extended to illuminate the ways in which Indo Caribbean art and artists negotiate the self-other divide in Afro Caribbean contexts.

In *Edouard Glissant and Postcolonial Theory*, Celia Britton notes that his "insistence on the ambiguous and constrained nature of the struggle to build a new mode of expression is theoretically illuminating," which helps us understand "a 'new language' outside the dominant one, a strategic relationship of resistance and subversion to the dominant language."[13] Recalling from the section above on Afro Caribbean art, we note that Glissant's notion of a "strategic relationship of resistance and subversion" was one of the driving forces in creating and circulating Afro Caribbean art in the early part of the twentieth century because it helped explain the manner in which these artists adapted European modernism to suit their needs.[14] Extending that same logic of national authenticity and, consequently, inclusion in the canon, Indo Caribbean art, one can argue, effectively engages modes of counterdiscourse. The artists discussed below exemplify the idea of *métissage* in the visual vocabulary by borrowing from and adapting local strains to resist Creole (Afro Caribbean) and hegemonic Indian (insular, Indo Caribbean) influences while subverting traditional Indian mythologies to better fit Caribbean contexts. That is to say, if *métissage* signals relationality with the land and with peoples of other races and cultures,[15] then it can be borrowed to explain the unstable and multiple identities that are constructed in the mediated spaces of self-other (Indo Caribbean artists in Afro Caribbean contexts), and we can add the idea of *chutney* as framing the scene on which this relationality works.[16] Such a maneuver helps explain a gendered, racialized, and sexualized space that allows for staging identity for the situated and diasporic Indo Caribbean artists that I discuss below.

Shastri Maharaj

Shastri Maharaj's painting (Figure 1) depicts a Lingam in a luminescent shade of blue with an eye drawn in black at the apex. The Lingam is a traditional, religious icon signaling Shiva's manifestation of energy and is often painted in blue to show its close connection to Shiva as Neela-Kantha—the blue-necked god. It is accurate to say that Indo Caribbeans incorporate more of Shiva imagery than of other Hindu deities. The bright blue shaft in the center of the canvas concentrates the viewer's gaze on the starkness of the image and then draws it upward to the single eye at the tip

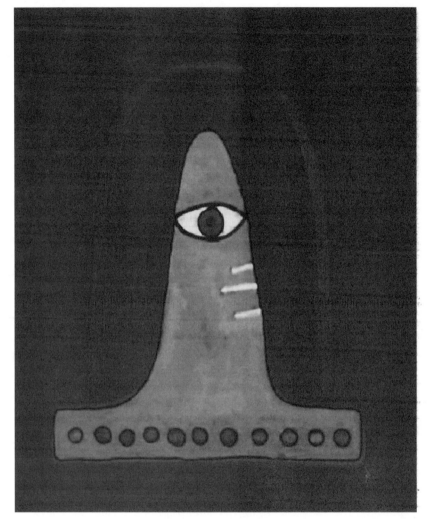

Fig. 1. Shastri Maharaj, "Blue Lingam" (acrylic on canvas, 1998). Used by permission of the artist.

of the shaft.[17] The Lingam is a bold assertion of presence, and the eye at the head suggests an omnipotent male gaze. But this forceful statement is subverted as the green sheath covering the Lingam controls the gaze. The domed shape of the stark Lingam also symbolically recalls the contours of temple architecture found in the Bihar region in India. The red dots at the bottom of the canvas are similar to an Indian floor decoration pattern called *rangoli*, a practice used extensively by Indians and Indo Caribbeans to signal the boundaries of sacred space. From a racial point of view, the dots enhance the religiocultural symbolism, almost suggesting a tantric ritual by drawing and arresting power by circumscribing sacred space much like totems in Afro Caribbean art. From an artistic point of view, the dots balance the illusion of matching the curved tip and the black eye at the apex of the Lingam and then draw the viewer's eyes to the curve of the green sheath, thus providing visual symmetry while also creating a dramatic contrast with the upright shaft.

The compelling assertion of a masculinized symbol in the Lingam is inescapable as it quickly signals an Indo Caribbean religious iconography. In a contemporary art context, the painting speaks to critics who are conversant with the meaning of the eye as gaze, but complicates that by sheathing and restraining that meaning.[18] In Maharaj's canvas one discerns a *chutney* and *métissage* moment wherein Hindu primal symbols are combined with a dialogic meaning that gestures toward a contemporary interpretation of the patriarchal gaze.[19] The masculine power of the Lingam is compromised by the powerlessness of the Indo Caribbean artist, who hybridizes a Hindu religious visual symbol with current discourses of patriarchy and subverts the final meaning through a modernist twist. It is an ironic reminder of what mainstream art critics had praised in Afro Caribbean artists such as Victor Manuel, Amelia Peleaz, Wifredo Lam, Carl Abrahama, and Eugene Good, for example, for wedding primitive symbolisms with modern art to visualize resistance, which were then authenticated as "Caribbean art." Applying the same evaluative standards, Maharaj's work should have found an entry into the global art scene instead of being exhibited locally in the Art Society of Trinidad and Tobago and in the Savannah Gallery in Anguilla. The "Blue Lingam" captures those very ideas seen as uniquely Caribbean—incorporating primitive, ancestral, and folk mythologies into modernist styles by deploying religious symbols to assert one's identity and create a subversive canvas. It can be argued that Maharaj positions himself as a male Indo Caribbean artist, who is intimately aware of the politics of exclusion.

Bernadette Indira Persaud

It is helpful in introducing Bernadette Persaud's work through her curatorial statement made during the 2000 exhibition to grasp her mood of

Fig. 2. Bernadette Indira Persaud, "Shiva Embracing the Other" (acrylic on canvas, 2000). Used by permission of the artist.

resistance, thus contextualizing the critical spirit behind her creative art-works. She writes:

> Concepts of art in our small postcolonial society [the Caribbean] tend to be extremely narrow and limited especially as they are articulated by a tiny cir-cle of art administrators and critics, who uphold outdated, academic or modernist doctrines of art once espoused in the Western mainstream. The pluralism of the contemporary international art scene is completely ignored by this dominant, elitist vision, which is equally oblivious of its own art community. . . . Our art [Indo Caribbean] is quickly dismissed, belittled, marginalized or subjected to inappropriate models of analysis. . . . Underly-ing this form of cultural arrogance is the simplistic assumption that all art, irrespective of its cultural sources is homogenous and has one universal aes-thetic appeal. Marxist analysis and feminist aesthetic theory have effectively demolished this myth of art that is devoid of race, gender, class, or sex.[20]

These words demonstrate her knowledge of current modes of art criticism and alert us to the institutionalized marginalization by an Afro Caribbean-centered art world.

The figure at the center of Persaud's canvas (Figure 2) stands against a fiery background and in a hypnotic fashion draws attention to itself. The title "Shiva Embracing the Other" is an allusion to *Ardhanarishvara*—or the myth of a fused Shiva-Sakti (Parvati)—wherein masculine and femi-nine energies are brought together. The *Ardhanarishvara* is a symbolic rep-resentation of powerful fused primal energies, usually invoked at a mo-ment of intense rage or crisis. It is not simple androgyny, as earlier West-ern critics had argued, but is a complicated expression of a gathering of primeval forces in readiness for war. As Ellen Goldberg argues in *The Lord Who Is Half Woman,* the body is made to do the work of culture by pro-viding new constructions of gender because the stereotyped passivity of the feminine is systematically challenged.[21] This nuanced and focusedly feminist explanation of the *Ardhanarishvara* myth is more in keeping with the curatorial statement that Persaud herself makes.

Shiva-Sakti stands tall and firm on the ground with a *Trishul,* Shiva's signature weapon that gestures to the artist's world and her nation (Guy-ana), which is split by the multiethnic, multiracial, and sexist politics on the eve of the 2001 elections when tensions between Indo and Afro Carib-beans had reached a breaking point. Here, the recognizable image of fire consuming the world as an effective form of resistance is a historical reminder of the revolt during days of plantation slavery and indentured labor. Persuad actualizes it as a nation being consumed by the fire of politicized racial hatred and rivalry. As the Shiva-Sakti figure stands half in light and half in darkness, it also signals the uncertain outcome of racial tensions within the body of the nation. However, in a contradictory move, Shiva's hand is raised in a gesture of universal peace, indicating and embracing another form of otherness—acknowledging the Christian, Islamic, and Hindu populations that comprise the many religions of Guyana. "Other" in Persaud's title taken together with the theoretical component of her curatorial statement noted above suggests that she is fully conscious both of racial and religious diversity and of refashioning gendered identity along the lines of continental feminists such as Toril Moi, who read androgyny not as sameness or negation of difference but as complicating received notions of gender. From a Caribbean discourse perspective, Persaud's canvas illustrates Glissant's view of the nonmonolithic nature of otherness, specifically underscoring the idea of *métissage* that posits gendered, Caribbean identity as always already hybridized, as resistant and subversive. Whether geographic or psychic, transformations often require vision and a certain violence, and here the juxtaposition of systemic categories of male/female, Indo/Afro Caribbean, peace/chaos is Persaud's vision of all these oppositions brought into play without resorting to simplistic cancellations. Maharaj asserted his male Indo Caribbean presence, however compromised by the sheath, but stands aloof and insular. Persaud, while equally assertive, is politicized, twining a feminist body with that of her nation's in contrast, acknowledging her identity as Indo-Creolized Caribbean, as belonging to both worlds and scripting those very markings on her gendered body. Persaud's painting is as much a visualization of Glissant's concept of *métissage* as it is a performative identity of a body made *chutney* by incorporating different religious and cultural sign systems.

Lucilda Dassardo Cooper

Lucilda Cooper's painting "Cosmic Dancer" (Figure 3) is sectioned off into two compartments. On the right is a traditional Shiva imagery—that of Nataraja, the dancing deity with a *yogini* (or mystical/ascetic female presence) at the right bottom corner creating a perception of energetic motion by giving the circular wheel its push. On the left is a pastoral scene with a

Fig. 3. Lucilda Dassardo Cooper, "Cosmic Dancer" (acrylic and water colors on canvas, 2001). Used by permission of the artist.

placid brook and tree-lined bank and a bird whirling in a colored configuration of energy. The two compartments are linked by the numerous blue lines (Shiva as Neela Kantha) emanating from Nataraja's circular, outer frame and moving toward the ball held in place by the bird on the left. The visual balance is maintained by the flow of blue and gold colors across both compartments, and representational symmetry is created by the circular lines connecting the two compartments.

The thematic connection between the two seemingly discrete images is evoked by the notion of transcendence. In the Hindu register, Nataraja traditionally performs a *tandavam,* a dance of destruction-creation that connotes transcendence, and in the Christian register, the bird is a traditional symbol of the soul's flight away from this mundane world. While there is no actual break between the two compartments, they are made distinct through their iconography. But the two separate religious registers (Hindu and Christian) are also connected by the blue (Indo) and gold (Christianized) lines flowing between the two images. The right side represents the strong influence of Shiva imagery, also seen in other Indo Caribbean artists thus far, but it has a twist in that Nataraja in a traditional dance pose needs the female figure to spin the wheel that provides the burst of energy to complement his sheer masculinity. While not as obvious as Persaud, Cooper here engages in a moment of *chutney* by re-presenting traditional mythology. Again, unlike Persaud or Maharaj, Cooper's engagement is peaceful, invoking a transition for the Caribbean to the United States through the metaphor of transcendence.[22] Cooper's painting in this light adds, dissolves, and creates an unimaginable juxtaposition of the self in order to represent the "I" at that moment of recognition. It is it eclectic and transitory and can be read as an innovative instance of *métissaged chutney*: an Indo Caribbean–gendered identity now anchored in New England.

Andrew Cheddie Sookrah

Andrew Sookrah, now living in Toronto, has a very different body of work. While we clearly saw Indo Caribbean imagery, icons, and systems of signification in Maharaj's, Persaud's, and Cooper's canvases, Sookrah's "Wallpaper Samurai" (Figure 4) hints at a different experiment with identity. This life-sized portrait belongs to a series of mostly nude men and women, and the bodies are clearly very stylized. The male figures in this series are well muscled, beautifully proportioned, and athletic in build; they exude an aloof and confident appeal; they are urban, cosmopolitan, and certainly contemporary. A Canadian art critic writes that this series has "existential giants. [Sookrah] paints nudes without skin. He paints the flesh and the soul of humans wounded by life and passions. His paintings tell us how to live life without denying ourselves."[23] Sookrah thus is not perceived as an ethnic, Caribbean artist but is absorbed into the body of the nation and claimed as a Canadian one.

The "Wallpaper Samurai" depicts a nude male body in the center of the canvas, with an orientalized wall hanging in the background, perhaps an indication of a memory of Indian and Chinese presences in the Caribbean. The title itself is interesting as it makes "Asian" an indeterminate category, while deliberately orientalizing and exoticizing along the lines of *chutneyfying* our perceptions of what is Asian in the Canadian-Caribbean context. The nude figure that dominates our vision has black-Latino features and leans forward in a lithe posture such that the well-defined mus-

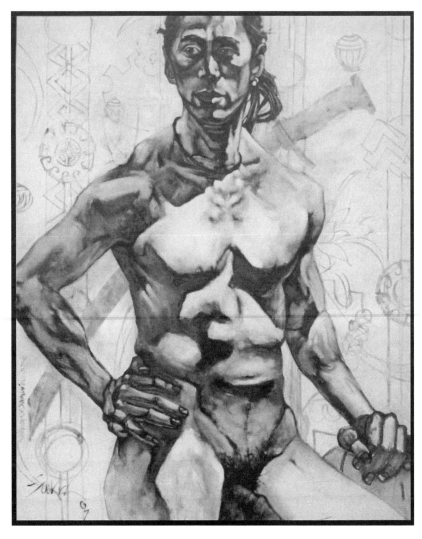

Fig. 4. Andrew Cheddie Sookrah, "Wallpaper Samurai" (oil on canvas, 2003). Used by permission of the artist.

cles of the arms and the legs hint at restrained power and energy. The *métissage*d body is perhaps another allusion to Guyana, his remembered home where multiraciality is a daily occurrence. Other than this, there is no direct reference to the Caribbean: that is, there is no religious symbolism, not even the uniquely adapted version of the modern. The portrait

stands alone and exudes a charged sexuality with desire emanating from
the male body.

Like Cooper, one can speculate that Sookrah also has borrowed from
North America. The male portraits in particular are reminiscent of Richard Bruce Nugent's work from the Harlem Renaissance. They reflect a re-
fined homoeroticism that is lacking in the portraits of female nudes.[24] It is
possible to speculate that homosexuality, because it is unspeakable (it carries a stigma of a strong social taboo) within the Caribbean, becomes im-
aginable, albeit in an artistic space. Interestingly, this portrait signals its
Indo-Afro Caribbeanness through lack: it defies an overt, aggressive, and
almost mandatory heterosexuality of the Caribbean to fashion in its place
tracings of homoeroticism in the outside world of Sookrah's Toronto.
Here I categorically state that I am not positing a homosexual identity on
the artist but rather speculate on the freedom to paint homoerotic subjects outside the boundaries of Guyana, thus subverting cultural imposi-
tions on Indo Caribbean identity through art. I mentioned Shani Mootoo
and Patricia Powell as authors who experiment with constructions of
hybridized, creolized identities. Both of them are important at this point
when speaking of Sookrah because they create gay, cross-dressing, and bi-
sexual characters that at one level refract the silenced reality of Caribbean
lives in diasporic literature and at another level experiment with gendered,
othered sexualities that are becoming part of global realities. Sookrah,
more than Cooper, falls into this global cosmopolitan continuum of home
and diaspora through his art by gracefully working through *chutney* and
métissage metaphors.

Conclusion

By examining two situated artists such as Shastri Maharaj and Bernadette
Indira Persaud in concert with two doubly diasporic ones such as Lucilda
Cooper and Andrew Cheddie Sookrah, both the sociocultural impulses
guiding their artistic vision and the limits exerted by the nation on one's
expression and imagination become noticeable. Maharaj from Trinidad
focuses on Hindu iconic emblems to assert the problems with exclusion of
Indo Caribbean presence amid the multiracial and multicultural chaos
of his national location. Persaud, artist and lecturer at the University of
Guyana, invests her figures with revolutionary energy by borrowing from
transplanted Hindu mythopoetics and contemporary Afro-Guyanese ra-

cialized politics. In contrast, Cooper, artist and local activist in Boston, represents figures from Hindu mythology, such as Shiva and Shakti, as carrying the potential for global harmony. And, Sookrah from Toronto, perhaps the most secular of the group, uses his diasporic distance to experiment with contemporary forms of identity as invested with sexuality and desire. All four artists reveal both a complicated dialogue with an imaginary sense of home matched with the realities of inhabiting that contested and undefinable space through lived realities.

NOTES

I thank Gurudev and Rohin Rajan for their inspiring encouragement as I wrote this essay. I am grateful to Lucilda Cooper, Andrew Cheddie Sookrah, Bernadette Indira Persaud, and Shastri Maharaj for generously sharing their artwork with me and for giving me permission to interpret them in my own fashion. I am obliged to them for not forcing me to abandon my critical interpretations. I thank Fairfield University and especially Johanna Garvey for supporting me with a Summer Faculty Research Grant, and Ranjanaa Devi and Ann Ciecko from the University of Massachusetts, Amherst, for inviting me to deliver a faculty lecture where I presented an earlier version of this argument. I am indebted to Marianita Amodio at Hamilton College for carefully preparing these works for publication. And I express my gratitude to Heike Raphael-Hernandez for inviting me to contribute to this innovative anthology.

1. I foreground the semiotic and theoretic impulses here. Semiotically, in not hyphenating Indo and Caribbean, I signal the same move made by Asian Americans in declaring their simultaneity of being both Asian and American. So, too, here it signals the autonomous identity of peoples of Indian origin in the Caribbean. The theoretical consists of seeing the Atlantic space in its entirety as capable of embracing Europe and the Americas into an imaginary Caribbean. I am grateful to the editors for sharing Lopez's essay from this collection, who quotes Antonio Benítez-Rojo to make this point: "The Atlantic is the Atlantic because it was once engendered by the copulation of Europe . . . with the Caribbean archipelago; . . . stretched between the *encomienda* of Indians and the slaveholding plantation, between the servitude of the coolie and the discrimination towards the *criollo.*" Antonio Benítez-Rojo, *The Repeating Island: The Caribbean and the Postmodern Perspective* (Durham: Duke University Press, 1996), 5. While Benítez-Rojo speaks to the Afro Caribbean question, I widen his idea to discuss the hybrid nature of Indo Caribbeans whose history of arriving in the islands and in North America is different.

2. Speaking of the different classes of Indian diasporas, Vinay Lal writes, "In

the nineteenth century, a large number of Indian were taken under conditions of savage exploitation, to various British colonies as indentured labor to work on sugar, tea, and rubber plantations, and the Indian populations of Fiji, Surinam, Mauritius, Trinidad, South Africa and numerous other places owe their presence in these countries to this particular circumstance. Diverse streams of the Indian population have fed into the Indian diaspora in the twentieth century: while a professional elite found its way to the United States, Australia, and other nations of the 'developed' West, the laboring poor were recruited to build the shattered economies of Britain, Holland, and Germany in the aftermath of World War II, and another strand of this working class has been providing for some years its muscle power to the Sheikdoms of the middle East." See Vinay Lal. "Reflections on the Indian Diaspora," 12 December 2002, available at www.sscnet.ucla.edu/southasia/Diaspora (retrieved 10 July 2005).

3. Veerle Poupeye, *Caribbean Art* (London: Thames and Hudson, 1998), 49. She continues that young Cuban intellectuals took this mood one step further in their 1927 manifesto, Grupo Minorista, which records, "Collectively or individually, our nucleus has fought and is still fighting for: the revision of false and out-moded values; for popular art, and in general, new art in all its diverse forms." Cited in ibid., 51. The major figures caught up in such sentiments were artists such as Wifredo Lam and Eduardo Abela, as well as the Cuban writer and cultural theorist Alejo Carpentier. Poupeye highlights the point that the intense interactions between and among artists, theorists, and politicians produced what soon became identifiably and uniquely Afro Caribbean art. For a slightly different selection of artist and brief critical commentaries, see Touring Exhibition Catalogue, *New World Imagery: Contemporary Jamaican Art* (Uckfield, UK: Beacon Press, 1994).

4. This is a trend that continues to this day as E. R. Gomez notes: "To those who live and work in the Caribbean—and to others in indefinite exile who remember their islands—the region is a gorgeous mosaic of magic and myth." E. R. Gomez, "Myth, Magic, and Mainstream," *ARTnews* 94 (Summer 1995): 112.

5. Ibid., 50. Poupeye points to a different kind of ideological influences: "Even though the Eastern Caribbean produced internationally acclaimed literary and political figures such as Aimé Césaire and the Trinidadian like C. L. R. James, developments in the visual arts were slower and comparatively modest, which may be explained by the lack of art patronage in these societies." Poupeye, *Caribbean Art,* 79.

6. Poupeye claims that "two aspects of popular culture—the religions and festival arts—are particularly important to the visual arts, as subjects and as sources of artistic production in their own rights" when reading Haitian primitive painters such as Hector Hyppolite, Robert Saint-Bryce, and Lafortune Félix (who was a Vaudou priest before he turned painter). Poupeye, *Caribbean Art,* 81. More recently, we have been reminded of such shared sensibilities in a historico-literary arena through Paul Gilroy's concept of the Black Atlantic.

7. Poupeye, *Caribbean Art,* 104.

8. It is beyond the scope of this essay to catalogue the instances where Naipaul has expressed, in fiction and in expository statements, his contempt for Afro Caribbeans and through opposition structured a bourgeois profile of Indo Caribbeans. And, he has paid absolutely no attention to Indo Caribbean art.

9. Lal made this statement in 1995. See "Reflections on the Indian Diaspora."

10. It is vital to understand the role of *chutney* in popular Caribbean culture because while Indo Caribbeans borrowed from Indian cinema that is circulating freely across the globe, Afro Caribbeans adapted freely from Hollywood. And, though *chutney* music and dance routines often bagged prizes during the Carnival contests, it remains a local phenomenon. Annie Paul from the University of the West Indies has commented on this innovative hybrid form. Poupeye writes that in contemporary times, Carnival (or *mas*) has created space for popular culture performative art forms through an intricate and dramatic combination of local religions, popular music, Rastafarian dance routines, and Hollywood-like stage productions. She claims that "the most spectacular case of overlap has been in the work of Peter Marshall (b. 1941), a theater designer, who revolutionized 'mas' in the early eighties and became one of Trinidad's most influential artists" by adapting styles and techniques from the *Star Wars* trilogy for his elaborate and technology-intensive Carnival king and queen presentation in *ManCrab* (1983). Quoted in Poupeye, *Caribbean Art,* 106.

11. *Chutney in yuh Soca,* March 1998, available at www.filmmakerslibrary.com (retrieved 29 June 2005).

12. Edouard Glissant, *Poetics of Relation* (Ann Arbor: University of Michigan Press, 2000), 34, original emphasis. Glissant's use of the word "errantry" carries his intent to say that "while not aimed like an arrow's trajectory, nor circular and repetitive like a nomad's, it is not idle roaming but includes a sense of sacred motivation" (211).

13. Celia Britton, *Edouard Glissant and Postcolonial Theory* (Charlottesville: University of Virginia Press, 1999), 3.

14. I am aware of the anachronistic basis of this statement. Glissant theorized the principle of *métissage,* and the word was not in usage when pronouncements about Caribbean art were being made. Benítez-Rojo presents this idea differently to say that the "spectrum of Caribbean codes [is] so varied and so dense that it holds the region in a soup of signs." Benítez-Rojo, *Repeating Island,* 12.

15. Glissant, like other postcolonial theorists, has noted that empires systematically posit otherness as the ground of exoticism. The first step in the Caribbean context is to acknowledge otherness through intermingling; thus identity, whether individual, communal, or collective, is also radically different from Western humanist definitions. Britton summarizes Glissant's explanations as follows: "The static polarity of the same and other gives way, in Glissant's relation theory, to a situation in which identity exists only as a shifting term in a network of multiple

relations with others who constitute it. Glissant defines this as a questioning of identity, in which it is the Relation to the Other that determines the self, but always in an open-ended way. It is based in interdependence rather than independence; hybridity, creolization, and the rhizome all reinforce this implication. Thus creolization makes our identities dependent on all possible 'mutual mutations' generated by this play of relations." Britton, *Édouard Glissant*, 34.

16. See the section on the combined influences of Indian and reggae music in John and Chris Gibson, *Soundtracks: Popular Music, Identity, and Place* (London: Routledge, 1991). See also Shalini Puri, who says that because of an undue emphasis on language of theory, "the issue of equality is displaced. A displacement of the politics of hybridity [is made in the name of] a poetics of hybridity." Shalini Puri, "Canonized Hybridities: Resistant Hybridities: Chutney Soca, Carnival, and the Politics of Nationalism," in *Caribbean Romances: The Politics of Regional Representation*, ed. Belinda J. Edmondson (Charlottesville: University of Virginia Press, 1999), 50. I contend that interrogating this displacement might challenge the almost formulaic association of cultural hybridity with the dismantling of the nation-state. For a similar idea but with a different focus, see Sunaina Maira, "B-Boys and Bass Girls: Sex, Style, and Mobility in Indian American Youth Culture," *Souls: A Critical Journal of Black Politics, Culture, and Society* 3.3 (Summer 2001): 65–86.

17. While traditional Hindus see the Lingam as a masculine emblem of all-powerful virility and do not equate it principally with the penis, many Western scholars have filled whole library shelves discussing the phallocentrism of this symbol.

18. In a slightly different context and without the restraint or subversion, but in the manner of asserting presence, Maharaj's work brings to mind Anish Kapoor's (U.K.) impressive sculptures, another diasporic artist, whose sphere "OM" was exhibited in the M. Sackler Gallery in the Smithsonian Institution in Washington, D.C. in 2000.

19. One wonders how much of the exclusion Maharaj feels when reading this: "Art is about making a statement informed by an awareness. . . . It is related to spiritual growth and primal ancestry." Artist's statement posted on the website of the Art Society of Trinidad and Tobago, where Maharaj's recent paintings were exhibited, November 2004, available at http://artsocietytt.org/maharajS.htm (retrieved 10 July 2005).

20. Bernadette Indira Persaud, Exhibition Catalogue, University of Guyana, Georgetown, 2000.

21. See Ellen Goldberg, *The Lord Who Is Half Woman: Ardhanarishvara in Indian and Feminist Perspectives* (Albany: SUNY Press, 2002).

22. The left side is interesting in that it shows unmistakable influences of the Hudson River School. Since Cooper was trained in Boston and has worked in the United States for over three decades, it is possible to speculate that *métissage* oc-

curred in a very different fashion and that she absorbed the sensibilities of her new home by incorporating the influences of the Hudson River School.

23. Juan Pascual-Leone, Conversation with artist, Toronto, 28 October 2002.

24. The homoeroticism in this canvas is unmistakable, especially in light of the Canadian reviewer's comment that "living life without denying ourselves" carries multiple valences.

Chapter 8

These Are the Breaks
Hip-Hop and AfroAsian Cultural (Dis)Connections

Oliver Wang

April 5, 2002, New York—Jin Auyeung, a rapper of Chinese American descent, wins his seventh week in a row on B.E.T.'s [Black Entertainment Television] Freestyle Fridays competition. He is only the second rapper in B.E.T. history to have completed all seven weeks without a loss. During the course of the competition, Jin is repeatedly attacked by his opponents with remarks that draw attention to his race, including:

> "I'm a star / he just a rookie / leave rap alone and keep making fortune cookies . . . In the hood / is where they'll find your body, dog / I'm the kid / you're just Mr. Miyagi." (vs. Sterling, Week 2)

> "What you wanna do? / Battle me / or sell me dollar batteries?" (vs. Skitzo, Week 3)

> "Who you supposed to be / Bruce Lee/ with his pants all sagging? / I'll murder you dog / they'll be no 'Return of the Dragon.'" (vs. Sean Nicholas, Week 7)

November 19, 2004, Philadelphia—I am in Philadelphia to appear on two different panels focusing on the role of Asian Americans in hip-hop. During the evening panel, held at the Asian Arts Initiative, African American activist Kenyon Farrow asks the panel whether or not the presence of Asian Americans in hip-hop represents a dehistoricizing or deracializing of the African American relationship to hip-hop. I briefly address Farrow's question in an entry on my personal weblog.[1] Farrow responds with an essay, "We Real Cool? On Hip-Hop, Asian-Americans, Black Folks, and Appropriation."[2] Within it, Farrow elaborates on his question at the panel:

"Since we live in this multi-racial state which still positions Blackness socio-economically and politically at the bottom, how does the presence of Asian Americans in hip-hop, this black cultural art form, look any different than that of white folks in Jazz, Blues, and Rock & Roll?"

March 15, 2005, San Francisco—Jeff Chang, a music journalist of Chinese American descent, appears on KQED FM's morning talk show, "Forum," to talk about his new book, *Can't Stop, Won't Stop: A History of the Hip-Hop Generation.* During the call-in portion, former University of California, Berkeley, Professor Cecil Brown phones in and asserts:

> The problem in the case of white journalists is even more insidious in the appropriation because they are stifling, they are taking the voice of the Black hip hopper. Who needs the voice of Chan [*sic*] giving us Black people? We need Black people expressing themselves, their voice, it's their hip-hop.[3]

The year 2004 represented an unprecedented time for public awareness around Asian Americans in hip-hop, almost all of it stemming from the debut release of Jin's *The Rest Is History,* the first rap album by an Asian American artist released on a major, corporate label.[4] This sudden publicity helped bring Asian American rappers out of a state of relative invisibility, but it also exposed undercurrents of racial tension between African Americans and Asian Americans. For much of the last fifteen and more years, it has become commonplace wisdom and belief that hip-hop culture represents an idealized space for multicultural cooperation and community building. Journalists and scholars alike have focused on hip-hop's massive appeal among youth globally, drawing attention to how, as an expressive form, hip-hop finds deep resonance with a wide array of communities spanning racial, gender, class, and other social lines. Few debate that hip-hop enjoys such large, diverse participation, but the idea that the culture's proliferation—and subsequent adoption—has been universally celebrated is an assumption that is increasingly being cast into doubt, as those three opening paragraphs attest. Rather than treat hip-hop as a space for universal inclusion, it is becoming increasingly clear that the participation of Asian Americans in hip-hop happens within a contested terrain that is inextricably linked to long-standing tensions between Asian Americans and African Americans. Therefore, hip-hop represents an opportunity for contact but also potential grounds for conflict.

This essay explores hip-hop as a social space where African Americans and Asian Americans encounter one another in both constructive and cautionary ways. In order to organize the range of issues present in such a topic, first I briefly summarize a history of Asian American rappers, focusing on how they have negotiated their race and ethnic identities within hip-hop's own racial paradigm. Second, I look at how the increasing prominence of Asian Americans in hip-hop, especially with the career of Jin, has brought out concerns around cultural appropriation and Afro-Asian race relations. Third and last, I hone in on a question that popular culture scholar George Lipsitz raises in discussing the kind of "cultural collusion and collision" that Asian Americans in hip-hop is an example of: "Which kinds of cross-cultural identification advance emancipatory ends and which ones reinforce existing structures of power and domination?"[5]

Since its emergence as a street culture from the South Bronx in the 1970s, hip-hop has evolved into a dynamic expressive form that has long drawn on a multitude of different cultural traditions and influences.[6] It is also, unquestionably, a Black cultural form, not only drawing from a range of African American and Afro-diasporic vernacular, musical, and other aesthetic traditions but also positioning within American society as clearly within a sociopolitical context of Blackness. In other words, hip-hop is inseparably tied into Black public culture.[7]

Those two statements are not, in any way, contradictory. Hip-hop can have its roots in Blackness yet also be the product of cultural encounters from outside Afro-diasporic influences. In an age of electronic media, contemporary cultures are almost always transformed when brought into contact with others. Neither are there "pure" cultural forms that have not been affected through hybrid practices or encounters. In this understanding, the term "Black" does not presume there is a 100 percent authentic Blackness out there any more than there is a 100 percent authentic "Asian Americanness" out there (the latter identity was a construction from its very inception as a term).[8] However, understanding and appreciating hip-hop's syncretic roots does not fundamentally change its relationship—especially in the popular imagination—to Blackness.[9]

With this in mind, one should also consider that just because culture integrates does not mean that people necessarily do. Popular culture can create opportunities for meaningful contact between communities, and culture often absorbs and expresses tensions not easily resolved through other social institutions like the government or an economic system. However, this does not mean that culture is able to actually resolve these tensions. Whatever potential might exist is only realizable through human and social will and dedication and, therefore, culture's emancipatory promise is not always (or often) realized.

In regards to hip-hop and the Asian American community, the waves of Asian American rappers from the early 1990s up through Jin's emergence reflect a series of changing perspectives and negotiations with race.[10] Given the relationship between hip-hop and Black public culture, there exists what one might call a "racial authenticity" within the public imagination whereas the idea of a "real" rapper is often automatically associated with Black faces. Non-Black rappers, especially Asian Americans,[11] create a visible break from that norm, thereby necessitating some form of negotiation or positioning to resolve the rupture.

Prior to Jin's emergence, I posit three distinct waves of Asian American rappers, each of which has pursued different negotiations of racial identities. The first wave, comprised of Asian American rappers from the early 1990s, were what I would call "Raptivists"—social activists who turned to hip-hop as a means to reach the public through popular culture. Influenced by both the radical racial politics of the 1960s Black Power and other social movements, as well as by the emergence of politicized rap groups like Public Enemy, Boogie Down Productions, and others, Asian American college students began to form their own groups including (but not limited to) the University of Washington's Seoul Brothers (Korean), University of California, Davis's Asiatic Apostles (Chinese and Filipino), San Francisco's Fists of Fury (Korean), Oberlin College's Art Hirahara (Japanese), and Rutgers University's Yellow Peril (Chinese). Most of these groups were highly politicized in their song content—for example, Fists of Fury rapped about interracial dating ("Sleeping with the Enemy"), Black/Korean relations ("Black Korea II"), and a racist educational system ("After School"). A quote from the latter should put into keen relief the kind of attitude and mission these artists undertook:

> First grade to college
> You're pushed to work hard,
> Get all A's on every report card;
> Your teachers will say,
> "Isn't he a bright child,
> Not like the Blacks,

Who always act wild."
Everyone expects you to be a genius,
Valedictorian when you're a senior
But, hey, brother, sister, haven't you heard?
Behind your back, they're calling you a nerd![12]

Raptivists performed mostly at Asian American collegiate and community events, and very few harbored ambitions to continue with their rapping careers after college.

By the mid-1990s, a new wave of Asian American rappers emerged, including Los Angeles' Key Kool (Japanese), Philadelphia's Mountain Brothers (Chinese), and the San Francisco Bay Area's Lyrics Born (Japanese). I refer to these artists as "Underground," reflecting a self-aware aesthetic of complex authenticity markers contrasting against "mainstream" or "commercial" artists. Underground artists have generally been more ambitious and committed than Raptivists and, as a consequence, their intended audience has been consciously developed to be more diverse than the Raptivists' more insular crowds. As such, Underground artists largely eschewed similar overt political or racial content[13] to what Raptivists engaged in. Instead, they favor more conventional hip-hop narratives—braggadocio, romance/sex, nostalgia—cast against a rhetoric of "the universal" where hip-hop is seen as belonging to a global community rather than specific racial groups. Not surprisingly, Underground artists largely avoid the rhetoric of racial pride (let alone exclusivity) in favor of appealing to the idea of "skills" (i.e., talent) as being the marker of authenticity rather than origin.

While these artists have found some success as independent artists, they have also had to struggle with finding a larger, mainstream audience. For example, the Mountain Brothers were briefly signed to Ruffhouse Records in 1997—no small feat considering that, at the time, Ruffhouse also had superstars such as Cypress Hill and the Fugees signed to their label. However, an anticipated Mountain Brothers album never materialized, mostly due to disagreements between the group and label, not the least of which was Ruffhouse's struggle to create a suitable marketing campaign for the group given their racial difference.[14]

By the late 1990s, a peculiar wave of Asian American rappers appeared, almost exclusively on the Internet: AZNs. "AZN" is a phonetic spelling of "Asian" that also signifies the adoption of urban, hip-hop-inspired vernacular.[15] Around 1999–2000, a flurry of AZN-related songs began to emerge online, using instrumental tracks from popular hip-hop songs but with new lyrics that expressed racial pride and superiority. The most famous example first circulated in 2000, a song called "Got Rice?" that was credited to AZN Pride.[16] Not only did the song adapt its title from the popular "Got Milk?" advertising campaign of the time, but also its instrumental track was taken from a hit song by the late rapper Tupac: "Changes." Using that familiar sound bed, the lyrics lie somewhere between self-pride and parody:

> It's the A-Z-N, nigga, fuck the rest,
> Dallas to New York, jigga, we're the best.
> Vietnam to Japan to Mongolia,
> Philippines to Taiwan to Cambodia
> Korea Ah Ah
> Hometown China, who you got, huh?
> You got shit, nigga feel the size,
> it's the A-Z-N better recognize.
> Got rice bitch? Got rice?
> Got food, got soup, got spice?
> Got brains like us? Got skills like us?
> Got cars, got clothes, got girls like us?[17]

On one level, the AZNs' desire to put their race front and center bears a passing similarity to the Raptivists, but the AZN understanding of race is considerably uncritical and problematic, most obviously evinced by the disturbing frequency of AZN rappers calling themselves and one another "nigga" with no apparent recognition of the racial implications of the term. As "Got Rice?" also suggests, many AZN songs also espouse racial identities that resemble self-generated caricatures. The AZN phenomenon has been a striking fusion of music, identity, and technology, but more research is needed, especially in collecting and analyzing demographic information on self-identified AZNs, many of whom exist anonymously within the Internet.

Since the late 1990s, a select few Asian Americans have risen to places of prominence in the public eye, including the Neptunes' Chad Hugo (Filipino), Linkin Park's Mike Shinoda (Japanese), and the Black Eyed Peas' Allan Pineda, aka Apl.de.ap (Filipino). However, the best-known Asian American rapper has been Jin Auyeung, who performs as simply "Jin."

Born to immigrant Chinese parents, Jin grew up in Miami and in the early 2000s relocated with his family to the Flushing neighborhood in Queens, New York.

Following his victories on the Freestyle Fridays competitions, Jin announced he had signed a contract with the record label, Ruff Ryders (a subsidiary owned by Virgin Records). Signing Jin was an unusual, risky move for the Ryders, not just because he was a virtual unknown outside of the BET audience but most obviously because Jin and the Ryders had to strategize a way to market an Asian American rapper to a largely Black and White rap audience, most of whom had never before seen an Asian American rap artist.

While the Underground artists sought to downplay race in favor of more universal ideals fixated on talent and aesthetics, Jin's strategy was to make race as prominent as possible in order to deny his potential detractors from raising it as an issue against him. His first single, "Learn Chinese," opens with Jin proclaiming, "Yeah, I'm Chinese. And what? The days of the pork fried rice coming to your door are over." That line is both a statement and a challenge, effectively daring his would-be critics to make race an issue. Not only that, but Jin symbolically kills off one dominant stereotype of Asian masculinity, the docile delivery boy, and replaces it later in the song with an equally flat caricature: the rough-riding Chinatown gangster.[18]

"Learn Chinese" was first released in the spring of 2004, and in between then and the eventual release of *The Rest Is History* in October of the same year, a deluge of press heralded Jin's debut. The quantity and quality of press Jin received was unusual for a new rapper. Hip-hop publications like *XXL* published features on Jin,[19] and so did many newspapers and even high-profile mainstream media outlets like the *New York Times Magazine*,[20] National Public Radio,[21] and *Newsweek*.[22]

In these features, Jin was well aware of the issues of race and authenticity surrounding him. In London's *Guardian* newspaper, Jin told reporter Dorian Lynskey, "Let's be honest, if I wasn't Chinese, the *New York Times* wouldn't have wanted to write about me. So I take it for what it is."[23] The observation was astute, as Jin recognized why the *New York Times*—or any of the other dozens of publications that ran stories on him—took notice: a story about "an Asian American rapper" laid out an instant and easy-to-understand narrative, that of the "outsider" (Jin) trying to make his way into the "inside" culture of Black hip-hop. Practically every story on Jin relied on this basic narrative, and while it netted him considerable press, race has been a double-edged sword because it is the one topic that Jin can never escape. As he himself noted, "It's a lose-lose situation. I talk about being Asian, they say I'm exploiting my history to get attention. If I don't talk about it, they say, 'He thinks he's black.'"[24] In other words, Jin's two choices are either to be a self-exploiting gimmick or a trespassing poseur, and for reasons that should be obvious, neither is desirable.[25]

With all of Jin's visibility, a backlash began to brew. Envy runs high in an industry as competitive as hip-hop, especially for new artists trying to distinguish themselves against one another. With Jin, however, the racial element created another, deeper layer of controversy and concern. Writer Kevin Kim summed up the core issue in his profile of Jin for *Colorlines Magazine*:

> Instead of trimming the tale's excesses or tracing the racism constraining Jin's every move, most observers turned to street-wise model minority myth. The protagonist was still stereotypically Asian, but this time the culture penetrated decidedly black. Asians were set against blacks ("Chinese in a black world," one suburban headline blared).[26]

The "Asian vs. Black" narrative that Kim observed formed the focus, for example, of the *Guardian*'s profile. Its subhead was telling: "Jin could be hip-hop's first Asian-American star—racism doesn't stop him."[27] Author Lynskey referred primarily to racism *within* the hip-hop community toward Asians, drawing on three examples: (1) Ice Cube's controversial 1991 song, "Black Korea,"[28] that referenced the Black/Korean tensions in Los Angeles prior to the L.A. rebellion of 1992; (2) the 2005 "Tsunami Song" recorded by New York urban radio station Hot 97, which mocked the Asian victims of the December 2004 Indian Ocean disaster using racially derisive language;[29] and (3) Jin's experience facing racist comments during MC battles such as the ones I detailed at the essay's beginning.

Lynskey puts the onus of intolerance onto other hip-hop performers, or, in the case of the Hot 97 incident, media gatekeepers. However, in focusing on Hot 97 or Ice Cube, Lynskey neglects to consider that Jin's most powerful antagonists are neither other rappers nor morning radio show hosts but hip-hop consumers and the record executives who base their decisions on what they think they see in the market. Jin—or any other non-Black rapper—has to convince both white and black hip-hop consumers that they are "authentic," despite their racial difference. Most record labels would hesitate to sign an artist unless they were reasonably assured of that acceptance as well. This creates a classic paradox: consumers cannot determine whether they will support an artist until there is music for them to listen to and weigh in on. And although artists usually have to rely on a record label to distribute the music to begin with, executives are wary of signing unknown acts until they have a sense of what the public thinks. That contradiction is sufficient to maintain a status quo that effectively keeps many non-Black rap artists from entering the market.

This is precisely why Jin's story earned so much coverage in the press—even mainstream publications that do not specialize in hip-hop coverage understood that Jin was an unusual artist. However, as Lynskey's article insinuated—and as Kim's essay observed—Jin's story became framed as a conflict between Asian and Black, and, not surprisingly, other pundits picked up on this thread and soundly critiqued it.

In the wake of Jin's press deluge, two essays were circulated on the Internet by December of 2004. The first to appear was "The Hype about Asian Rappers Reveals Low Standards for Asian Americans in Race Politics," by Tamara Kil Ja Kim Nopper, a self-described "writer, researcher, educator, and activist living in Philadelphia." A few weeks later, an essay by New York activist Kenyon Farrow was also circulated via email and then later posted on the online journal, *Chickenbones*: "We Real Cool?: On Hip-Hop, Asian-Americans, Black Folks, and Appropriation." Both essays use Jin's popularity as a jumping-off point to challenge assumptions made around Asian American participation in hip-hop.

Nopper targets the idea that Asian American rappers and spoken word artists "are politically more subversive than those who act like 'model minorities.'"[30] Although she believes that Asian American adoptions of Black cultural practices are read as inherently "political" acts since they go against the grain of assimilation paths into Whiteness, Nopper counters that often what is being espoused in the rhetoric of these rappers and poets hardly contradicts a status quo that upholds capitalist exploitation, misogyny, or anti-Black racism. In specific reference to Jin, she notes that some of his rhymes use sexist language and asks, "Are people supposed to embrace Jin as proof of Asian American cultural pride and 'subversiveness' because he battles other male rappers with words that are fucked up towards women?"[31]

Farrow has similar points to make in his essay, arguing that participation in hip-hop is not necessarily a road to racial solidarity. In accusing Asian Americans of appropriating hip-hop, Farrow suggests that they may be little different from nineteenth-century White minstrels who aped elements of Black style and culture as a way to affirm White supremacy and denigrate Blackness. He asks:

> If first-generation white European immigrants like Al Jolson could use min-strelsy (wearing blackface, singing black popular music and mimicking their idea of Black people) to not only ensure their status as white people, but also to distance themselves from Black people, can Asian Americans use hip-hop (the music, clothing, language and gestures, sans charcoal make-up), and everything it signifies to also assert their dominance over Black bodies, rather than their allegiance to Black liberation?[32]

Farrow is arguing against the assumption that hip-hop's multiracial following is a sign of solidarity between other people of color (who participate in or appropriate hip-hop) and the interests of Black Liberation. Instead, Farrow urges people to "un-assume that because we're all up in hip-hop that we're all on the same page. Let's un-assume that because you might try to look like me or sound like me (or how you think I do both), that we are working towards the same goal, or that we even have the same enemy."[33]

Clearly, Farrow is interested in issues beyond just the realm of hip-hop. For him, hip-hop is a focal point, a battle site if you will, where larger tensions and conflicts manifest on a smaller scale. Like Nopper, he is arguing against the belief that cultural crossings are inherently positive or progressive acts, but they need to be critically interrogated before such claims can be made. Nopper's concerns echo Farrow's when she writes, "Asian Americans getting involved in Black cultural domains like spoken word and hip hop doesn't translate into Asian Americans actually having a radical politic," by which she means a politic that seeks to undermine or critique "social mobility, assimilation, capitalism and anti-Black racism."[34]

There are some looming concerns with both Farrow's and Nopper's essays. While accepting that they were publicly circulated personal essays rather than scholarly articles, both make serious claims without offering much supportive evidence. For example, Nopper asserts, "Are we supposed to embrace Asian Americans who use spoken word and hip hop to depict Black people as politically selfish, jealous, divisive, and uncultured, which are all statements and gestures that support white hostility towards Blacks and related claims of 'reverse racism'?"[35] Some level of example—even anecdotally—would have bolstered her argument, especially since there is considerable evidence that stands contrary to her claim.[36]

Likewise, Farrow's comparison of Asian American hip-hoppers with White minstrels fails to offer enough concrete examples to warrant such an analogy, save for Farrow's observation that, at the Philadelphia panel, there were "Asian youth with [dread]locks and hair teased out (and often chemically treated) to look like afros!"[37] Certainly, the aping of Black hairstyles can serve as an apt example for uncritical adoptions of ethnic culture, but that is far from making a case that Asian Americans are just latter-day minstrels. Given the complex history of minstrelsy in America, especially in relation to Black/White relations,[38] invoking the term begs for a more nuanced argument to prove its point.

This said, both essays insightfully warn against conflating cultural participation in, or appropriation of, Black culture with either a critical appreciation of Black experiences or lived, social interaction with Black communities and individuals. I would further extend this critique to say that hip-hop is hardly alone in the situation; popular culture can too easily serve as a proxy for actual human interaction and contact, leading to the kind of politically problematic relationship that Lipsitz has described as "escapes into postmodern multi-culturalism."[39]

On these specific issues, Nopper and Farrow are speaking to difficult truths that need to be understood and appreciated. Questions of cultural exploitation and appropriation become all the more relevant in an era where, within a global marketplace, cultural forms are easily transformed into commodities that can be produced, sold, and consumed at the speed of media. In particular, Nopper points out that "in this stage of capitalism, ethnicity is a hot commodity,"[40] drawing attention to both how malleable ethnic identity has become in contemporary culture, as well as the reality that "ethnicity" itself has become less tied to generational practices and traditions and more associated with symbolic markers (for example, henna tattoos) and gestures (for example, mimicking Black slang) that can be easily consumed or copied. While, on the surface, these casual adoptions of culture may seem harmless, they can easily lead to a state of dangerous *un*consciousness that Lipsitz warns against: "To think of identities as interchangeable or infinitely open does violence to the historical and social constrains imposed on us by structures of exploitation and privilege."[41]

This is precisely the flashpoint that concerns Nopper, Farrow, and others who are cautious about assigning the cross-cultural participation of Asian Americans in hip-hop as an inherently libratory action. In those cases—such as the AZNs—where those crossings lack critical awareness of larger racial issues, they only serve to highlight both historical and contemporary inequalities between communities. It is no revelation to note that there have been immense conflicts and tensions between African American and Asian American communities, many of them arising out of the ways in which the two groups have been played off one another to advance the cause of White supremacy and sustain patterns of systemic social inequality. Though Farrow does not go far enough in proving the case that Asian American rappers are equivalent to White minstrels in either material or even symbolic ways, he is more accurate in arguing that Asian Americans have often benefited—intentionally or not—from the legacy of discrimination against African Americans that stems back to colonial slavery and beyond. As Susan Koshy cogently argues in her essay, "Morphing Race into Ethnicity: Asian Americans and Critical Transformation of Whiteness," there are key historical moments where Asian Americans—when given the option—have tried to position themselves closer to White privilege and away from solidarity with Black communities.[42] Hers is a sobering study of how the hegemony of racial inequality is perpetuated through the active participation of marginalized groups and not just the will of the oppressor.

However, it is important to resist the temptation to perceive AfroAsian cultural crossings as worst-case scenarios, where Asian Americans are presumed to be consuming Black culture and style in one breath, while exhaling invectives and criticisms of African Americans in the next. Few things in culture are rarely so (if you pardon the cliché) black and white. Understanding the nuances is not simply for the sake of accuracy, but it can also open up the space of political possibilities rather than a series of fatalistic dead-ends.[43] For example, I argue that the concern about AfroAsian cultural relations is not that Asian American rap artists or fans hold viciously derogatory views of African Americans but, rather, the reverse: that some Asian Americans romanticize the African American experience and believe that their participation in hip-hop brings them closer in solidarity with African Americans.

Jin himself attempted this in his song "Same Cry" from *The Rest Is History,* suggesting that African Americans and Asian Americans have more in common than they think, specifically through the struggles and tragedies they have faced. For example, he rhymes about the Tiananmen massacre and the SARS epidemic, but his third set of verses most specifically attempt to forge cross-cultural understanding:

Stuck between a rock and a hard place,
Thinkin 'bout the refugees that went to see Gods face.
Sixteen thousand miles across the ocean tides,
Some died, some got lucky and survived.
I wouldn't call it luck, they reached their destination
Modern-day slavery without the plantation.
Them sneakers on ya feet cost a hundred a pop,
My people's making 15 cents a day at sweatshops,
To make them kicks so you can look good
Think we open restaurants 'cause we cook good?[44]

To be sure, "Same Cry" has its share of problems, especially in comparing refugee experiences to American slavery. Though refugees fled to the United States under the most adverse of conditions, Africans were forcibly removed and brought to America as slaves. Though both are reflective of dire circumstances, the conditions of migration, especially in relation to power and privilege, are vastly different between the two.

However, "Same Cry" is clearly meant to be a bridge between communities, flimsy as the construction may be. I am not suggesting that good intentions equal good politics. However, in addressing Lipsitz's question about discerning between cultural crossings that "advance emancipatory ends" versus reinforcing "existing structures of power and domination," the desire of these artists to work and speak cross-culturally is entirely relevant, and the desire for Asian American hip-hop fans to think of rap music as a way to bridge experiences between themselves and other communities—especially Black—cannot be easily dismissed, either.

After all, one reason Asian Americans (among many other communities of youth around the world) have taken so strongly to hip-hop (besides for its pleasures as a cultural form) is because it has come to represent a form of alterity that marginalized groups identify with. This holds as true for Algerian youth in Paris as it does for Korean youth in Tokyo as it does for Maori youth in Auckland. That desire to identify with hip-hop's outspoken politics of identity can provide the basis for the *beginning* of a potential dialogue between different groups. It has the *potential* of bridging the gulf created by historical structures of inequality or interpersonal conflicts. Obviously, these dialogues are not guaranteed to achieve "emancipatory ends" simply on the basis of intent, but they are an attempt to bridge commonalities between communities that share long histories of disenfranchisement and marginalization.

Postscript: May 20, 2005, New York

Jin tells AllHipHop.Com, "No more studio for me," and records a song "I Quit" that announces his retirement.[45] He does not elaborate on his reasons, though he asserts that it was not for poor record sales (his album, *The Rest Is History*, sold modestly at around 100,000 units—not a disaster, but far from being a success). On one of his personal websites, he closes his retirement announcement with, "Just remember: I wasn't the first. And I certainly will not be the last."[46]

It was ironic to receive word of Jin's retirement while I was completing this essay. After all, it was Jin's unique rise into prominence that catalyzed many of the issues discussed above. With his departure, it is once again the case that no Asian American rappers are signed to a major label. This is not an inherently "bad thing"—one would be hard pressed to argue that there *needs* to be an Asian American rapper situated in the industry. However, it does serve as a reminder that the Asian American presence in hip-hop is tenuous at best, especially at the level of the recording industry where Asian Americans are anything but entrenched, either symbolically or structurally.

If the history of Asian American rappers suggests anything, it is that race still matters in hip-hop. Fears around its wholesale deracialization, while understandable given how other Black music has been appropriated throughout the twentieth century, are yet to be realized in hip-hop. For the foreseeable future, the relationship between hip-hop and Blackness will still remain normative, though there are provocative shifts happening on a smaller level within newly budding hip-hop subcommunities.[47] Furthermore, as Jin's experience shows us, if and when Asian Americans begin to take a more public role in shaping and representing hip-hop, this will likely invite challenges and questions about what their involvement means for hip-hop and for the larger backdrop in AfroAsian cultural connections and relations.

It must be said that hip-hop, despite its long-standing cross-cultural appeal, is not an ideal space in which AfroAsian relations should be forged and developed. As an expressive form that has flourished in an era of electronic media, hip-hop has become easily consumable from the comfort of one's private home. Enjoying hip-hop may be a commonality that people share with others, but as I have stressed throughout, it does not inherently compel human interaction simply through the act of consumption. Obviously, the same can be said of most cultural forms that have been commodified, but the political traditions of hip-hop have created false expectations for its worth as a tool for social organizing and cross-cultural coalition building. Hip-hop *can* serve that function in the hands of astute and forward-thinking social activists,[48] but it cannot be assumed that it always will.

In short, hip-hop is no panacea to solving tension and conflicts between African Americans and Asian Americans. Where I do see some potential, though, is the way in which hip-hop has and will define the cultural experiences of several generations of young people in America. It has been the dominant cultural force of the last twenty years, and as its popularity continues to grow, it forms a cultural foundation that, ideally, individuals from different communities can relate to and share. Again— shared cultural habits do not erase historical enmities, and they cannot resolve larger structural inequalities. They are merely a starting point—an opportunity for conversation or even confrontation. What is important here is the opening of communication, without which the possibility for change and transformation cannot exist.

The last thing I want to stress is the need for more research on Asian Americans in hip-hop from the perspective of the audience. My essay, as well as those by Nopper, Farrow, and others, tends to focus on Asian American artists, and while the perspectives of cultural producers are certainly important, they cannot be presumed to have the same views or values as consuming audiences. This shortcoming in existing scholarship reflects the ways in which much hip-hop research is based around methodologies of lyrical or other textual analysis; but what is needed is more ethnographic and similarly qualitative data that examines what hip-hop means to the youth who actively consume it. If hip-hop can offer the potential for communities to forge meaningful contact and dialogue, it would behoove future scholars to find ways to gather the opinions and testimonials of different youth groups to determine what hip-hop means to them and their aspirations for (or against) cross-cultural connections.

NOTES

The development of this essay and its arguments owes much to conversations I have had in the last year with several colleagues and peers, especially Jeff Chang, Tamara Nopper, Jared Sexton, and Ronnie Brown.

1. Oliver Wang, "He's Your Chinaman," *Pop Life*, 22 November 2004, available

at http://www.o-dub.com/weblog/2004/11/hes-your-chinaman-jin-jin-everywhere .html (retrieved 27 July 2005).

2. Kenyon Farrow, "We Real Cool? On Hip-Hop, Asian-Americans, Black Folks, and Appropriation," *ChickenBones,* November 2004, available at http://www .nathanielturner.com/werealcoolkenyon.htm (retrieved 27 July 2005) .

3. Cecil Brown, Phone-in comment, "The History and Future of Hip Hop" *Forum with Michael Krazny,* KQED 88.5FM, San Francisco, 15 March 2005, available at http://www.kqed.org/epArchive/R503151000 (retrieved 27 July 2005). Note how Brown conflates—at the very least, confuses—Chang as a "white journalist."

4. As opposed to released on a small, independent label.

5. George Lipsitz, *Dangerous Crossroads: Popular Music, Postmodernism and the Politics of Place* (New York: Verso, 1997), 56.

6. See Jeff Chang, *Can't Stop, Won't Stop: A History of the Hip Hop Generation* (New York: St. Martin's Press, 2005). Chang's discussion of hip-hop's origins in the South Bronx is one of the most comprehensive histories compiled to date.

7. See Tricia Rose, *Black Noise: Rap Music and Black Culture in Contemporary America* (Hanover, NH: Wesleyan University Press, 2004), chapter 2. Also see Imani Perry, *Prophets of the Hood: Politics and Poetics in Hip Hop* (Durham: Duke University Press, 2005), chapter 1. Both Rose and Perry discuss, at length, the indelible relationship between hip-hop and African American/Afro-diasporic cultural traditions.

8. Blackness and Whiteness may exist as concepts for racial identities, but there is no equivalent "Asianness." The pan-ethnic ties that bond Asian Americans to one another is based on a shared, conscious political will but not necessarily common cultural or historical similarities. As such, Asian American political solidarity—to say nothing of a unified cultural identity—is fractured at best, making it difficult to accurately speak about an "Asian American community" that is truly inclusive of that group's internal diversity and differences. See Yen Le Espiritu, *Asian American Panethnicity* (Philadelphia: Temple University Press, 1992).

9. See Perry, *Prophets of the Hood,* chapter 1, for an extended discussion about reconciling hip-hop's hybrid roots with its connection to Blackness.

10. This section is largely adapted from my essay: Oliver Wang, "Asiatic Static: Race, Authenticity and the Asian American Essay," in *Alien Encounters: Popular Culture in Asian America,* ed. Thuy Linh Nguyen Tu and Mimi Nguyen (Durham: Duke University Press, 2006). In that essay, I expand in far more historical detail on the adaptive strategies that different Asian American rappers have taken in negotiating their racial identities when faced with hip-hop's racial authenticity.

11. Differences between African American and Asian American men, in particular, manifest in striking ways in the realm of the symbolic. If contemporary Black masculinity is associated with stereotypes of hypermasculinity and hypersexuality, physical aggression, and the underclass, these stand in almost diametric opposition to so-called model minority stereotypes of Asian masculinity: effete or

asexual, passive, middle class. In other words, one could argue that what largely defines Asian masculinity is the absence of traits associated with Black masculinity. See Kobena Mercer, "Black Masculinity and the Sexual Politics of Race," *Welcome to the Jungle: New Positions in Black Cultural Studies* (New York: Routledge, 1994), 131–170; Yen Le Espiritu, "Ideological Racism and Cultural Resistance," *Asian American Women and Men* (Thousand Oaks, CA: Sage, 1997), 86–107. (Thanks to Shannon Steen for reminding me of this obvious dichotomy.)

12. Fists of Fury, "After School," unreleased demo, 1993.

13. There were exceptions to this, notably Key Kool's single about the World War II incarceration of Japanese Americans called "Reconcentrated."

14. The Mountain Brothers eventually released their debut album, *Self, Vol. 1*, through their own independent label in 1998, though they were able to get their video, "Galaxies," onto MTV—one the first Asian American rap artists able to do so.

15. The "AZN" name was one of several kinds of cultural markers that these youth deployed. Another popular convention was spelling sentences using random uppercase and lowercase lettering, such aS ThiS pHRaSe heRe.

16. It is unclear if "AZN Pride" is the name of a group because the term became an all-purpose, generic name given to many different songs recorded in a similar style as "Got Rice?" For example, an online search for songs by "AZN Pride" would call up dozens of different songs that were clearly recorded by different artists. For the song's lyrics, refer to http://www.asianjoke.com/pictures/got_rice.htm.

17. AZN Pride, "Got Rice?," 2000.

18. However limited Jin's politics may be in "Learn Chinese," he is most certainly conscious of the circulation of racialized stereotypes about Asianness and Asian malehood in particular, and "Learn Chinese," in its own bombastic way, goes about trying to offer a shotgun spray's worth of correctives. This includes everything from a critique of the mainstream American media apparatus ("this ain't Bruce Lee/ ya'll watch too much TV") to single-serving size tidbits of Asian American history ("we should ride the trains for free/ we built the railroads") to the reclamation of racial epithets as an act of pride ("stop/ the chinks took over the game"). The video for the song, which appeared on all the major rap video outlets, mirrored many of the same ideas in its imagery, with the camera following Jin into a Chinese restaurant kitchen, posh gangster den, and street block filled with Asian-influenced racing cars. The street scenes are interesting, too, because elsewhere in the video most of the people we see are Asian, but on the street Jin is surrounded by a conspicuously multiracial crowd, in particular, the Fugees' Wyclef Jean—the song's producer—who stands next to Jin in these shots, making explicit the idea that Jin is able to move freely through these different cultural spaces without out contradiction.

19. Mr. Parker, "Golden Child," *XXL* (September 2002): 158–162.

20. Ta-Nehisi Coates, "Just Another Quick-Witted, Egg-Roll-Joke-Making, Insult-Hurling Chinese-American Rapper," *New York Times Magazine*, 21 November 2002, 55.

21. Derek John, "Asian-American Rapper Jin Makes Hip-Hop History," *Day to Day. NPR*, 26 October 2004, available at http://www.npr.org/templates/story/story.php?storyId=4126877 (retrieved 27 July 2005).

22. Lorraine Ali, "A Whole New Rap," *Newsweek*, 8 November 2004, 56.

23. Dorian Lynskey, "Straight outta Chinatown," *Guardian*, 3 March 2005, 15.

24. Jim Farber, "Jin's a Tonic," *New York Daily News*, 17 October 2004, 20.

25. These poles reflect competing logics around cultural crossings within hip-hop: people either desire full and open access to hip-hop (the logic of the market system) or take up defensive stands around it (the logic of cultural parochialism). Finding a middle ground between the two extremes is difficult since advocacy for one often has the effect of only emboldening the other to strike back defensively.

26. Kevin Kim, "Rapping Chinatown," *Colorlines Magazine* 7.4, Winter 2004, available at http://www.arc.org/C_Lines/CLArchive/story7_4_03.html (retrieved 27 July 2005).

27. Lynskey, "Straight outta Chinatown," 15.

28. Richard Harrington, "*Billboard*'s Hot Refrain: Editorial Decries Ice Cube's 'Racism,'" *Washington Post*, 20 November 1991, D7.

29. David Hinckley, "'Tsunami Song' Fallout: 3 Suspended, 2 Fired," *New York Daily News*, 2 February 2005, 80.

30. Tamara Nopper, "The Hype about Asian Rappers Reveals Low Standards for Asian Americans in Race Politics," *Azine*, 3 December 2004, available at http://www.aamovement.net/art_culture/poetry/standards 1.html (retrieved 14 March 2006).

31. Ibid.

32. Farrow, "We Real Cool?"

33. Ibid.

34. Nopper, "Hype about Asian Rappers."

35. Ibid.

36. For example, prominent Asian American spoken word artists such as Chicago's now-defunct I Was Born with Two Tongues and Minneapolis' Bao Phi have explicitly talked about their commitment to social justice causes in partnership with other communities of color, especially African Americans. Likewise, in over thirteen years of researching and writing on Asian American rap artists, I have never conducted or read a single interview where Asian American rappers have "depicted Black people as politically selfish, jealous, divisive, and uncultured," as Nopper asserts in "Hype about Asian Rappers." While this may be how certain media outlets have chosen to frame narratives around Asian American rappers (such as Lanskey's profile on Jin for the *Guardian*), in my experience, it has never been the case where the artists themselves have expressed such views.

37. Farrow, "We Real Cool?"

38. See Eric Lott, *Love and Theft: Blackface Minstrelsy and the American Working Class* (New York: Oxford University Press, 1995).

39. Lipsitz, *Dangerous Crossroads*, 63.

40. Nopper, "Hype about Asian Rappers."

41. Lipsitz, *Dangerous Crossroads*, 62.

42. Susan Koshy, "Morphing Race into Ethnicity: Asian Americans and Critical Transformation of Whiteness," *Boundary* 2.28 (2001): 153–194.

43. Sylvia W. Chan, "From Coolies to Courvoisier: Asian Americans and the Failure of Orientalism" (currently being prepared for publication), does an exemplary job of discussing the crucial differences between Orientalism within a white, colonial context and Orientalist gestures performed by African Americans within contemporary hip-hop and R@B songs and videos. Chan argues that treating all Orientalisms as the same threatens to flatten an understanding of power and inequality that could effectively "prevent the possibilities of unities-in-difference—the alliances and coalitions needed to work towards a liberatory politics."

44. Jin Auyeung, "Same Cry," *The Rest Is History*, Compact Disc, Virgin Records, 2005.

45. Strong Nolan, "Jin Says Rap Career Is Over, Records 'I Quit,'" *Allhiphop.com*, 20 May 2005, available at http://allhiphop.com/hiphopnews/?ID=4412 (retrieved 27 July 2005).

46. Auyeung, "Same Cry."

47. See Jon Caramanica, "Emo Rap: Up from the Underground," *Spin*, 12 February 2004, available at http://www.spin.com/features/magazine/2004/02/emo_rap_up_from_underground/ (retrieved 27 July 2005). In this intriguing article, Caramanica chronicles the rise of mostly white hip-hop audiences oriented around specific rappers such as New York's Aesop Rock and Minnesota's Slug. See also Bakari Kitwana, "The Cotton Club: Black-Conscious Hip-Hop Deals with an Overwhelmingly White Live Audience," *Village Voice*, 24 June 2005, available at http://www.villagevoice.com/music/0526,kitwana,65332,22.html (retrieved 27 July 2005). Kitwana also discusses the rise of predominant white rap audiences and weighs in on the implication of what this means for hip-hop's identity politics.

48. See Kate Bowman, "Turning Rhymes into Votes: Political Power and the Hip-Hop Generation," *Sojourners*, June 2004, available at http://www.sojo.net/index.cfm?action=magazine.article&issue=sojo406&article=040638 (retrieved 27 July 2005).

Part III

Performing AfroAsian Identities

Chapter 9

Racing American Modernity

Black Atlantic Negotiations of Asia and the "Swing" Mikados

Shannon Steen

> It is here in the Pacific that the future drama of our expanding commerce will be enacted. The play of rival forces now finds the Pacific for its stage.
>
> —*San Francisco Chronicle*, 31 August 1925, on the occasion of the first nonstop flight between California and Hawaii

I.

In the spring of 1939, in a New York humbled by the economic losses of the Depression, and confronted by the specter of German fascism, Japanese imperial expansion, domestic isolationist pressures, and the racial inequities of Jim Crow, Broadway producer Michael Todd staged a hit show, *The Hot Mikado* (Figure 1). A spin-off of the enormously successful *Swing Mikado* (1938) staged by the Federal Theater Project (FTP) with a black cast the previous year (Figure 2), Todd's "hot" version brought the house down every night with a startling joke: as the African American actor Eddie Green opened a telegram announcing the impending arrival of the Japanese emperor, he exclaimed in consternation, "It's in Japanese!" and then remembered in delight, "Oh! *We're* Japanese!"

What was the cultural resonance of a black actor's claim to *be* Japanese? Green's punch line illuminates how American modernity was precariously forged on a continent uncomfortably situated between two differently racialized, cross-oceanic cultures—the Atlantic and the Pacific. The joke

Fig. 1. (*top*) Act II finale, *The Hot Mikado*. Billy Rose Theatre Collection, The New York Public Library for the Performing Arts, Astor, Lenox and Tilden Foundations. Fig. 2. (*bottom*) Katisha and the Mikado cakewalk, Act II, *The Swing Mikado*. Courtesy of the Library of Congress, Federal Theatre Project Collection.

imagined America's future through its relationship to Asia, while carrying its black Atlantic present into that negotiation. The creation of a swing adaptation of *The Mikado* seems at first glance a perfect example of Joseph Roach's circum-Atlantic performance—one that contributes to an "oceanic interculture" founded on the "diasporic and genocidal histories of Af-

rica and the Americas."[1] Indeed, the swing *Mikado*s Americanized a quintessentially British cultural product through white fantasies of African
American expressive forms. But these fantasies did not just reinforce the
circum-Atlantic basis of U.S. national identity. The disparate visions in the
swing *Mikado*s of an implied black Pacific culture were used to perform
the permeability of what David Palumbo-Liu has called the "racial frontier" constituted by America's westernmost border.[2] In other words, Asia
was figured in the productions as the site through which the United States
would create a modern status distinct from that of Europe, and blackness
was used as the vehicle through which Asia could be Americanized.

In response to the heavy reliance on the racial binary that has effaced
the influence of Asian American presence on U.S. racial structures, Claire
Jean Kim has offered instead a racial "triangulation"—a system in which
Asians are positioned "between" black and white Americans with respect
to qualities of virtue, intellect, and enterprise but positioned entirely re-
motely from black or white Americans by virtue of their seeming "foreign-
ness."[3] How might our models of race, modernity, and nationalism in
America change if we adopted alternative racial geometries like Kim's? I'd
like to use the swing adaptations of *The Mikado* to suggest here my own
alternative model. These shows demonstrate how distinct racial categories
were deployed against one another within white fantasies of difference in
an attempt to shore up the racial and geopolitical boundaries of the American nation-state in the late 1930s, a time in which the United States tried
aggressively to consolidate its own status as a power in the modern world.
Specifically, they challenge us to scrutinize the effect America's relationship to Asia had on the creation and implementation of racial categories.
In these performances, one racialized geopolitical entity—an already internalized black Atlantic culture—intersected and buttressed national and
racial identities challenged by another, newly emergent but equally racialized geopolitical entity, the Asian/Pacific.[4]

As David Palumbo-Liu and others have noted, the United States of the
early twentieth century viewed East Asia as an arena through which it
could compete against the European colonialist powers in order to become one of the elite global powers. As the United States attempted to
extend its cultural, economic, and military influence in East Asia, white
America mobilized, and in some cases altered, images of African Americans in order to manage anxieties raised by Asia and Asian American immigration. Gilbert and Sullivan's 1885 original had satirized contemporary
English attitudes toward sexuality and capital punishment by projecting

those tensions onto Japan, a projection itself enabled by the forcible opening of Japanese trade to the West in 1853 that produced an England awash
in Japanese trinkets. The swing adaptations of the 1930s used a set of
primitivist cultural references to re-project the Orientalist parody of Gilbert and Sullivan's original onto the American cultural scene through the
associations of swing with blackness. While the Victorian British fascination with Japan had similarities to that of swing-era America (indeed,
these similarities allowed for the musical to "play" to both audiences), it
contained significantly less anxiety, as Japan had not yet become a potential naval and imperial power in 1885 when the original show premiered.
While they similarly intended to parody Japan, the 1930s productions did
so at the expense of African Americans. The new adaptations did not simply use black actors to translate *The Mikado* to an American context, however, but staged a chain of incomplete racial displacements to perform a
national racial context that was at once black, white, and Asian.

Intended as novel and comic relief, the chaotic, competing fantasies of
race and nation in the two swing *Mikado*s drove one of the most fascinating theatrical rivalries of the late 1930s. Once both shows opened in New
York in the spring of 1939, playing in theaters located across the street
from one another, they became the talk of the town and the hits of the
season, and their competition even forced a scrutiny of government intervention in commercial trade that prompted some critics to call for the
closure of the FTP itself.[5] Trumpeted in print everywhere from the *New
Yorker* to *Time* magazine, the "Battle of the Black *Mikados*,"[6] as it came to
be known, performed a densely concatenated series of American racial anxieties and pleasures and invented a spectacular way of thinking through
various challenges to domestic and foreign racial and national stability.
Using the black cultural associations of the swing era, the shows staged a
series of fantasy journeys across the Pacific, which beckoned to an America attempting to invent its modernity by shrugging off its associations
with Europe. The FTP's *Swing Mikado,* for example, staged an Edenic
island paradise associated with anthropologically inspired fantasies, in
which the romantic heroine Yum Yum was transformed into the Black
Narcissus prominently displayed in the pages of *National Geographic,* in
which Gilbert's bumbling tailor Ko Ko was recreated in the stinging words
of one reviewer as a "Japanese Stepin Fetchit," and in which the maniacal
Mikado was ridiculously recostumed in the perceived sumptuary excesses
of Polynesian aristocracy. The commercial *Hot Mikado,* in contrast, depicted a swinging Japan colonized by African Americans and overrun by

Cotton Club aesthetics. Featuring a striped Mt. Fuji, streetlamps hung with enormous dice, costumes that parodied the 1930s' couture craze for *japonaiserie,* and governed by Bill "Bojangles" Robinson as a tap-dancing Mikado, the designs of the commercial Broadway show crossed racialized aesthetics such that Gilbert and Sullivan's Titipu was populated by "Japanese Jitterbugs." In both cases, the crossing of Orientalist with primitivist tropes manifested the hyperbolic fear of the global displacement of whites by Asians in the face of Asian immigration and Japanese imperial power— a fear partially discharged by the presence of black actors, who served as a wily, genuine "American" self that could resist the tide of the Yellow Peril.

II.

In the late 1930s, the United States faced an Asian/Pacific that it contemplated through disparate and sometimes competing fantasies. As a result, the Pacific constituted the most malleable and unstable border that confronted the United States, racially and physically. The Pacific Islands, in particular, constituted a space of chaotic racial semiotics; anthropological ideologies and immigration policies, for example, produced indeterminate notions of whether or not Pacific Island inhabitants were Asian Orientals or primitive savages. The swing *Mikado*s were staged on the heels of a range of American policies: the National Origins Act of 1924 that had halted Asian immigration to the United States altogether, and which also created the racial category "Asian" by conflating Japanese, Chinese, and Korean nationals and barring them from legal integration into the American economy; the Tydings-McDuffie Act of 1935, which made the Philippines an independent state, thereby subjecting its citizens to the immigration controls of the National Origins Act from which they had previously been exempt; the rapid acceleration of American foreign investment in China by 600 percent from the mid-1910s to the mid-1930s; and perhaps most important for the *Mikado* productions, the apprehensive attempt to control Japan's imperial expansion, which the latter justified specifically on the grounds of intervening in Western incursions into China.[7]

By 1939, the year the two swing *Mikado*s opened in New York, Japan had already invaded Taiwan, Korea, Mongolia, and Manchuria and was feared to intervene in America's economic agenda in China. In response, U.S. Secretary of State Cordell Hull renounced the 1911 Treaty of Commerce with Japan in retaliation for its colonization of China, paving the way for the later trade embargoes that would prompt the 1941 bombing of Pearl Harbor.[8] As the popular and critical acclaim of the swing *Mikados* grew, reports of Japan's activities in the Pacific crept ever closer to the front page. When the Mikado strode onstage in 1939, then, to declare, "From every kind of man obedience I expect," the joke was considerably more unnerving than in its first utterance in 1885. Until, that is, those words were put into the mouth of a *black* actor. That crucial locution unconsciously returned the specter of Japanese imperialist ambition safely to the edges of consciousness by ridiculing it through primitivist and minstrelsy tropes.

White racial anxieties regarding Asians by no means exceeded those toward African Americans during the Depression. The severe economic crises during the 1930s renewed fears of black radicalism as African Americans suffered more extreme effects of the economic downturn than did their white counterparts.[9] The effect of the Depression on African Americans was so palpably worse than on white Americans that the latter feared that "Harlem would go radical" and turn to open rebellion to alleviate the economic disparity for which the attempt at middle-class private enterprise had failed. In fact, 1930s Harlem was ripe for civil unrest. The economic discrepancies of the Depression intensified the problems of segregation and political disenfranchisement, and the routine, dehumanizing practices of police brutality, withholding of health and social services, and punitive and discriminatory housing practices finally erupted in a riot in 1935.[10]

The overwhelming popularity of the *Mikado* adaptations was eventually exploited by protest groups over the exclusion of black Americans from symbolic and economic integration into the American mainstream. The leftist revue *Pins and Needles* capitalized on the shows' notoriety to demonstrate against the refusal by the Daughters of the American Revolution (D.A.R.) to rent Constitution Hall in Washington D.C. to Marian Anderson for a recital (the first African American woman to attempt to perform in that hallowed space). In *Pins and Needles'* "Red Mikado," the Three Little Maids from School carried fans conspicuously marked "Made in China" while they sang "Three little D.A.R.s are we / Filled to the brim with bigotry," and spurted blue blood when pricked by Ko Ko's sword.[11] Playing on the racist implications of the swing *Mikado* adaptations, the revue used the spectacle of happy black Asians to protest the fact that the D.A.R. had no problems with consuming the products of racial others, while continuing to exclude them from white public space.

Born of the mutual influence and cooperation of black and white musicians in the spirit of New Deal pluralist optimism, swing was positioned in the shows to maintain the cultural integrity of the United States and, moreover, to act as a cultural export that could aid the American penetration of the Pacific. As David Stowe has noted, swing had been perceived since the 1920s not merely as an authentic American cultural product but as its preeminent form. The most popular musical and cultural form of the late 1930s, it produced a range of responses to American black/white internal racial relations, as it was alternately relished and feared as sweeping aside notions of racial separation and the last vestiges of sexual propriety that remained in the wake of the Roaring Twenties and flapper culture. Projecting Gilbert and Sullivan's Orientalist parody onto America, the new adaptations not only engaged swing to ridicule old-fashioned sexual mores but also titillated audiences with the specter of miscegenation raised by swing culture itself. Swing constituted one of the first instances of desegregation, and in doing so paradoxically maintained racial and other divisions:

> In its simultaneous challenge and acceptance of dominant racial, sexual, and cultural hierarchies and of large-scale industrial consolidation, swing acted out larger cultural impulses at the same time that it modified them. Swing was widely perceived, and understood itself, as both Other and Self— at once marginal and similar to an "ideal picture of America," the defining of which was a central cultural achievement in the years in which swing flourished.[12]

Although swing was notable for its collaborations between black and white bandleaders, composers, and musicians, some of its practitioners nevertheless saw it as a form devised by white musicians trying to legitimate jazz from its associations with the perceived lewd sexuality of the Cotton Club and the illegality of the Prohibition speakeasy. While interracial couples might dance together at the Savoy Ballroom in Harlem, the world outside the swing clubs continued to reinforce segregation. Swing, as Stowe points out, instantiated a central American racial paradox: the interpenetration of racial groups on the one hand that enabled the fantasy of pluralism and constituted one of the primary national myths of early-twentieth-century America, and the rigid maintenance of racial boundaries that belied that myth on the other.

The foundation for the black Pacific crossing of the swing *Mikados* had already been laid within the FTP by other swing revues. In 1936, the vaudeville unit of San Francisco (a racially desegregated company) produced *Swing Parade,* a globe-trotting spectacle set in exotic locales like the Hawaiian islands and an African jungle (the design for all of which was inspired by issues of *National Geographic*), and which culminated in a meal in Chinatown that led to the display of the recently completed Golden Gate Bridge, itself a portal to the Pacific funded through the federal auspices of the Works Progress Administration (WPA).[13] The FTP had mounted several "straight" productions of *The Mikado* over the course of the 1930s, and the production teams that designed Gilbert and Sullivan's Orientalist spectacle often also created other exotic extravaganzas. The design team Maxine Borowski and Alexander Jones, for example, created a *Mikado* for the FTP in New York in 1936 and later went on to design the 1938 Negro unit revue *Swing It.* Both *Swing It* and *Swing Parade* contained Chinese characters—the latter in scenes set in Chinatown, in which white actors played Chinese characters in yellowface; the former in the black vaudevillian actor Al Young, who perpetuated the vaudeville tradition of black actors playing Chinese characters. When drafting his production team for the commercial *Hot Mikado,* producer Michael Todd poached the FTP talent pool and recruited Nat Karson—whose last major success had been the "Voodoo" Macbeth staged for the FTP by Orson Welles and John Houseman in 1936—to design the sets and costumes. In other words, by the time the swing *Mikados* were staged in 1939, the foundation had been laid within theatrical production systems for the crossing of Orientalist and primitivist tropes on the level of both content and design, and the creative teams responsible for staging the shows were already well versed in both forms of exoticism.

Exactly how *The Mikado* came to swing is a bit of a mystery. Although a black minstrelsy troupe had performed *The Black Mikado, or the Town of Kan-Ka-Kee* in Boston in 1886,[14] and a jazz adaptation of Gilbert and Sullivan's classic had been staged in Berlin in the early 1930s, these productions appear not to have influenced the American swing versions of 1938–1939. Harry Minturn, the Chicago director of the FTP, needed a show for his Negro-unit actors and capitalized on the current swing rage. Minturn produced the FTP's *Swing Mikado* in Chicago in the fall of 1938, where it went on to provide the biggest box office hit the midwestern unit of the FTP ever saw. At some time that fall, the FTP considered selling the rights for the show to a private concern, at which point New York producer Michael Todd, who already had a straight *Mikado* to his credit, became interested in acquiring it. But the FTP was reluctant to give up one of its hits and abandon its actors, who would no longer be assured of work once the show went into commercial production.

The FTP's adaptation wasn't a complete rewriting of Gilbert and Sullivan's original. Although the stage design reproduced the "coral island" of the South Seas made popular by Margaret Mead in the 1920s, the show relied musically on the complete original score and lyrics. While it is difficult to discern from the sheet music exactly how "hard" Arthur Sullivan's music was swung in practice (swing being, like jazz, a largely improvisational form whose textual notation only suggests its rhythmic and melodic parameters), for the most part adapters Gentry Warden and Charles Levy retained his chord progressions and only slightly changed the underlying rhythms of his orchestrations. These encores of Gilbert and Sullivan's most famous tunes were performed in swing and maintained the minstrelsy show practices that were beginning to die out in live performance (although their cinematic counterparts were to prove to have greater longevity),[15] as did the choreographic elements of the production. Nanki-Poo's claim of "patriotic sentiment" in "A Wandering Minstrel" was accompanied by a tap-dancing chorus, and the Mikado's entrance in act two during "Let the Punishment Fit the Crime" featured him and Katisha cakewalking in front of a swaying chorus.[16]

While the actors were black and the music and staging derived from African American cultural forms, the swing productions still maintained the Orientalist framework of Gilbert and Sullivan's original. By designation of music, lyrics, and staging, these black actors *were* Japanese. Both adaptations maintained the paradoxical disavowal of the Japanese status of its characters located in Gilbert's original libretto. In the swing versions, as in the original, the performers persistently reiterated that they both were and were *not* Japanese. One of Yum Yum's friends laments at the seemingly immanent execution of Nanki Poo that "I would sigh into my pocket handkerchief, if only the Japanese *used* pocket handkerchieves!" Like Eddie Green's delighted discovery that, "Oh, *we're* Japanese!" in *The Hot Mikado*, this simultaneous statement and disavowal of Japanese identity to some extent simply points to the pleasurable blurring between actor and character that constitutes theatricality itself—that the actor both is and is not the character she performs. But the racialized nature of this disavowal in the swing adaptations, in which black actors alternately claimed and denied their Japanese identities, performed particular cultural work with respect to retaining racial boundaries.

Musically, both shows maintained the aural framing device "Miya Sama," Sullivan's Orientalist leitmotif for the show that opens both the overture to *The Mikado* and the second act. Originally sung by the Toka-gawan army attempting to hold on to the last vestiges of feudal, Shoganate rule in the late 1860s, "Miya Sama" was introduced to Sullivan by Algernon Mitford, a member of the British diplomatic corps in Japan in the opening years of the Meiji period.[17] As Michael Beckerman has observed, Sullivan altered this melody, characterized by the pentatonic *ritsu* scale that has become one of the primary markers (if not, indeed, the predominant aural stereotype) of the Far East, in fragmented, inverted, or otherwise altered form throughout the score. To this day, the song's open-fifth inter-vals are used in Western representations to signify Asia musically (for example, "Bali Ha'i" from *South Pacific*, "A Hundred Million Miracles" from *The Flower Drum Song*, the Buddhist prayer from *The King and I*, and the wedding ceremony from *Miss Saigon*). This Orientalist leitmotif weaves throughout the show, creating a framework on which the other forms that Sullivan exploited to great effect—the madrigal, the patriotic march—could hang.[18] In creating the overture to the show, Sullivan care-fully highlighted the numbers that featured open-fifth intervals and cre-ated in effect what Beckerman refers to as "an aural, pseudo-Japanese scrim" through which the rest of the show is heard. This scrim was used, he writes, as a "primal defense" against the alien, fascinating presence of the Japanese in the midst of Victorian England.[19] Variously understood to denote meaningless nonsense, military fervor, or "the foulest song ever sung in the tea-houses of Japan,"[20] "Miya Sama" induced the projection of classic Orientalist tropes: inscrutability (through its Japanese lyrics), belli-cose pride (through its associations with the Tokagawan rebellion), and the lust for flesh and blood that underwrote both throughout the operetta.

These Orientalist tropes structure not only the quality of the music in the operetta but the text of the show as well. Beckerman points out that *The Mikado* contains a striking number of violent images and references —more than any other in the Gilbert and Sullivan repertoire.[21] Ko Ko temporarily convinces Yum Yum to delay her wedding when he announces an ancient law that demands the wife of an executed man be buried alive. The Mikado later pleasurably describes Ko Ko's fate for killing the heir to the throne as "something humorous, but lingering, with either boiling oil or melted lead."[22] When he describes his trumped-up execution of Nanki Poo, Ko Ko paints a particularly gruesome portrait for the Mikado's pleasure:

Now you'd have said the head was dead
(For its owner dead was he).
It stood on its neck, with a smile well-bred,
And bowed three times to me![23]

Ko Ko's fantasy unites the trope of bloodthirsty Oriental to the stereotype of obsequious, ever-smiling Asian servility embodied by Ko Ko himself:

Though trunkless, yet
It couldn't forget
The deference due to me."[24]

If Ko Ko's execution story unites the tropes of bloodlust and servility, Yum Yum's lovely aria of the second act, "The Sun, Whose Rays Are All Ablaze," reveals the manner in which sexual desire was constructed to underwrite imperialist ambition within Orientalism. The charming song cloaks the threat of incipient Japanese imperialism behind the surface of the Lotus Blossom façade, especially in the choruses:

First Chorus:
I mean to rule the earth, as he the sky;
We really know our worth, the sun and I!

Second Chorus:
Ah, pray make no mistake, we are not shy;
We're very wide awake, the moon and I![25]

The anxieties here of a threat by the Land of the Rising Sun to the Empire on Which the Sun Would Never Set were offset by Sullivan's lovely, haunting melody and softly pulsating orchestration on the one hand, and by Gilbert's dialogue that ushers in the song on the other. Just before she sings the aria, Yum Yum casually remarks, "I am indeed beautiful. Sometimes I sit and wonder, in my artless Japanese way, why it is that I am so much more attractive than anybody else in the whole world. Can this be vanity? No! Nature is lovely and rejoices in her loveliness. I am a child of Nature, and take after my mother."[26] Japan is rendered "artless" by virtue of Yum Yum's narcissism, absurdly defended as it is through a Romantic pastoral rhetoric that Gilbert simultaneously parodies.[27] Through Yum Yum, Gilbert depicts a Japan obsessed with physical beauty ("I am so much more attractive than anybody else in the whole world"), with effete, nostalgic Romanticism ("I am a child of Nature"), with social standing and imperial ambition ("I mean to rule the earth as he the sky"), and finally with an indirect, coy revelation of its sexuality ("make no mistake, we are not shy"). The Lotus Blossom, though vain and ambitious, was pastorally unthreatening when sexually fulfilled.

The Orientalist connotations of the music and lyrics were crossed with primitivist conventions in the staging of both productions: in the FTP version, the traditional mincing steps of the Three Little Maids from School broke down into trucking when the actresses performed the swing rendition of Sullivan's famous tune as an encore. The combination of Orientalist and primitivist tropes induced some tripping over racialized terminology for reviewers. Alternately delighted and confused by the kind of racial crossing inaugurated by the interpolation of primitivist staging conventions into the Orientalist sensibilities of *The Mikado*, reviewers unwittingly echoed the doubled racial signification of the term "Savoyard." Originally denoting the Savoy Theatre opened by Richard D'Oyly Carte (the producer behind Gilbert and Sullivan's shows) in 1881, Savoyard came to stand for quintessential Gilbert and Sullivan: the style of music, the crisp performances of the singers, Gilbert's precise staging, and the sense of Englishness that encompassed the whole endeavor. The term later came to include Gilbert and Sullivan groupies who vigilantly watched for and hotly contested any production unfaithful to Gilbert's exact stage business in the absence of international copyright protection that would have ensured delivery of the genuine Savoyard experience.

The earnings of the Savoy Theatre, which housed Gilbert and Sullivan's premieres after 1881, enabled D'Oyly Carte to open the Savoy Hotel in 1889, which, with its technological wonders like telephones, in-room plumbing, and elevators, quickly became a landmark symbol of elite, modern elegance and cosmopolitan sophistication. This latter sensibility was "swung"—and blackened—with the 1926 creation of the Savoy Ballroom in Harlem. Originally a black enclave, the ballroom quickly became known for the racial mixing that characterized both its Lindy-Hopping clientele and the orchestras that played there, memorialized in Benny Goodman and Chick Webb's 1934 hit "Stomping at the Savoy."[28] Michael Todd, who was consciously aware of the Savoy connection, physically manifested this black Atlantic transformation of the term when he drafted "Whitey's Lindy Hoppers" (Figure 3), a group of elite dancers from the club vetted by one of its bouncers, to perform a special number in front

Fig. 3. Whitey's Lindy Hoppers, *The Hot Mikado*. Billy Rose Theatre Collection, The New York Public Library for the Performing Arts, Astor, Lenox and Tilden Foundations.

of the pagoda gates of the palace in the first act of the *Hot Mikado* that reviewers dubbed the "Japanese Jitterbug." Significantly, the dancers were billed in the program as Whitey's Jitterbugs, using the "white" slang for swing dance rather than the preferred black term "Lindy Hop." The phrase "Japanese Jitterbug" then, denoted the Asian/Pacific context for a white renaming of a black dance form, for a set of dancers known for the performance in a black nightclub whose own name had been appropriated from the D'Oyly Carte Savoy, and who now danced in front of a fantastic Cotton Club pagoda.

In this way, Savoyard in the swing *Mikado*s confused reviewers and demonstrated the permeability of racial boundaries between black, white, and Asian. This tripartite understanding of race, connected through the term "Savoyard," underwrote the reception of the pieces, both positive and negative. For the FTP *Swing Mikado* in Chicago, reviewers consistently blurred the origins as to which Savoy—London theatre and hotel, or Harlem ballroom—the shows primarily referred. Some reviewers were frustrated by the interpolation of swing Savoy into the Orientalist tropes such as those exemplified by Yum Yum and Ko Ko, which they considered the apex of traditional (i.e., white) Savoyard standards. Some, like Gail Borden, were furious that Gilbert and Sullivan's original Orientalist intentions were supplanted by the new primitivist adaptation, a criticism she leveled particularly at the actor Herman Greene who played Ko Ko in the FTP *Swing Mikado*. Borden argued that the mixed conventions obscured the original Orientalist references and that the primitivist staging interfered with the "genuine" Savoyard experience that relied on Orientalist depictions of Japan; Greene's portrayal of Ko Ko was seen to be especially guilty of such a failure. Borden argued that while he managed to be a "likable and genial gent" despite his "vaudeville impression" of Ko Ko, Greene failed in the role precisely because he was forced into a character convention that Borden read as incommensurate with Ko Ko's properly Orientalist qualities: "[He] is amusing in the manner of a Japanese Stepin Fetchit, but is, thanks to the direction, far from the character of the cringing little tailor that was Gilbert's Lord High Executioner."[29]

Borden attempted through her objection to maintain a rigid separation of racial groups, but director John McGee's instincts were right on the nose with respect to conflating the "cringing" qualities of the Orientalized Ko Ko with the Stepin Fetchit convention. The "cringing little tailor" Ko Ko is elevated by the people of Titipu into a social role that he cannot perform effectively and from whose social lapses much of the humor of the operetta ensues: his bumbling impersonation of aristocratic behavior serves only to emphasize his humble origins and ensures the delivery of his beloved Yum Yum into the arms of Nanki Poo (his narrative opposite: the real prince slumming as a wandering minstrel). The interpolation of Stepin Fetchit—of racist projections of black servility—into this already classist parody of social elevation, of "putting on airs," was actually quite a close fit.[30] The original parody of classist English social etiquette relied on the Orientalist stereotype of an obsession with social rank and the Western fascination with what was seen to be the Japanese terror of "loss of face."[31]

The use of black actors in *The Mikado* literalized the thinly veiled subtext of the class issues and the appetites for sex and violence that buttress its plot. The Japanese were perfect targets for a parody of sexual mores—

for example, the façade of modesty used to stereotype Japan could only cloak a rampant desire lurking barely beneath. This putative desire was manifested through the use of swing music with its associations with moral depravity and black actors who were coded as sexually lascivious from before they even took to the stage. Orientalism and primitivism were deployed as polar discourses to highlight the sense of hypocrisy surrounding sexual mores. Orientalist appetites for sex were seen to be determined by rigid social conventions, as opposed to primitivist appetites that were perceived to issue forth directly from the body without regard for social restraint. Whereas the primitive's relationship to the body is wholly without social order, the Oriental's corporeal response is rigidly determined by it.

The shifting racial identities staged in both swing *Mikado*s performed a function similar to that which Eric Lott ascribes to blackface minstrelsy: mediating heavily policed racial boundaries by staging an aversion to black and Asian Americans along with the "love and theft," in his trenchant phrase, of their cultural forms. But where antebellum blackface minstrelsy involved white men actually "blacking up"—physically inhabiting a racist fantasy of black psychic, social, and physical life—the swing *Mikado*s enacted a somewhat different phenomenon. Remaking what is in effect a yellowface performance—Gilbert and Sullivan's original *Mikado*—the swing adaptations staged white audiences watching black performers enact a combination of blackface and yellowface conventions.

The mapping of primitivist tropes onto Orientalist ones that the swing *Mikado*s enacted demonstrates the crossing of racial boundaries that Lott has argued are crucial to their separation. The historical fact, he contends, "of white men literally assuming a black self continues to occur when the lines of race *appear* both intractable and obstructive, when there emerges a collective desire (conscious or not) to bridge a gulf that is, however, *perceived* to separate the races absolutely."[32] The form of racial impersonation of the swing *Mikado*s, in which blackness was deployed to stand in for American international influence in the Asian/Pacific, eased the sense of racial instability enacted through the kind of bridging Lott describes. The black/Asian inhabitation enacted two racialized, colonialist fantasies that were played off against one another to create a pleasurable, impossible tension that produced the "joke" of the shows: imagining African Americans that could happily, unproblematically, *be* Japanese and at the same time staging a Japan that could relax and enjoy its newly black American culture. Retrospectively, the performances' own hyperbolic excesses can be seen to empty out categories of race. But the black/Asian doubling that buttressed the punch line of the performances—that the only thing more ridiculous than the Mikado is a *black* Mikado—underscored, policed, and reinvested the separation of those categories, even while offering the impossibility of ontological claims about them. The fluidity of racial crossings in these performances, of course, also points to the seemingly infinite adaptability of dominant racial strategies—strategies that are shaped and molded to confront nearly any perceived threat to racial stability and national cohesion and might.

III.

The swing *Mikado*s demonstrate not only how racial identities are historically located and underpinned by attempts at national self-conception but also that conceptions of "race" are formulated within the relationship between domestic and international racial mappings. As James Clifford argues in *Routes*, "The currency of culture and identity as performative acts can be traced to their articulation of homelands, safe spaces where the traffic across borders can be controlled. Such acts of control, maintaining coherent insides and outsides, are always tactical."[33] The tactical articulations of home in *The Swing Mikado* and *The Hot Mikado* used African American cultural forms to epitomize Americanness in the face of the racial presence of Asia that loomed off its western shores, and which seemed to offer both a threat to national coherence and the opportunity for international preeminence.

The *Mikado* adaptations of the 1930s accomplished exactly what the New Deal leaders hoped the FTP would: they brought about the amelioration of the plight of joblessness by bringing work to those without it and also were beacons of better times, by staging the fantasy of America's future across its western ocean, through their mixing of black, white, and Asian cultural forms. This optimism was manifested most clearly in the outrageous gold trousers embroidered with Chinese dragons that Nat Karson designed for Bill Robinson as the titular monarch (Figure 4). *New York Times* critic Brooks Atkinson (one of the most influential theater critics of the twentieth century) went so far as to suggest that Robinson's Mikado should be erected as the privileged American icon for the 1939 World's Fair. Atkinson argued that "probably it would be a good thing to raise a

Fig. 4. Bill Robinson as the Mikado. *The Hot Mikado.* Billy Rose Theatre Collection, The New York Public Library for the Performing Arts, Astor, Lenox and Tilden Foundations.

statue of Bill Robinson on top the Hall of Music like the rugged worker who bestrides the Soviet Pavilion. . . . Bill's eyes are as magnetic as his feet, and his pants are a dream of better times."[34]

That Robinson as the Mikado should be seen by one of the most prominent theater critics of the day as the preeminent American national symbol staged internal racial difference as an attempt to master international racial difference. The joke encoded in his performance as the black Mikado engaged a kind of reciprocal racial mapping and domination. It domesticated Japanese imperial menace by projecting it onto the spectacle of happy black Americans and simultaneously Americanized Japan by projecting the physical exhilaration of swing culture onto it. This crossing of black Atlantic and Asian/Pacific racial connotations confronted America's neocolonialist present, a crucial moment in the negotiation of shifting geopolitical power, of old versus new colonialism. The spectacle of a swinging Japan manifested the nineteenth-century European scramble for African land and transformed it into the American commercial penetration of Asia. The swing *Mikado*s, personified by Bill Robinson's magnetic feet and dreamy trousers, his tap-dancing and Orientalist costume, embodied American tenacity in the face of overwhelming bad fortune—the economic failures of the Depression, internal racial struggle, Japanese imperial menace—while simultaneously discharging these problems through the cheerful, determined march into the future, into the Asian/Pacific.This forceful, vivid, spectacular manifestation of America's black Atlantic present challenged its Asian/Pacific future head on.

NOTES

For my reconstruction of *The Hot Mikado,* I have relied largely on newspaper accounts from the scrapbook and clippings files on the show in the Billy Rose Theatre Collection at the New York Public Library for the Performing Arts (hereafter "NYPL"), container MWEZ x n.c. 15,554 and" *The Hot Mikado* 'Clippings' File." For the Federal Theater Project's *Swing Mikado,* I used the Production Bulletin file for the show located in the Federal Theater Project Archive at the Library of Congress (LCFTP).

1. Joseph Roach, *Cities of the Dead: Circum-Atlantic Performance* (New York: Columbia University Press, 1996), 4.

2. David Palumbo-Liu, *Asian/American: Historical Crossings of a Racial Frontier* (Stanford: Stanford University Press, 2000).

3. Claire Jean Kim, "The Racial Triangulation of Asian Americans," in *Asian Americans and Politics: Perspectives, Experiences, Prospects,* ed. Gordon H. Chang (Stanford: Stanford University Press, 2001).

4. The term "Asian/Pacific" here denotes the simultaneous presence of both Asian and Pacific Islander cultures, often conflated within generalized racial accounts.

5. The first and only attempt to create an American national theater, the Federal Theater Project (FTP) was beset by controversy from its inception. A branch of the Works Progress Administration (WPA), the FTP was designed to ameliorate the plight of unemployed professional theater artists across the country. Signifi-

cantly, the FTP was divided into "leagues" organized by region and by ethnic grouping. Consequently, the FTP produced "Negro" plays (of which *The Swing Mikado* was one effort), Yiddish plays, plays in the American Southwest, and others. As with the WPA generally, the FTP came under national scrutiny and was eventually dismembered for its supposed "interference" in the operation of fair marketplace competition. For more information on the FTP, see Hallie Flanagan, *Arena: The History of the Federal Theatre* (New York: Arno Press, 1980); Barry Witham, *The Federal Theatre Project: A Case Study* (New York: Cambridge University Press, 2003); Glenda Gill, *White Greasepaint on Black Performers: A Study of the Federal Theatre, 1935–1939* (New York: Peter Lang, 1988); Rena Fraden, *Blueprints for a Black Federal Theatre, 1935–1939* (New York: Cambridge University Press, 1994).

6. For the following account of the "Battle of the Black *Mikados*," I am indebted to a series of newspaper articles on the matter in the NYPL. See also Stephen M. Vallillo, "The Battle of the Black *Mikados*," *Black American Literature Forum* 16.4 (Winter 1982): 153–157.

7. For accounts of shifting U.S. immigration policies toward its Pacific Island territories, see David Palumbo-Liu, "Pacific America," in Palumbo-Liu, *Asian/ American: Historical Crossings of a Racial Frontier* (Stanford: Stanford University Press, 2000), 17–42; Lisa Lowe, *Immigrant Acts: On Asian American Cultural Politics* (Durham: Duke University Press, 1996), 1–36; for policies regarding Hawaiian residents, see Ronald Takaki, "Raising Cane," *Strangers from a Different Shore: A History of Asian Americans* (Boston: Little, Brown, 1989), 132–178.

8. See Jonathan G. Utley, *Going to War with Japan, 1937–1941* (Knoxville: University of Tennessee, 1985); Akria Iriye, *The Origins of the Second World War in Asia and the Pacific* (New York: Longman, 1987).

9. E. Franklin Frazier, "Some Effects of the Depression on the Negro in Northern Cities," in *Black Communities and Urban Development in America 1720–1990*, Vol. 6: *Depression, War, and the New Migration, 1930–1960*, ed. Kenneth L. Kusmer (New York: Garland, 1991), 17–28.

10. See *The Complete Report of Mayor LaGuardia's Commission on the Harlem Riot of March 19, 1935* (New York: Arno Press, 1963).

11. Frederick S. Roffman, "D'Oyly Carte Tradition vs. 'The Hot Mikado,'" *New York Times*, 2 May 1976, D15.

12. David W. Stowe, *Swing Changes: Big-Band Jazz in New Deal America* (Cambridge: Harvard University Press, 1994), 2–3.

13. LCFTP, Production Bulletin: *Swing It*.

14. Rena Fraden, *Blueprints for a Black Federal Theatre, 1935–1939* (New York: Cambridge University Press, 1994), 188.

15. Eric Lott reports in *Love and Theft* that souvenir programs from the minstrelsy shows frequently exhorted patrons to "refrain from requesting encores," a practice generally encouraged at the FTP performances. See Eric Lott, *Love and*

Theft: Blackface Minstrelsy and the American Working Class (New York: Oxford University Press, 1993).

16. The *Hot Mikado* altered the original more substantially. While none of the chord progressions were changed, Sullivan's entire score was put into swing time, and some of the major songs had entirely new lyrics, topically adapted for the *Hot Mikado* by Dave Greggory and William Tracy. For the most part, while altered lyrics included predictable references to current politics and celebrities (as in the revamped "Let the Punishment Fit the Crime" in which Bill Robinson sang, "Joe Louis is gotta/ Be Vice Mikado/ If I go for a third term"), the new words also attacked the class-conscious, the vain, and the snobbish. See NYPL, Souvenir Program: *Hot Mikado,* "Topical Lyrics," and LCFTP, W. S. Gilbert, script for *The Mikado.*

17. Paul Seeley, "The Japanese March in 'The Mikado,'" *Musical Times* (August 1985): 465.

18. Musicologist Michael Beckerman has argued that even Yum Yum's "The Sun, Whose Rays" (often considered the apex of English loveliness) contains elements of the Miya Sama riff in the oboe line. See Michael Beckerman, "The Sword on the Wall: Japanese Elements and Their Significance in *The Mikado,*" *Musical Quarterly* 3 (1989): 303–319.

19. Ibid., 318–319.

20. Seeley, "Japanese March," 455.

21. See Beckerman, "Sword on the Wall," 315–316. I am indebted to his work in cataloguing the violence in *The Mikado.*

22. Gilbert and Sullivan, *The Mikado,* 78.

23. Ibid., 74.

24. Ibid.

25. Ibid., 53–54.

26. Ibid., 52–53.

27. See Beckerman, "Sword on the Wall," 305, for a similar suggestion that "the general fascination for the Oriental which prevailed during the nineteenth century . . . remains a lively but largely underexplored facet of the Romantic Movement."

28. For a more detailed analysis of the Savoy Ballroom as a site at which black and white racial tensions were mediated, see Brenda Dixon Gottschild, *Waltzing in the Dark: African American Vaudeville and Race Politics in the Swing Era* (New York: St. Martin's, 2000), 71–75.

29. LCFTP, Gail Borden, "Negro Unit Jazzes up Opera 'Mikado.'"

30. See Eric Lott, "Stepin Fetchit," in *The Oxford Companion to African-American Literature,* ed. William L. Andrews et al. (New York: Oxford University Press, 1997), 697.

31. Dorinne Kondo has noted the idea of "face" as "the stereotypic 'Oriental' trope, signifying a presumed Asian preoccupation with social reputation." See

Dorinne Kondo, *About Face: Performing Race in Fashion and Theater* (New York: Routledge, 1997), 24–26.

32. Eric Lott, "White Like Me: Racial Cross-Dressing and the Construction of American Whiteness," in *Cultures of United States Imperialism,* ed. Amy Kaplan and Donald Pease (Durham: Duke University Press, 1993), 475.

33. James Clifford, *Routes: Travel and Translation in the Late Twentieth Century* (Cambridge: Harvard University Press, 1997), 7.

34. Brooks Atkinson, "The Play: Bojangles Robinson and 'The Hot Mikado' Take a Trip to the World's Fair," *New York Times,* 23 June 1939, 26; emphasis mine.

Chapter 10

Black Bodies/Yellow Masks

The Orientalist Aesthetic in Hip-Hop and Black Visual Culture

Deborah Elizabeth Whaley

I remember my brother and his friends, after seeing the movie *Revenge of the Dragon,* sport "num-chucks." It became popular to be around Asians. Bruce Lee represented the underdog in his films. He was the David fighting against the white male Goliath who had privilege and position. My brother and his friends attached themselves to the idea of Bruce Lee and what he represented.
> —Black American artist Deborah Grant, 2004

We had no role models for finding identity. We followed what the blacks did. Within the whole Asian American identity, part of the black identity came with it. Usually when you say Asian American, you are going to have some aspect of the Black experience, too.
> —Japanese American activist Rie Aoyama, 1995

In the fall of 2004, a subsidiary of Music Television (MTV), Video Hits One (VH1), aired a special on the top new trends in music video. Among the program's top one hundred, one could watch the reoccurring use of Asian culture among hip-hop musicians in their videos. While commentators cited signs of Asian ethnicity as now "hot" in the twenty-first century for rap and R&B artists alike, there was an acknowledgement of its use in early music video as well, such as in 1980's punk rock musicians The Vapors' "Turning Japanese" video.[1] The Vapors' video is visually and linguistically startling. While swaggering a sword in front of women dressed as Japanese geishas, the group members sing: "I think I'm turning 'Jap-a-nese-a,' I think I'm turning 'Jap-a-nese-a,' I really think so . . . no sex, no drugs, no wine, no women . . . everyone around me is a total stranger, everyone around me looks like a cyclone ranger, everyone." There was also mention in the VH1 special of Madonna's video for the song "Nothing Matters," where she performs in the wardrobe of a Japanese geisha, and R. Kelly's video for "Thoia Thoing," where he performs as a Japanese warrior. Most of the commentary on the VH1 special remained in the realm of tongue and cheek comedy concerning pop and hip-hop artists' appropriation or sampling of Asian and Middle Eastern music. However, one commentator went from jest to racial stereotype when he looked into the camera while making suggestive phallic movements and said, "I think it's odd that Black guys are trying to make themselves Asian in music video because you know the thing about Black guys. And, you know the thing about Asian guys. All I can say is they've lost their minds." Here, the white commentator's phallic fantasy serves as an example of the sexual views of Black and Asian men in popular imagination. Through the Occidental gaze, both groups are objects of racial and sexual misrepresentation in various forms of minstrelsy for the masturbatory consumption of the dominant culture. Yet, it seems that while blackface minstrelsy is largely a part of popular culture's shameful past, or is at least seen as unacceptable, playing Asian, also known as "yellowface," is gaining enormous momentum in popular music, especially in hip-hop music and Black visual culture.

This essay explores the tactical performance and representation of the imagined "Oriental" in hip-hop and Black visual culture. I am especially concerned with the epistemological and material consequences of Orientalism in the realm of ideas (theory) and Black American and Asian American social relations. The music video, art, and film examples explore how and why facets of what cultural critic Edward Said theorizes as Orientalism is a reoccurring trope in contemporary Black visual culture.[2] For Said, Orientalism constitutes the projection of white European ideologies onto people of Middle Eastern and Asian descent. Orientalism in practice attaches itself to binaries of the Western hemisphere as civilized, pure, chaste, and democratic versus the Eastern hemisphere as uncivilized, exotic, hypersexual, and authoritarian in order to rationalize the subjugation of an imagined Orient. I thus examine how and why claimed knowledge of "Asianness" constructed as Other and aesthetic constructions of things perceived as Asian in the Black, popular imaginary, may or may not result in a different power effect as compared with its typical use and deployment in mass culture by the dominant U.S. culture.[3] The tactical performance of the "Oriental" not only poses a representational dilemma replete with contradictory racial, ethnic, and national signifiers but also opens up questions about the multiple meanings of its precarious usage by Black Americans who perform these images.

Dimensions of AfroAsian cultural productions are a growing area of popular culture studies, Asian American studies, and Africana studies. However, the majority of this work focuses on facets of shared cultural production, such as hybridity and multiplicity, or the Asian appropriation and rearticulation of hip-hop culture. Conversely, while there is an immense amount of scholarly work on the performance of blackface minstrelsy and facets of Orientalism by the dominant culture, the performative characterization of Asian racial and ethnic groups by Black Americans remains underexamined in the literature. Textual examples of Orientalism in hip-hop and Black visual culture provide speculative answers to the following questions. If the tactical use of Orientalism reifies white identity in its European/Anglo deployment and renders Asian and Asian American subjects fetishized and marginalized in representation, what is one to make of this representational projection by the Black subject? Given the subjugation of Black Americans within hegemonic power relations and the assumption of our identity as always-already stable and fixed, what does it mean when Black hip-hop musicians seek to obscure their Black skin with yellow masks? If the presentation of Orientalism in Black visual culture mirrors misrepresentations by the dominant culture, is their performance only a matter of representational racism? Does the construction of the "Oriental" in Black visual culture obstruct or help to facilitate solidarity and cultural crossroads between people of Asian and African descent in the United States?

To begin, I explore the phenomenon of Black bodies wearing yellow masks in contemporary music video as a process of racial skinning.[4] The performance of racial skinning in Black music videos appears to work as a venture in repairing a fragmented identity that allows Black bodies to create and consume Eastern exotica free from the perceived confines of racialized Blackness. While a significant number of popular Black musicians construct and project Orientalism in hip-hop music video via yellowface, Asian American and Black American artists in the 2004 exhibition *Black Belt* seek to rearticulate and fracture such Orientalist iconography, thereby creating oppositional viewpoints and subjects. In the final example I consider the narrative of the film *Romeo Must Die* (2000), which grapples with the problems that arise when Black Americans, Chinese, and Chinese Americans seek to transgress racial-ethnic barriers in alliance. *Romeo Must Die* presses beyond the polemic and transformative art showcased in *Black Belt,* as it illustrates how Orientalism and pathological ideologies of Blackness obscure racial and ethnic understanding and continuously rupture the potential for sustained alliances between people of the Asian and African diaspora. The goal of this essay is therefore textual and material, insofar as I extract representations from three forms of visual culture —music representation, material culture, and film—to articulate Black American and Asian American cultural, political, and social crossroads. An exploration of these various cultural forms allows for an interrogation of how people of African descent via mass-produced production invoke Asia as a signifier to fulfill Occidental desires. More than an unmasking of such forms of representation, the intent of this interrogation is also to reveal how the very same forms of cultural production—that is, visual and hip-hop culture—can exist as a formable site of transformation within the realm of representation and in social relations.

I. Racial Skinning and the Performance of Orientalism in Hip-Hop Music Videos

In the "Oriental Mirage," Roger Benjamin argues that Orientalists or those who use claimed knowledge of the East to construct visual representations of the imaginary Orient, usually end up producing an illusory image of their created, exotic Other.[5] Throughout history and in art, performance, and the cinema, the employment of yellowface and an Orientalist aesthetic conjures gender-specific caricatures of Asia embedded within the popular imagination.[6] As cultural critic Lisa Lowe writes, the ramifications of such presentations may shape public policy and fuel a sentiment of Asian Americans as foreign Others.[7] The calculated Orientalist aesthetic in recent Black music videos draws on four primary strands of representation akin to the Orientalist aesthetic and Oriental mirage: (1) the sexualized, yet virginal Japanese geisha; (2) the South Asian Indo-chic;[8] (3) the Chinese kung fu warrior; and (4) the use of Asian languages as an iconographic fashion statement detached from specificity of meaning and etymological usage.

Depictions of these representations are abundant in hip-hop. For example, in the music video "Girls, Girls, Girls," rapper Jay Z serenades a group of women inside the hallway of a squalid, urban hotel. In the video, Jay Z stands next to a woman of Asian descent who wears a red silk dress with a dragon appliqué on the side, while he raps the following lyrics: "I had this Chinese chick, but I had to leave her quick, because she kept bootlegging my shit." Rapper Busta Rhymes' and singer Mariah Carey's "All that I Want" video takes the viewer inside what appears to be a brothel, where Rhymes receives an erotic massage by several scantily clad women who are physically marked as Asian. In Mya's "Me and You," Monica's "Just Another Girl," and RES's "Vision," the three R&B performers dress as Japanese geishas while performing seductively on stage. Mya, Monica, and RES wear kimonos, chopsticks in their hair, and exaggerated eyeliner to emphasize an almond eye shape, and they mimic rhythmic movements associated with geisha performance. Hip-hop's Truth Hurts's "Contagious" and the queen of hip-hop Mary J. Blige's "You Are My Everything" invoke trendy Indo-chic by mixing Middle Eastern and South Asian iconography as the setting for their videos and as their choice of wardrobe. Blige wears a jewel on her forehead, henna tattoos, and a sari, while Hurts belly dances, wearing a *bedleh*[9] alongside a group of similarly dressed women in a harem. The hip-hop and R&B group TLC wear yellowface in their music video "Girls Are Talking," where singers T-Boz and Chili mask as "Asian" women as they travel through the settings of several Third World countries.

Female rapper Missy Misdemeanor Elliott's video "I'm Really Hot" uses the setting of a mythical Chinatown as a dangerous excursion to violence, fantasy, and sexuality. For Elliott's video, two groups of androgynously styled women of African and Asian descent have white painted makeup on their faces, wear black and red tuxedos, and engage in a karate duel. Elliott's video is more complicated and contradictory than the ones of her hip-hop peers, insofar as the visual signifiers she uses blur racial and gender identities. Her video re-creation of the kung fu film genre also places women, as opposed to men, at the center of its narrative, which creates a departure from the ways the genre has historically displaced female subjects. Despite the transgressive and reconstructive gender and racial signs in Elliott's video, Orientalism still wreaks havoc via a visual iconography of sporadic signs of Asian language characters and the use of Chinatown as an ethnic and geographic periphery.

One might deconstruct these music videos in terms of their multiple meanings and various audience receptions and come to less strident conclusions. However, given that these and many other hip-hop artists mimic people and cultures of the Asian diaspora via Black yellowface exclusively, without any representations of other ethnic groups in these popular Black music videos, their performances lean strongly toward calculated Orientalism. In all of these instances, the performers do not work through Black identity, as Fanon observed about Black identity fragmentation and formation, via a white mask but, rather, via a yellow mask.[10] So, what are we to make of this mask? As many scholars in cultural studies and studies of consumption have shown, the dominant culture consumes Black culture in excess, while at the same time actively denying that Black Americans have a distinct culture. Theorist Melville Herskovitz explains this as the "myth of Negro past," where the dominant culture renders African-derived and Black cultural forms invisible in order to promote the cultural hegemony of the white power structure.[11] Cultural critics Vijay Prashad and Robert G. Lee argue separately in their texts on Asian American cultural production and popular representation that although history construes Black Americans as having no culture or as having lost their culture with the slave trade, in contrast, history depicts Asian Americans, especially Chinese Americans, as inhabiting an abundance of culture.[12] Black Americans and Chinese Americans share a history of being the objects of racial and ethnic parody in the nineteenth century through the minstrel performances of Euro-ethnics. Yet, for Black hip-hop musicians in the twenty-first century, Black-yellowface works as a conduit through which Asian ethnic representations—however distorted—stand in for a naïve sense of a romanticized culture positioned outside of the Otherness of Blackness.

The cultural skinning and masking as seen in these music videos serve two primary purposes. For male music artists such as Busta Rhymes and Jay Z, Orientalism's Passive Doll and Dragon Lady obviously provide the fulfillment of sexual fantasy. Black women musicians like Mary J. Blige, Truth Hurts, and TLC, however, appear to use yellowface as a timeless racialized mask to travel through other worlds—whether geographically or sexually—as an imagined, hyperfeminine, and sexual Other. Conversely, for artists such as Mya, Monica, and RES, the Japanese geisha performance provides a sexualized space never afforded to Black women in popular representation: that is, as simultaneously a sexual object and as chaste. While popular culture depicts Black women as Jezebels, Sapphires, and Mammies, rarely has the popular imaginary shown them as at once virginal and as an object of sexual desire. This representation of the Japanese geisha has salience in Black music video because the other stagnate representations of Asian American women are too parallel to those of Black women. In the popular imagination, hypersexual Jezebel parallels Suzy Wong; Sapphire is just as bitchy, evil, and conniving as Dragon Lady; and Mammy is as sacrificing, passive, and asexual as the Asian American female servant.[13] Perhaps not transparent in the multiple meanings behind Black male and female musicians' performance of the Orientalist aesthetic in music video is what is at stake concerning this form of racial, ethnic, and gender parody.

Although problematic, I am less concerned with these artists' propagation of stereotypes than I am interested in the purpose these representations serve for hip-hop musicians and audiences. To typify a group based on exaggerated, distorted, and stagnant characteristics is certainly troubling. Yet, what concerns me here is how these specific representations of Orientalism collide with ideas of Blackness in the popular imagination, and how they shape the construction of Black popular identity in visual culture and in social relations. Although it may not appear on the surface that these forms of parody are intended for racist consumption like white Americans' blackface and yellowface minstrelsy, these representations, like other forms of Orientalism, fantasize, project, and marginalize vis-à-vis parochial signs of the East, regardless of the actual diversity and heterogeneity of Asian and Asian American people.[14] In their racialized performance of ethnic caricatures, Black yellowface in music videos does not provide new ways of seeing and enacting social relations between people of the Asian and African diaspora. Their use does not contribute to, connect to, or even pretend to unite with the existing struggles of people of Asian descent or to understand the culture that is the object of the parody and consumption. Rather, Black musicians' yellowface provides the dream of culture without a perceived consequence—one naively construed as untouched by whiteness and imperialism through a distorted Black popular imaginary.

It is probable that many overlook these tropes of Orientalism because the musicians' Blackness appears to provide a free cultural pass into the East in a way that makes such traveling appear as a benign form of cultural borrowing of one marginalized group from another marginalized group. Black musicians' yellowface indirectly contributes to the power relations that seek to relegate Asians and Asian Americans as perpetual foreigners. Further, their bodies repeatedly act as instruments to perform typical forms of Orientalism that the dominant culture has propagated as natural and audiences view as pleasurable. As cultural critic George Lipsitz argues, "Nonwhite people can become active agents of white supremacy as well as passive participants to its hierarchies and rewards. One way of becoming an insider is by participating in the exclusion of other outsiders."[15] In view of this, the means by which people of the Asian and African diaspora invoke counternarratives to Orientalism's popular mischief becomes increasingly vital to examine.

II. Whose Ice Is Colder?: AfroAsian Corridors and Contestation

In juxtaposition to the general deployment of Orientalism in hip-hop music video, the Studio Museum of Harlem's (SMH) exhibition *Black Belt* provides shifting and contradictory racial and ethnic signifiers that convene to render race unintelligible, the Black and Asian American subject unmarked through hybrid masquerade, and Western imperialism unstable. SMH's curator Christine Kim explains that the exhibition places Black American fascination with kung fu, Asian American fascination with hip-hop, and the cross-pollination of cultural moves across and between the Black and Asian diaspora at its center.[16] The installations work singularly and as a whole to suggest cultural mixing and borrowing as a means by which complicated and new understandings of identity replace the Orientalist's colonialist fantasies.

Black Belt displays the work of artist Iona Rozeal Brown, for example, who pictures defiant subjects in brownface. The brown mask only partially covers the subjects' faces, revealing prototypical markers of Orientalism—for example, the Japanese geisha as seen through Western eyes— mixed with hip-hop iconography and insurgent Black youth oppositional stances. In Brown's painting "Blackface #0.50" (2001), a geisha in brownface looks matter of factly at the spectator and raises her middle finger, while another woman shyly hides behind her with the same dress and style. Another geisha figure in "Blackface #3" (2002) dons an afro with two protruding afro combs emerging from each side of the woman's head to suggest urban, Black, and Asian cultural crossroads. "Down-Ass Emperor Qianlong" (2003) presents a young male wearing a combination of emperor and hip-hop clothing, such as a gold embroidered and richly red satin cape, box hat, Fubu t-shirt, braided hair, baggy jeans, sneakers, and a silver chain with a Korean character charm, while he slumps in an ornate chair that rests on an "Oriental" rug. The subject's gestures and his body language are obviously aggressive; his facial expression disrupts any pleasure a spectator might take in the typical fantasy gaze at Orientalism. Brown's images use racial markers, but neither of these subjects bears markings of one stagnant racial interpretation. Instead, Brown's paintings use and mix stereotypes, Asian ethnic signs, and hip-hop culture to remark on the complex histories of imperialism and cultural appropriation within Black and Asian cultural configurations. In so doing, Brown creates interethnic corridors into the diverse and global subculture of hip-hop. Since there is a blurring of the ethnic configuration of the subjects via brownface in the artist's work, the mixture of ethnic markers, such as Asian and Black, and the mixture of cultural forms, such as hip-hop and Asian ethnicities, create new, rather than timeless, subjects for spectators.

In his installation "The Art of the Battle" (2003), artist Rico Gaston uses photographic frames of Bruce Lee, Mohammed Ali, rappers Nas and LL Cool J, burning crosses, Black stereotypes, and snapshots of children with boxing gloves to fuse various forms of Asian and Black political struggle. In the photos, red is the background color, which intimates an oppositional stance of anger. Gaston's collage of digital photos, according to the artist, creates an unapologetic political challenge to other forms of political art by using images of stereotypes and resistance as "sonic cadences."[17] David Chung's "Study for Bruce" (2003), David Dao's "Twin Dragons" (2000), and Patty Chang's "Death of the Game" (2000) use different mediums—watercolor, sketch art, and digital media—to claim Bruce Lee as an iconic figure of double consciousness and kung fu as a site of Black and Asian political contestation. The three pieces illustrate how kung fu films can at once unite people across the Asian/African diaspora, while at the same time presenting how, in many of these films, the two groups were in competition with each other and became pawns of white colonialist manipulation. The latter artists' resurrection of actor and martial arts artist Bruce Lee recognizes Asian American masculinity in comparative opposition to Dr. Fu Manchu and Charlie Chan caricatures. The three art pieces refigure Lee in terms of a strategic gender identity that negotiates hegemonic masculinity, engages in the politics of ethnic affirmation, and defies the asexual or sexualized gaze projected on Bruce Lee throughout his career.[18] In *Black Belt*, Bruce Lee is often the iconic subject repositioned as a political sign that struggles to divorce itself from Western imperialism and colonialist notions of Asia, Asian Americans, and their subsequent subjugation in the United States.

In Glenn Kaino's painting "Bruce Leroy's Kung Fu Theater" (2000), Afro-Asian corridors and contestation are productively reconstituted through the cultural politics of articulation.[19] In his piece, Kaino uses the name of a character from the 1985 Black/Asian kung fu film *The Last Dragon*, Bruce Leroy, in a strategic manner. While the name suggests ethnic and masculine fusing, Kaino's use of the name in his piece, which rests on a marquee with bright lights along a square parameter, implies performative questions: Are Black and Asian identities a theatrical spectacle on display for the dominant U.S. culture? Are kung fu films the stage where Blacks and Asians resist or acquiesce to the dominant culture? In a roundtable conversation with SMH artists, Kaino reflects about his participation in the *Black Belt* exhibition and answers the question that "Bruce Leroy's Kung Fu Theater" indirectly poses when he confesses: "I've been considering, in my artwork, how, within this postmodern culture of recycling, referencing, and sampling, we can actually be progressive." Kaino then remarks how exhibitions such as *Black Belt* walk a thin line between contestation and nostalgic voyeurism by asking, "How can we create new ideas and meanings in a way that doesn't fall back to an old cycle, where we repeat our past mistakes at the price of giving old, bankrupt ideas a second run?"[20] For Kaino, then, the recycling of kung fu icons and characters provides a window into how this genre created connections between Black Americans and Asian Americans. At the same time, Kaino is self-reflexive about the potential lack of change in their discursive deployment; therefore, he asks artists and spectators to acknowledge the unpredictable effects of these images' circulation.

Taken as a whole, *Black Belt* reframes Orientalism and repositions Black and Asian subjects as participants in a complex popular history rather than as blank canvases waiting for Western Orientalism to inscribe its masturbatory fantasies of the East onto its surface. Indeed, the visualization of *Black Belt*'s cultural work is artfully present in David Hammons's installation "Whose Ice Is Colder?" (1991). In this installation, Hammons juxtaposes a simile of an American flag painted in red, black, and green with the Korean flag. The flags hang above blocks of dry ice, and their parallel positioning resurrects signs of Black and Korean nationalism. Hammons's installation questions the utility of weighing oppression and counterproductive competition between Black Americans and Korean Americans—henceforth the title "Whose Ice Is Colder?" The experiences of Black and Korean Americans, Hammons's installation suggests, cannot move toward the politics of liberation represented in the imagery of the flags if they continue to exhibit an identity politics of resentment and rivalry. The ice blocks underneath the two flags are equal in size and temperature. It is up to the people who comprise the social relations behind the imagery to shift away from the type of racial skinning seen in hip-hop music videos and pass the strife acted out between the two groups in urban locations. The cultural work of *Black Belt* thus emanates from all of the artists' ability to redistribute signs of Orientalism and combine Asian and Black cultural forms to point to the possibilities of those signs to also create an emancipatory cultural politics of race, ethnicity, sexuality, class, and nation.

III. Lessons from a Second Daughter and First Son: Afro-Orientalism in the Wake of Kung-Fusion

I conclude with a brief analysis of the film *Romeo Must Die*, which is a film that visualizes the work necessary for the political articulation in social relations that *Black Belt* presents to spectators through art and that elides the makers of, and performers in, hip-hop music videos. Ron Silver, the producer of the *Matrix* series, masterminded *Romeo Must Die*. In an interview, Ron Silver shares that the film is a modern-day, hip-hop *Romeo and Juliet* story that matches the action scenes of the *Matrix* and reveals what happens when two cultures, in this case the East and the West, meet.[21] Significant about this statement is that for Silver, Black Americans and hip-hop culture signify the West, and Chinese Americans in the United States signify the East. This suggests that, despite citizenship and generational status, the popular imagination creates ways of seeing people of the Asian diaspora as perpetual foreigners, even in the minds of those with the best of intentions to produce a counternarrative. Further, Silver's reference to hip-hop as a signifier for Western hemispheric culture reveals his perception of the subculture as an assimilative commodity detached from its African and Latino diasporic center. Still, *Romeo Must Die* shows how, in the midst of kung-fusion, collisions between Black Americans, Chinese, and Chinese Americans do not easily translate into political allies, but how under the right circumstance—as the word "articulation" suggests—they could form meaningful alliances.[22]

The film's narrative concerns the economic and territorial competition between a wealthy Black American family, the O'Days, and a wealthy Chinese family, the Sings, in Oakland, California. Both families own equal parts of waterfront property in downtown Oakland until a white business conglomerate approaches the two families to sell their property for $360 million in order to build an NFL football field stadium and sports center. To make this happen, both sides must also convince the surrounding Chinese American and Black American businesses to sell their property. The two families thus set about the work of destroying their own communities and the livelihood of their people in order to vie for the monetary payoff promised by the white conglomerate. In the midst of their dealings, sons of both families—Po Sing (Jon Kit Lee) and Collin O'Day (D. B. Woodside)—end up dead, and it appears on the surface that each group is responsible for the other's loss. Soon after, the first son of Mr. Choy (Henry O), Han (Jet Li), and the second daughter of Mr. O'Day (Delroy Lindo), Trish (late hip-hop singer Aaliyah), begin a friendship in the name of finding out who is responsible for each of the families' losses. Their tenuous relationship deteriorates with the demise of Po and Collin, which incites paranoia and distrust in the minds of both camps, thus resulting in an all-out war between them and a consecrated effort to keep Trish and Han apart. As the film ends, the spectator learns that, fueled by jealousy and insecurity, Mr. O'Day's right-hand man Mack (Isaiah Washington) killed Collin, and Mr. Sing's right-hand man Kai (Russell Wong) killed Po. Mack had viewed Collin as an obstacle to his promotion within the O'Day family, and Kai had felt that Po would be unable to take on the responsibilities of the Sing family business.

Romeo Must Die is a throwback to the kung fu films of yesteryear made modern by glossy cinematography, computer-enhanced action scenes, and a slick hip-hop soundtrack. The story between the Sings and the O'Days is not a new one; the power structure manipulates the two groups, and members within their own camp are able to deceive them for reasons encouraged by envy and an insatiable thirst for power. Mack and Kai are able to deceive those in their community because the two families fail to realize that they are likely more productive as partners in struggle than as enemies in competition for the scraps of modern capitalism offered by the dominant white power structure. To their detriment, the O'Days and Sings only work together to the extent where they would benefit and not challenge each other to give up or share power and resources. There is no respect between the two cultures, and there is no attempt to mend the circumstances that keep their people in a subjugated position. The camps do exactly what modern capitalism and its proponents wish for them to do: to destroy each other, thus making it impossible to work side by side in struggle, and to deny each other's humanity, thus remaining embittered and embattled economic and social enemies.

Black Belt exhibition contributor Latasha Nevada Diggs bemoaned the anticlimatic love story between Trish and Han, and film and cultural critic Cynthia Fuchs's review of the film interprets the economic rivalry between the two families as implausible. Comparatively, cultural critic James Kim explains *Romeo Must Die*'s polarization of Black American, Chinese, and Chinese American men by arguing that the film displays the former through the lens of distorted hypermasculinity, while the latter succumbs to symbolic castration that presents itself in the form of Asian/Asian American male helplessness.[23] The film is not without problematic gender representations and narrative liberties, although in many instances, *Romeo Must Die* transgresses as much as it contains. On the one hand, women are scantily clad sexual objects in nightclubs; on the other hand, they are independent subjects who collaborate with men on both ends of the social justice crusade. Asian characters remain within the parameters of stagnant tradition (Mr. Sing), are ill prepared in the throes of modernism (Han), or are often punished for crossing racial and sexual borders (Po). Many of the Black American male characters are excessively violent (Mack), yet others are multidimensional (Mr. O'Day and Collin).

Despite *Romeo Must Die*'s murky forms of representation, a metacritique of social relations depicted in the film—however imperfect in terms of its narrative structure—is fruitful. As cultural critic Herman Gray argues, analyses of popular culture must press beyond issues of inclusion, representation, and identity to grasp "how culture matters politically and how politics matter culturally."[24] As Mack tells Han in a physical altercation, "Listen, Romeo, it's been fun and all, but now, you gotta die." In other words, through a postmodern prism, the answer to their predicament does not exist within a romance, positive representations of Black Americans, Chinese, and Chinese Americans or romantic notions of unity between Black Americans and Asian Americans. *Romeo Must Die* illustrates that AfroAsian alliances must be more than strategic; they must exist as defiant to the power structure and *maneuver* strategically.

If, as Stuart Hall writes, "hegemonizing is hard work," then the counter-hegemonic implications of an AfroAsian bloc similarly requires constant hard work, reiteration, and affirmation.[25] The result of this would disrupt current forms of Black American Orientalism and begin the work of producing its revolutionary counterpart: an Afro-Orientalism. Such a formation would draw and learn from our shared and divergent histories, political cleavages and political alliances, and cultural exchanges and cultural standoffs to make the world anew for historically marginalized peoples.[26] Unlike Orientalism, Afro-Orientalism uses a part of the troublesome namesake (i.e., Orientalism) as a signifying practice to infer a critical mode of thought and action in defiance to Western Occidentalism. Cultural critic Bill Mullen describes Afro-Orientalism as constituting new and transformative social relations between people of the Asian and African diasporas to the ends of long-term social change. In the wake of kung-fusion, a move toward Afro-Orientalism would demand a fundamental movement away from the Black bodies and yellow masks of music video, would press beyond the hybrid representations of AfroAsian popular culture seen in *Black Belt,* and would intervene in the toxic social relations that the film *Romeo Must Die* reveals as our downfall.

NOTES

1. Several other examples of Orientalism in music video include the punk rock group Red Rockers' video for their song "China," rock musician David Bowie's "China Girl," and Sting's recent collaboration with Algerian singer Cheb Mami in the video for the song "Dessert Rose," where visual and audible signs of Asia serve as ethnic spice.

2. Edward Said, *Orientalism* (New York: Pantheon, 1978).

3. Black popular culture consists of cultural products made, produced, and disseminated by Black people or products with largely, although not exclusively, a Black and/or urban audience in mind. On definitions of Black popular culture, see Stuart Hall, "What Is This 'Black' in Black Popular Culture?," in *Black Popular Culture,* ed. Gina Dent (Boston: Beacon Press, 1994); Gena Caponi, *Signifying, Sanctifying, and Slam Dunking: A Reader in African American Expressive Culture* (Amherst: University of Massachusetts Press, 1999).

4. I use the term "skinning" to define a process of appropriating cultural forms in isolation of their relevant cultural, social, and political meanings and contexts. Skinning, therefore, represents the separation of a cultural form from its cultural function.

5. Roger Benjamin, *Orientalism: Delacroix to Klee* (Auckland City: Art Gallery of New South Wales, 1997), 7.

6. See Jachinson Chan, *Chinese American Masculinities: From Fu Manchu to Bruce Lee* (New York: Routledge 1999); Sonia Shah et al., *Dragon Ladies: Asian American Feminists Breathe Fire* (Boston: Beacon Press, 1999); Robert G. Lee, *Orientals: Asian Americans in Popular Culture* (Philadelphia: Temple University Press, 1999).

7. See Lisa Lowe, *Immigrant Acts: On Asian American Cultural Production* (Durham: Duke University Press, 1996).

8. On the commodification of South Asian music and ethnicity, see Sunaina Maira, "Henna and Hip Hop: The Politics of Cultural Production and the Work of Cultural Studies," *Journal of Asian American Studies* 3.3 (2000): 329–369. See also an essay by Kevin Miller, "Bollyhood Remix," which is available on the Institute for Studies in American Popular Music website, http://depthome.brooklyn.cuny.edu/ isam/S04Newshtml/Bollyhood/Bollyhood.htm (retrieved 20 February 2004).

9. A *bedleh* is the traditional clothing worn by belly dancers. In Arabic, the word *bedleh* means suit. This style of dress generally consists of a beaded bra, belt, and long, flaired, chiffon skirt.

10. Frantz Fanon, *Black Skins/White Masks* (New York: Grove Press, 1991).

11. Melville Herskovitz, *Myth of the Negro Past* (Boston: Beacon Press, 1958).

12. Vijay Prashad, *Everybody Was Kung Fu Fighting: Afro-Asian Connections and the Myth of Cultural Purity* (Boston: Beacon Press, 2001); see also Lee, *Orientals.*

13. On these representations, see Shah, *Dragon Ladies*; see also Mary E. Young, *Mules and Dragons* (New York: Greenwood Press, 1993).

14. On blackface minstrelsy, see Eric Lott, *Love and Theft* (Oxford: Oxford University Press, 1995); David Roediger, *The Wages of Whiteness: Race and the Making of the American Working Class* (New York: Verso, 1999). On yellowface minstrelsy, especially minstrelsy directed at Chinese American men, see John Kuo Wei Tchen, "Believing Is Seeing: Transforming Orientalisms and the Occidental Gaze," in *Asian/America: Identities in Contemporary Asian American Art*, ed. Margo Machida, Vioshakha desai, and John Tchen (New York: Asia Society Galleries, 1994), 12–25.

15. George Lipsitz, *The Possessive Investment in Whiteness* (Philadelphia: Temple University Press, 1998), viii.

16. Christine Y. Kim, "Afro as I Am," in *Black Belt*, ed. Christine Kim (New York: Studio Museum in Harlem, 2004), 27.

17. Rico Gaston, "The Art of the Battle," in *Black Belt*, ed. Christine Kim (New York: Studio Museum in Harlem, 2004), 42.

18. On Chinese American masculinity, stereotypes, and the cultural and masculine signs of Bruce Lee, see Chan, *Chinese American Masculinities*, 73–95.

19. "Articulation" describes the process of two different entities, which, at specific historical moments, may converge to create a new social process that has the possibility to provide divergent or new meanings. On the theory of articulation, see Jennifer Slack, "The Theory and Method of Articulation in Cultural Studies," in *Stuart Hall: Critical Dialogues in Cultural Studies,* ed. David Morley and Kuan-Hsing Chen (New York: Routledge, 1996).

20. Glenn Kaino, "Roundtable Conversation," in *Black Belt,* ed. Christine Kim (New York: Studio Museum in Harlem, 2004), 17.

21. Silver makes this statement in the special edition DVD set interview: *Romeo Must Die,* dir. Andrzej Bartkowiak (Warner Home Video, 2000).

22. I borrow the term "kung-fusion" from Prashad, *Everybody Was Kung Fu Fighting.*

23. James Kim, *"The Legend of the White-and-Yellow Black Man: Global Containment and Triangulated Racial Desire in* Romeo Must Die," *Camera Obscura* 19.1 (Fall 2001): 152.

24. Herman Gray, *Cultural Moves: African Americans and the Politics of Representation* (Berkeley: University of California Press, 2005), 3.

25. Stuart Hall, "For Allon White: Metaphors of Transformation," in *Stuart Hall: Critical Dialogues in Cultural Studies,* ed. David Morley and Kuan-Hsing Chen (New York: Routledge, 1996).

26. On the meaning of Afro-Orientalism, see Bill Mullen, *Afro-Orientalism* (Minneapolis: University of Minnesota Press, 2004), xv–xvi. Mullen theorizes Afro-Orientalism as an ideological intervention and as a practice of shared political action in the name of cultural and social transformation.

Chapter 11

The *Rush Hour* of Black/Asian Coalitions?
Jackie Chan and Blackface Minstrelsy

Mita Banerjee

Hollywood has always had a vexed relationship to the history of ethnic communities in the United States. There is a strange ambivalence in Hollywood classics introducing—and hence mainstreaming—ethnic presences on what might well be defined as a white screen. The appearance in the 1930s of Charlie Chan, the "Oriental" detective, signaled at once Hollywood's recognition of an Asian presence in the United States and its containment of this presence in terms of ethnic stereotype. Jessica Hagedorn describes this stereotypical figure of Charlie Chan as the "inscrutable, wily Chinese detective with his taped eyelids and wispy mustache. . . . The sexless, hairless Asian male. . . . Yellow peril. Fortune Cookie Psychic. . . . Invisible. Mute."[1] In the character of Charlie Chan, the dominant culture's dismissal of Asian men's "effeminacy" converged with the beginnings of the idea of the model minority even though this term—historically— would not emerge in U.S. political rhetoric until three decades later. Hollywood may thus well be considered a litmus test of immigrant presences registering in popular culture. It is the ambivalence between presence and containment, between real immigrant and Hollywood simulacrum, with which this essay is concerned. Given this tension between the material and the celluloid image of ethnicity, I propose that films such as *Rush Hour* (1998) can be deconstructed by reading them through alternative discourses such as mural art, an art in which interethnic coalitions are politicized and not only, as in *Rush Hour*'s narrative, commodified.

Rush Hour revolves around the uneasy coalition between Carter, an African American policeman who is not taken seriously even by his own colleagues, and Lee, a Chinese cop who has been sent to the United States to rescue Hong Kong Consul Han's daughter, who has been kidnapped by an Asian gang. The film's humor is drawn from the fact that Carter and Lee are being forced by police and government officials to team up against their own will and better judgment. The film pivots on their ability to turn this necessity into a virtue of black/Asian coalitions.

Incidentally, even Charlie Chan had a sidekick, and it is by no means a coincidence that this sidekick was a black imbecile. From the very beginning, then, Hollywood has "simulated" Asian characters, as well as the possibility of their coalitions with other ethnic groups, especially African Americans. Even in Charlie Chan, the Oriental model minority (*avant la lettre*) takes shape against an idiotic blackface. It is this differentiation in presence—and in the degree of mainstreaming—that in turn marks the screen as white. The referent of this coalition continues to be the dominant community, which remains unseen—a community whose crimes are solved by an Asian detective whose condescension toward his black sidekick mirrors the dominant culture's own.

Both Chan's and his black sidekick's registering on the American screen, I argue, must be seen in terms of the filmic narrative's indebtedness to a fundamental—and fundamentally racist—theatrical form: the performance of minstrelsy. What is crucial here is that films such as *Charlie Chan and the Jade Mask* indicate the simultaneity of blackface and yellowface minstrelsy. What is even more crucial, however, is that the Asian character's straining of the confines of the minstrel form is enabled by the black character's adhesion to and his entrapment in minstrelsy in its most traditional form. It is hence interesting to explore the tension between blackface and yellowface minstrelsy. Historically, because minstrely was a reaction to ethnic presences in the United States, yellowface emerged only in the second half of the nineteenth century, when an increase in especially Chinese immigration triggered anti-Asian sentiment. *Rush Hour,* however, suggests that the relationship of yellowface to blackface is not merely one of mere mirroring or of temporal sequence. Rather, the film implies that the "copy" (yellowface minstrelsy) is in fact more dynamic than the "original" (blackface minstrelsy). Whereas blackface performance remains static, a mere springboard for yellowface to signify upon, yellowface minstrely emerges as more complex and ambivalent. My concern in this essay is twofold: I draw attention to Hollywood's simulacrum of black/Asian coalitions, a simulacrum that is, I propose, fundamentally ahistorical; and I read the filmic narrative against the grain to emphasize the historicity and the historical coalition that the narrative denies.

If, as Vijay Prashad has argued, the spirit of a people-of-color coalition, especially an alliance between blacks and Asians, is that "everybody is kung fu fighting," the 1998 blockbuster film *Rush Hour* signals the failure of what Prashad has called "kung-fusion"—the search for a "new skin" that would counter strategic essentialism through a productive confusion of racial markers and allegations.[2] But this new skin remains absent from *Rush Hour,* a film that leaves the opposition between "the model" and "the undesirable" intact. The search for a new skin is crucial for an envisioning of AfroAsian coalitions for a number of reasons. First, a new skin would upset the distinction between desirable Asian immigrant and unwanted blackness. Second, the idea of a "skin" being simultaneously black and Asian would highlight the depthlessness of any racial markers. If the practice of minstrely reduces race to mask, the new skin reverses this process and retranslates the mask into lived experience. Crucially, the idea of a new skin would suggest that blackface and yellowface are no longer two separate minstrel masks imposed on blacks and Asians by a white mainstream. Rather, in an appropriation of such imposition, the ethnic subject performs a simultaneity of allegiance: wearing both blackface and yellowface and performing both as presences, not mere caricatures, the ethnic subject is black and Asian at the same time, desirable and undesirable.

If Prashad argues that the very practice of cultural fusion, of interethnic coalition building, alters the identities of those who engage in them, however, *Rush Hour* gives us the coalition with the ethnic ingredients intact: it reinscribes stereotypical identities under the guise of coalition building. *Rush Hour* is thus what I would call a mock black/Asian coalition—a coalition that serves the purpose of a whiteness which remains unseen.

To illustrate the racial politics of a positive "kung-fusion"—the possibility of ethnic coalition building not based on identity politics and racial purity—Prashad focuses on the person of Bruce Lee. Prashad thus emphasizes the necessity to look at the politics *off* screen, not the filmic narratives in which Lee was featured. I would argue, however, that to separate the filmic from the material might ultimately leave the films themselves unchallenged. Rather than separate the actor from the film, then, I seek to draw attention to the ways in which films like *Rush Hour* can be deconstructed through the material setting (such as the city of Los Angeles) which they evoke.

Where Bruce Lee, off screen, can be seen as an exponent of an alternative politics of antiracist resistance, a resistance not based on identity politics but on cross-race solidarity, he was nevertheless required to adopt the mask of yellowface minstrelsy in his films. According to Prashad, "when

Bruce's bravado took him to Hollywood in 1966 to play Kato in *The Green Hornet,* his role did nothing to challenge the stereotypes of the alien 'Heathen Chinee' within America. As Kato, Bruce was welcome to be the mysterious clown, and sidekick."[3] There is thus a tension between the actor and the filmic narrative. Even as this tension is, to some extent, also present in the career of Lee's successor in Hollywood, Jackie Chan, Chan has been mainstreamed to a degree that was denied to Lee. Crucially, while Bruce Lee, as Prashad emphasizes, went to Hong Kong due to his frustration of being assigned only the role of the yellowface minstrel, Jackie Chan's direction has been the opposite. The requirement of mainstreaming—of entering the American cultural imaginary—was that Lee, against the grain of his own extrafilmic politics, enter the codified visual hierarchy of American film, a hierarchy which, in keeping with its stage legacy, relegated ethnic characters to the form of minstrelsy.

Where Lee returned to Hong Kong, Chan engineered his own mainstreaming in terms of American popular culture—terms, however, which he, unlike Lee, was able to manipulate rather than succumb to. Chan's move from Hong Kong to Hollywood culminated in his inclusion in Hollywood's Walk of Stars. Ironically, this move into mainstream began with Chan's *in*ability to live up to the man whose successor he was to become: Bruce Lee himself. Not fitting into the mold of the heroic kung fu fighter, Chan created his own fusion of comedy and martial arts—a style, even more important, that was modeled on none other than Buster Keaton. Chan's entry into the American mainstream begins with a cultural fusion: the fusion of the Hong Kong kung fu tradition with American comedy.

If I have argued above that every instance of an ethnic character's achieving of cultural dynamism, of representational complexity, will have to be negotiated against the haunting of the American screen by the theatrical form of minstrelsy, Jackie Chan's filmic performance is a counter-representation not only of Bruce Lee but also of Charlie Chan himself. It could be argued that Chan's acting style and the choreography of his martial arts sabotage the filmic scripts into which they are inserted: the minstrel's acting, so to speak, is indicative of the *absence* of minstrelsy, of the artist's own literacy in American popular culture and his ability to manipulate this culture for his own purposes. Yet, it may be argued that, in keeping with Prashad's analysis of Bruce Lee, this cultural fusion of martial arts and Buster Keaton remains invisible to anyone not familiar with Chan's biography or attuned to the art of Buster Keaton echoed in Chan's acting. Even so, Chan's parodic acting style as sabotage of minstrelsy upsets the dichotomy between actor and filmic narrative on which Prashad's reading of Bruce Lee, for reasons having to do with Lee's own biography, has to be predicated. Chan's choreography is a detail that enables us to deconstruct the filmic script by contextualizing it. Yet, what about the filmic narrative itself? Chan may deconstruct the script of minstrelsy through his acting style, but the script remains. What, moreover, is the role of interethnic alliances for this script?

It is significant that the filmic narrative appropriates the idea of Afro-Asian coalition building but does so in highly reactionary terms. *Rush Hour* introduces a fake black/Asian politics, which, unlike that of Bruce Lee, is decidedly not antiracist: it is a black/Asian coalition premised on racialist structures of thought. Real-life coalition building can hence not only be contrasted to but also signify on Hollywood's simulacrum of ethnicity—a simulacrum on which I will dwell more closely than Prashad does in his account of Bruce Lee's presence on the American screen. I am interested in the insight this simulacrum may reveal into the unconscious of the dominant culture itself. As Eric Lott has argued in his groundbreaking study on minstrelsy and the American working class, minstrelsy was long understood as a self-evidently racist form. Lott proposes that an inquiry into the performance itself can yield conclusions not just about the black community that minstrely disenfranchises, but on the very mainstream who is anxious to perpetuate this disenfranchisement. As Lott observes:

> The culture that embraced [minstrelsy], we assume, was either wholly enchanted by racial travesty or so benighted, like Melville's Captain Delano, that it took such distortions as authentic. I want to suggest, however . . . that there was a range of responses to the minstrel show which points to an instability or contradiction in the form itself.[4]

Similarly, *Rush Hour* may yield conclusions about Hollywood's own political "instability." If minstrelsy is a containment of the dominant culture's racial anxieties, the film suggests that the possibility of black/Asian coalitions must be stemmed off through caricature. If the continued presence of minstrelsy on Hollywood's screen implies that racial anxiety has not waned, this anxiety, as *Rush Hour* indicates, may have taken a new turn: it is no longer a suspicion merely of black or Asian presences but a fear of these presences entering into a coalition with each other.

Hence Jackie Chan's mainstreaming may be symptomatic of a particu-

lar historical moment, a moment in which Asian capital may be more desirable than a familiar black presence. By mainstreaming a man who has
long been a star of Hong Kong's own highly profitable movie industry—
an industry, it must be remembered, with a global dissemination—Hollywood can in fact be seen to have its cake and eat it, too. By including
Jackie Chan, Hollywood has also entered a valuable coalition with film
industries outside the United States. Chan, within the filmic narrative and
outside it, embodies the desirability of Asianness for U.S. investment. It
is small wonder, then, that the terms spelled out by Hollywood for such
an inclusion are rather favorable. In *Rush Hour,* Hollywood offers inclusion to Jackie Chan by ameliorating the racialist politics of yellowface.
Where Bruce Lee was confined to a script of minstrely that could have
not been more depthless, Chan's yellowface can be said to parody itself in
Rush Hour. Although the film allows the performance of the "Asian cop
as yellowface minstrely" to deconstruct itself, this deconstruction can be
achieved only through maintaining the tradition of blackface minstrelsy as
both depthless beyond repair and idiotic. This is the transition from Bruce
Lee's *Enter the Dragon* to Jackie Chan's *Rush Hour:* the Chinese character
may still be a minstrel, but his minstrelsy, ironically, is superior to that of
his black sidekick.

These parameters notwithstanding, both blackface and yellowface minstrelsy are masterminded by whiteness. It is this vexed relationship between mainstreaming and minstrelsy that also needs to be investigated.
Yet, who is being mainstreamed in *Rush Hour?* Even as Jackie Chan's role
exceeds that of the minstrel, his mainstreaming takes place, as it were, "on
the back of blacks." It could thus be argued that Chan mirrors the role of
Jewish American minstrels at the beginning of the twentieth century. As
Michael Rogin has argued, minstrel performers such as Al Jolson in the
1927 legendary film *The Jazz Singer* entered the American mainstream by
participating in a racist social imaginary: the very imaginary that minstrelsy was predicated on. The Jew became American by becoming racist
in American terms, and he became a white American by donning blackface. As Rogin writes, "Blackface as American national culture Americanized the son of the immigrant Jew."[5] It is significant for the purpose of
my argument that, prior to Michael Rogin's discussion (to which I return below), minstrelsy has always been investigated as solely a black-and-
white phenomenon. Rogin introduces into this equation—or, rather, the
opposition between dominant culture and subordinate nonculture—a
third ethnicity whose relationship to the mainstream is determined by the

practice of minstrelsy. *Rush Hour* can be seen as adhering to the same triad of mainstreaming—the Jew becomes white through blackface—by substituting Asianness for Jewishness. What if not Jewish immigrants but Asian immigrants and nonimmigrants are being mainstreamed through minstrelsy? At the same time, given the racial classification of Asians in the United States, this mainstreaming of Asianness does not quite result in whiteness. If in *The Jazz Singer* the Jew becomes white by donning blackface, in *Rush Hour* the yellowface minstrel is able to deconstruct the depthlessness of his own minstrel mask by establishing a contrast to the continued depthlessness of blackface. At the end of *Rush Hour,* the Asian has not (like the Jew) become white through the practice of minstrelsy, but he has at least become a desirable immigrant presence which can potentially be Americanized.

Like *The Jazz Singer, Rush Hour* is predicated on the mainstreaming of immigrant cultures and races accomplished through minstrelsy. Chan's identity in its complexity and its hybridity takes shape against the background, *through,* a black minstrel. Where the black minstrel played by a black man remains static, the Asian's multifacetedness takes shape against this lack of movement. Minstrelsy's premise of the threat of black masculinity is still at the core of *Rush Hour,* even as this threat has now been rendered even more ridiculous. For example, Carter, the African American policeman played by Chris Tucker, insists on taking every comment of his white female partner, Officer Johnson, as a sexual advance: "Johnson, if you want to go on a date with me, you don't have to wait on a list like every other woman."

Where the black Other remains a stock character, the Chinese subject moves *into* the American mainstream. Chan's is a mainstreaming that, ironically, does not lead to an unqualified (and hence, ultimately, to white) Americanness. Lee is being mainstreamed, a process that reinforces the static quality of Tucker's blackface minstrel mask. This mainstreaming stops short of the Asian's complete Americanization. Even more ironically, as the film closes, the mainstream is a Chinese one: Tucker and Lee are on a plane to Hong Kong. It is here that the genres in which *Rush Hour* participates may be well worth considering. In the genre of the kung fu movie, especially in its Jackie Chan brand, the norm is Hong Kong. Even if Chan's presence verges on Americanness at the end of *Rush Hour,* this Americanness is by no means synonymous with white Americanness, and Chan goes back to China at the narrative's end. *Rush Hour's* is a mainstreaming, then, in which Chan, the Asian visitor, becomes the equivalent of Asian investment in the United States: both are highly welcome. The Asian is desirable because he has been Americanized to a degree (an Americanization achieved through blackface minstrelsy), and he can now go home again. Thus *Rush Hour* indicates that we may have to speak of degrees of mainstreaming and that mainstreaming is not always synonymous with the acquisition of whiteness or white privilege.

But how is this Americanization achieved? In Rogin's analysis of *The Jazz Singer* as much as in *Rush Hour*, Americanization is inextricable from the Other's initiation into American popular culture. *Rush Hour* inscribes the process of Americanization through the ubiquity of American popular culture.

Yet, there is an interesting tension in the narrative between Americanization and African Americanization in *Rush Hour*. Through Carter, Lee is being initiated not just into American culture but into African American subculture:

> *Lee* [Turns on the radio, smiles]: Beach Boys.
> *Carter*: Oh hell no. You didn't just touch my goddamn radio.
> *Lee*: The Beach Boys are great American music.
> *Carter*: The Beach Boys'll get you a great ass-whoopin'. Don't ever touch a black man's radio, boy. You can do that in China but here you'll get your ass killed down here, man. Let me show you real music. [Changes the station to rap music; starts moving] Now, can you do that to the beach boys? Hell no!

It is at this point that, even though at first glance *Rush Hour* and *The Jazz Singer* seem to differ tremendously, there is a striking similarity in them: in both instances, Americanization is synonymous with African Americanization. The Jewish immigrant, as Rogin argues, becomes American by performing jazz. Even if in *Rush Hour* African American culture is epitomized by rap, not jazz, the structure of Americanization or African Americanization remains. It is thus small wonder that Lee should be taught to perform American culture in an African American voice:

> *Lee* [Sings]: War. What is it good for, absolutely nothing. Sing it again, you all.
> *Carter*: It ain't you all, it's y'all.
> *Lee* [Tries]: Y'all.
> *Carter*: Man, you sound like a karate movie. Y'all!
> [Lee is making an effort]

Carter [Pointing to his stomach]: Say it from right here with some soul.
   Y'all.

Ironically, there is a sense here in which the minstrel performer is being taught African American authenticity by the black man himself. Seen in this light, Lee's would thus be a minstrel performance. Once again, even as both the Asian and the black characters of *Rush Hour* are ultimately minstrels of white cultural imagination, Lee's role is a dynamic one whereas Carter's is not. Lee is a minstrel *performer,* where Carter is only a minstrel.

Rush Hour's narrative can thus be seen as an ironic replay of the history of black/Asian relations in the United States. Carter's attitude to his Asian "partner," Lee, moves from open antagonism to a grudging acknowledgment. The film signifies on a history of black/Asian relations in the United States even as it distorts these relations, and it dismisses the role of whiteness in bringing about the increasing tension between black and Asian communities that the film seeks to transcend through humor. The idea that black/Asian alliances are being portrayed by the filmic narrative as being imposed from above (the white police captain *orders* Tucker to team up with Lee) and as being imposed by whiteness is in fact a blatant denial of historical reality. Historically, the white mainstream has brought about not the coalition between blacks and Asians but their antagonism. The enmity between black and Asian communities was the outcome of a mainstream politics of divide and rule, which pitted an allegedly "dysfunctional" black community against an Asian model minority. This historical genealogy is completely absent from the film, which portrays black/Asian antagonism as an outcome of these communities' own racial myopia. Ironically, *Rush Hour* can be read as the mainstream's attempt to make up for its own historical failures: it reconciles the very communities for whose mutual suspicion this mainstream is responsible in the first place. Race relations are thus played out in popular culture.

It is crucial to read *Rush Hour* against the background of the history of black/Asian relations in the United States. Significantly, these relations came to a head in the very city in which the film is set: Los Angeles. How, then, does *Rush Hour* signify on the L.A. urban uprising? How do the parameters of this historical event modify the message of the film? Crucially, the race relations described in *Rush Hour* mirror black/Asian antagonism and its eruption into violence, as well as the role of whiteness in this antagonism. The L.A. urban uprising seems inseparable from this practice of the dominant culture of pitting the dysfunctional black subject against the Asian model minority. In *Rush Hour,* black dysfunctionality is still in place, as is the script of minstrelsy. In fact, the presence of Carter as the black cop can be seen as metonymical of popular culture's inclusion of ethnic minorities only in nominal terms. The inclusion of blackness is ridiculed by the filmic narrative; the black man is included as a minstrel character who *plays* a police officer. Carter is a minstrel at the white police chief's disposal, blissfully unaware of the fact that he is being functionalized by whiteness. While the filmic narrative suggests that this functionalizing of blackness indexes only Carter's having to "baby-sit" his Chinese colleague so the latter does not interfere with the FBI operation of getting Consul Han's daughter back, I am interested in a more abstract politics of racial containment that *Rush Hour* can be said to inscribe. The foundational premise of minstrelsy is that minstrelsy constitutes the performance of "nonsense" by a black character, and a performance that is being masterminded by white imagination:

> *Chief* [On the phone to the FBI]: Even if I had an extra man, who would want such a bullshit assignment? It's a disgrace to me. It's a disgrace to my department. It's a disgrace. . . . [Carter is seen walking past] Dan? I'm sending someone right over.

Carter is thus a token presence, a presence that leaves the assumption of black dysfunctionality untouched and leaves unthreatened the assertion that blacks cannot be integrated into the structures of law and order because they cannot tell its basic parameters apart. As Carter proclaims, "We're L.A.P.D.—we're the most hated cops in the whole world. My own mama she ashamed of me. She telling everybody I'm a drug dealer." What this assertion of hatred alludes to and leaves out at the same time is the precedence of racial hatred in the Rodney King assault. Crucially, this precedent is doubly disavowed in *Rush Hour* because it is being referred to by a black character, and because it is decontextualized, dehistoricized. Even more strikingly, the violence perpetrated by the L.A.P.D. is attributed by the filmic narrative to a *black* policeman. The cause of the world's hatred of the L.A. police, *Rush Hour* asserts, is a black man's actions:

> *Chief:* Two officers were shot [in your operation], one man lost a pinkie.
> *Carter:* Didn't nobody die.
> *Chief:* You destroyed half a block.
> *Carter:* That block was already messed up.

The violence of the L.A.P.D. has thus been turned by Hollywood into a topos of popular culture, but into a topos which is profoundly ahistorical and which distorts the historical precedent itself.

If the L.A. uprising was predicated on an opposition between black and Asian communities, between an allegedly dysfunctional minority group and an Asian minority that was perceived as a stand-in for whiteness, *Rush Hour* leaves this very opposition untouched. This opposition between Asian model minority and dysfunctional blackness is enacted in *Rush Hour* without its violent effects: *Rush Hour* is the reconciliation of Asian and black communities in mainstream popular culture.

It is thus impossible to read *Rush Hour* without taking into account the L.A. riots: impossible because, as a host of critics have argued, the L.A. urban uprising was the eruption of an antagonism that had been building for years. It is no coincidence that *Rush Hour* should be set in Los Angeles and that it should dehistoricize the city by failing to allude to its civil unrest. Crucially, *Rush Hour* can be read as a sequel of this unrest: white society, ironically, could be said to make up for its own responsibility in the tensions leading up to the social unrest by reconciling blacks and Asians. Even more significant, however, is that this reconciliation is strongly at odds with the fact that the filmic narrative upholds the very binary that led to the antagonism in the first place: the Asian is still the model minority, and blackness is still dysfunctional.

The scenario of L.A. civic unrest, I argue, was itself predicated on a politics of ethnic surrogation. This surrogation, in *Rush Hour*, is all the more powerful because the filmic narrative suggests that there *is* no white mainstream. Against such an assertion, however, I want to trace a disembodied white voice—a voice that emanates, alternately, from a black and a yellow body. This disembodiment of voice, in fact, is in keeping with the traditional framework of minstrelsy: the whiteness of the voice is disavowed through blackface, the act of a white subject speaking as an ethnic one. In *Rush Hour*, what Prashad has called the "kung-fusion" of the senses results from the disembodiment of whiteness: we never know whether the ethnic subject speaks as itself or as a surrogate for whiteness. *Rush Hour* works precisely through the effect of this undecidability. It is significant that in *Rush Hour*, a white mainstream could be said to play out its own encounter with ethnicity through surrogate ethnic bodies. The bearer of this white gaze, the temporary "stand in" for whiteness, however, shifts from Asian to black body and back again. Ironically, while the white characters in the filmic narrative seem to be sympathetic, or at least indifferent, to the Chinese trespasser, Carter's is a racist response. As Carter tells Lee, who has just stepped off the plane in Los Angeles:

> *Carter:* I'm detective Carter. Do you speak any English? [Lee looks at him] Do you understand the words that are coming out of my mouth? [Points to his mouth] [Lee smiles] I can't believe this shit. First, I get a bullshit assignment, now Mr. Rice-a-Roni doesn't even speak American.

Through the politics of surrogation, a white mainstream can have its cake and eat it, too: it can pose as racially progressive or at least benevolent and nevertheless live out its racism through the surrogate of a black body. It is in this white mimicry of "Chineseness" performed by a black subject that historical ignorance converges with racist attitude. Hong Kong, as the film's opening makes clear, was a British colony; Carter's assumption that Lee does not speak English is hence also a symptom of his own historical ignorance.

Ironically, the filmic narrative thus suggests that there is no white gaze on Chan's yellow body; the white detectives have no interest in him. I argue in contrast that this gaze has only been disembodied: it is Carter who looks at Lee, as it were, through white eyes, or, conversely, the dominant culture looks at an Asian Other through blackface. The form of blackface, however, remains the same: Otherness is being stared at not from behind blackface but nevertheless through black eyes. The structure of minstrelsy remains, yet it is being used to different ends: minstrelsy helps a mainstream norm cope with the multicultural reality surrounding it, as well as with the multiethnic dystopia of Los Angeles. The traffic chaos of L.A.'s streets becomes a metaphor for its multiethnic dysfunctionality—a dysfunctionality from which whiteness is curiously absent. As Lee tells his kung fu student Soo-Yung, before she leaves with her diplomat father for the United States:

> *Lee* [Subtitled in English translation]: Don't worry, America is a friendly place. [Cut to L.A. traffic]
> *Driver no. 1:* Get the hell of my way.
> *Driver no. 2:* You moron.

In *Rush Hour,* the politics of ethnic surrogation cut both ways: the dominant culture looks through black eyes at a yellow body, and an Asian model minority protects the mainstream from African American dysfunctionality. In this instance, too, Hollywood could be said to be haunted by history, a history that *Rush Hour* sets out to deny. David Palumbo-Liu's account of the L.A. civic unrest showed that media coverage of the event focused on Asian bodies protecting white property. *Time Magazine* featured the picture of a Korean American wearing a Malcolm X T-shirt with the caption "By any means necessary" and fending off a blackness that was wreaking havoc on public space and private property. Crucially for my purposes here, the wearing of a Malcolm X T-shirt by a Korean American was interpreted by *Time Magazine* not as the sign of a coalition between blacks and Asians—a coalition that might lead to a healing of the rift expressed in the L.A. riots—but resulted instead in a de-racing of Malcolm X's slogan. Not only is the phrase "By any means necessary" divorced from the movement for African American liberation, but also Malcolm X's words are used against the black community that *Time Magazine* conceives of as dysfunctional. And, what is even more crucial, the use of Malcolm X against African Americans is achieved through the surrogate body of a Korean American. As Palumbo-Liu points out, "An icon of Black Power has been uprooted from its historical specificity and appropriated now seeming to sanction and even prescribe counterviolence against blacks and others who might threaten the dominant ideology. That is how the words of Malcolm X have . . . come to legitimize protecting property from blacks?"[6] In the complex image of an Asian man protecting Asian (and white) property from a violent black community, there is hence a complex history of race relations in the United States. In this instance, as in the filmic narrative of *Rush Hour,* whiteness manages to remain unseen because of a politics of ethnic surrogation. Palumbo-Liu writes:

> An Asian body occupies the foreground in this narrative; blacks are present as second-level images (Malcolm X on the T-shirt). Whites, however, are invisible, somehow not part of "this" America. Thus what is missing in the narrative implicated by this photo/text is any inquiry into the structure of an economic system that historically has placed Asians against blacks and Latinos.[7]

Time uses an Asian body as a stand-in for whiteness (an Asian protecting white property), even as this politics of surrogation is disavowed through the Asian wearing a Malcolm X T-shirt: in a sad irony, whites defend their own property through a Korean who has been made to don blackface through wearing a Malcolm X T-shirt. Both *Rush Hour* and *Time*

Magazine dehistoricize the possibility of black/Asian coalitions. Both pit the Asian against the black, even as one reinscribes the opposition between the two and the other centers on the forced coalition between a black cop and a policeman from Hong Kong. Like the media's Asians protecting white property from blacks running amok, Jackie Chan (with or without a Malcolm X T-shirt) enforces law and order on American soil, whereas his black minstrel partner destroys half a city block. Chan ultimately protects white property from a blackness that is out of control. Both Asian men are surrogates for a white mainstream that remains unseen.

If *Rush Hour* signifies on the L.A. urban uprising without acknowledging this historical precedent of its own evocation of black/Asian antagonism, it may be useful to contrast the film with an art form that openly engages the history of the city itself. In a very immediate way, mural art signifies on the very buildings it is inscribed upon, and hence also on the material geography of the city itself. Murals supply the context and reality of black/Asian coalitions that *Rush Hour* refuses to provide. L.A. murals can thus be seen as an alternative text to *Rush Hour.*

How might the interaction between filmic narrative and its social and urban geographical setting shed light on the film itself? There is a tension, I believe, between the reactionary multiethnicity of the filmic narrative and the multiethnicity of Los Angeles itself, a multiethnicity that mural art represents. The film can be said to participate, as the opening shot of L.A. traffic indicates, in the genre of dystopic narratives associating L.A.'s multiethnicity with social dystopia and dysfunctionality. To resist this coding of multiethnicity as dystopic, *Rush Hour* needs to be inserted into a wider continuum of ethnic artistic production, a production centering on the urban space and social topography of Los Angeles itself.

Incidentally, one scene of *Rush Hour* takes place against the background of a mural painting, "Hollywood Jazz 1945–1972" (1990) by Richard Wyatt. Where *Rush Hour* contains and neutralizes the spirit of a people of color coalition by framing the black/Asian encounter through the form of minstrelsy, California mural art is exemplary of an alternative multiethnic coalition. Mural art, in the very spirit of Prashad's definition of a progressive kung-fusion of identity politics, defies cultural purism even as it portrays ethnic faces on L.A.'s city walls. Mural artist Keith Sklar has described his own painting, "Mitzvah: The Jewish Cultural Experience":

> People in the mural are local Bay Area people, such as Harvey Milk, Gertrude Stein and Rabbi Heschel—he was a local activist rabbi who for years

marched with Martin Luther King, Jr. Then there are local Jews who are Asian, Black, and Chicano in the mural. So it breaks apart a stereotype of what it looks like to be Jewish. These are not converted people. These are people who grew up that way.[8]

Just as Sklar fuses black and Jewish faces, *Rush Hour* could have fused black and Asian faces in a positive way but fails to do so. Where the filmic narrative sets out to authenticate the black/Asian cop alliance through the mural against whose background the scene is shot, I argue that the mural in fact disauthenticates the reactionary politics of *Rush Hour*.

At first glance, there seems to be congruence between the mural's message of multiethnicity, of ethnic reconciliation, and the filmic narrative's dialogue. Lee's message, in any case, seems to be a call for cultural enlightenment. This plea for enlightenment, however, is directed not at the mainstream—a mainstream that, as I argue throughout this essay, remains absent from the film—but the black minstrel:

> *Lee*: Not being able to speak is not the same as not speaking. You seem as if you like to talk. I like to let people talk who like to talk. It makes it easier to find out how full of shit they are. [Smiles] [After a pause] We're both full of shit.

This dialogue of reconciliation is pronounced against the background of mural art. Mural art seems to index within the logic of the narrative only the topos of L.A.'s multiethnicity, not the much more profound message of interethnic coalition building which this essay is about.

Wyatt's L.A. mural shows us a multiethnic reality that the film capitalizes on, but whose political edge it ultimately denies. Where the filmic narrative of *Rush Hour* includes mural art only as local color, and a local color characterized by the token presence of ethnicity, I am interested in mural art's comment on *Rush Hour* as a Hollywood cultural production. If the film includes the mural as backdrop, I propose that through this backdrop, the filmic narrative itself might be deconstructed. As Wyatt has described his mural: "Hollywood has a huge, legendary history of jazz. There have been a lot of jazz clubs. I couldn't show all the artists who performed during that period (1945–72). Instead, in the background, I created the illusion of etched names for some of the others, so everyone got some recognition."[9] At this point, we have come full circle back to Rogin's analysis of *The Jazz Singer*. The form of jazz, like the form of mural art, is predicated on an interethnic dialogue. Muralizing the history of jazz, Wyatt at the same time implicitly addresses the issue of interethnic encounters. What is the relationship, however, between Wyatt's take on such encounters and that of *Rush Hour*? The echo that the filmic narrative creates between the mural and the film itself is a false one. The mural suggests that ethnic artists can reverse Hollywood's appropriation—and commercialization—of ethnicity: Wyatt retranslates Hollywood's containment of a music that had originally been African American back into noncommercial mural art, an art that restores to jazz the idea not only of historicity but also of cultural complexity—a cultural complexity which, I have argued throughout this essay, is entirely absent from *Rush Hour*. If we deconstruct the filmic narrative through the mural, both Chan's and Tucker's presences may in time be reappropriated by mural artists as part of a genealogy of black and Asian presences and of black/Asian coalitions. Mural art may redeem what Hollywood set out to appropriate.

Where Wyatt's mural restores, against the grain of the filmic narrative, the historicity of ethnic communities and the genealogy of interethnic coalition building, *Rush Hour* goes on to deny this very historicity. What is surprising, and surprisingly reactionary, about *Rush Hour* is that there is no sense of a Chinese American community. Lee is being initiated, as the film opens, by being taken to Mann's Chinese Theater, not Chinatown. As Carter tells him, "I wanna show you something first. Look familiar? Just like home. I ain't never been to China, but it probably look like this." Even as Chinatown is of course ambivalent as the site of both tourist exoticism and the lived complexity of the Chinese American community, Chan's entering into the United States is blocked, as it were, by being led into a maze of mainstream simulations of Chineseness.

Where Chinatown does surface in the film, it is contained as exterior to the U.S. nation space. It is through its association with gang culture that Chinatown is inscribed, not as an American space[10] but as a polluting link to overseas Chinese warlords. The violence of gang culture is shown to be random, disinterested. It is as Asian as it is systemic, and it is embodied by Juntao, the stereotypical Asian criminal:

Chauffeur: Is there a problem, officer?
Juntao: No problem. [Shoots him] Just rush hour.

The film evokes a transnational alliance of crime, and its face is Asian. Robert Lee suggests that the "contemporary yellow peril [is] the invasion of new Chinese immigrants and their gangs."[11] Even as this matching of illegality and race is seemingly neutralized by the film's protagonist, a Chinese cop, the exteriority of the Asian remains. As Robert Lee has argued, yellow peril and model minority are sides of the same coin: "The model minority has two faces. The myth presents Asian Americans as silent and disciplined; this is their secret to success. At the same time, this silence and discipline is used in constructing the Asian American as a new yellow peril."[12] If Juntao is a bad Asian and Lee is a good one, they are both exterior to the nation. The Asian cop helps the CIA solve its problem with Asian ethnicity and then goes back to China. In the end, moreover, it matters little that Juntao was not the mastermind of his own crimes and that the crimes were instigated by the British ambassador to Hong Kong, a white man. What remains is the script of Oriental delinquency perpetuated by the filmic narratives. In the case of both Juntao and Lee, the filmic script thus ultimately denies Asian originality: both the Oriental's committing the crime and his fellow Asian's solving it have to be masterminded by whiteness.

Now, after a discussion of the tension between actor and filmic script, where I zoom in on the filmic narrative itself, I end this essay by zooming out from that narrative. Even if *Rush Hour* can be deconstructed through the contexts provided by the L.A. urban uprising and mural art, respectively, its politics are still based on minstrelsy. Minstrelsy can be upset through these alternative discourses, but, from the perspective of a mainstream audience, its script in *Rush Hour* may still remain in place. I believe that is only in his own film, *Shanghai Noon*, a film which he himself directed, that Jackie Chan is able to combine the "Asian (American) fusion" of his martial arts choreography and an acting style that is indebted to American mainstream comedy with a filmic script that is not predicted on blackface or yellowface minstrelsy. In *Shanghai Noon*, the Asian enters as cowboy, the most striking embodiment of white American masculinity. *Shanghai Noon* restores the element of originality that is missing in *Rush Hour*, and it renders visible in the obviousness of the title's allusion the cultural fusion on which the film is predicated. Chan has given Gary Cooper an Asian face. Where the indebtedness of his acting style in *Rush Hour* to Buster Keaton's comedy remains unseen to any but Jackie Chan aficionados, the title of *Shanghai Noon* in its pun emphasizes the director's and lead actor's own cultural literacy in American popular culture—a popular culture which, Chan implies, by far exceeds the form of minstrelsy.

In the filmic narrative that *parodies* American racial scenarios—scenarios determining the minstrelsy of *Rush Hour*—the Asian Other reappears not only as native but also as Native American, a Native American who goes on to don a cowboy disguise. This postethnic and/or multiethnic scenario truly lives up to Prashad's definition of "kung-fusion." In *Shanghai Noon,* unlike in *Rush Hour,* filmic narrative and off-screen coalition building converge. Yet, it is significant that Chan's is a multiethnic tricksterism, not a multiethnic utopia based on interethnic coalitions. Moreover, blackness remains curiously absent from the American West. Can the new skin of Prashad's kung-fusion never be put on celluloid, then? We may perhaps dwell on the act of Chan's multiethnic tricksterism in *Shanghai Noon.* If in the form of minstrelsy, the putting on of ethnic masks was the prerogative of the white performer, this prerogative has now been appropriated by an "Asian" actor whose very performance demonstrates his cultural literacy and hence makes him American. Such multiethnic masking proves that mainstreaming can be achieved by practices other than minstrelsy. The cowboy has reentered the American scene, and his face is rainbow-colored.

NOTES

1. Jessica Hagedorn, *Charlie Chan Is Dead: An Anthology of Contemporary Asian American Fiction* (New York: Penguin, 1993), xxii.

2. Vijay Prashad, *Everybody Was Kung Fu Fighting: Afro-Asian Connections and the Myth of Cultural Purity* (Boston: Beacon Press, 2001), x.

3. Ibid., 128.

4. Eric Lott, *Love and Theft: Blackface Minstrelsy and the American Working Class* (New York: Oxford University Press, 1993), 15.

5. Michael Rogin, *Blackface, White Noise: Jewish Immigrants in the Hollywood Melting Pot* (Berkeley: University of California Press, 1996), 6.

6. David Palumbo-Liu, *Asian/American: Historical Crossings of a Racial Frontier* (Stanford: Stanford University Press, 1999), 184.

7. Ibid., 185–186.

8. Robin Dunitz and James Prigoff, *Painting the Towns: Murals of California* (Los Angeles: RJD Enterprises, 1997), 102.

9. Quoted in ibid., 206.

10. As Nayan Shah has suggested in his study of perceptions of San Francisco Chinatown at the turn of the twentieth century, "The vivid and visceral narration of the midnight journey through Chinatown became one of the standard forms of knowledge used in both medical and popular accounts to establish the truth of

Chinatown as the preeminent site of vice, immorality, degradation, crime, and disease." Nayan Shah, *Contagious Divides: Epidemics and Race in San Francisco's Chinatown* (Berkeley: University of California Press, 2001), 29.

11. Robert Lee, *Orientals: Asian Americans in Popular Culture* (Philadelphia: Temple University Press, 1999), 197.

12. Ibid., 190.

Chapter 12

Performing Postmodernist Passing
Nikki S. Lee, Tuff, and Ghost Dog in Yellowface/Blackface

Cathy Covell Waegner

Nikki S. Lee, the Korean American photographer, darkens her face to plunge into the African American hip-hop scene in the Bronx; the artistic result is snapshots of herself cheerfully embracing her role as a "homegirl," literally being embraced by "rap gangstas." Paul Beatty's outrageous, politically incorrect African American hero in the novel *Tuff* (2000) plays that he is "starring in one of those Chinese gangster movies"[1] when he grotesquely executes a dog. In Oriental masquerade, R. Kelly and a large troupe of African American back-up singers dance with Asianized hip-hop movements in his fleshly MTV video *Thoia Thoing*. The short film *Tokyo Breakfast*, which pretends to be the pilot of a Japanese sitcom, depicts an entire Japanese family, including the grandfather, as hip-hoppers, gleefully rappin' through their daily life, affectionately calling each other "nigga." And Ghost Dog, an abused African American ghetto youth, becomes an unlikely and dedicated samurai in the satirized Mafia milieu of modern-day Jersey City in Jim Jarmusch's stunning 1999 film *Ghost Dog*.

These disparate case studies in different genres, linked in a variety of ways to pop culture, reflect a growing trend in yellowface/blackface impersonation which I would like to call "playful postmodernist passing." After looking at these case studies more closely, I distinguish this playful postmodernist passing from the generally black-to-white phenomenon more conventionally associated with the term "passing" in which discovery could have dire social and legal consequences, as well as show how it moves beyond a version of minstrelsy in which blackface is used as a hegemonic device to amuse by denigrating the Other.[2] I then draw some working conclusions about the contemporary trope of passing in light of some current theory on "polyculture" and "performative acts," suggesting that the trope offers a certain amount of personal empowerment for the cultural self and provides the impulse for new polycultural art forms in the twenty-first century.

Joyful Trespassing

Born in 1970 in Kye-Chang, South Korea, Nikki S. Lee immigrated to the United States in 1994, receiving an M.A. in photography in 1999. As an immigrant newcomer to the New York art scene, she was quickly able to give herself profile in a series of what she calls "projects," disguising her ethnicity, profession, and gender as, for example, a Puerto Rican, strip dancer, and drag queen. Her blend of photojournalism, self-portraiture, and performance art produces the vivid snapshots of the "Hip-Hop Project," which form an outstanding part of the *One Planet under a Groove: Hip-Hop and Contemporary Art* exhibition which displays the hybridity of the hip-hop world in its ingesting and even shaping of international culture. The exhibition began at the Bronx Museum of the Arts (2001), moved to Minneapolis (2002), and crossed the Atlantic to Munich, Germany (2003–2004). The Hip-Hop Project photograph featured most frequently in the exhibition critiques[3] depicts Lee in elegant "blackface" as one of five young African Americans on the back seat of a car, all wearing du rags, bling bling, or designer sunglasses, making hip-hop "yo" gestures with tattooed hands on their way to a block party. Lee is obviously physically well integrated into the group—more specifically, into the arms of a handsome male hip-hopper.

Exhibition viewers quickly find themselves puzzling over several questions: Do the hip-hoppers know that Lee is in disguise? Do they realize that they are taking part in an art project? With a glance into the hip-hop milieu in which Lee is so snugly ensconced, viewers perceive the passing on one level as "authentic" but nonetheless suspect that the photos are largely staged. Indeed, the fellow hip-hoppers are in complicity with Lee's immersion, giving their consent beforehand to being part of her project.[4] This manipulated reality, which fits in with the current trend for reality television, offers what could be called postmodernist "willed authenticity" —a voyeuristic glimpse into lived experience, the artificiality of its media staging remaining nonetheless undisguised. Surely, this is exactly the hybrid effect that Lee is aiming to achieve. The viewer plays along with Lee's game and is rewarded for this: as Lee interweaves the improvised with the planned or rehearsed in her performance, the slightly ironic slippage between them can, as Elin Diamond suggests in a performance theory context, beneficially reveal "concealed or dissimulated conventions."[5]

Viewers also find themselves asking how these photographs can possibly be attributed to Lee, who serves as a *sujet* in the pictures. How can she be both experiencing the hip-hop milieu and recording it?[6] Are the snapshots taken by random bystanders? If not, is the actual photographer also dressed as a hip-hopper to blend into the scenario? In fact, some of the photographs were taken by bystanders, but most by undisguised friends of Lee who are not professional photographers. The snapshot character is deliberately preserved by use of an inexpensive automatic focus camera.[7] Unlike most photographic self-portraits, these pictures reveal little about the artist. Instead, the stereotypes used to determine socioethnic groups are encoded and foregrounded. Lee's performed immersion into the largely African American hip-hop world of the Bronx parallels her placing herself informally on the "other" side of the camera; both movements suggest that ethnicity, role, (self-) identification and "authenticity" are negotiable. Lee's switch from agent (photographer) to subject, like her transformation from Asian to African American, appears fluid and easy.

Hip-hop with its "cross-cultural portability"[8] lends itself particularly well to Lee's performance of Asian to African American passing. Indeed, the origins of hip-hop, commonly perceived as African American, lie in a fusion of African American, Caribbean, and Asian strands. The African American fascination with the Asian in the 1970s, exemplified in the Bruce Lee and martial arts cult, deeply affected the hip-hop movement. This influence is also reflected in the *One Planet under a Groove* exhibition, which features ethnically hybrid installations such as breakdancing on a kalideoscopic mandala background, breakdance as somo wrestling, "Kanji Wildstyle" hip-hop grafitti in Oriental script, and the rapper's hood reminiscent of the *hijab* (headscarf) in Islamic culture. One installation links Tupac and the packaging artist Christo with a visualization of the pun "(w)rap." The pun could be applied to Nikki Lee's disguised play of identities, which a German reviewer sees as subversive, as "cheekily undermining" the supposed African American monopoly on hip-hop.[9] But Lee is finally neither a mere recorder nor a guerrilla; as a *proclaimed player,* she enjoys poetic license, as it were, to move freely between the ethnicities and social groups, her allegiances as temporary as her makeup.

What about the "air of condescension" that some reviewers have seen being involved in Lee's shape-shifting feats, despite her dedicated, "vivid

theatricality"? These reviewers are uncomfortable with the possible arrogance and lack of essence in her pranksterism: "Looking at the snapshots
that document her masquerade, one can't help but experience a little frisson, wondering what, in fact, is left after all the studied camouflage is
stripped away."[10] The evocation of this "frisson," I claim, is a deliberate
part of Lee's multifunctional, intentionally naughty, but never disrespect-
ful, postmodernist act. A more disturbing criticism of Lee's undertaking
lies in the sociopolitical implications of her cross-cultural trespasses; the
artifice and playfulness of her mimicry can be seen as part and parcel of
her privilege as an artist: "It is clear, Lee is not the person against whom
the Fifth Avenue boutiques barricade their windows with thick sheets of
plywood. . . . She can hang, braided and disenchanted, with the hip-hop
heads, but at the end of the day she leaves them behind and goes back to
being a popular artist whose photos hang in major museums."[11] This critical approach, however, serves to polarize "art" and "reality," a distinction
that runs counter to the postmodernist thrust of crossing and breaking
down borders in all spheres as a liberating, on the whole socially healthy,
experience.

Tuff's Politically Incorrect Yellowface

A mirror image of Lee's joyful and sly but respectful blackface masquerade
is embodied in Tuff, the ethnically blasphemous black protagonist of Paul
Beatty's novel of the same name set in thoroughly intercultural Spanish
Harlem. Beatty, whom reviewers have dubbed "the poet laureate of the
hip-hop generation" and Rachel C. Lee calls a "postmodern ethnic,"[12] laces
his novel with snapshots of Tuff's AfroAsian passing. With ghetto ventril-
oquism, nineteen-year-old Tuff imitates a cinematic Cantonese accent
when he impersonates a Chinese film villain; he chuckles in his "Ming the
Merciless laugh"[13] as he releases a piranha into his fishbowl. Tuff's key
leisure-time activity is watching classic Asian films, often reacting with
comically maudlin empathy, as when he realizes he would have to eliminate his wife before he could slip into the protagonist's role in the 1942
Ozu film *There Was a Father*: "If you think about it, Landa, all I have to do
is kill you and this movie be just like me and Jordy's life. Father and son
against the world."[14]

The protagonist's often sadistic, occasionally sentimental appropriation
of Asian film stereotypes is accompanied by a not entirely ironic influence

of the samurai culture. His quoting from Yoshikawa's famous samurai epic *Musashi* is one of the scarce but significant "straight" moments of Beatty's satirical novel: "Extend the circle, its edges go to the ends of the universe. . . . Shrink the circle, it becomes the size of your soul."[15] The image of the circle becomes a leitmotif, as when Tuff creates harmony in jail by being the midpoint of a "disjointed circle" of gang members, imagining the ghost of Musashi Miyamoto "filling in its gaps" by beautifully wielding his samurai stick.[16]

His thoroughly politically incorrect friends (and enemies) usually deflate his moments of relatively earnest passing: when Tuff's voice "tak[es] on a clichéd Chinese lilt" as he proclaims, "It's like a finger pointing away to the moon: don't concentrate on the finger or you will miss all that heavenly glory," his buddy gruffly cuts him off with "Enough with *Enter the Dragon* bullshit."[17] And their offensive anti-Asian comments such as "so the largest black company is owned by a Chink?" and "let him go, you slant-eyed bitch!" are part of the novel's discourse.[18]

In addition to performing Asian movie and epic stereotypes, Tuff also immerses himself in Japanese video games, acting out real-life quarrels through the mediation of virtual highjinks. Fittingly named "Rotundo" in a bloody ninja game with elaborate swordplay, the overweight protagonist is coolly conquered by Kashmira, an assassin played by Tuff's wife Yolanda, who is furious with him for having sought arrest: "Before he could assume a defensive crouch Kashmira decapitated him." Bruce Lee's elegant leaps and swift jabs of the 1970s movies and magazines, which Tuff has always consumed avidly, have been transformed into the game figures' grotesque "flurry of secret moves" and the players' hyperkinetics of "intricate joystick-button combinations."[19]

The climax of Tuff's yellowface performance is reached when he vanquishes a formidable professional wrestler in a sumo-wrestling event that the narrative voice calls a "Japanese minstrel show." Dressed in the traditional costume of satin belts which necessarily leave his huge buttocks exposed and "hoist . . . his paunch almost to his nipples," the obese Tuff enters the arena, fascinated with being "in the presence of so many men his size." The ghetto youth is in the midst of campaigning for city council and could have used this public event as mere promotional grist for his campaign mill, but instead he takes the bout surprisingly seriously, using a combination of Harlem street moves and strategies gleaned from kung fu movies to win. Given the appropriate name of *Kuroyama* or "Black Mountain," he feels as if he has stepped out of the screen of an Asian film as "the unassuming hero in a martial-arts movie: trained by wind, trees, and the monkeys, the country bumpkin makes a name for himself"[20] and even considers undergoing professional initiation into the sumo troupe as he studies his *Science of Sumo* book.

Movies, video games, magazines, and handbooks are not the only source of Tuff's knowledge of Asian culture; the woman who raised him and is sponsoring his political campaign is a Japanese American, Inez Nomura, born in a World War II internment camp, who became a Malcolm X groupie and a Marxist Harlem activist. As an optically striking participant in the front row of Malcolm X's weekly rallies, she proved her ethnic allegiance by mouthing his chant "I'm a field Negro."[21] Now her Orientalism is asked for: in order for Tuff to prove Japanese heritage to become a sumo wrestler, she would have to, as the coach tells Tuff, "sign an affidavit swearing she was your mother."[22] This would mean an official and legal ethnic passing that goes a step too far for Tuff, just as he refuses to "pass" into the political establishment when he is wined and dined by third parties wanting to instrumentalize him as "their" candidate.

As Tuff moves through the derelict housing projects of Spanish Harlem, interacting with and defending the junkies, dropouts, and felons, often of mixed ethnicity and sexual persuasion, the reader realizes that the unlikely candidate indeed has a charismatic populist touch that justifies his reputation as a rising folk-hero samurai. He even begins to adopt a modern samurai strategy of negotiation rather than violence when he helps his friends talk their way out of a bank robbery arrest. On election day, however, he commits political hari-kari by failing to vote for himself, then gleefully voting for "the surnames he thought sounded Jewish" for the judgeships,[23] and finally letting his little son Jordy flip the rest of the polling booth switches according to the toddler's whims. Tuff spends the last of his campaign money, $2,000, to become a patron of the alternative Theater for Classic Cinema with an engraved plaque on the back of a seat. He opts for keeping his passing within the realm of the vicarious world of the cinema rather than in his foster mother's polycultural political arena.

Staged Passing and Parodic Strategies

Before turning to Jim Jarmusch's film protagonist Ghost Dog, who, in contrast to Tuff, shows a different face of postmodernist passing by playing the role of a samurai in deadly earnest, I scrutinize two examples of staged passing in popular consumer culture.

Consider the recent R. Kelly music video (2003), ambiguously entitled *Thoia Thoing* to arouse both Asian and sexual associations, exemplified by Kelly's erotic caressing of a samurai sword handle. The best-selling African American R&B singer, illustrating the Orientalized beat by Asianizing his hip-hop gestures, is joined by a troupe of black female singers and dancers with their pronounced curves clad—very scantily—in Asian clothing, their faces painted white in geisha-girl style. Stereotypical Asian features such as martial arts, tea ceremony, kimono hairstyle, slanted eyes abound. The women's role is clearly that of serving/servicing the men in the video as exotic accessories, very different from Nikki Lee's purposeful use of her body as an aesthetic text.

The hodge-podge Asian mixture suits the panoply of professional quick cuts in time to the music. The MTV video with its chant-like rhythm obviously appeals to young viewers and listeners, for whom the Internet even offers a download of the music for their cell phone ring. The lyrics of the song, however, describe a pickup at a club and the lovemaking aftermath, interestingly enough without the slightest specific reference to Asian exoticism, not even the reference to "circus" performance fitting that bill: "Tattoo on her back, lovin' the way she work it; body movin' like she's dancin' in the circus." Would young Asian or African American women not take offense at Kelly's appropriation of the woman's body of both ethnicities? An informal student survey of young people who designated their ethnicity as Asian or African American suggested that they, astonishingly, did not in fact feel offended.[24] Their reaction to this video, which older viewers would no doubt tend to find in gloriously bad taste, was to dismiss its appropriations as a feature of a genre with its own rules for reception: "It's just an R. Kelly video," for example. Not unlike Nikki Lee in her modality as a proclaimed player, however, the singer deliberately calculates "poetic license" into his work, autographing his lyrics with reference to his personal rhythm and blues fame, the second "R" in this excerpt referring to R. Kelly himself: "One day without me and she's shaking like a fiend (ah); y'all tell me, what's R&B without the R (ah)?" Kelly's viewers, I conjecture, do *not* perceive the video as a modern minstrel show, if minstrelsy is defined as black or yellowface that amuses through degrading another ethnicity. Through its casually eroticized yellowface exaggerations, R. Kelly's *Thoia Thoing* even parodically comments on an earlier, charged context. Within the broad context of fluid postmodernist passing for entertainment consumption, I venture the hypothesis that sophisticated (or jaded?) young spectators do not find the perfomance by Kelly and his black geisha girls degrading because they view Kelly's hyperbolical stereotyping with a considerable amount of ironic distance, though, as CD sales indicate, clearly taking pleasure in his consummate performance.

The more obviously comic—but, according to the student survey, potentially more offensive—short film *Tokyo Breakfast* depicts a three-generation Japanese family stylizing themselves as hip-hoppers, dressing and moving ghetto-style in their tastefully furnished Japanese home. The mother raps while she cooks in her high-tech stainless steel kitchen, and even the grandfather uses hip-hop gestures when speaking Japanese. The hip-hop insider form of address "nigga" becomes the leitmotif of the film, with the characters punctuating every sentence with the word, calling each other and themselves "niggas" in a Japanese accent. Not least because of the Japanese credits, *Tokyo Breakfast* masquerades as a Japanese product satirizing the Eastern (Asian) consumption of Western (African American) popular culture, made for the Japanese TV audience. Many Internet forum participants discussing the film believed it to be the pilot for a real Japanese sitcom.[25]

However, the viewers of *Tokyo Breakfast* were tricked! The video was actually created by two white American filmmakers, Mike Maguire and Tom Kuntz, former directors for MTV. The film passes as a clip from a Japanese sitcom.[26] In an email from one of the directors, we learned that this presentation of the Japanese obsession with Western culture—an engrossment which Jones and Singh call with reference to African American cultural products "the consumption of a fetishized blackness in Asia"[27]—was disguised as intraethnic, deliberately meant to con the viewer into thinking that such a heavy-handed satire could be popular in its home country of Japan. The Internet debate as to whether the film, ostensibly produced in the Far East, is a comedy or a racist flick attests to the tricky success of their undertaking. The directors maintain that their intention is in a broad sense didactic: to show that the Japanese obsession with Western culture can "backfire when they don't know the complete story behind what they're adapting."[28] Later I point out how this film hovers dangerously on the brink of modern minstrelsy.

The yellowface masquerade in Jim Jarmusch's remarkable film *Ghost Dog* is perhaps as hyperbolic as the passing performed in the other film clips, but it is completely different in focus.[29] The African American hero has become an unlikely samurai in a Jersey City 'hood. His daily solemn perusal of the eighteenth-century guidebook of the samurai code, *Haga-kure,* is intermittently projected on screen with voiceover reading. The hauntingly atmospheric soundtrack by RZA and the Wu-Tang Clan from the Asian African American jazz-inflected hip-hop scene enhances Ghost Dog's application of samurai ethics to modern-day violence. Donning his rapper's hood, Ghost Dog passes into social invisibility, becoming a hit-man for the satirized Mafia bosses meeting in the tawdry backroom of a Chinese restaurant and mismanaging their control of racialized neighbor-hoods. Unlike Nikki Lee, whose impersonation of a black hip-hop groupie is planned and ephemeral, Ghost Dog, a brutalized child of the ghetto, internalizes the ancient samurai code, managing even to dignify the karate kicks and elaborate samurai flourishes of his gun as part of his act. In my opinion, viewers find themselves drawn to this potentially ridiculous loner through his understated but powerful performance.

In my other case studies, the staged nature of the passing performance was emphasized by the encoded presence of an audience or consumers; in *Ghost Dog* there is, in addition to the cinema spectators, an intrafilm audience of improbable disciples in Pearline, a young black girl who reads the books he recommends—notably the Japanese epic *Rashomon*—and the African ice cream vendor Raymond, who speaks only French but shares Ghost Dog's thoughts. They watch and understand his last stand as the rebellious retainer against his Mafia lord who has proved so undeserving of Ghost Dog's samurai fealty. The caricatured Mafia "family" members are the counteraudience to these insiders. Instead of reflecting a postmodernist attitude that approves of lateral and creative ethnic interactions, these Italian Americans consider other ethnicities an inferior mix, as in this parodic dialog among four of the leaders, a veritable minstrel show complete with mocking mimicry thinly veiling their subliminal fascination:

Sonny Valerio: What the f— is his name?
Louie Botticelli: Ghost Dog.
Sonny Valerio: Ghost Dog?! . . .
Louis Botticelli: A lot of these black guys today, these gangsta-type guys, they all got names like that they make up themselves.
Sonny Valerio: He means like the rappers . . . they all got names like that . . . my favorite was always "Flavor Flav" from Public Enemy. [Valerio then raps a few lines theatrically]
Ray Vargo: It makes me think about Indians; they got names like Red Cloud,

Crazy Horse, Running Bear, Black Elk. [He moos loudly in a deadpan
version of an elk]
Old Consigliere: Yeah, Indians, niggers, same thing.

The irony that Sonny then summons his hitman "Sammy the Snake"—
whose name is no less metaphorical than "Ghost Dog"—to eliminate the
tactically undesirable African American escapes these four. The gunman
and a cohort commissioned to "whack" or "neutralize" Ghost Dog mistakenly try to kill Ghost Dog's Native American acquaintance. In their frustration at not locating the elusive and undefinable quarry, they substitute a
gratuitous slaughter of Ghost Dog's beloved flock of carrier pigeons—his
samurai army—whose beautiful flights above the sordid city like animated Asian paintings have provided a cinematic and symbolic point of
view at key points in the film.

The deliberate transparency of Nikki Lee's cross-ethnic playfulness, the
blatant inappropriateness of Tuff's, the consumer appeal of R. Kelly's and
the trickiness of *Tokyo Breakfast*'s are "replaced" in the person of Ghost
Dog by a dignified, albeit unlikely, merging of what he seems to consider
his African American body and his Asian self. The representations of race
and passing in these case studies are deployed in disparate media and cultural contexts and with different aims for audience reception—and no
doubt received differently by viewers and readers who align themselves
with particular ethnicities—but they can meaningfully be compared with
regard to their performed passing impulse and instrumentalization of parodic strategies.

From Danger to Complicity

Most of us associate the term "passing" with a movement from black to
white, from a race socially and legally discriminated against to the economically and politically more powerful white race chiefly during bygone
times of blatant racial inequality and the judicial determination of race.
Passing was eminently dangerous, and discovery could easily prove to be
life-threatening. The slave narrator's escape to freedom frequently hinged
on a daring passing maneuver, as in the dramatic transracial and transgen-
der story of Ellen and William Craft, who managed to escape to the North
with the light-colored Ellen disguised as a young white slave master, her
husband serving as the master's slave. Giulia Fabi's recent study of the rise

of the African American novel reveals the importance of the trope of passing as a thematic and narrative device at the heart of the early novels.[30]
Fabi's image of "tres-passing" refers not only to the forbidden entry of
mulattos and mulattas into the white world of privilege and personal freedom but also to the quite recent intrusion of those literarily troublesome
African American narratives into the canon of accepted nineteenth- and
early twentieth-century novels. The Harlem Renaissance novels, written
long after emancipation could have eliminated the necessity for passing,
continued to include the physical danger—after all, light-skinned Clare
Kendry in Nella Larsen's *Passing* (1929) plunges (or is pushed?) to her
death at least partially because of her immersion in the white world—but
placed more emphasis on the psychological price paid by the passer.
Clearly, the existential urge to pass was still present at this time in a binary,
racialized society despite the rearticulated pride in "New Negro"-ness.
Other motivations for passing emerged and are still potent in conventional passing narratives, such as romantic involvement with a member of
another race or opportunity for professional advancement or the thrill of
cultural slumming.[31]

Passing was dangerous not only for the passer but also for society and
its status quo in general, since passing threatened the "objective" foundation of the dominant white majority. It was jeopardized by the creativity
of the passer, who had necessarily to forge a "coherent, plausible [but in-
vented] narrative"[32] to account for his or her present and past positions;
this revealed a person's skill as a storyteller at the same time that it undermined the hegemonic control exercised by what Toni Morrison famously
calls the "master narrative." Capturing the spirit of postmodernism, the
discourse of passing—past and present—reveals the limitation of the essentialist view of identity; as Elaine Ginsberg succinctly (and admittedly
somewhat paradoxically—does one "truth" replace another?) puts it, passing "discloses the truth that identities are not singularly true or false but
multiple and contingent."[33] When Nikki Lee forms artworks out of her
self-transformation, she is making explicit and visual what other passers
have perhaps accomplished unwittingly and invisibly, without the knowing gaze of the gallery visitor.[34] Lee is creating a new story, which shows
that, like for other passers, her "history is a work in progress"[35] beyond the
identity category predetermined by a relatively fixed social and ethnic
hierarchy. As I have shown, she and all the other postmodernist passers
we have dealt with—including the largely silent Ghost Dog, whom we
often follow voyeuristically in the film—require an audience to read her

and their own stories (or histories), to witness and even participate in the code-switching performance, be it as a music video downloader or a conned Internet forum contributor.

Minstrelsy and Lateral Passing

But do the categories of black/white/yellow not remain despite the passer's code-switching? Before considering how the polyculturalists might respond to this question, we can elucidate the ways in which the post-modernist passing impulse can be distinguished from minstrelsy, even though sharing certain performance strategies. Recent scholarship has indicated that the phenomenon of minstrelsy—both as the undeniably most popular form of public entertainment in the nineteenth-century and as a long-term, culturally pervasive force—is much more complex, with a far deeper impact than previously suspected. A relevant aspect here is the dialectic between adulation and scorn, which led to the white minstrels and their audiences being fascinated by the African American culture (or, rather, what they believed were songs, dances, instruments, verbal tactics, attitudes of the African Americans) and taking pleasure in ridiculing it. The negative component of ridicule alone cannot account for the many decades of economically successful minstrelsy in blackface (both black on white and black on black), including many tours to Europe, Australia, New Zealand, even China, Japan, and Indonesia. The partially immigrant audience in the United States was able to laugh at itself as well when stereotypical whisky-guzzling Irishmen and sauerkraut-devouring Germans (along with exotic "Injins," "Chineemen," and the "Jap-oh-knees")— all portrayed by blackface actors—shared the stage with the caricatures of African Americans. Robert C. Toll points out that between 1865 and 1867 at least eight major minstrel companies, calling themselves "The Flying Black Japs," performed extravagant takeoffs on the tour of the Imperial Japanese Acrobats in the United States.[36] In 1877 Bret Harte and Mark Twain wrote a minstrel-influenced play based on Harte's widely read poem "The Heathen Chinee." Tuff's uninhibited political incorrectness thus draws on a long tradition. Wherein lies the difference, however, between the minstrels' derision and Tuff's irreverence?

A productive focus of minstrelsy scholarship since the groundbreaking 1970s has been the black-on-black minstrelsy in the latter half of the nineteenth century. Most of these African American minstrel troupes wore blackface, exaggerating their mouths with a broad outline of white make-up and marked red lips, the large, gaping mouth having become an icon of minstrelsy. Given the competitive minstrel market and the already cod-ified audience expectations, the black minstrels were obliged to continue the character stereotypes as well, such as the ignorant, low-comedy fool or the pretentious urban dandy; furthermore, the managers of the black troupes were often, and increasingly, white. There was, however, a mini-mum amount of room for ironic inversion, which is now being recovered in research;[37] the window of irony has been opened wide to the "signify-ing"[38] of such comic egalitarian narratives as *Tuff,* in which the characters' political incorrectness is equally applied to all the ethnicities rather than being a tool of a dominant one. *Tokyo Breakfast* hovers on the verge of media minstrelsy, particularly because of the whiteness of the filmmakers and their position of superiority in conning their audience. But in show-ing a humorous Japanese inscription of African American cultural ges-tures, the film depicts a lateral passing in which a flash of the white skin (of the filmmakers) behind the blackface of the yellow skin is deliberately relinquished. The white superiority remains chiefly on the level of media trick; the didacticism intended in pointing out the pitfalls of the Japanese when, in Kuntz's words again, "they don't know the complete story behind what they're adapting" aligns the white directors with the African Ameri-cans as U.S. "insiders"—but a certain uneasy feeling remains that Kuntz and McGuire's satire borders on condescension, with the two film produc-ers as contemporary, behind-the-scenes media minstrels.

Polycultural Porousness versus Code-Shifting

Developing a theory of "polyculture" as a replacement for "multicultural-ism," Vijay Prashad would like to see the binary basis (black/white; yel-low/black) for racial distinction eliminated.[39] Prashad finds the approach of multiculturalism, albeit liberal and well-meaning, nonetheless racist and essentialist in that it presupposes separate ethnicities that have iron-clad, distinct identities and histories. He feels that the porousness and intermingling—both diachronic and synchronic—of ethnicities should be foregrounded. His particular version of polyculture is Marxist, stress-ing the history of economic and class oppression among the ethnicities, particularly—in America—the Asian immigrant adoption of patterns of racism discriminating against African Americans. The pattern that solidified during the Cold War era—that is, the Asian American serving as a "model minority" anchored hierarchically between the dominant white majority and the African Americans at the bottom[40]—is to a certain extent and in some geographical areas and social groupings being reshuffled, with more black/Asian American interaction.[41] Claire Jean Kim's engagé work, using the Black-Korean conflicts in New York City in the early 1990s as a case study, however, shows how the larger context of racial power constellations, including white-dominated political strategies, needs to be understood before improved grass-roots relationships among the "minority" ethnicities can be expected.[42]

In the discussion of African American/Asian encounters at the MESEA (Multi-Ethnic Studies, Europe and the Americas) conference in Thessaloniki, Greece, in June 2004, the wish was uttered for the "passing of passing," for a time when racial distinction would be insignificant. The Marxist polyculturalists would oppose this, however, as a Euro/American-centered, utopian "universalism," seeing it as one of "the pallid, unilateral declarations of a world beyond race."[43] They would prefer to harness the dynamism of intermixture and cultural complexity, the "recombinant political and affective potentialities of racial significations and identifications."[44] In their polycultural utopia, cultural communities would demand acknowledgment, but the hierarchy of racial supremacy would be absent; these communities would thus "move between the dialectic of cultural presence and antiracism."[45] The advantage of "polycultural strife," according to this school of thinking, is that it privileges larger "social transformation" over "small, individual gains."[46]

Our postmodernist passing certainly reveals the porousness of the culture lines between the ethnicities, but the very notion of "passing" seems to embody a reliance on ostensibly static difference, which Prashad would not willingly espouse, and in music video examples with their "hype of hybridity" there is a decontextualization of ethnic passing to which a historical materialist would object. Aesthetic rather than anthropological passing reigns here. Nonetheless, the passing impulse suits the polycultural spirit of matter-of-course dynamic interaction. A link between the older social models in which passing made sense and a postmodernist polyculture in which passing is taken for granted lies in the mobilization of *performance.* Judith Butler has taught that "one *does* one's body"[47] in a constant series of performative acts which constitute one's gender; I would like to extend this to ethnicity,[48] which of course in postmodernist theory is commonly viewed as constructed rather than given. These performative acts can glide into salutary boundary crossing during which "ethnicity can be performed or enacted, donned or discarded."[49] Performance thus becomes a kind of invigorating code-shifting, transmogrifying the passer into a skilled artist rather than a menacing trespasser. The act of passing defuses the racial difference, which even in our times is still often fixed and charged in real-life social confrontations. Passing also means personal empowerment, as the passer, with dexterity and awareness, exercises control over the cultural self, in the best mass-media cases minimizing or purposefully implementing the "cultural management" of international commercialism. Granted, passing still involves a certain amount of risk—not the risk of social and judicial punishment of earlier passing, but the challenge of forging a flexible cultural profile in which potential loss is outweighed by increased personal freedom and versatility and by gains in the imaginary. Surely, these benefits cannot be classified as the trivial "small individual gains" dismissed by Prashad.

Performing in Butler's sense does not rely on a form of simple double-consciousness in which the subject is deliberately taking on a role perceived to be separate from his or her authentic identity. In postmodernist passing, it is just as difficult to separate performing subjects from their roles as it is in Butler's gender creation. However, the artificiality of the cultural crossing is deliberately stressed in our examples of ethnic passing, enabling parody to become an effective instrument. Yet this is not the disparaging blackface of minstrelsy or the sardonic yellowface of cartoons that evokes laughter by mocking and ridiculing a race perceived as lower on the social scale. The parody of the latest passing narratives includes a strong dose of "signifying" on earlier serious passing and blackface traditions. Furthermore, the laughter includes the parodist, like Tuff; or deliberately plays to and with the consumer's stereotypes, as in *Thoia Thoing*; or involves a revealing media con, as in *Tokyo Breakfast*. The magic of Ghost Dog's convincing passing as a samurai lies in the constant foregrounding of the artificiality of his undertaking, reinforced by the grotesque comedy of the inept and racist characters he is surrounded by, in combination with the beauty of his utter dedication to his role. Thanks to such performers as Nikki Lee and Ghost Dog, passing has become a polycultural art form of the twenty-first century.

NOTES

1. Paul Beatty, *Tuff* (New York: Vintage, 2001 [2000]), 73.

2. I fully realize the risk involved in defining the term "passing" as *including* disparate techniques such as masquerade, disguise, yellowface/blackface performance, and con. As my argument in this essay shows, the postmodernist passing urge can be realized through these different strategies. However, "minstrelsy," still semantically preconditioned, inscribes a hierarchical concept of race that goes against the grain of the lateral modes of ethnic passing considered here. Susan Gubar coins the attractive term "racechanges" in her encyclopedic book *Racechanges: White Skin, Black Face in American Culture* (New York: Oxford University Press, 1997) to refer to the broad "traversing of race boundaries, racial imitation or impersonation, cross-racial mimicry or mutability, white posing as black or black passing as white, pan-racial mutuality" (5). Her scope is much larger than mine, however, and as it includes "minstrelsy," which I attempt to see as being only parodically "signified on" in my case studies, I prefer my term of "postmodernist passing" to refer to the recent phenomenon under discussion here.

3. Villa Stuck, *One Planet under a Groove: Hip-hop und Zeitgenössische Kunst* (Munich: Villa Stuck, 2004 [press documentation of exhibit, 18 October 2003 to 11 January 2004]); I am certainly grateful to Michael Buhrs, head of exhibitions at the Villa Stuck Museum, for supplying me with these critiques, many of which were displayed at the fine exhibition. The photo is also featured as a large color plate in the exhibition catalog: Bronx Museum of the Arts, *One Planet under a Groove: Hip-hop and Contemporary Art* (New York: Bronx Museum, 2001), 57. This photograph, among others, can be viewed on Lee's agent's website: www.tonkonow.com (retrieved 1 March 2004).

4. I kindly thank Ms. Lee's agent, Leslie Tonkonow, for this information given via email on 4 March 2004.

5. Elin Diamond, ed., introduction to *Performance and Cultural Politics* (London: Routledge, 1996), 5.

6. This question is also posed by Malcolm Beith, "It's a Hip-Hop World: How a Movement Shaped and Absorbed Global Culture," *Newsweek,* 10 November 2003, 60.

7. Tonkonow, email.

8. Beith, "It's a Hip-Hop World," 60.

9. "Ein Spiel der Identitäten, das die Originalität der afroamerikanischen Bewegung frech unterläuft." Anna Eckberg, *Applaus* [event magazine for Munich, Germany], November 2003, n.p.

10. All the quotations so far in this paragraph are from Sarah Valdez, "Art in America," April 2002, available at www.findarticles.com/p/articles/mi_m1248/is_4_90/ai_84669359 (retrieved 1 February 2005).

11. Chisun Lee, "Portrait of the Assimilartist," *ColorLines,* Fall 2002, available at www.alternet.org/story/13858 (retrieved 1 February 2005).

12. Rachel C. Lee, drawing on Frederick Buell, labels Paul Beatty a *"postmodern ethnic"* (Lee's emphasis), who realizes that ethnicity is a nonreferential act. Rachel C. Lee, "Blackface and Yellowface: Costly Performances or Coalitional Enactments?," in *Literature on the Move: Comparing Diasporic Ethnicities in Europe and the Americas,* ed. Dominique Marcais, Mark Niemeyer, Bernard Vincent, and Cathy Waegner (Heidelberg: Universitätsverlag C. Winter, 2002), 147.

13. Beatty, *Tuff,* 132.

14. Ibid., 254.

15. Ibid., 77–78.

16. Ibid., 181.

17. Ibid., 47.

18. Ibid., 54, 61.

19. Ibid., all three quotations 191.

20. Ibid., all quotations 193–200.

21. Ibid., 66.

22. Ibid., 201.

23. Ibid., 252.

24. Two students at the University of Siegen, Caroline Schneider and Benjamin Marienfeld, conducted an informal survey of Asian and African American students on both sides of the Atlantic and Pacific (approximately thirty interviewees), as well as German fellow students (forty informants), to record young people's reactions to the modes of "passing" in three of our case studies.

25. The film premiered at Ohio Indie Film Festival, November 2001. For samples of the Internet debate, see the Japan Forum, www.jref.com/forum/archive/index.php/t-748.html (retrieved 10 May 2004) and article posted 5 July 2002 at www.milkandcookies.com/article/1040/ (retrieved 10 May 2004), which labels the film "a Japanese version of the Osbournes."

26. In the Schneider and Marienfeld interview, most student interviewees fell into Maguire and Kuntz's trap. The ethnicity of the filmmakers was not an issue for some respondents, however, who considered the film with its rollicking use of the epithet "nigga" in bad taste, no matter what the source or audience. Other interviewees enjoyed the exaggeration in the film, finding that it reflected their notion of "ironic Asian humor." One participant even viewed the Asian co-option of the epithet "nigga" as defusing the racialized term: "Asians present the word *nigga* in a friendly, 'natural' way."

27. Andrew F. Jones and Nikhil Pal Singh, eds., guest editors' introduction to *The Afro-Asian Century,* special issue of *positions* 11:1 (2003): 4.

28. Email from Tom Kuntz, 24 February 2004; the filmmaker continued: "We knew we were going to post the film on the web, and didn't want people to know

that the film was done by some clever filmmakers. . . . Instead we wanted people to be confused . . . so we put the title at the beginning which makes it look like a real TV show pilot from Japan. Needless to say, we were very surprised at how much attention the film got." We thank him for his candid information.

29. Perhaps the most surprising response in the Schneider and Marienfeld survey was the Asian students' reaction to *Ghost Dog*. The African American students tended to find Ghost Dog's transformation into an African American ghetto samurai "convincing," whereas the Asians did not. Perhaps the passing *into* the viewer's culture must meet with different standards of acceptability.

30. Giulia Fabi, *Passing and the Rise of the African American Novel* (Urbana: University of Illinois Press, 2001).

31. The widely viewed and highly acclaimed film *The Human Stain,* based on Philip Roth's 2000 novel, shows the continuing interest in "serious" passing. The secret of college professor Coleman Silk's passing from African American to Jewish to preserve his relationship to a white woman and to further his academic career slowly emerges.

Spike Lee's *Bamboozled* (2000) shows "cultural slumming" as the most likely motive for the television producer Dunwitty to become a "wigga" (or "white nigga"). See also my "Rap, Rebounds, and Rocawear: The 'Darkening' of German Youth Culture," in *Blackening Europe: The African American Presence,* ed. Heike Raphael-Hernandez (New York: Routledge, 2004), 249–271, for a discussion of white "cultural adulation" of blackness.

32. Maria Carla Sanchez and Linda Schlossberg, eds., *Passing: Identity and Interpretation in Sexuality, Race, and Religion* (New York: New York University Press, 2001), 2.

33. Elaine K. Ginsberg, *Passing and the Fiction of Identity* (Durham: Duke University Press, 1996), 4.

34. In an exciting study of the events leading to *Plessy v. Ferguson* in light of performance theory, Amy Robinson points out that "passing" in the nineteenth-century political sense depended on the performance being invisible. Amy Robinson, "Forms of Appearance of Value: Homer Plessy and the Politics of Privacy," in *Performance and Cultural Politics,* ed. Elin Diamond (London: Routledge, 1996), 239–261. Just the opposite is true for postmodernist passing. According to Robinson, it is the spectator who manages a "successful pass" (241) by failing to realize the con. In my case studies, the complicity of the intranarrative and extranarrative spectators is required.

35. Ginsberg, *Passing and the Fiction of Identity,* 4.

36. Robert C. Toll, *Blacking Up: The Minstrel Show in Nineteenth-Century America* (London: Oxford University Press, 1974), 94.

37. Annemarie Bean, for instance, describes the way black female minstrels at the turn of the century impersonated black males on stage, reclaiming minstrelsy's stereotypical, ridiculous "urban dandy" as a sophisticated "'race man' worthy of

the upcoming Jazz Age." Annemarie Bean, "Black Minstrelsy and Double Inversion, Circa 1890," in *African American Performance and Theater History: A Critical Reader,* ed. Harry J. Elam Jr. and David Krasner (New York: Oxford University Press, 2001), 181.

38. David Krasner points to "signifying" as the climax of strategies for African American performers dealing with "minstrelsy's insidious representations": "Black performers have negotiated, subverted, incorporated, resisted, challenged, and ultimately 'signified'—the black rhetorical strategy of inversion, parody, and innuendo—on the pervasive minstrel image." David Krasner, "Afterword: Change Is Coming," in *African American Performance and Theater History: A Critical Reader,* ed. Harry J. Elam Jr. and David Krasner (New York: Oxford University Press, 2001), 346.

39. Robin D. G. Kelley's essay, "People in Me," *ColorLines* 1:3 (Winter 1999): 5–7, appears to be the source of the term "polycultural."

40. Robert G. Lee, *Orientals: Asian Americans in Popular Culture* (Philadelphia: Temple University Press, 1999), has an excellent chapter on the development of the concept of the "model minority" ("The Cold War Origins of the Model Minority Myth," 145–179).

41. The popular Jackie Chan films, notably *Rush Hour* (1998) and its sequel *Rush Hour 2* (2001), show how popular film types, such as the "crazy cop duo" genre, can cleverly reflect such a paradigmatic change—and yet remain mired in stereotypes.

42. Claire Jean Kim, *Bitter Fruit: The Politics of Black-Korean Conflict in New York City* (New Haven: Yale University Press, 2000). Kim refers specifically to the Flatbush Boycott in 1990.

43. Jones and Singh, guest editors' introduction, 8. A logical problem here, of course, is that it is impossible to speak of a "we" of a particular ethnic group if the commixture is as thorough as the polyculturalists insist.

44. Ibid., 8.

45. Vijay Prashad, "Bruce Lee and the Anti-imperialism of Kung Fu: A Polycultural Adventure," in *The Afro-Asian Century,* special issue of *positions* 11:1 (2003): 54. See also the more direct theoretical statement in Vijay Prashad, "From Multiculture to Polyculture in Asian American Studies," *Diaspora* 8:2 (1999): 185–204.

46. Prashad, "Bruce Lee," 81.

47. Judith Butler, "Performative Acts and Gender Constitution: An Essay in Phenomenology and Feminist Theory," in *Performing Feminisms: Feminist Critical Theory and Theatre,* ed. Sue-Ellen Case (Baltimore: Johns Hopkins University Press, 1990), 272; my emphasis.

48. Judith Butler's approach to gender construction has been applied to ethnicity in some recent "performance studies" literature, such as in Diana R. Paulin's fine essay, "Acting out Miscegenation" in *African American Performance and Theater History: A Critical Reader,* ed. Harry J. Elam Jr. and David Krasner (New York:

Oxford University Press, 2001), 251–270. In addition, Krasner clearly summarizes recent understanding of the term "performativity" as shifting emphasis away from playwrights to relations among authors, performers, and audiences, informed by the language of the body (Krasner, Afterword, 345–350.)

49. Ginsberg, *Passing and the Fiction of Identity,* 4. One of the "fathers" of modern performance studies, Richard Schechner, emphasizes "fluidity" and "play-fulness," which we have already mentioned as essential for postmodernist passing, as common denominators in the many sectors of his very diverse field: "Any call for or work toward a 'unified field' is, in my view, a misunderstanding of the very fluidity and playfulness fundamental to performance studies." Richard Schechner, "What Is Performance Studies Anyway?," in *The Ends of Performance,* ed. Peggy Phelan and Jill Lane (New York: New York University Press, 1998), 361.

Part IV

Celebrating Unity

Chapter 13

Persisting Solidarities

Tracing the AfroAsian Thread in
U.S. Literature and Culture

Bill V. Mullen

AfroAsian Solidarity: Literary Roots

In July of 1946 Zora Neale Hurston wrote to her friend Claude Barnett in a political rage. The source of her anger was U.S. President Harry S. Truman, specifically Truman's penchant for bloodthirsty foreign policy. "I am amazed at the complacency of [the] Negro press and public," she wrote to Barnett, perhaps goading a little the president of the Associated Negro Press, the country's first Black news service:

> Thruman [*sic*] is a monster. I can think of him as nothing else but the BUTCHER OF ASIA. Of his grin of triumph on giving the order to drop the Atom bombs on Japan. Of his maintaining troops in China who are shooting the starving Chinese for stealing a handful of food. Of his slighting the Inauguration of the new nation of the Philipines [*sic*] by nothing bothering to be present. Of his lynching all the able Japanese under the guise of "War Criminals." War is war, but these men are being lynched for it without a murmur of protest from the Negro population of the U.S. . . . Do we not see that we any any [*sic*] too prominent Negro being morally lynched with everyone of those able Japanese. WE are being taught a lesson and given a horrible example through that. Is it that we are so devoted to "good Massa" that we feel that we ought not to even protest such crimes? Have we no men among us? If we cannot stop it, we can at least let it be known that we are not deceived. We can make any party who condones it, let alone orders it, tremble for election time. What are we, anyway?[1]

This singular anti-imperialist outburst, on display in the Claude Barnett Papers and in Carla Kaplan's *Zora Neale Hurston: A Life in Letters*, disrupts popular and often persuasive critical narratives that draw Hurston as a willing accomplice in conservative or racist U.S. political schemes. Yet Hurston's letter above could not be clearer: U.S. foreign policy against Asians is genocidal and racist and implicitly an attack on Black Americans. In a rare moment of solidarity, Hurston joined at least ideological arms with authorial contemporaries—and sometimes literary foes—like W. E. B. Du Bois, Langston Hughes, Paul Robeson, William Patterson, and Richard Wright, all of whom spent part of 1946 raging against the expansion of the U.S. empire into Asia and exhorting Black Americans to do something about it. Like these other writers, Hurston finds reason and room for a solidarity of analogy: Chinese under the legacy of Western imperialism are, as African Americans in the United States, a minority subaltern—just as Du Bois observed, while walking the streets of the 1930s Shanghai, how the colonial partitioning of the city reminded him of the streets of the Jim Crow South. Indeed, it is interesting to consider how Wright and Hurston—erstwhile mortal enemies on matters political after his blind and savage review of *Their Eyes Were Watching God* and her sneering dismissal of his Communist sympathies in *Uncle Tom's Children* —could *either* have written this letter in 1946, the year Wright abandoned the United States entirely for France, exhausted and estranged by the nation's predatory wanderlust directed against people of color at home and around the world.

Hurston's letter is thus an effective symbol and reminder of the at times surprising, yet enduring, expressions of solidarity in writing by African Americans and Asian Americans, a solidarity whose contours are explored in this essay. Indeed, Hurston's example foregrounds several features of this theme. First, pro-Asian sympathies in writings by African Americans often constitute a specific form of internationalist thought rooted in an appreciation of racial solidarity that disregards hemispheric divisions. AfroAsian internationalism in nineteenth- and twentieth-century African American writing is rooted in a cyclical appreciation of common racial interests, on the one hand, and in the deleterious global effects of U.S. interests in people of color everywhere, on the other hand. Second, for African Americans in particular, both events in Asia and the treatment of Asian countries by the United States have often been used as a reflective mirror to assess U.S. racial conditions. For example, Hurston's insistence that the Truman administration's decision to drop the atomic bomb on

Japan was a "high tech lynching" reminiscent of domestic treatment of Blacks echoed in an Asian vein the "Double Victory" theme inaugurated by the Black press during World War II—fight (German) fascism abroad, defeat racism at home. Third, AfroAsian literary collaboration is a distinctive and logical continuation of this solidarity theme. Well before the groundbreaking *Yardbird* anthologies of the 1970s, products of AfroAsian collaboration between West Coast writers Ishmael Reed, Sean Wong, Frank Chin, and others, African American writers had recognized Asian and Asian American politics and culture as sources of their own dynamic, evolving, and innovative literary experiment. The printed word and music have been especially fruitful arenas to explore and demonstrate these ties.

Examining the continuity and contiguities of AfroAsian alliance in U.S. literature and culture also serves to underscore a dissenting theme from a cultural consensus a book like this one seeks to challenge—namely, that Blacks and Asians have historically perceived each other as enemies or just plain can't "get along." As Vijay Prashad and others have argued, Afro-Asian affiliation, cultural borrowing, and exchange present a dialectical and synthetic model of transraciality that abolishes comfortable and discreet categories of "racial," "ethnic," or even "disciplinary" modeling. In this essay, therefore, I hope to trace some of the "roots and routes," not just of what some have come to call a "Black Pacific" linkage between Blacks and Asians but a set of disparate, overlapping, intersecting historical vectors that have consolidated AfroAsian interests and experiences.

Yardbird Lives

In a recent essay titled "The Yellow and the Black," African American writer and publisher Ishmael Reed recalls a 1969 party to celebrate the publication of *19 Necromancers from Now,* an anthology of primarily African American writers edited by Reed (though the book included an excerpt from Chinese American writer Frank Chin's novel *A Chinese Lady Dies*). At the party, Reed remembers, four writers, later known as the "Four Horsemen" of Asian American literature, met for the first time: Shawn Wong, Frank Chin, Jeff Chan, and Lawson Inada. Reed had invited the four to do a special issue for *Yardbird* magazine, Reed's own dynamic, energetic forum for multicultural writing. The resulting publication, *Yardbird 3,* precipitated the publication of Shawn Wong's novel *Homebase* under Reed's own publishing imprint, Reed and Cannon Publishing. As

Cheryl Higashida has noted, Reed's collaboration with Wong and Chin and the emergence of AfroAsian publishing collaboration were part of a larger "coalition building" endemic to post-1965 multiethnic literary movements. According to Higashida, Reed's Yardbird Publishing Company became a signal moment for Asian American writers who were seeking venues for challenging hegemonic conceptions of Asian American culture.[2] This literary collaboration reflected more disparate late-1960s political currents, like the formation of San Francisco–based Red Guard units in Asian Pacific American communities, modeled on the Black Panther Party cells in Oakland, a moment to which I will return.

Though neither Higashida nor Reed does so, however, it would be a mistake to argue that something like AfroAsian literary collaboration was "born" out of the Yardbird moment. Its roots are deeper still, enmeshed in nineteenth- and early-twentieth-century experiments in affiliative thought, especially by African American writers seeking national, international, and even transnational modes of cooperation that might alleviate the pressures of racial and economic isolation in the United States. The first cultural and intellectual contact points were established by nineteenth-century African American nationalists looking to Asiatic sources in antiquity as a means of recuperating a racial identity beyond the sphere of classical "Western" models. As Wilson Jeremiah Moses has noted, and as Martin Bernal has documented in detail, Black "contributionist" and Egypocentric thoughts of the nineteenth century were predicated on analyzing Egypt, North Africa, and the Mediterranean region as crossroads of Asiatic and African cultures.[3] Jupiter Hammon, Alexander Crummell, and even Frederick Douglass used Asian antiquity as a touchstone for the "roots" of AfroAsiatic civilization. Their interest in "Eastern" byways for the development of Black culture was often linked to a restorative conception, in particular of Ethiopia as the ancestral home, or "Zion," of the Black diaspora. These linkages, the foundation of what Moses calls "Afrotopic" Black thought, underpinned much of the imaginative work of early Black nationalists to conceive of a racial nation with nonwhite sources at its root.

It was W. E. B. Du Bois who most completely and coherently synthesized these nineteenth-century Black intellectual currents with something like a secular program for "divining" AfroAsian solidarity. In both his much neglected early literary work and his nonfiction writing on Asia, Du Bois after 1900 conceived the "color line" quite literally as both separating and bridging peoples of Black and Asian descent. Du Bois was initially stirred toward engagement with Asian politics and culture by the formation of the Indian National Congress in 1885. It drew his interest in two very specific directions: toward the study of scholarship on the AfroAsian roots of classical antiquity and toward a theory of what might be called Pan-Asian-African unity. In *The World and Africa: An Inquiry into the Part Which Africa Has Played in World History,* published in 1947 but presenting the culmination of a lifetime of study, Du Bois drew on nineteenth-century Egyptocentrist and Afrocentrist thought, especially that of Alexander Crummell, composing an argument that anticipated Martin Bernal's *Black Athena*: "The Greeks, inspired by Asia, turned toward Africa for learning, and the Romans in turn learned of Greece and Egypt." Du Bois also rendered the Western Renaissance a colonial enterprise, meant to efface Black and Asian contributions to world culture: "Without the winking of an eye, printing, gunpowder, the smelting of iron, the beginnings of social organizations, not to mention political life and democracy, were attributed exclusively to the white race and to Nordic Europe."[4] Du Bois's outrage at white supremacist historiography was fueled by eugenics theorists like Lothrop Stoddard and Madison Grant, whose World World I era tomes, *The Rising Tide of White World Supremacy* and *The Passing of the Great Race,* respectively, argued for the literal and figurative elimination of the colored races. Du Bois's brilliant and polemical *Darkwater,* a series of essays on internationalist themes, published in 1920, in fact riffed off Stoddard's aquatic theme; the two would meet later in a debate on eugenics theory in 1929 in Chicago.[5]

In the realm of the secular and the social, Du Bois after 1900 was a tireless interpreter of the possibilities of Black-Asian kinship. In 1906, after Japan defeated Russia in an inter-imperialist war for territory in Manchuria and Korea, Du Bois celebrated the event as "the first time in a thousand years a great white nation has measured arms with a colored nation and has been found wanting."[6] The war also provided Du Bois occasion to rewrite his infamous Color Line thesis from *Souls of Black Folk* as a hemispheric theory: "The magic of the word 'white' is already broken, and the Color Line in civilization has been crossed in modern times as it was in the great past. The awakening of the yellow races is certain. That the awakening of the brown and black races will follow in time, no unprejudiced student of history can doubt."[7] By 1914, Du Bois was again revising his Color Line thesis to articulate a specific call for racial solidarity along East-West lines. In "The World Problem of the Color Line," Du Bois wrote: "All over the world the diversified races of the world are coming into close and closer contact as never before. We are nearer China today than we were to San Francisco yesterday."[8]

The literary culmination of Du Bois's emerging Pan-AfroAsianism, and perhaps his most neglected text until recently, is his 1928 novel *Dark Princess*. Depicting the story of an African American medical student named Matthew Townes, who becomes lover and political collaborator with an aristocratic Indian princess, Kautilya, the book is a loosely veiled allegory of post–World War I AfroAsian efforts at internationalist collaboration and national liberation struggle. The princess is part of a circle or cell of Asian émigrés operating in Berlin to foment political revolution, tinged by Soviet policy on ethnic nationalism. Matthew arrives in Berlin— where Du Bois studied Marx and Engels as a graduate student in the 1890s —ripe for expressing personal insult and outrage after his medical schooling is blocked in the United States by racist, exclusionary policies. Matthew and the princess travel back to the United States, where he works as a train porter, she as a boxmaker. He becomes involved briefly in a Garvey-style nationalist movement while the two of them continue to imagine an international movement that unites workers of the world. Du Bois literally records this cross-racial, self-determination movement as a flight of fancy: the book ends with the princess giving birth to a son, who is heralded as the "messiah to all the darker races" of the world. *Dark Princess* is an inordinately complex rendering of Black, Asian, and Soviet-influenced liberation struggles narrated as a revolutionary romance.

Du Bois's novel anticipated the 1930s' escalation of African American interest in and support for Asian liberation struggles. Two examples are Langston Hughes and Richard Wright. As he recounted in his autobiographical *I Wonder as I Wander*, Hughes, like Du Bois, was positively drawn to AfroAsian internationalism by trips to the Soviet Union, China, and Japan during the 1930s.[9] As did Du Bois, Hughes developed a prophetic revolutionary poetic voice when moved by China's liberation struggles in particular. "Roar China" was first published in *Volunteer for Liberty* on September 6, 1937, and was later republished in the Communist Party's *New Masses* on February 22, 1938.[10] The poem was written at a moment of intense civil war within China between nationalist and Communist forces and on the cusp of fullscale war with imperial Japan. The poem was literally concurrent with Hughes's better-known, more celebrated poems about the Spanish Civil War, like "Song of Spain." "Roar China" shares with that poem a passionate dedication to anti-Fascist, pro-Communist politics here in the specific service of an underdog nation which Du Bois himself once deridingly described as the "Uncle Tom" of Asia. Hughes's poem wills China to reject its colonial past and is something like a pep talk for a nation besieged. I excerpt two passages to demonstrate:

> Roar, China!
> Roar, old lion of the East!
> Snort fire, yellow dragon of the Orient,
> Tired at last of being bothered.[11]

> Laugh, little coolie boy on the docks of Shanghai, laugh!
>   You're no tame lion.
> Laugh, child slaves in the factories of the foreigners!
>   You've no tame lion.
> Laugh, child slaves in the factories of the foreigners!
>   You're no tame lion.
> Laugh—and roar, China! Time to spit fire![12]

Hughes's grandiloquent appeals to Black readers at home to hone an internationalist sensibility was arguably the thrust of Richard Wright's exile period, which also grounded itself in sympathy for Asian national liberation struggles. Perhaps the least read and least discussed of all of Wright's exile books, *The Color Curtain,* is a riveting, sui generis account of Wright's attendance at the momentous 1955 Bandung Conference in Indonesia.[13] The conference was a major meeting of twenty-nine African and Asian countries seeking to build mutual support for national independent movements. Wright attended the conference on the heels of his travels to Ghana in support of Kwame Nkrumah's government recorded in his 1953 book *Black Power.*[14] At Bandung, Wright offered a more difficult and less successful rendering of AfroAsian solidarity. The book's enthusiasm for Asian self-determination movements is overshadowed by Wright's anti-Communist dis-ease with China's presence at the meeting. Wright wrote the book at a moment of heightened contradiction for himself because by 1955 he had become a firm anti-Stalinist. The book is also tainted by Wright's contradictory relationship with the idea of the "West." What Paul Gilroy calls aptly Wright's "negative loyalty" to Western cultural, political, and spiritual life is confounded by Wright's naïve suspicions about religious-based societies like Muslim Indonesia, his pragmatic faith in technological development, and his own premonitions about the need for the "Third World" to enter something like modernity. *The Color Curtain* is one of the most complex works in the AfroAsian literary genealogy of the United States. It is a landmark text for understanding post-1945 AfroAsian linkages in the United States. Ironically but importantly, the book nearly vanished after poor reviews and poor sales still during Wright's lifetime, symptomatic of both the book's limitations and Wright's gradual eclipse from public interest in the United States as he stayed abroad.

And yet, those African American writers and intellectuals of the Cold War who were persistently in search of new modes of international and transnational solidarities duly noted Wright's presence at Bandung in particular. A key moment in the development of 1960s AfroAsian liberation efforts—one that corresponded with Wright's appearance at Bandung—was the case of Robert F. Williams. Williams, a one-time autoworker in Detroit and leader of the NAACP branch in Monroe, North Carolina, his hometown, was chased into exile by the FBI in 1961 after attempting to shelter a white couple during a race rebellion in Monroe. He fled to Canada, then Cuba, where he became first an ardent supporter and then critic of Fidel Castro's socialist revolution. Living in Cuba from 1961 to 1966, Williams was visited by African American political and cultural workers from the United States, including Amiri Baraka, whose shift from Beatnik sensibility to proto-Black Nationalism was in part triggered by both Williams's and Cuba's example. In 1966, disillusioned with Castro for not speaking out on behalf of Black nationalism in the United States, Williams and his wife Mabel moved to Beijing at the invitation of Chairman Mao, with whom Williams had initiated mail correspondence several years earlier. Indeed, Mao's famous 1963 "Support for the American Negroes in Their Struggle against Racial Discrimination and for Freedom and Equal Rights," released and distributed worldwide,[15] was literally provoked by a written request by Williams. Williams's arrival in Beijing in 1966, where he lived until 1969, became a real and symbolic exemplar of the desire for African American and Asian American race rebels seeking to forge international affiliations. One iteration of this was the resurgent interest in the Cultural Revolution and the writings of Mao as touchstones for the Black Arts Movement. Mao's famous 1942 "Talks at the Yenan Forum on Art and Literature"[16] became the subject of study circles in Black Arts centers like Detroit, an example of what Black Arts poet and theorist Larry Neal called "useable elements of Third World culture" for the building of Black Arts.[17] "What we demand is unity of politics and art," wrote Mao, "of content and form, and of the revolutionary political content and the highest possible degree of perfection in artistic form. . . . We must carry on a two-front struggle in art and literature."[18] Revolutionary art and literature were to be judged "on the basis of actual life and help the masses to push history forward."[19] In an extraordinary bit of AfroAsian congruence, Williams lectured in Beijing on the significance of Mao's Yenan talk for Black artists in the United States, citing as example of "Yenan"-style art "progressive new protest jazz" and Frank Greenwood's all-black theatrical production in Los Angeles of Claude McKay's 1919 sonnet "If We Must Die."[20] Back in the United States, Black cultural workers like Baraka and Detroit's Woodie King forged all-black theater companies dedicated to cultural self-determination and a Black Arts version of a "two-front struggle in art and literature."

It was not long after these literal examples of transnational influence that Ishmael Reed's *Yardbird* appeared on the West Coast as a new manifestation of something that might be called in retrospect "proto-multiculturalism." As Reed recounts, California itself, with its history of Mexican *indigenos,* Asian miners and railroad workers, Japanese and Philipino farm workers, and African American migrants was a natural source for a new conception of interethnic collaboration.[21] Los Angeles and San Francisco became the obvious flashpoints for new forms of AfroAsian collaboration. Still inspired by events like China's Cultural Revolution and anticolonial struggles across Africa, especially Ghana and the Congo, young Asian American and African American radicals formed nearly concurrently the I Wor Kuen (IWK) and the Black Panther Party. While the history of the latter is well known, IWK, a Cantonese name meaning "Society of the Harmonious Righteous Fist," played an equally important role in determining the direction of Asian Pacific American political culture in vanguard Leftist circles from New York to California, likewise stirring Afro-Asian interchange in the arts. In a foundational history of IWK, Fred Ho, a former member, recounts that IWK first formed as a revolutionary collective in New York City in November, 1969.[22] Just months earlier, in San Francisco, the Red Guard Party had formed, a collection of Asian American street youth formerly members of Leway (from the name "Legitimate Ways") formed in 1967. Leway, like the Black Panther Party, developed study cells for Mao's Third World writing.[23] After it had formed, both IWK and the Red Guard Party organized "Serve the People" programs based on the Black Panther Party Survival Programs. While the organizations did not share membership, they offered a similar revolutionary,

Third World, working-class orientation to young African and Asian Pacific Americans, simultaneously combating racial and economic hardships in their respective communities.

Clearly, this political modeling influenced the formation of proto-multiculturalism championed by Reed, Sean Wong, and other participants in earlier AfroAsian collaboration in New York and the Bay Area. For example, in addition to Reed's Yardbird publications and books, the early 1970s featured AfroAsian collaborations like *Time to Greez! Incantations from the Third World*, a poetry anthology edited by Asian American poet Janice Mirikitani, and others, including work by a wide ethnic variety of authors. As Cheryl Higashida has noted, *Time to Greez!* was published by Glide Publications, part of Glide Church, a multiracial San Francisco institution headed by Mirikitani and African American minister Cecil Williams.[24] The progressive, multicultural paradigms offered by Glide, Yardbird Publishing, and Reed's Before Columbus Foundation became in many ways the dominant ones for 1970s cultural production in colored communities; accordingly, AfroAsian collaboration in the arts deepened across the decade. Filipino performance poet Jessica Hagedorn, later better known for her novels *Dogeaters* and the *Gangster of Love*, co-founded the West Coast Gangster Choir with African American authors Thulani Davis and Ntozake Shange.[25]

In jazz, the 1970s produced a number of emerging collaborative Afro-Asian strands: Chinese American musician and composer Fred Ho picked up his first baritone saxophone at the age of fourteen, joined the Nation of Islam two years later as Fred3X, later joined I Wor Kuen, and began to filter the "free jazz" pioneered by writers and composers like Archie Shepp into a hybrid sound and dialectical politics which were mutually informing. Ho formed the Afro-Asian Music Ensemble and began adopting historical Filipino, Chinese, and other East Asian worksongs, love songs, and anthems of national independent to traditional "jazz" instruments and radically contemporary arrangements. He also tapped the spirit and rhetoric of Bandung-era Third World Internationalism in his work. His early recordings with the Afro-Asian Music Ensemble include *Underground Railroad to My Heart*, a compilation of antiracist, anti-imperialist songs bridging AfroAsian interests, and later, *The Black Panther Ballet Suite*, a multimedia tribute to the Black Panther Party. Ho maintains fidelity to principles of both Yenan and the Black Arts Movement, seeking to foster spaces for Third World cultures and autonomous networks of support for AfroAsian artists and writers. In his essay "Fists for Revolution," a personal

and social history of I Wor Kuen and the League of Revolutionary Struggle, Ho articulates his vision for building "independent militant, not non-
profit, organizations and resources . . . in all the many visual, spoken word,
musical and theatrical expressions and forms to promote revolutionary
consciousness."[26]

Ho represents the Left vanguard of AfroAsian collaboration in jazz that
also produced dynamic cultural institutions and new talent in the wake of
late 1960s, early 1970s AfroAsian collaborations. Again the San Francisco
Bay Area was central to this merger. The 1980s saw the development of the
West Coast Kearney Street Workshop and Asian Improv Records initiated
by Asian American jazz pianist Jon Jang and bassist Mark Izu, among others. These progressive cultural institutions were testing grounds for the
production and distribution of "Asian American Jazz." Mindful and respectful of the development of jazz as an African American vernacular, the
Kearney Street Workshop continued the spirit of autonomous culture and
community-center building inaugurated by early Black and Asian Pacific
American organizations like IWK. The AfroAsian cast to the institutions
finds echo in other African American–centered cultural groups like the
Combahee River Collection that became the impetus for the formation of
Kitchen Table Press, perhaps the most important feminist multicultural
publishing house in contemporary U.S. culture. In short, the continuity
and persistence of AfroAsian solidarity and exchange is an easily marked
line from the mid-1950s to the present. In the last section of this essay I
discuss in brief the contours of this exchange at present.

Postscript

The legacy of Bandung and Third World AfroAsian solidarities remains
vital in the work and lives of numerous contemporary U.S. writers of African and Asian descent. Some of these writers are veterans of "first wave"
AfroAsian solidarity of the 1960s; others are post-1960s innovators, rekin-
dling and recuperating historical forms of AfroAsian solidarity. New Orleans–based poet Kalamu ya Salaam, a veteran of both the Black Arts
Movement and the Congress of Afrikan Peoples, is a co-founder of Runa-
gate Multimedia publishing company and founder and director of Neo-
Griot Workshop, a New Orleans–based Black writer workshop. He has
published several books of poetry and spoken word CDs. He also is col-
laborating with Fred Ho on the Afro-Asian Arts Dialogue, a music/spoken

word duet that pays tribute in part to the legacy of AfroAsian solidarity. In his poem "We Don't Stand a Chinaman's Chance Unless We Create a Revolution," Ya Salaam pays explicit tribute to the legacies of Bandung and China's seizure of state power:

> You don't stand a chinaman's chance
> Is what people used to say to define hopelessness
> You don't stand a chinaman's chance
> Used to be a definition of a loser
> But after Mao & crew did their do
> A chinaman's chance got so good
> That nobody played that number anymore.
>
> Regardless of the problems and perplexities
> Of China's current state at least they got a chance,
> A future & the whole world recognizes that.[27]

Maya Almachar Santos is a Filipina American poet and artist from Seattle. In 1997, she became a founding member of the Isangmahal arts collective, poets and artists in residence at the Northwest Asian American Theater. Isangmahal means "one love" in Tagalog. Santos's work expresses the urgency of the survival of the culture and political will of colored or marginalized peoples. It is a plain expression of Third World internationalism in which Tagalog and English become a radically hybrid lingua franca. This is from her poem "self-rebolusyon":

> Kalayaan
> Kasi mamabuhay ang katipunan
> Demokratikung Pilipino movement
> Raise up yo fist and labian
> Cuz this be the continuation
> Our breath the duration
> Like the incessant path to liberation
> To escape existential situations
> Bob Marley called it a "redemption song"
> Kinda like, "ang bayan kong pilipinas,"
> I press pause and ask the annihilating question,
>
> "what happened to our world war II veterans?"[28]

Finally, a major player on the Minneapolis/St. Paul Twin Cities hip-hop and spoken word scene is Thien-bao Thuc Phi. Born in Saigon, Vietnam, he was raised in the Phillips neighborhood of South Minneapolis. He has twice won the Minnesota Grand Poetry Slam and won two poetry slams at the Nuyorican Poets Café in New York. He is the only Vietnamese American man to have appeared on HBO's *Russell Simmons Presents Def Poetry*. Bao Phi describes himself as a "straight up ghetto-raised hip hop fan. Never a hustler or a street kid or a banger, but a ghetto nerd who grew up in hip hop—and I didn't necessarily always like it."[29] Yet he has written profoundly and provocatively of the complex intersections of AfroAsian exchange in the breeding arena of hip-hop where stereotypes of both African Americans and Asian Americans are abolished and challenged and where ethnic remixing is a potentially liberatory project for men (and, he argues, for women). Bao Phi's vision of a hip-hop future across the color line is not only a pragmatic response to hip-hop's globalization (after all, rap has even caught the popular imagination of the People's Republic of China), but also a very personal dream of extending the AfroAsian legacy into a public sphere where it can compete or combat popular misconceptions about the nature of AfroAsian relationships. For every Jackie Chan/ Chris Tucker collaboration that reduces Black and Yellow to popular cardboard cut outs—what Fred Ho calls the "chop suey" approach to Afro-Asian collaboration—Bao Phi suggests the need and space for serious, engaged, "saturated," as Larry Neal might call it, AfroAsian social movements and cultural forms.

AfroAsian solidarity has always been future-oriented, anticipating the declining significance of whiteness, the globalization and communion of the colored world, and the prospects for diminished essentialist or separatist social programs. It is debatable where each of these is in ascent or decline. What is not debatable is that AfroAsian solidarity needs a constant reorientation to itself. The constant threat of historical erasure of the coalition building of ethnic communities necessitates an urgent, disciplined commitment to a "useable" AfroAsian past. It is toward the preservation and continuity of this past that this essay is dedicated. Like this book, it hopes to make the constant, shifting lines of AfroAsian solidarity past and present more visible to those who seek to sustain them.

NOTES

1. Hurston's letter to Barnett may be found in the Claude Barnett Papers, Claude Barnett Collection, Chicago Historical Society, Chicago, IL, Box 289, Folder 25. It is published in *Zora Neale Hurston: A Life in Letters*, ed. Carla Kaplan (New York: Anchor Books, 2002), 546.

2. Cheryl Higashida, "Not Just a 'Special Issue': Gender, Sexuality, and Post-1965 Afro-Asian Coalition Building in the *Yardbird Reader* and *This Bridge Called My Back*," in *Afro/Asia: Revolutionary Political and Cultural Connections between African-Americans and Asian-Americans*, ed. Fred Ho and Bill V. Mullen (Durham: Duke University Press, forthcoming).

3. See Martin Bernal, *Black Athena: The Afroasiatic Roots of Classical Civilization: The Archaeological and Documentary Evidence* (New Brunswick: Rutgers University Press, 1991).

4. W. E. B. Du Bois, *The World and Africa: An Inquiry into the Part Which Africa Has Played in World History* (New York: Viking Press, 1947), 20.

5. The debate between Du Bois and Lothrop Stoddard was held in the Chicago Coliseum in March 1929. Du Bois's remarks were reported in the *Chicago Defender*, 23 March 1939. A pamphlet titled *Report of the Debate Conducted by the Chicago Forum: "Shall the Negro Be Encouraged to Seek Cultural Equality?" Affirmative: W. E. Burghardt Du Bois . . . Negative: Lothrop Stoddard . . . March 17, 1929 Fred Atkins Moore, Director of the Chicago Forum"* was published in Chicago in the same year.

6. W. E. B. Du Bois, "The Color Line Belts the World," *Collier's Weekly*, 20 October 1906, 20.

7. Ibid.

8. W. E. B. Du Bois, "The World Problem of the Color Line," *Manchester* (NH) *Leader*, 16 November 1914.

9. Langston Hughes, *I Wonder as I Wander* (New York: Rinehart, 1956).

10. See "Roar China!" in *The Collected Poems of Langston Hughes*, ed. Arnold Rampersad (New York: Knopf, 1995), 198.

11. Ibid.

12. Ibid., 199.

13. Richard Wright, *The Color Curtain* (Jackson: University Press of Mississippi, 1994).

14. Richard Wright, *Black Power: A Record of Reactions in a Land of Pathos* (New York: HarperCollins, 1995).

15. Mao Tse-Tung, "Statement Supporting the Afro-Americans in Their Just Struggle against Racial Discrimination by U.S. Imperialism (August 8, 1963)," *People of the World, Unite and Defeat the U.S. Aggressors and All Their Lackeys* (Peking: Foreign Language Press, 1967).

16. Mao Tse-Tung, "Talks at the Yenan Forum on Art and Literature (May 23,

1952)," in *Mao Tse-Tung: An Anthology of His Writings,* ed. Anne Fremantle (New York: Mentor Books, 1962), 254–259.

17. Larry Neal, "The Black Arts Movement," in *The Norton Anthology of African American Literature,* ed. Nellie Y. McKay and Henry Louis Gates Jr. (New York: W.W. Norton, 1997), 1963.

18. Mao, "Talks at Yenan," 259.

19. Ibid., 254.

20. Robert F. Williams, "Speech, 25th Anniversary of Mao's 'Talks at the Yenan Forum on Literature and Art,'" box 3, Robert Franklin Williams Papers, Bentley Historical Library, University of Michigan, Ann Arbor, MI.

21. Ishmael Reed and Al Young, eds., *Yardbird Lives!* (New York: Grove Press, 1978), 14.

22. Fred Ho, "Fists for Revolution: The Revolutionary History of I Wor Kuen/ League of Revolutionary Struggle," in *Legacy to Liberation: Politics and Culture of Revolutionary Asian Pacific America,* ed. Fred Ho, Carolyn Antonio, Diane Fujino, and Steve Yip (New York and San Francisco: Big Red Media and AK Press, 2000), 3.

23. Ibid.

24. Higashida, "Not Just a 'Special Issue,'" 29.

25. Ibid., 30.

26. Ho, "Fists for Revolution," 13.

27. Kalamu ya Salaam, "We Don't Stand a Chinaman's Chance Unless We Create a Revolution," in *Afro/Asia: Revolutionary Political and Cultural Connections between African-Americans and Asian-Americans,* ed. Fred Ho and Bill V. Mullen (Durham: Duke University Press, forthcoming).

28. Maya Almachar Santos, "self-rebolusyon," in *Afro/Asia: Revolutionary Political and Cultural Connections between African-Americans and Asian-Americans,* ed. Fred Ho and Bill V. Mullen (Durham: Duke University Press, forthcoming).

29. Thien-bao Thuc Phi, "Yellow Lines: Asian Americans and Hip Hop," in *Afro/Asia: Revolutionary Political and Cultural Connections between African-Americans and Asian-Americans,* ed. Fred Ho and Bill V. Mullen (Durham: Duke University Press, forthcoming).

Chapter 14

Internationalism and Justice
Paul Robeson, Asia, and Asian Americans

Greg Robinson

I [just sang] Chinese and Hebridean folk songs to illustrate a point that is very close to my heart these days—
the likeness of the music of various peoples. . . . This was
brought home to me in Scotland . . . in many of my concerts I would find the Chinese and the African and the
Scotch chaps exchanging their music on the flute and on
the bagpipes and on the xylophone, and they all came
out the same way. So it was very interesting and so the
Chinese songs are very much like our African melodies,
and the languages are very close. I think I've done it once
before in the church—it might be amusing—I always
say in Chinese "Hao bu hao," which means "How do you
feel?" You can't say "Hao bu Hao"; you have to say
"Haaaaoooo *BUUU* Haaoo" (laughter) and you answer
"xie xie"—"thank you very much. Very well." In the African language I know there is something very close to
that. It goes "Aka *AKA* ingwah": try that 'Aka *AKA* ingwah—Haaooo *BUUU* Haaoo.'"

— Paul Robeson, concert at AME Zion Church,
Harlem, ca. 1950

Am I an American? I'm just an Irish, Negro, Jewish,
Italian, Spanish, French and English, Russian, Chinese,
Polish, Scotch, Hungarian, Litvak, Finnish, Swedish, Ca-
nadian, Greek and Turk and Czech and Double Check
American.

— Paul Robeson as the lead singer in
Earl Robinson–John Latouche,
"Ballad For Americans," 1939

Throughout the twentieth century, African Americans have looked beyond the United States to the world stage. Seeing themselves as part of a non-white world majority—in some cases, such as W. E. B. Du Bois and Richard Wright, even as the vanguard of that majority—they associated themselves with anticolonialist and democratic struggles in many areas of the world. The power of their identification can be demonstrated in a number of instances, such as African Americans' sympathy for India's campaign for independence from British rule in the first half of the twentieth century (and, conversely, the influence of Gandhi's theories of nonviolent struggle on African American civil rights activists), their moral and financial support for Ethiopia following the Italian invasion in 1935, and later their concern for South Africa and the leadership of the anti-Apartheid movement in the United States during the 1980s. A number of recent historical studies, notably those of Brenda Gayle Plummer, Penny von Eschen, and Thomas Borstelmann, have underlined the role of internationalist thought in the African American community and its role in shaping not only black community attitudes but also government policy toward other nations, particularly in the nonwhite world.[1] More specialized studies, notably those of Sudarshan Kapur, Reginald Kearney, and Mark Gallichio, have revolved around Black internationalism in its connection with Asia.[2]

The political activism of Paul Robeson during the 1930s and 1940s, and in particular his cultural and political engagement with East Asia and with the Asian diaspora, represents a fascinating case study of Black internationalism. Robeson was probably the most popular and visible African American of the 1930s and 1940s. He was a celebrated stage actor, the first black movie star, an internationally famous folk singer, a champion athlete, a lawyer, a powerful speaker, and a linguist conversant in anywhere from ten to twenty-five languages. Robeson was and continues to be primarily known for his interest in international politics, chiefly as an uncritical supporter and admirer of the Soviet Union and of the U.S. Communist Party. Because of his sympathy for communism, plus his advocacy of civil rights, Robeson suffered severe repression during the Cold War years when he was vilified in the press and targeted for boycotts by conservative groups. When Robeson gave a concert at Peekskill, New York, in 1949, concertgoers were attacked and beaten by right-wing vigilantes. During the 1950s, Robeson was blacklisted, harassed by the FBI, and denied a passport by the State Department. As a result, Robeson (who had been the highest-paid black entertainer in the nation during the prewar years) was effectively unemployed for ten years, while his health was ruined by the ordeal.

Although it was Robeson's advocacy of friendship with the Soviet Union that aroused the greatest public attention and controversy, his primary interest on the international scene during the 1930s and 1940s was in Africa, whose nations were then engaged in a developing movement for independence from European colonial rule. Robeson's principal organizational affiliation during that period was as co-chair of the Council for African Affairs (CAA), a New York–based group that served as an information clearinghouse on Africa and which campaigned for an end to colonialism. Most of Robeson's public speeches were made at meetings of the CAA or in the name of the council, and the CAA organized Robeson's concert tours to help in fundraising.

Robeson's interest in Africa and in its liberation was based on a powerful cultural foundation. This in itself is hardly surprising. Robeson's wife, the writer and ethnologist Eslanda Goode Robeson, was a prominent student of African cultures.[3] Furthermore, Robeson came of age as a thinker during the 1920s, a time when, as David Levering Lewis and other scholars have observed, the black artists and writers of the Harlem Renaissance brought a rich sense of the use of cultural politics to the struggle for civil rights. Cultural nationalists, seeing the route to political enfranchisement blocked, urged a strategy of black equality through cultural self-assertion. Africa served as a central spiritual rallying point for nationalists, notably Marcus Garvey, who attracted millions of followers with his vision of black pride and a redeemed African fatherland.

Nevertheless, Paul Robeson raised the conjunction between art and politics to a new level. Unlike many black Americans of his day, Robeson considered himself fundamentally African in character. He referred to himself frequently as an Afro-American and took great pride in his ancestry—he commented that sometimes he felt like he was the only Negro in the United States who did not want to be white.[4] With the encouragement of his wife, Robeson engaged in intensive, though unsystematic, study of African languages, sculpture, and music at the School for Oriental Languages in London, the city that served as his home base throughout much of the 1930s. These studies and his contacts with Africans in England persuaded him that if people of African ancestry could learn and rediscover Africa's rich cultural heritage and contributions, which had been obscured by European racism, they would gain the self-confidence required to throw off colonialism in Africa and white domination in the United States.

A corollary of Robeson's feelings of identity with Africa and his hopes that a cultural revival would catalyze the liberation of its people was his sense that the interest of Africans (and thus African Americans) lay in co-ordination with other oppressed groups, particularly those which he felt had powerful cultural traditions from which they could draw strength. For example, Robeson was a fervent admirer of Jewish culture and devoted significant attention to building coalitions between Blacks and Jews in the United States. He also supported India during its struggle for independence from Great Britain in the years surrounding World War II.

Nowhere, however, was Robeson's particular fusion of cultural politics and political struggle more apparent than in his attachment to China and its effect on his ideas. Starting in the early 1930s, Robeson began to learn about Chinese culture, an interest he retained for decades. Although, unlike his wife, Robeson never traveled to China, he bought books on Chinese art and politics, intermittently studied Chinese language, and interviewed Chinese opera singers and artists.[5] He many times expressed his desire to analyze his ideas about China in an extended work, and while he never produced any formal work on the subject, Robeson communicated his passion in endless casual discussions and by performances of folk songs in his concert programs.

Robeson drew from his discoveries about China the fundamental conclusion that Africans were spiritually (and hence politically) more kindred with Asia than with the West. As he stated in an article, " [The Chinese are] artists concerned mainly with [the] inner development of *man*. . . . Long ago this most ancient of living cultures assigned soldier and warrior and glorious *hero* to lowest rank—and the scholar stands first—certainly there is no question of fundamental rightness of the latter."[6] Robeson expressed great (and from a current-day viewpoint, somewhat excessive) admiration for the capacity of the Chinese to absorb Western science and technology alongside their particular philosophical and cultural systems, and thereby reinforce rather than surrender their traditional communitarian values. On several occasions he advised young Africans to study China and the Far East as a model to use in their own struggle with modernism. While they could adapt the technical and mechanical knowledge of the West, they should look to the East for "fundamental values of humanity." As he stated in an interview in autumn 1935:

> The trouble with the American Negro is that he has an inferiority complex. He fails to realize that he comes of a great ancestry linked with the great races of the Orient. . . .
>   I am more than ever convinced that the African civilization dates back to

the times when Oriental culture, including that from China, began to influence the Western world. I believe that where the Afro-American made his
mistake was when he began trying to mimic the West instead of developing
the really great tendencies he inherited from the East. I believe the Negro
can achieve his former greatness only if he learns to follow his natural tendencies, and ceases trying to master the greatness of the West. My own instincts are Asiatic.[7]

However, Robeson's insistence on the close resemblance between the
spiritual values of Chinese and African culture, and his admiration for the
"profundity" of Chinese culture, is problematic. The cultural connections
he cited were generally superficial and based on an extremely generalized
and ahistorical view of both African and Asian cultures. On the one hand,
he clearly wished to free himself and his readers from internalized colonization and a feeling of inferiority vis-à-vis European and European-
American civilization by reminding them of alternate, and nonwhite,
models of society and sites of culture. On the other hand, by positing a
stark opposition between Western technology and a unitary Eastern spiri-
tuality and wisdom, Robeson bought into familiar Western Orientalist
images of Asia as a land of exotic and mystical wisdom.

Robeson's cultural interest in China grew in tandem with his developing political consciousness during the 1930s. He was already deeply disillusioned about life in the United States and Western Europe by the beginning of the decade as a result of the harsh racial prejudice he had experienced, and he began speaking of the necessity for African Americans to
follow a different path. His respect for Russian culture, along with his feeling of sympathy with the Chinese and other cultures he considered non-
Western, gave him a new sense of himself as an artist. As he stated in an
interview in mid-1933:

I will not do anything that I do not understand. I do not understand the
psychology or philosophy of the Frenchman, German or Italian. Their history has nothing in common with my slave-ancestors. So I will not sing
their music, or the songs of their ancestors. . . . But I know the wail of the
Hebrew and I feel the plaint of the Russian. I understand both, as I do the
philosophy of the Chinese, and I feel that they have much in common with
the traditions of my race. And because I have been frequently asked to present something other than Negro art, I may succeed in finding either a great

Russian opera or play, or some great Hebrew or Chinese work which I feel I shall be able to render with the necessary degree of understanding.[8]

Shortly afterward, Robeson traveled for the first time to the Soviet Union. While en route, he passed through Germany, then at the dawn of the Hitler period, and he was deeply shaken by what he observed of Nazi racial attitudes. Conversely, his experience in Moscow and on the tours he was given in the Soviet Union persuaded him that the Communists had abolished poverty and conquered racial prejudice. While in Moscow, Robeson met Jack and Si-Lan Chen, the children of Eugene Chen, a Jamaican of mixed African and Chinese ancestry who had been a minister in Sun-Yat Sen's government. The willingness of the Chinese nationalists to offer black men positions of such prominence greatly impressed Robeson, and he returned from Russia with a heightened political consciousness. The events of the Spanish Civil War further politicized him. He was deeply impressed by the international mobilization of anti-Fascist groups, in which the Communists were prominently represented, to fight in defense of the republic. In January 1938, he traveled to Spain and sang concerts for the members of the Abraham Lincoln battalions.

Robeson seems not to have reacted immediately to the Japanese invasion of China in summer 1937. Nevertheless, beyond the cultural and race-based kinship Robeson felt with the Chinese, he clearly felt that China was part of the larger cause of freedom in the world. Certainly, the occupation of the country by a pro-Fascist Japan and the leadership of the Chinese Communist Party in the national resistance movement encouraged Robeson, like other progressives, to draw comparisons with the plight of the Spanish Republic. (In the same way, the African American intellectual and activist Langston Hughes, who had previously supported the Republican forces in Spain, published a pro-Chinese poem, "China, Rise," in the left-wing magazine *The New Masses*). Thus, on his return home to London from Spain, when Robeson was approached by representatives of the Chinese government for support, he agreed to attend a Save China rally in London and to sing at a fundraiser. A few months later, in response to another plea from Chinese representatives, he made a public statement of solidarity: "Greeting to the Chinese people who are so heroically defending the liberties of *all* progressive humanity."[9]

Still, whatever Robeson's genuine willingness to serve the anti-Fascist cause, China was not a central concern of his at this time. Robeson's

efforts were an adjunct of the dozens of fundraisers and supportive activities he undertook on behalf of the Spanish Republic before its fall in early
1939. In summer 1938, the U.S. Communist Party published an anti-Japan-
ese pamphlet called "Is Japan the Champion of the Colored Races?" The
pamphlet mentioned Robeson prominently as an American Negro and
underlined the warm reception he had received in the Soviet Union. In
a footnote, the pamphlet mentioned that Robeson was a sponsor of the
China Aid Council of the American League for Peace and Democracy (itself a Communist Party front group).[10] Although Robeson was not himself
responsible for the juxtaposition, it is no doubt symbolic of China's subordinate place in his program.

It was not until the end of 1939, two years after the Japanese invasion,
that Robeson became active in the Chinese cause. Although he never explained the roots of his commitment, the timing of his shift suggests a tension in his political views. Robeson returned to the United States in fall
1939, shortly after the outbreak of World War II in Europe, and spent the
war years in the United States. There he continued his support for the de-
posed Spanish republic through the Joint Anti-Fascist Committee to Aid
Spanish Refugees and threw himself into the African independence movement through the Council of African Affairs.[11] By this time, the signing of
the Nazi-Soviet Non-Aggression Pact had shattered the Popular Front of
the 1930s and had caused thousands of anti-Fascist activists to abandon
the Communist Party. Robeson himself refused to give up his unswerving
support for the Soviet Union. Instead, as the party line changed in the
wake of the pact from support for international mobilization against fascism to calls for workers to oppose the "imperialist war," Robeson followed suit. He denounced the English and French war efforts, expressed
support for Russia's invasion of Finland, which he termed defensive in
nature, and during 1940 and early 1941 participated in rallies and made
public statements against American defense mobilization and aid to Great
Britain. In early 1941 he recorded Earl Robinson's satirical antiwar "Spring
Song."

However, if Robeson was publicly silent about Hitler and fascism in
Europe in accordance with the dictates of the party, at the same time
he chose to escalate his involvement in the movement for Chinese freedom. This strongly suggests that support for China made it possible for
Robeson to continue his anti-Fascist commitment without challenging
the party line. (Although the Communist Party still officially supported
China's struggle against the Japanese occupation, party members seem to

have considered the China war a distant "local" conflict, subordinate to the European question, and did not offer significant support to the Chinese war effort).[12] In early 1940 Robeson became a public sponsor of the Committee to Aid China and appeared at a rally for the China Defense League, where he called for an end to the Japanese occupation.[13] In addition, Robeson enrolled in a Chinese-language course at Columbia University (his law school alma mater), with the idea of integrating Chinese songs into his concert repertory as an expression of solidarity.[14] He would continue to study Chinese off and on for several years. During the war years, Chuh Shih, the director of the Chinese Institute in America, agreed to tutor Robeson in Chinese pronunciation. Robeson, intrigued by his tutor's interest in the United States, suggested that he learn the song "Old Man River" from the musical *Show Boat,* which Robeson had popularized and which remained his signature tune (with lyrics he himself altered), in order to gain insight into the problems of black Americans.[15]

In early 1941, Robeson agreed to appear at a number of events on behalf of the China War Relief. For example, he appeared at "Stars for China," a Philadelphia benefit, in May 1941.[16] His actions sparked a major controversy when the Washington Committee for Aid to China invited him to headline a "Night of Stars" benefit at Constitution Hall. The Daughters of the American Revolution, who owned the hall, refused to admit a black performer, as they had famously done two years previously in the case of Marian Anderson. A support committee of prominent liberals, including Eleanor Roosevelt, quickly secured another hall for the event, which agreed to waive its segregation policy for the occasion. When Mrs. Gifford Pinchot, who was leading the support committee, discovered that the China Relief organization was giving half the event's proceeds to the National Negro Congress (a Communist-backed civil rights group which Robeson had made his principal vehicle of activism), she and Mrs. Roosevelt withdrew their support on the rather specious grounds that it would be an insult to ask Robeson to sing in a segregated hall.[17]

Despite the contretemps and withdrawal of sponsorship, Robeson agreed to sing at the event. That evening he made use of his Chinese fluency to sing a new repertoire of Chinese military anthems that had been arranged (and presumably translated) by Liu Liang Mo, a Christian Socialist from Shanghai who was close to the Communist Party. After fleeing China, Liu had settled in New York, where he organized the Chinese People's Chorus to sing at rallies and thereby instill patriotism and cultural pride in Chinese Americans.

A few weeks after the concert, Robeson joined Liu and the Chinese People's Chorus to record an album entitled "Chee Lai: Songs of New China," which was released on the Keynote label. Robeson sang four Chinese songs —one in Chinese, one in English, and two in both languages—preceded by his spoken commentary. The title song, which Liu had popularized in China, Robeson described as "a song born in the struggle of the brave Chinese people."[18] ("Chee Lai" would later be adopted as the Red Army's official song, and after the Communist Party's takeover of China in 1949 it became the national anthem of the People's Republic of China). Robeson also sang "Feng Yang," a classic beggar's folk song, to which he rather doubtfully ascribed a contemporary political significance: "This is a true Chinese folk song about a place called Feng Yang. It tells of the long suffering of the Chinese people, or the invasion and continued misery and of the hope for eventual freedom."[19]

Robeson and Liu continued their close association during the succeeding years, during which time Liu worked on behalf of the United China Relief and began a regular column for the African-American newspaper the *Pittsburgh Courier*. In his first column for the *Courier*, Liu wrote that Robeson's recording of Chinese songs "is a strong token of the solidarity between the Chinese and the Negro people."[20]

In June 1941, Nazi Germany invaded the Soviet Union. Robeson quickly resumed his advocacy of alliance against fascism. His support for China, though relegated to second place by his interest in a Second Front to aid the Soviet Union, did not altogether disappear. During the war years, he continued to speak at United China Relief rallies. For instance, in March 1944, Robeson spoke at a Sun Yat-Sen Day Tribute in New York City in which he called China the "Promise of a New World." Robeson claimed that the recognition of China as one of the four great powers (a recognition that was, in actual fact, foisted on an unwilling Stalin by Franklin Roosevelt) demonstrated that the war was one of liberation from "the Hitlerite doctrine of master and inferior races."[21] During the postwar years, Robeson praised the Chinese Communists several times for fighting hunger and removing European-imposed discrimination from China. He hailed the creation of the People's Republic after the victory of the Red Army in 1949 and publicly praised the regime of Mao Tse-Tung for its efforts to end poverty and feed the population in China.[22] As a sign of his solidarity, he used Chinese songs in his concert repertory.[23]

Robeson also expressed an interest in Korea. Like the Chinese, the Koreans were engaged in struggling for liberation from Japan. In May 1942, the East and West Association, an American-Asian friendship organization directed by novelist and militant Pearl S. Buck, invited Robeson to speak at a pro-independence rally in New York titled "Korea and the United Nations." Robeson performed a Korean folk song at the meeting (according to the program, the song was "Do Rah Gee Tah Ryung," the "outing song"). After Korea won its independence from Japan in 1945, he spoke publicly on behalf of the Communist regime of Kim Il Sung, and at the end of the decade he opposed U.S. intervention in the Korean War. Recalling his earlier singing appearance on behalf of Korean independence, he urged blacks not to fight their "brothers" in Korea.[24]

In tandem with his growing political commitment to Asian freedom during the 1940s, Robeson began to concentrate on the struggles of Asian Americans. Ironically, despite his concern for Asian liberation, earlier, during the 1930s, Robeson had been silent about racial discrimination against people of Asian ancestry, especially on the West Coast. While this can be explained to a certain extent by Robeson's lack of familiarity with West Coast race relations, it also reflects his cultural politics. Just as Robeson sought freedom for Africa and saw himself as an African, he seems to have envisioned Chinese (and other Asian) Americans as primarily Asian in their identity, and not as fellow Americans. Indeed, despite the evidence of his friendship for individuals, notably actress Anna May Wong, Robeson even expressed a certain scorn for Westernized Chinese as divorced from their cultural heritage and national struggle. In 1934, he wrote that American Negroes looking at Africa and wondering what such lands of savagery and squalor had to do with them were as ignorant as Chinese students in the West who wondered what the "chaos of conflicting misgovernments and household gods and superstition" had to do with them.[25] He privately told a friend, "If necessary I will die for Africa, but what should Africans care about American Negroes when most of them are Americans in culture? Can one expect a Chinese in China to be as concerned about the Chinese in San Francisco as about his own neighbors?"[26]

Still, if Robeson remained aloof from the plight of Asian Americans, both his talent and his insistence on racial equality made him widely admired among young Asian Americans. One Nisei newspaper columnist rhapsodized about Robeson's singing at a recital at the University of California, Berkeley:

Inadequate vocabulary of your writer fails to describe the rich simplicity of Mr. Robeson's voice as well as his ability to hold the audience spellbound to his very last notes. The magnitude of his voice actually made this reporter forget the presence of the campus cuties at his sides all evening. Of all the meetings attended by yours truly in the Men's gym, apparently this Negro baritone's recital equalled if not surpassed the brilliance and the dynamic eloquence of President [Robert] Sproul's speeches. In short, Mr. Robeson's voice decidedly has obscured your talented reporter's best shower bath singing into oblivion.[27]

Meanwhile, the editors of the San Francisco Japanese American daily *Nichi Bei* reported exultantly on Robeson's victorious suit against the proprietor of a Bay Area café that had excluded him from the establishment on racial grounds.[28]

During the war years, however, Robeson developed a growing interest in the condition of Asian Americans. To a certain degree, Robeson's commitment seems to have grown out of his activism on behalf of Chinese liberation. In 1941, he sang a benefit at Bryn Mawr College in Pennsylvania to raise money for scholarships for Chinese students stranded in America by the war, and in his speeches on behalf of China Relief, he praised the repeal of the Chinese Exclusion Act. However, this connection should not be overstated. For example, Robeson expressed his sympathy on various occasions with Americans of Asian ancestry as laborers and as fellow victims of discrimination.[29] For instance, in a letter in 1943, he stated that the future of African Americans was "bound with the future of the great masses of the American people, including the forces of labor, the Mexicans, the Chinese, the American Indians."[30] In a speech shortly afterward he praised "the workers from Mexico and from the east—Japan and the Philippines—whose labor has helped make the west and the southwest a fruitful land."[31]

Perhaps the strongest proof of Robeson's separation between Asians and Asian Americans is the fact that his strongest connections were not with Chinese Americans but with Japanese Americans, whom he easily disassociated from the hated Japanese enemy. In February 1942, as widespread pressure built up for the expulsion of all Japanese Americans from the Pacific Coast, liberal California congressman John Tolan announced that his Committee on Defense Migration would open hearings on the Japanese situation. Robeson, then in California, was approached by the sculptor Isamu Noguchi, who had founded a progressive group called Nisei Writers and Artists Mobilization for Democracy. Noguchi asked Robeson to appear before the commission as part of a blue-ribbon panel of prominent non-Asians who would testify to the loyalty of Japanese Americans and thereby help avert mass evacuation. Robeson readily volunteered to testify to the loyalty of Japanese Americans.[32] Shortly thereafter, President Franklin D. Roosevelt signed Executive Order 9066, authorizing the Army to remove and exclude civilians from the West Coast. The order made mass evacuation a fait accompli, and the idea of a celebrity panel was dropped. Robeson's promise of action nonetheless impressed many Nisei intellectuals.

Robeson continued, moreover, to keep himself informed of the conditions of the Nisei in the years that followed. In 1946, he publicly opposed the Canadian government's movement to deport thousands of citizens and residents of Japanese ancestry to Japan. As a sign of his solidarity, Robeson signed on as an honorary life member of the Japanese Canadian Committee for Democracy.[33] Meanwhile, he sang and spoke before Japanese American audiences on several occasions. In April 1946, he gave a concert in Salt Lake City, then home of the Japanese American Citizens League (JACL), to an audience composed in significant part of Japanese Americans. Although he did not refer directly to the Nisei in his remarks, he spoke out in favor of "equal economic rights" for all races: "It seems to me that America would have to pause and readjust her thinking, when you consider that nowhere else in the world do Negroes, Spanish-Americans or others have to apologize because of their color."[34] This, Robeson said, was the chief difference between fascism and the Soviet system, which melded all people into a brotherhood that recognized no racial distinctions. His talk was widely reported in the Nisei press. Community reaction was so favorable that a coalition of Japanese American groups in Chicago invited Robeson to be a guest speaker at a testimonial banquet honoring Nisei veterans on Memorial Day, 1946. At the banquet, which was heavily publicized in the Nisei press, Robeson strongly denounced racial discrimination in America as a Fascist doctrine and reminded the veterans that the victorious struggle against fascism had to be extended to the home territory. "Your fight is my fight," he told the veterans.[35]

The following year, Robeson returned to Salt Lake City to give another concert. After the concert he granted an interview to Larry Tajiri, editor of the JACL newspaper *Pacific Citizen*. Tajiri, an outspoken liberal and a prominent partisan of collaboration between Japanese Americans and African Americans, reported that Robeson was "sharply aware of the evacuation and of wartime prejudice against the Nisei. He said he would like to include a Japanese song in his program, a song of the common people to help fight discrimination against Americans of Japanese origin. It is all part of one problem, he noted, this matter of discrimination and it may be the foremost question facing us today in the atomic age."[36]

Robeson seems not to have found a Japanese American song to his liking, for he did not add one to his repertoire. However, he came into contact with the problems of the Nisei again in 1948 when he became a founding member of the Progressive Party and a prominent supporter of Henry Wallace's presidential candidacy. At the party's founding convention in Philadelphia, Robeson joined forces with a group of activist delegates, including Dyke Miyagawa and Chiye Mori, representatives of the Nisei for Wallace (subsequently called Nisei Progressives), to lobby for civil rights planks in the party's platform.[37] The Progressive Party agreed to endorse voting rights for African Americans and the elimination of Jim Crow laws. It also went on record in favor of evacuation property claims for former Japanese American internees, the repeal of discriminatory land and fishing laws against Japanese aliens, and equal immigration and naturalization rights.[38] The platform also called for an end to housing discrimination and laws banning intermarriage, which targeted both groups. In conjunction with the Wallace campaign, Robeson organized a concert tour in Hawaii to benefit the International Longshore Workers Union. There the largely Asian American workforce gave him what he later called the warmest reception of his life. Upon his return to the mainland, Robeson told a union meeting how impressed he had been to see "workers from all over the world who have become part of the American way of life, building a decent home and a decent way of life for their children and for themselves in the Islands of Hawaii."[39] He concluded his comments, typically, by connecting activism with music: "I managed to learn some of the songs of the people from the Philippines, of the Japanese Americans."[40]

To conclude, Robeson's activism, although sometimes naïve and uncritically pro-Stalinist, reveals his broad internationalism and generous humanism. He fervently believed in the liberating potential inherent in international coalitions of oppressed groups and in the strength to be derived from an exploration of their cultures. While his cultural nationalism was sometimes simplistic (he contrasted the European as an "intellectual" culture on one side and on the other listed among the "natural" cultures the African, Chinese and—allied with the Chinese through the Tartars—the Russian), his theories offered a welcome alternative to white racial arrogance in both political and cultural terms. His solidarity with Asia and his willingness to speak out against discrimination made him a genuine hero to people of all races. Even in the 1950s, when he was silenced by the government and stripped of his passport, he remained a popular figure in Asia, and birthday celebrations were scheduled by groups not just in Communist countries but also in other nations such as India and Japan.[41]

Robeson's attachment to Asia was paralleled by and informed his solidarity with Asian Americans. Although their struggles were never as central an area of interest for Robeson as those of other minorities or of Africans—when he gave his litany of oppressed groups in speeches, he tended to mention blacks first and foremost, then Jews, then Spanish-speaking people[42]—he welcomed them as fellow workers and victims of racial bias. Within the United States, Asian American civil rights groups looked to him as a supporter. The Chinese Hand Laundry Alliance in New York invited him to their rallies during the war.[43] Japanese American and Japanese Canadian newspapers devoted a number of articles to his activities in the years surrounding the war.[44] When Robeson was threatened, they joined him. Among those who attended Robeson's Peekskill concert were numerous Japanese Americans. Even though they were warned about the violence that would ensue, they believed that, as Robeson had told them at their veterans' banquet in Chicago three years before, "My fight is your fight."[45]

NOTES

1. Brenda Gayle Plummer, *Rising Wind: Black Americans and U.S. Foreign Affairs, 1935–1960* (Chapel Hill: University of North Carolina Press, 1996); Penny von Eschen, *Race against Empire: Black Americans and Anticolonialism, 1937–1954* (Ithaca, NY: Cornell University Press, 1997); Thomas Borstelmann, *The Cold War and the Color Line* (Cambridge: Harvard University Press, 2002).

2. Marc Gallichio, *The African American Encounter with China and Japan: Black Internationalism in Asia, 1895–1945* (Chapel Hill: University of North Carolina Press, 2000); Sudarshan Kapur, *Raising up a Prophet: The African-American Encounter with Gandhi* (Boston: Beacon Press, 1992); Reginald Kearney, *Afro-American Views of the Japanese: Solidarity or Sedition?* (Albany, NY: SUNY Press, 1998). The works of Vijay Prashad, which defy easy categorization, centrally address African American cultural connections with Asia.

3. See, for example, Robert Shaffer, "Out of the Shadows: The Political Writings of Eslanda Goode Robeson," in *Paul Robeson: Essays on His Life and Legacy,* ed. Joseph Dorinson and William Pencak (Jefferson, NC: McFarland, 2002), 98–112.

4. Paul Robeson, "I Don't Want to Be White," *Chicago Defender*, 26 January 1935, reprinted in *Paul Robeson Speaks!*, ed. Philip Foner (Larchmont, NY: Brunner/Maazel, 1978), 91.

5. Charles Blochson, "Paul Robeson: A Bibliophile in Spite of Himself," in *Paul Robeson: Artist and Citizen*, ed. Jeffrey Stewart (New Brunswick, NJ: Rutgers University Press, 1998), 244. According to Robeson's son, it was the famed Russian director Sergei Eisenstein who encouraged Robeson's Chinese studies and educated him in the history of Chinese theater. Paul Robeson Jr., *The Undiscovered Paul Robeson: An Artist's Journey, 1898–1939* (New York: Wiley, 2001), 245.

6. Martin B. Duberman, *Paul Robeson* (New York: Knopf, 1988), 199–201, 174–175.

7. Paul Robeson, interview in the *Sunday Times*, New Brunswick, NY, 27 October 1935, reprinted in Edwin P. Hoyt, *Paul Robeson: The American Othello* (Cleveland: World, 1967), 60.

8. "Paul Robeson on Music," interview in the *Wall Street Journal*, 23 August 1933, 3.

9. Duberman, *Paul Robeson*, 644.

10. Communist Party of the United States of America, "Is Japan the Champion of the Colored Races?," Pamphlet, 1938(?), Left-Wing Literature Collection, Baldwin Library, University of Connecticut, 40.

11. Ron Ramdin, *Paul Robeson: The Man and His Mission* (London: Peter Owen, 1987), 109.

12. Larry Ceplair and Robert Englund, *The Inquisition in Hollywood: Politics in the Film Community, 1930–1960* (Berkeley: University of California Press, 1983), 64. A typical article on U.S. policy in a party journal devoted most of its length to attacking the Lend-Lease law and aid to Britain as "reactionary" and "counterrevolutionary" and advocating a shift in policy: "Strangulation of the people's forces in Latin America must give way to cooperation with them, deepening their crusade for education and sovereignty. The ominous pressure on China's United Front must give way to a policy of helping China defeat the invader. That, and the chance of redirecting the whole course of affairs in Europe, giving true hope to its imprisoned and silenced, depends on cooperation with the USSR." Joseph Starobin, "American Foreign Policy," *New Masses* 38.9 (18 February 1941): 4.

13. Ramdin, *Paul Robeson*, 109.

14. William Theodore du Bary, "Living Legacies," *Columbia Magazine* (Spring 2002): 28.

15. Chuh Shih, *Chinese American Understanding: A Sixty Year Search* (New York: China Institute in America, 1988), 213. In the final verse, Robeson replaced Oscar Hammerstein's lyric "I gets weary and sick of trying/ I'm tired of living and scared of dying" with "I keeps laughing instead of crying/ I must keep fighting until I'm dying."

16. A picture of the event is reproduced in Susan Robeson, *The Whole World in*

His Hands: A Pictorial Biography of Paul Robeson (Secaucus, NJ: Citadel Press, 1981), 131.

17. Duberman, *Paul Robeson*, 251–252.

18. Paul Robeson, commentary on "Chee Lai," in Paul Robeson, *Chee Lai: Songs of Free China*, LP (New York: Keynote Records, 1941).

19. Paul Robeson, introduction to "Feng Yang," in Paul Robeson, *Chee Lai: Songs of Free China*, LP (New York: Keynote Records, 1941).

20. Gallichio, *African American Encounter*, 159.

21. Paul Robeson, "China: Promise of a New World," speech delivered as Sun-Yat Sen Day Tribute, reprinted in *Paul Robeson Speaks!*, ed. Philip Foner (Larchmont, NY: Brunner/Maazel, 1978), 155.

22. In 1951, Robeson applied for a passport in order to attend a celebration of the second anniversary of the People's Republic of China. The visa was denied. Dorothy Butler Gilliam, *Paul Robeson: All-American* (Washington, DC: New Republic Books, 1976), 160.

23. Robeson frequently sang what he called the "Chinese Children's Song," and in his famed 1958 Carnegie Hall concert he sang the Edward Eliscu-Jay Gorney song "The Four Rivers," which advocates peaceful coexistence among the people of the United States, England, China, and the Soviet Union. Paul Robeson, *Paul Robeson at Carnegie Hall*, LP (New York: Vanguard Records, 1958).

24. Paul Robeson, "Here's My Story," *FREEDOM* (May 1951), reprinted in *Paul Robeson Speaks!*, ed. Philip Foner (Larchmont, NY: Brunner/Maazel, 1978), 274. See also Lawrence Lamphere, "Paul Robeson, *Freedom* Newspaper, and the Korean War," in in *Paul Robeson: Essays on His Life and Legacy*, ed. Joseph Dorinson and William Pencak (Jefferson, NC: McFarland, 2002), 133–142. Robeson offered support to other Asian nationalist movements as well. In 1954, he praised Vietnamese Communist leader Ho Chi Minh as the "Toussaint L'Ouverture of Indo-China" (Lamphere, "Paul Robeson," 140). In a 1947 speech, Robeson expressed his support for Asian decolonization and his concern over "the brutal Dutch Aggression against the Indonesian Republic." Paul Robeson, speech to Alpha Phi Alpha, 5 October 1947. Reel II, Paul Robeson papers, Schomburg Library, New York City.

25. Paul Robeson, "I Want to Be African," reprinted in *Paul Robeson Speaks!*, ed. Philip Foner (Larchmont, NY: Brunner/Maazel, 1978), 88.

26. Marie Seton, *Paul Robeson* (London: Dennis Dobson, 1958), 87, cited in Gilliam, *Paul Robeson*, 78.

27. George Jobo, "Campanile Chimes," *Nichi Bei*, 14 February 1941, 1.

28. "Robeson Wins Café Suit," *Nichi Bei*, 5 January 1941, 1.

29. See Mark D. Naison, "Americans through Their Labor: Paul Robeson's Vision of Cultural and Economic Democracy," *Ominira* 1.1 (Spring 1999), available at www.hartford-hwp.com/archives/45a/432.html (retrieved spring 2004).

30. Foner, *Paul Robeson Speaks!*, 146.

31. Ibid., 244.

32. Letter, Isamu Noguchi to Carey McWilliams, 18 February 1942, Box 1, Carey McWilliams papers, Hoover Institution, Stanford University, Stanford, CA.

33. "Great Basso-Baritone Approves JCCD, Becomes Life Member," *New Canadian*, 16 November 1946, 1.

34. "Robeson Performs in Salt Lake City," *Utah Nippo*, 8 April 1946, 1.

35. Associated Negro Press Dispatch, 1 June 1946. See also *Pacific Citizen*, 2 June 1946, 1.

36. Larry Tajiri, "Vagaries," *Pacific Citizen*, 4 March 1947, 4.

37. For Nisei progressives, see Martha Nakagawa, "Rebels with a Just Cause," *Rafu Shimpo*, 11 December 1997, 1: 4.

38. Ibid. The Supreme Court's *Oyama* and *Takahashi* decisions during the 1947–1948 term effectively halted application of discriminatory land and fishing legislation against "aliens ineligible to citizenship," and the 1952 McCarran-Walter Immigration Act, which provided immigration and naturalization rights to Japanese, eliminated the existence of such a category. The Japanese Evacuation Claims Act, passed by Congress in summer 1948, granted token compensation for property losses to internees.

39. Foner, *Paul Robeson Speaks!*, 163.

40. Ibid.

41. For example, the radical Japan-born activist Ayako Ishigaki, in her book *Saraba waga Amerika: jiyu to yokuatsu non 25-nen [25 years in America]* (Tokyo: Senseido bukkusu, 1972), included a photo of Robeson and devoted prominent attention to deploring his persecution as an example of American injustice.

42. See, for example, Paul Robeson, speech at Rally of Council on African Affairs, New York, 25 April 1947. Reel II, Paul Robeson papers, Schomburg Library, New York City.

43. Renqiu Yu, *To Save China, to Save Ourselves* (Philadelphia: Temple University Press, 1992), 121.

44. See, for example, a report on Robeson's appearance at the University of British Columbia in Vancouver, where he spoke of discrimination against Blacks in Canada: "Mr. Robeson, it is well known, is famous for his theatrical gifts, both legitimate and on the screen. But to many he owes no less of his public stature to his vigorous leadership in the fight against racial prejudice in America." "Paul Robeson in Vancouver," *New Canadian*, 20 January 1945, 1.

45. Among those present were Lewis Suzuki, Toshi Ohta Seeger, and Chiye Mori. Mori left a harrowing account of the violence and racial slurs directed toward the Nisei. Chiye Mori, "Peekskill, NY, September 5," *Bandwagon* 2.8 (October 1949): 8–10.

Chapter 15

"Jazz That Eats Rice"
Toshiko Akiyoshi's Roots Music

David W. Stowe

Just two years after the Negro slaves were emancipated in the United States, Emperor Meiji became the Emperor of Japan. So, the Japanese people and Black American people started for the New World, of which they never knew, almost at the same time. . . . And those two peoples had to abandon their old traditions, of which they were ashamed when they compared them to the old European traditions. . . . That is why we Japanese can easily understand everything the American Black people are doing.
—Yui Shoichi, quoted in E. Taylor Atkins,
Blue Nippon, 2001

In 1974, Toshiko Akiyoshi began performing and recording a big band she had formed two years earlier with her husband, Lew Tabackin. After more than twenty years in the business, the pianist felt it was time for her to repay jazz by bringing her Japanese heritage to the music. Based in New York City for most of her career in the United States, Akiyoshi relocated to Los Angeles. Within a few years the band was acclaimed, winning prestigious *Down Beat* readers' and critics' polls. By 1980, when Akiyoshi won the magazine's awards for best big band, arranger, and composer, her group was regarded as best jazz orchestra in the world. Her ascent in the jazz world was remarkable, even in a musical history filled with extraordinary prodigies and rapid climbs.

This decision linked Akiyoshi to an important mythology of American popular music, positioning her in what I call the unstable ethnic triad. Its best-known example is staged in the 1927 film, *The Jazz Singer*, starring Al Jolson as a Jewish immigrant boy who escapes the clutches of his Orthodox Jewish heritage and assimilates as a Caucasian American through a symbolic identification with African America. Jolson enacts this transformation musically by performing minstrel "jazz" songs and visually by donning blackface and wig.[1] The Mardi Gras Indians of New Orleans—social clubs of young African Americans who adopt Indian names and don Indian costumes—serve as another, more subtle example of the unstable ethnic triad. By constructing an imaginary racial identity that plays on actual historical creolization, they disrupt the dominant American black/white racial binary. These "Indians" are celebrated in Wynton Marsalis's *Blood on the Fields* as agents who serve to mediate between white owners and black slaves and as purveyors of survival skills and the natural world.[2]

I.

In Japan, a comparable ethnic triad has underscored the quest for musical authenticity. Following its forced opening to the West by the U.S. Navy in the 1850s, Japan had fashioned a modern nation with one foot in Asia and one foot in the West. These identifications had shifted back and forth at various times to suit the national interest of the state. Japanese jazz developed within these oscillations. The music had reached Japan quite early, before 1920, transmitted via transpacific ocean liners. The 1920s saw a "Jazz Age" every bit as vigorous as its American counterpart, driven by the popularity of social dance in commercial ballrooms in Tokyo, Osaka, and Kobe. The first jazz coffeehouses were established, and musicians found abundant work in the recording industry, film, and radio. Shanghai provided stimulating offshore stomping grounds for Japanese musicians who rubbed shoulders with musicians from America. But cultural nativism was ascendant during the rise of ultranationalism of the 1930s. In 1937, jazz was suppressed as "enemy music" and dancehalls were shuttered. During the war, jazz was actually pressed into service as propaganda meant to weaken the resolve of American troops tuning in to Japanese broadcasts.[3]

After the war, jazz became an important symbol, along with candy and gum, of U.S. benevolence to its shattered foe. Japanese musicians found many opportunities to hear and play with American military musicians, creating a so-called Jazz Boom in the early 1950s. The quest for Japanese musical authenticity took on a new urgency during the 1960s, as Japan began to flex its economic muscles. Influenced by currents of cultural nationalism emanating from the United States, young Japanese musicians stressed their racial solidarity with African Americans. Taking to heart W. E. B. Du Bois's 1940 formulation—the "social heritage of slavery; the discrimination and insult . . . binds together not simply the children of Africa, but extends through Yellow Asia and into the South Seas"—these musicians emphasized their affinities for American people of color.[4] As Taylor Atkins has shown, Japanese players had long been troubled by their perceived inability to put a distinctive innovative mark on a musical form that above all prides itself on originality. If African American cultural nationalists were correct that the racialized self was the source of musical authenticity, Japanese selves had much to offer. They could provide the elusive ground of authentic music.[5]

Akiyoshi herself was of an earlier generation and had developed her musical reputation prior to the 1960s. Born in 1929, she had grown up in Japanese-occupied Manchuria, where her father owned an import-export business. Her family lost everything in the war and returned to Japan destitute. Relocating to Kyushu, the family faced the universal experience of trying to establish a life in the ruins of war. The teenaged Akiyoshi answered a notice for a pianist at a local dance hall and learned on the job.[6] She developed rapidly as a jazz player. Two years after the dance hall gig, she moved to Tokyo with the goal of playing jazz professionally. Pianist Hampton Hawes, who led an army band in Yokohama during 1953–1954 and exerted a large influence on the Tokyo jazz scene, observed her in Ginza. "That little chick in a kimono sat right down at the piano and started to rip off things I didn't believe, swinging like she'd grown up in Kansas City," he recalled.[7] Akiyoshi established herself as a leading Japanese jazz modernist, influenced by bebop, uninterested in commercial success. Then came her big break. She was noticed by pianist Oscar Peterson and producer Norman Granz, who recorded her with an all-star American combo in Tokyo. The resulting LP was widely praised and won her a scholarship to the Berklee College of Music, in Boston, the most important American institution for jazz musicians.

Akiyoshi began performing and recording in a variety of small groups, some with Charlie Mariano, a sax player she met at Berklee. After her marriage to Mariano broke up, Akiyoshi faced the challenge of surviving as a jazz musician and single mother in the unforgiving milieu of New York City. She scraped by playing gigs at Greenwich Village jazz clubs. There she struck up a friendship with the prodigious Charles Mingus, who eventually hired her. By the early 1970s, though, like even the most established American jazz artists, Akiyohi's career was floundering. "I came to the point where I started doubting about my meaning of existence as a jazz musician," she later said. "I had the belief that I should try to create something from my heritage, something unique enough that I could maybe . . . return something *into* jazz, in my own way, not just reap the benefits of American jazz."[8] With her second husband, Tabackin, a player of dazzling skill on both tenor sax and flute, she relocated to Los Angeles, where Tabackin had steady work with the *Tonight Show* band. Rehearsal space was cheaper—$3 an hour at the musicians' local rather than $25—an important consideration for a fledgling big band. Two years later, the band would record *Kogun,* an album that marked the beginning of its critical and popular ascent in both Japan and the United States.

The years leading up to the formation of the Akiyoshi-Tabackin band were notable for racial polarization on both sides of the Pacific. In the United States, hard bop and free jazz dovetailed with the civil rights and black power movements, stressing an aesthetic of freedom. Musicians like Charles Mingus, Archie Shepp, and Miles Davis made explicit currents of Black Nationalism that had remained latent in earlier periods. In an important article in *Down Beat* and in his classic *Blues People* (1964), writer LeRoi Jones (later Amiri Baraka) developed an influential argument about the inextricable links between blues, jazz, and working-class African American life. Blues and jazz were a direct outgrowth of the social experience of African Americans, he insisted, and the music could not be properly performed or interpreted without direct access to those forms of experience.[9]

In Japan, a new generation of jazz musicians was making similar claims about the possibilities of a distinctively Japanese jazz. Musicians like Togashi Masahiko were working to articulate a Japanese jazz aesthetic, along with critics like Yui Shoichi. "Right now this is a new global trend that is coming to rule jazz," wrote Yui. "Even in America, blacks are aiming for black jazz, whites for white jazz; and in Europe, as well, in Spain and West Germany different national hues using the diction of jazz are being worked out. It is certainly reasonable that Japanese musicians are in a hurry to 'create Japanese jazz.'"[10] The crucial challenge was to discover a Japanese analogue to the blues, a vernacular musical form rooted in the historical experience of the people, expressive of social and political resistance, with continuing cultural vitality. Japanese musicians had long employed what

Atkins calls "strategies of authentication," such as replicating the exact styles of favorite American artists or sojourning in foreign cities like New York and Shanghai. A new strategy of the 1960s was to incorporate traditional instruments, tone colors, or formal principles that would mark the music as distinctly Japanese.[11]

Akiyoshi was no stranger to these aesthetic currents. In the early 1950s, she had speculated about the links between African American identity and jazz. "How do you play the blues that way," she once queried Hampton Hawes, the first American to discover her talent. "How can I learn to play them so authentically?":

> *Hawes*: I play the blues right because I eat collard greens and black-eyed peas and corn pone and clabber.
> *Akiyoshi* [Sighs]: Where can I find that food? Do I have to go to the United States to get it?

Hawes was kidding; "All you need is the feeling," he admitted.[12] A decade later, in New York, Akiyoshi played with perhaps the most outspoken black nationalist in jazz. Though Mingus frequently intimidated his sidemen, the diminutive Akiyoshi held her own during her ten months in the band. The two remained loyal friends: Mingus was one of the few in the audience of Akiyoshi's Town Hall recital of 1967; the following year she visited him in the hospital during a period of mental collapse.[13]

II.

Whatever she may have learned about music during her stint with Mingus, it was Mingus's own hero, Duke Ellington, whom Akiyoshi credited with inspiring interest in exploring Japanese music in jazz. She began at roughly the time Ellington died, in 1974. "Spiritually, since I started writing for big band, my main influence is Duke Ellington," she explained in 1976:

> One of the reasons that I truly admire and respect him — aside from his being a great writer—is that his music was deeply rooted in his race and he was proud of his race. That encouraged me to draw some heritage from *my* roots. Jazz in this country comes from European and African music, but there was never anything Oriental.[14]

As a Japanese woman, Akiyoshi occupied a complicated position in 1970s jazz. Her ancestry disrupted the black/white racial binary so dominant in the jazz community. In 1976, just after the release of *Kogun* in the United States, Akiyoshi described the challenge of working in what was considered a quintessentially American idiom:

> Not only I am not an American, I am a minority race. I believe in seeing things the way they are, and for minorities, it's hard in this country. If I were a male American and wrote a hundred tunes, if 30 of those tunes were super and the rest mediocre, I could get by. It's possible for an American male writer. But in my case, I can't afford that. Whenever I write, each one has to be good.[15]

Akiyoshi was not a member of an American minority group, of course; she was a Japanese national, not a Japanese American. Being Japanese rather than Chinese or Korean placed Akiyoshi in an even more complex category. Japan and the United States have experienced deep political and cultural ambivalence since the 1853 appearance of Commodore Perry's "black ships" in Tokyo Bay. Ever since, the United States has represented both Self and Other to Japanese, serving both as a model and a nemesis. At times Japanese have emphasized their Asianness ("Greater Asian Co-Prosperity Sphere" of the 1930s and 1940s, for example), at other times their kinship to Europe and America. Modern Japan had clearly been shaped by U.S. imperialism and Japan's fascination with the West. But Japan's own imperial ambitions had shaped much of the Asian world militarily and economically. In addition, the late 1960s saw a strong anti–Vietnam War movement in Japan. As the Akiyoshi-Tabackin band was drawing increasing attention, Japan was demonstrating its newfound economic might vis-à-vis the United States. The mid-1970s were also the heyday of a Japanese genre called *nihonjinron,* which offered theories for the distinctiveness, and often superiority, of Japanese society, culture, and physiology.[16]

Furthermore, Akiyoshi was distinctive in jazz not just for her nationality: women have long struggled to achieve recognition in jazz. "Masculinity is one of the essences that jazz music has to have, for my taste—you know, hard-driving," Akiyoshi herself acknowledged.[17] She had to work through both of these categories as she pondered her future:

> Jazz is American music. And I thought, here I am, I'm a Japanese and a woman, and the woman part is not that important I think, but here I am

Japanese and a jazz player and playing in New York. . . . And I look at it and then have to really think about where my position is, what my role will be. And somehow it looks kind of pathetic and comical, the fact that there is a Japanese little girl trying to play jazz . . . and I felt very insignificant.[18]

Akiyoshi's Japanese identity was not the only racial factor affecting the direction of the band; co-leader Tabackin's whiteness also played a part. Like many cultural milieus, the New York jazz community was sharply polarized during the late 1960s and early 1970s. "New York was very strange because there was almost like a Black revolution happening," Tabackin recalls. "Martin Luther King was assassinated earlier and Malcolm X and it was very difficult for white jazz musicians."[19] In response, big bands had emerged as refuges for white jazz musicians, according to Akiyoshi, as "the entry to the starting gate."[20] For Tabackin, this entailed a major reorientation of his style. "Before I came to New York, I had never played in any big bands and had no desire to play in them," he explained. "I came from a small group background. And when I came to New York, all of a sudden— especially since I'm a white player—I found myself in big bands, although I couldn't even read a chart."[21] Because he was in charge of hiring musicians for the band, Tabackin's musical perspectives had a ripple effect beyond his own featured soloing; he effectively shaped much of the musical personality of the ensemble. In choosing a big band as her musical vehicle, Akiyoshi located herself in an older tradition of African American racial pride in jazz stretching back to the 1920s.[22]

Ironically, it was Tabackin's virtuoso abilities on the flute that created one of the band's most conspicuous forms of sonic Japaneseness. Along with the *koto,* the most widely recognized Japanese traditional instrument is the *shakuhachi,* a five-hole bamboo flute held vertically and played from the end. Though Tabackin never played the instrument, his mastery of European flute enabled him to achieve a wide range of musical effects that simulated the sound of the *shakuhachi*: microtone smears, flutter-tongued bursts, glossolalic cries. "Lew has a French model flute (open-holed) that enables him to do this," explained Akiyoshi. "He listened to a lot of shakuhachi music. His abilities are so incredible, he can *sense* the music." "I am forced to come up with different devices to try to perform her music," added Tabackin. "I might have to employ certain techniques, like using the overtone series in a different manner and some quarter-tone effects."[23]

Tabackin's shakuhachi-like stylings, and the band's distinctive use of flute sections more generally, were only one of several ways in which Akiyoshi brought Japanese sounds into the music. We can group the Japanese musical traces into four categories: first, the use of actual Japanese voices and instruments; second, the use of Japanese timbres and tone colors, like Tabackin's flute playing, even if produced on Western instruments; third, the use of rhythmic, harmonic, and melodic elements influenced by Japanese techniques or principles; fourth, the inspiration of themes drawn from Japanese history. Following John Corbett, we can distinguish these influences into the categories of decorative Orientalism (or "contemporary chinoiserie") and conceptual Orientalism. Decorative Orientalism refers to the incorporation of Asian or quasi-Asian musical elements; conceptual Orientalism suggests the use of aesthetic principles or compositional procedures derived in some way from Asian precepts. Akiyoshi's repertoire includes elements of both.[24]

Juxtaposition—the assembling of ostensibly unrelated musical ingredients into a musical collage—is one of the most striking of Akiyoshi's techniques. She accomplishes it primarily through the deployment of Japanese instruments or voices. Often it is the preternatural upward sliding howl (to Western ears) of Noh vocals and accompanying drummers' calls, as at the opening of *Kogun* and the last section of *Minamata*. The voices are accompanied by the *otsuzumi* and *kotsuzumi,* the distinctive drums used to punctuate Noh—one with a sharply cracking report, the other with a more resonant tom-tom sound. With its origins in Buddhist chant, Noh singing, known as *yokyoku* or *utai,* retains a deeply solemn, introspective quality. "The special voice quality of noh singing originates in the abdomen," explains ethnomusicologist William Malm; "Graces and vibratos are added to the tone to give it variety. The pronunciation of the words is an abstraction of ancient styles and further removes the plays from the everyday world."[25] *Utai* and the cries of the *tsuzumi* players represent perhaps the most exotic Japanese musical sound for non-Japanese and for many Japanese as well.

In "Kogun" and "Children of the Universe," Akiyoshi juxtaposes *utai* and *tsuzumi* against Tabackin's flute in a counterpoint that melds smoothly into the ensemble theme. Other times Akiyoshi juxtaposes a child's or a woman's voice, as at the beginning of *Minamata,* and the many passages of survivors' diaries read into *Hiroshima—Rising from the Abyss.* Subtler than the juxtaposition of actual Japanese instruments or voices is Akiyoshi's use of Japanese timbres and tone colors. "I have used some Japanese instruments, but that's a very obvious infusion," she says. "If people listen very closely to my writing, they can hear a lot of more subtle infusion." The inspiration came to her during a period of self-examination in New York, when she was reading widely in Japanese literature:

> Anyhow, one night I was writing a tune called *Sumie,* a simple melody 12 bars long (but not a blues). I lay down on a bed and I began to hear this traditional Japanese *gagaku* [classical music] sound. It's a form of very close harmony; and I heard it with a melody in my mind, repeating and repeating, and this Japanese sound matched it very well, in my head. It sounded very musical and very natural to me.
>
> I had the idea of writing this sound for trumpets. . . . Years ago in Japan, I used to hear trumpet players doing a lot of note-bending, both upward and downward. You have to slide into and out of things, using the valves very carefully.[26]

Also in the trumpet section, Akiyoshi likes to use very close voicings, having the first, second, third, and fourth trumpets playing within a whole tone or minor third of each other.[27] She also uses massed flutes, rare in jazz bands. At times, the band achieves a kind of static, suspended quality reminiscent of the mouth organ, or *sho,* used in traditional Japanese court music to provide a harmonic matrix based on tone clusters. This is especially pronounced in the first section of *Minamata,* where the arco base and unusual combinations of reeds playing long, suspended chords give a sense of stasis, and cymbal rolls wash over the ensemble, evoking the waves of a fishing village.

In his analysis of traditional Japanese music, Malm distinguishes between the vertical conception of Western music that emphasizes harmonic sequences and the horizontal conception of most non-Western music organized through complex scales or rhythmic systems.[28] Likewise, Akiyoshi describes her own approach to ensemble sections in what she calls "layers of sound":

> In other words, I will have one thing, then I will hear another that goes along with it. It's just like a photograph with a double exposure, you know? . . . *Kogun* . . . is a good example. I have one melody that represents almost a 2/2 kind of time feeling. A very timeless kind of feeling, with a lot of glissando. But then I have the brass and rhythm sections doing something in an entire different idiom, a Western idiom, with a very strong rhythmic feel.[29]

This approach to rhythm and phrasing is crucial. Akiyoshi attributes some of her rhythmic approach to her Japanese background:

> Years ago, [drummer] Shelly Manne was talking about dissonance. . . . Originally it would be played like this (snaps fingers in medium four) . . . but then you would feel like (imitates sliding horns, with tempo cut in half) . . . like a spacing. This is very Oriental thinking. Rather than counting the time, you feel the time and you learn it. . . . I feel this is a very natural way in jazz, which would have a swing feeling but would also have this spacing.[30]

"The beat is different," she explains elsewhere. "It's more circular, arched, rather than an up or downbeat."[31] In articulating the notion of a distinctive Japanese sense of rhythm, Akiyoshi aligned herself with Japanese musicians and critics who were keen to identify an authentic Japanese musical aesthetic in terms of culturally specific concepts of space, silence, or interval (referred to in Japanese as *ma* or *kukan*).[32]

Between sonic juxtapositions and distinctive approaches to ensemble arrangement, phrasing, and rhythm, we recognize both decorative and conceptual Orientalism. But how were these formal principles transmitted to Akiyoshi? What is the source of Akiyoshi's grounding in Japanese music? Her musical education was Western:

> When I went to school in Japan, from kindergarten to grammar school, high school, and so on . . . all association I had with musical schooling was Westernized. It happens with all my generation and younger. Western music is not really foreign, and on top of that I was studying piano since I was six, so that added more to it.
>
> The only relationship I had with Japanese music was from my sister. She was a student of Japanese traditional dance, and she was quite good at it. I used to hear the music when she was studying, so I was familiar with the music in that relationship. Also, my father was a student of Noh, the Noh play.[33]

During her first years in the United States, Akiyoshi found herself typecast as a stereotypical geisha girl, often donning a kimono in television appearances in shows like *What's My Line?* and with Steve Allen. Producer George Weiner described her in liner notes he wrote for her second album as being "pretty as a lotus flower, as gentle and sweet as [a] cherry blossom."[34] Perhaps it's accurate to say that both jazz and traditional Japanese music represent borrowed traditions for Akiyoshi: one through immersion in nightlife, the other absorbed in the bosom of the nuclear family.

III.

Beyond the use of Japanese sonorities or musical principles is Akiyoshi's investigation of Japanese history as a compositional thematic. Here I focus on three works representative of Akiyoshi's early, middle, and late periods: *Minamata*, recorded in 1976; *Kourakan Suite*, recorded at Carnegie Hall in 1991; and *Hiroshima—Rising from the Abyss*, a three-part suite recorded live in Hiroshima in 2001.[35] All three are examples of program music, pieces that describe or narrate a story through sound. All are at some level concerned with cultural change, with the impact of modernity, migration, or technology on the lives of Japanese people. And they are responses to particular issues salient in Japan during the years in which they were composed.

Minamata is a three-part suite recorded in the year the band was just beginning to generate enthusiasm and interest among American critics and listeners and during a period of extreme national introspection in Japan, reflected in the popularity of *nihonjinron*. Its title refers to a fishing village in Kyushu, not far from Akiyoshi's ancestral home, whose people were devastated by mercury poisoning. Beginning in the 1950s, residents began to show symptoms of a degenerative disease that began with numbness in the extremities and ended in loss of vision, hearing, bodily control, and ultimately mental incapacity. More than three hundred people died while another twelve hundred developed symptoms. The disaster inspired one of the earliest citizens' movements, resulting in numerous lawsuits against the corporation responsible for discharging the mercury compounds, and ultimately a comprehensive antipollution law was passed in 1967. The Minamata movement provided an influential model for other citizens' groups to push for redress from corporations or the state.[36]

Akiyoshi structures her nearly twenty-two-minute piece in three parts: "Peaceful Village," "Prosperity and Consequences," and "Epilogue." The piece begins with a girl's voice intoning: *mura ari sono nao Minamata to iu* ("There is a village called Minamata"), suggesting a folk tale to come. We hear the peaceful stasis of the first five minutes give way to the frenetic bebop sound of the middle part, which alternates spiky ensemble figures with solos by tenor sax, alto sax, trombone, and again tenor. The use of pedal points builds tension as each solo comes and goes. In the thirteenth minute we hear the suggestion of Noh *utai* counterposed with sliding brass figures. The *utai* appears again in the twentieth minute with the band, set over spare accompaniment of walking bass and drums, joined by dissonant collective improvisation. Also at that point, the band executes a series of dramatic breaks and rests, followed by even more powerful *utai* vocals (by Hisao Kanze of Tokyo, chief of the Kanze school of Noh). The final minute features the voice again, riding over the suspended chords of the piece's opening, gravely intoning the words spoken at the beginning by the girl. One reading of the narrative seems clear: traditional ways invaded and deranged by technology, followed by a kind of restitution. When the deep, gravelly *utai* voice swells in the final minutes of the suite, the section called "Consequences," it is not difficult to hear it as a rebuke from the ancestors, or perhaps an utterance of judgment from the spirit world.[37]

Akiyoshi's most recent extended work for big band, *Hiroshima—Rising from the Abyss*, shares some of the thematic and structural features of *Minamata*. Also written in three parts, its trajectory narrates a story of manmade devastation ("Futility–Tragedy") followed by shocked witness ("Survivor Tales") and survival and recovery ("Hope"). Unlike *Minamata*, Akiyoshi here eschews *utai*, Japanese instruments, and even tone colors. Though he plays some flute, Tabackin avoids *shakuhachi*-like stylings. Rather, a prominent place is given to a Korean musician, who plays a traditional Korean flute, or *taegum*, which produces a distinctive buzzing tone due to a membrane-covered hole. But the Japanese nature of the piece is unmistakably inscribed, due to the juxtaposition of readings from the "Mother's Diaries" of the Hiroshima Memorial Museum. Read in Japanese by a woman, the entries provide a series of testimonies of the atomic bomb: student factory workers dying, bodies covered with keroid; children sent off by train to safer locations while their parents died; a daughter who never returned from a hiking trip to eat the peach her mother saved for her. The readings occur over a somber C tonic tone sounded by bass and trumpet, evoking an air raid siren, interspersed with fluttering phrases from the *taegum*, sounding vaguely like a struggling bird. Akiyoshi chose the Korean flute both for its unique sound ("It doesn't exist anywhere else," Tabackin explains, "definitely not in Japanese music") and for the fact that a significant proportion of the fatalities from the two atomic bombings—perhaps forty thousand total—were Koreans conscripted to work in war factories.[38]

Hiroshima—Rising from the Abyss premiered at a Hiroshima auditorium on 6 August 2001, the first anniversary of the bombing in the new millennium. The impetus came from a Buddhist priest from Hiroshima, a long-time fan of Akiyoshi. The priest sent her some material, including a book of photos taken three days after the bombing. Akiyoshi recalls:

> I have never been shocked that much in my life. The effectiveness of this bomb was indescribable. I thought, "I can't write about something like this." I couldn't see the reason or the meaning. But I was turning the pages, and on one page there was a young woman. She was in the underground, and she wasn't affected. She came out, and she looked so beautiful. She's got a little smile, a fantastic smile. And when I saw that, I said, "I can write that!"[39]

In Part II, after the diary readings, the instruments enter one by one—first trumpet, then flute, then tenor sax, followed by trombone and baritone sax—over a subdued but swinging rhythm section. It is as if survivors are emerging from rubble, voicing their reactions, then joining in an ever-expanding dialogue that crescendoes to a fortissimo collective improvisation and ensemble section at the end. Seven chime notes signal the beginning of Part III, followed by two uttered statements of hope: luxuriant trees and grass returning ahead of schedule, people healthy and strong. "This is our message to the world from Hiroshima, with love and hope," ends the second, "no nuclear and atomic weapons, and peace on earth." A throbbingly eloquent tenor solo by Tabackin comprises the rest of "Hope."[40]

If *Minamata* and *Hiroshima* mourn the impact of technology and war on the daily lives of ordinary people, *Kourakan Suite* is a celebration of Japanese cultural pluralism. As is true for many of Akiyoshi's explicitly Japanese-themed compositions, the piece was written on commission, for the city of Fukuoka, in Kyushu. It marks the discovery in the late 1980s of an ancient guesthouse, known as a *kourokan* (the U.S. title gets the spelling wrong) full of artifacts of travelers from Persia who made their way to Japan. The piece has very few Japanese accents; rather, the prevailing musical tinge is Latin. The opening section offers hints of Arab melody before the piece settles into a vamp in 6/4 time, conga drums accompanying an extended piano solo by Akiyoshi. As the band reenters in the sixth minute, the meter gradually shifts into 4/4, and the band swells to accompany a Tabackin tenor statement. The mood changes abruptly in Part II, "Prayer," ushered in by a gong and Tibetan clattering cymbals (*gsil snyan*) and large earth-shaking trumpets (*dung chen*). Two minutes into the section, a woman's solo voice enters, singing a wordless spiritual. After another two minutes, the band commences a stately Ellingtonian shuffle beat, supplying lush harmonies upon which Tabackin unleashes one of his more impassioned saxophone orations. The band rides this for more than six minutes, ending in a large collective shout chorus.

Akiyoshi described the piece as a celebration of a Japanese multicultural past. "And so we found out that migrations to Japan had come not only from Korea and China but also from far away, from the Near East, the silk roads," explained Akiyoshi. "This showed we have so many different people." She wrote the opening theme to reflect this: "not really Japanese, not really American, and not really Near Eastern." Judging from the liner notes, Akiyoshi was in effect creating a multicultural Japan in the image of her own adopted country. "These people from the Near East came into a strange country, Japan, looking and hoping for happiness and prosperity," the notes assert. *Kourakan Suite* "was indeed, vividly, graphically multicultural, for Toshiko was trying to visualize and dramatize the experiences of feelings of these people from a far land renewing themselves in Japan."[41] In fact, this account is highly romanticized; though the *kourokan* artifacts did reveal the extent of Nara and Heian Period Japan's involvement in Silk Road trade, the historical building was a facility for receiving foreign embassies and merchants, not a sort of proto-Ellis Island entrepot for immigrants traveling from the Asian mainland.

As with *Minamata* and *Hiroshima—Rising from the Abyss,* however, this theme fit the Japanese zeitgeist. During the late 1980s and early 1990s, debates over multicultural Japan were very much in the air. There was both an internal and an external context for Japanese soul-searching. Externally, there were the well-publicized remarks of Prime Minister Nakasone in 1986 that ethnic minorities bring down the intelligence level of the United States. More significant, though, were efforts by a range of minority groups within Japan to win full rights of citizenship. Along with ethnic Koreans, Chinese, Okinawans, and other resident aliens living in Japan, *burakumin* (members of a vestigial low-caste group) and *Ainu* (Native peoples of Hokkaido) worked diligently during the 1980s to secure redress against social and economic discrimination and win full rights of citizenship. By the 1990s, "the burgeoning and very visible demand for minority rights had laid to rest any notion that Japan was a one-dimensional, ethnically homogeneous society."[42] In this context, then, Akiyoshi's *Kourakan Suite* appears as a sonic usable past, a celebration of differences only recently acknowledged in the Japanese nation. But the language and categories used to describe these differences sounded like the classic image of the Unites States as a land of liberty and opportunity, beckoning to the downtrodden and persecuted.

Less obviously, *Kourakan's* theme connects to Akiyoshi's personal history. Visiting Manchuria for the first time in nearly half a century, she first realized that her family was of a "privileged class," on the dominant side of a social system not unlike Jim Crow. "There was a separation between the Japanese and Chinese communities," she recalled in retrospect. "There were Japanese schools, Japanese stores and a Japanese hospital. I can't remember any Chinese students, but in high school, my piano teacher was Chinese."[43] Akiyoshi received some of her formative training in Western music from a colonial subject of Japan. In this context, she experienced both ethnic diversity and racialized discrimination.

As a Japanese woman enmeshed in a male-dominated musical form shot through with nationalist accents, Toshiko Akiyoshi occupies a singularly complex position. Growing up with the privileges of an imperial occupier, she imbibed one form of musical education at school, a radically different one at home. She came of age in a nation devastated and occupied by its imperial nemesis, a nation it had simultaneously admired and resented for nearly a century. As a teenager returning to her ancestral home, Akiyoshi entered yet another musical world, an African American hybrid, whose inspiration and encouragement led her out of her native country. Caught up in the currents of cultural nationalism of the 1960s, she took inspiration from Duke Ellington, both a committed race man and an American patriot, incidentally aligning herself with a quest for Japanese jazz authenticity taking place in her homeland.

Like the Mardi Gras Indians, Al Jolson's jazz singer, and other embodiments of the unstable ethnic triad in American music, Akiyoshi has made cultural in-betweenness a kind of aesthetic signature, juxtaposing music of Europe, African America, and Japan. At one point Akiyoshi thought that her Japanese accents might set a future direction for jazz, like Brazilian music, but eventually realized, "It's more of a special effect."[44] In Akiyoshi's work, though, Japanese musical elements are more than decorative effects; they shape both the music's formal construction and its thematic imperatives. Her composing and bandleading call into question easy assumptions about artists and their respective cultural traditions. Arguments about essentialism in music—if and how ethnic or racial identities are expressed through musical forms—has generated voluminous scholarship in recent years.[45] In Akiyoshi's case, traditional Japanese music was as much a borrowed tradition as jazz. Her native musical tongue was Western art music.

Ultimately, the effort to align her musical styles with her ethnic background collapses, as it usually does, under the weight of its own historical and logical contradictions and in the face of irrepressible creative impulses.

NOTES

My thanks to Taylor Atkins and Shannon Steen for perceptive comments on earlier drafts of this article. The title of this chapter comes from Ono Masaichirô, quoted in E. Taylor Atkins, *Blue Nippon: Authenticating Jazz in Japan* (Durham: Duke University Press, 2001), 245.

1. David W. Stowe, *How Sweet the Sound: Music in the Spiritual Lives of Americans* (Cambridge, MA: Harvard University Press, 2004), 170–195; Michael Rogin, *Blackface, White Noise: Jewish Immigrants in the Hollywood Melting Pot* (Berkeley: University of California Press, 1996), 73–120.

2. George Lipsitz, *Dangerous Crossroads: Popular Music, Postmodernism and the Politics of Place* (New York: Verso, 1994), 72, 74; Reid Mitchell, *All on a Mardi Gras Day: Episodes in the History of New Orleans Carnival* (Cambridge, MA: Harvard University Press, 1995), 113–130; David W. Stowe, "The Diasporic Imagination of Wynton Marsalis," in *The Black Urban Community: From Dusk Till Dawn*, ed. Gayle Tate and Lewis Randolph (New York: Palgrave Macmillan, 2006).

3. E. Taylor Atkins, *Blue Nippon: Authenticating Jazz in Japan* (Durham: Duke University Press, 2001), 45–163.

4. Du Bois quoted by Kwame Anthony Appiah, *In My Father's House*, in *The American Intellectual Tradition*, Vol. II, ed. David A. Hollinger and Charles Capper (New York: Oxford University Press, 2001), 478.

5. Atkins, *Blue Nippon*, 222–264.

6. Michael Bourne, "Rising Hope: Toshiko Akiyoshi's Deep Reflection on Hiroshima," *Down Beat* (July 2003): 45–46.

7. Hampton Hawes quoted in Atkins, *Blue Nippon*, 182.

8. Leonard Feather, "East Meets West, or Never the Twain Shall Cease: Toshiko Akiyoshi and Lew Tabackin," *Down Beat* (3 June 1976): 16.

9. Scott Saul, *Freedom Is, Freedom Ain': Jazz and the 1960s* (Cambridge, MA: Harvard University Press, 2003), 6; LeRoi Jones, *Blues People: Negro Music in White America* (New York: Morrow Quill, 1963); LeRoi Jones, "Jazz and the White Critic," in *Keeping Time: Readings in Jazz History*, ed. Robert Walser (New York: Oxford University Press, 1999), 255–261.

10. Atkins, *Blue Nippon*, 244, 249–250.

11. Ibid., 12.

12. Ibid., 19.

13. Gene Santoro, *Myself When I Am Real: The Life and Music of Charles Min-*

gus (New York: Oxford University Press, 2001), 192; Atkins, *Blue Nippon,* 208; Fred Jung, "A Fireside Chat with Toshiko Akiyoshi," 20 April 2003, available at www .AllAboutJazz.com (retrieved 15 June 2004).

14. Bourne, "Rising Hope," 46. Akiyoshi vociferously denies that Japanese musicians or critics had anything to do with her turn toward Japanese roots music. E-mail from Toshiko Akiyoshi, 28 September 2004. Ellington had also drawn inspiration from Asia. One of his most admired late pieces, *The Far East Suite* (1966), incorporates some of the same Orientalist musical effects Akiyoshi would later include in her own writing for big band.

15. Feather, "East Meets West," 38.

16. James L. McClain, *Japan: A Modern History* (New York: Norton, 2002), 623–624; Atkins, *Blue Nippon,* 257.

17. Feather, "East Meets West," 18.

18. From an interview in the film *Jazz Is My Native Language: A Portrait of Toshiko Akiyoshi* (Rhapsody Films, 1983). This passage is also quoted in Atkins, *Blue Nippon,* 240.

19. Jung, "Fireside Chat with Lew Tabackin."

20. Leonard Feather, "Toshiko Akiyoshi: Contemporary Sculptress of Sound," *Down Beat* (20 October 1977), 15.

21. Feather, "East Meets West," 16.

22. Asked about the predominately white personnel of her bands, Akiyoshi observed that African American musicians with the necessary skills to play her music were highly in demand and frequently not available or affordable. E-mail from Akiyoshi, 28 September 2004.

23. Peter Rothbart, "Toshiko Akiyoshi," *Down Beat* (August 1980), 15; Feather, "East Meets West," 17.

24. John Corbett, "Experimental Oriental: New Music and Other Others," in *Western Music and Its Others: Difference, Representation, and Appropriation in Music,* ed. Georgina Born and David Hesmondhalgh (Berkeley: University of California Press, 2000), 170–173.

25. William P. Malm, *Traditional Japanese Music and Musical Instruments* (Tokyo: Kodansha, 2000), 129. Originally published 1959.

26. Feather, "Toshiko Akiyoshi," 14.

27. Feather, "East Meets West," 17.

28. Malm, *Traditional Japanese Music and Musical Instruments,* 102.

29. Feather, "Toshiko Akiyoshi," 14.

30. Ibid.

31. Rothbart, "Toshiko Akiyoshi," 14.

32. Togashi quoted in Atkins, *Blue Nippon,* 258.

33. Feather, "East Meets West," 17.

34. Atkins, *Blue Nippon,* 208.

35. Toshiko Akiyoshi Jazz Orchestra, *Insights* (BMG, 1976); Toshiko Akiyoshi

Jazz Orchestra, Carnegie Hall Concert (Columbia 48805, 1992); Toshiko Akiyoshi Jazz Orchestra, *Hiroshima—Rising from the Abyss* (True Life, 1000082, 2002).

36. Timothy S. George, *Minamata: Pollution and the Struggle for Democracy in Postwar Japan* (Cambridge, MA: Harvard University Press, 2001). First published in 1969, Ishimure Michiko's eloquent expose helped establish the powerful narrative surrounding the Minamata tragedy; see Michiko Ishimure, *Paradise in the Sea of Sorrow: Our Minamata Disease,* trans. Livia Monnett (Kyoto: Yamaguchi, 1990).

37. Other interpretations are possible, of course; the suite could narrate the devastating impact of organic mercury on an individual, the frenzy of neurological breakdown followed by death. *Minamata*'s opening line was recited on the recording by Akiyoshi's eleven-year-old daughter, Michiru.

38. Jung, "Fireside Chat with Lew Tabackin"; McClain, *Japan,* 626.

39. Bourne, "Rising Hope," 46.

40. *Hiroshima—Rising from the Ashes* was released in the United States two years after its recording in Hiroshima, and only because Akiyoshi herself found a label to bring it out. In fact, none of her recordings have been released in the United States since 1994. "Since then, we have three recordings for BMG Japan, but BMG American never picked them up," she says. "Lew always said that I am demographically challenged." Jung, "Fireside Chat with Toshiko Akiyoshi"; Ben Ratliff, "Remembering Hiroshima, in a Farewell Performance," *New York Times,* 21 Oct. 2003, E5.

41. Akiyoshi, Carnegie Hall Concert, liner notes.

42. McClain, *Japan,* 68.

43. Bourne, "Rising Hope," 45.

44. Feather, "Toshiko Akiyoshi," 15.

45. The literature is extensive, but in addition to Atkins' *Blue Nippon,* two recent persuasive interrogations of racial essentialism in music are Ronald Radano, *Lying up a Nation: Race and Black Music* (Chicago: University of Chicago Press, 2003), and Michael D. McNally, *Ojibwe Singers: Hymns, Grief, and a Native Culture in Motion* (New York: Oxford University Press, 2000).

Chapter 16

Kickin' the White Man's Ass
Black Power, Aesthetics, and the Asian Martial Arts

Fred Ho

To even the casual observer of the martial arts community in the United States, there is undeniably a significant representation of African American and Latino participants and aficionados, perhaps in greater numbers and intensity than that of Asians. I noticed this sociological phenomenon as a young teenager during the 1970s while attending the popular martial arts movies in deteriorating inner-city movie theaters in and around Boston's Combat Zone–Chinatown area and in the then-seedy Times Square area of New York City. In the audiences of these cheap theaters, often with double and triple features, sat black, brown, yellow, and white youth, mostly male, enjoying the martial arts mayhem of Hong Kong–imported B-grade action films.

Later as I became both producer and creator of large-scale theatrical works, I especially came to notice the magnitude of martial arts skill, generally exceeding other ethnicities, possessed by young African Americans and Latinos whom I saw in my auditions for my martial arts and music/theater productions beginning in the mid-1990s.

And from martial arts tournaments to Ultimate Fighting events across the United States, the presence of blacks and browns is large.

As a popular cultural genre, the Asian martial arts have attracted possibly one of the widest multicultural cross-sections of urban youth. The Asian martial arts join the later sociocultural phenomenon of hip-hop as a site of intercultural recreation, creation, and identity construction: a sociocultural dynamic that really took off in the late 1960s and early 1970s, not coincidentally, but as I assert in this essay, in direct relation to the upsurges of the Third World national liberation movements across the planet and in the U.S. oppressed-nationality communities.

Why the attraction of Asian martial arts for black and brown youth in U.S. society? The Asian martial arts have continually been an area where nonwhite dominance is uncontested. The huge impact of the late Bruce Lee and the release of his film *Enter the Dragon* (1973) projected "non-whites" as flawed heroes who could kick the butts of physically powerful and sometimes armed white males. In *Enter the Dragon*, with its promotions by the major film studio Warner Brothers and widespread screening in thousands of movie theaters across the United States, audiences were introduced to an unlikely trio of martial arts protagonists—two of the three were not white, but one an Asian and the other an African American: Lee (played by Lee), Roper (played by white actor and martial arts student John Saxon), and Williams (played by black U.S. karate champion Jim Kelly).

The character Williams is a black militant, who beats up two white cops when he is stopped in a typical case of racial profiling and soundly defeats a white New Zealand martial arts champion in martial arts competition. In a flashback that reveals Williams's past, we see him at a black karate training session and in the background a black nationalist flag of red, black, and green, set on the continent of Africa with a cobra emblem (à la the Symbionese Liberation Army). When Williams is approached by the movie's principal villan, Han, a renegade Shaolin monk, to join his drug cartel, the militant Williams declines. It is clearly established from the beginning that Williams's political consciousness is very high. When the white con man and get-rich-quick scheming Roper comments about how he has heard that Han "likes to live big," Williams replies, pointing to the poverty shanties surrounding them in Hong Kong harbor, "Yeah, well, they don't live so big over there. Ghettos are the same all over the world: they stink." When I first heard this, at the age of sixteen, I let out an inner howl of "right on!" Williams is modeled on a "bad boy" quick-talking Muhammad Ali–type character. When asked by Han if he is prepared to accept defeat, Williams replies in typical Ali style, "I'll be too busy lookin' good." Though Williams is soon killed in the story of the film for refusing to join the villianous Han's cartel, he is killed not by a white, but by the Asian Han, who must be brought to justice by Lee.

Of course, it is the great Bruce Lee who dispatches the formidable white martial artists. In the case of *Enter the Dragon*, he disposes of O'Hara (played by white martial artist/actor Bob Wall). In *Return of the Dragon*, it is U.S. karate champion Chuck Norris in a duel of cinematic symbolic proportions held in the Roman Coliseum. Few could overlook or ignore the political symbolism of such a showdown between the East (Lee) and the white West (Norris).

In the early 1970s, the U.S. war in Southeast Asia had reached a turning point, and it was clear to all but the most deluded that the Vietnamese National Liberation Front would achieve decisive military victory over both the U.S.-supported South Vietnamese government and the U.S. military forces themselves. Worldwide, it was an era of intense and victorious anticolonial and national liberation struggles sweeping Africa, Asia, Oceania, the Caribbean, and Central and South America (the so-called Third World). It seemed that the darker, "colored" peoples of the world were rising up and beating their former colonial "white" masters in the United States and Western Europe. In the United States, the antiwar movement opposed U.S. intervention into Southeast Asia particularly, but many also supported the aspirations of national self-determination by other Third World peoples worldwide. Large sections of the African American and Latino American communities declared solidarity with the Vietnamese, as well as identified and supported the struggles of Third World people. Indeed, many in the United States of Third World ancestry adopted the sobriquet "Third World" as a way to collectively identify with the struggles in their ancestral homelands as connected to their own struggles in the United States as so-called minorities or so-called people of color (or oppressed nationalities, which is the term I prefer to use).

African American world heavyweight champion boxer Muhammad Ali, when refusing to be drafted into the U.S. Army, borrowed the slogan from the Student Non-Violent Coordinating Committee (SNCC) and its Black Power leader, then Stokely Carmichael, proclaiming his reason for draft resistance to be "No Vietnamese ever called me nigger." Among Chicanos, major demonstrations against the U.S. war and its draft were held and became a tradition still commemorated today as the August 29th moratorium in honor of police-slain Latino journalist Rueben Salazar, killed during a demonstration in 1970 by Los Angeles police.

Obvious political "readings" can be made of the "nonwhite" Third World beating, defeating the "white" First World as a statement of anti-imperialist and nationalist pride. Even Bruce Lee has been quoted as saying that he explicitly and consciously made the choice to show whites beaten and defeated by Asians.[1] What becomes abundantly clear to the black and brown male teenager is the fact that in this film, for the first time, powerful whites are defeated by nonwhites, the same nonwhites who, for the most part, have been disparaged, underestimated, and treated as outcasts in media portrayals and in U.S. society. And especially in the case of Bruce Lee, the nonwhite man is yellow (Asian), speaks with an accent, is proud of his Chinese heritage, and has a highly masculinized "ripped" body that shames and slights those of any past or current white screen star. Lee unabashedly displayed his body, unlike today's out-of-shape and overweight white martial arts stars like Steven Seagal who are covered up and always fully clothed on screen. It was also abundantly clear that Lee was the "real deal," instead of the cinematic fakery so prevalent with to-day's white Hollywood action stars who rely on stunt doubles, camera tricks, special effects, and editing instead of actual physical prowess and fighting capability. Even the more comical buffoonery of Jackie Chan is given credibility by his reputation of doing his own stunts and suffering serious injuries at times. The legend of Bruce Lee was partly built on his being frequently "tested" from the streets to movie sets by would-be chal-lengers who initially doubted Lee's authenticity but soon regretted their mistaken assumption.

Bruce Lee, as an Asian American actor, was all too familiar with the sting of white racism, having been passed over on numerous occasions for Hollywood roles. The most well-known incident was the selection of white actor David Carradine over Lee to play the lead character in the tele-vision series *Kung Fu* in the early 1970s.

The world of the martial arts through these movie imports, often over-dubbed with the silliest of voiceovers, offered for the first time a heroic world not populated by whites but by a Third World people, specifically the Chinese. The Chinese were seen by black and brown youth as a people with a long and glorious history that extended further back than the his-torical greatness of Europe, including knowledge and ways not monopo-lized or dominated by white Europeans such as the martial arts. As a teen-ager during this time, I had many long conversations with an African American junior high school English teacher of mine, Marilyn Lewis (who joined the Nation of Islam and recruited me into the movement) about black interest in revolutionary China. It was she who offered this analysis. Many of the young teenage African Americans I was involved with at this time were taking up Chinese and Asian martial arts, which furthered their interests in other facets of Chinese and Asian history and culture. I re-member in the pages of *Black World* magazine, a nationwide forum edited by Hoyt Fuller for black nationalist culture and politics, how articles and essays appeared, promoting interest in the Chinese revolution, including an on-going series by writer John O. Killens about his travels in the People's Republic of China. I also remember when the great African American drummer Max Roach told me that he and other black activists and radical intellectuals were interested in how the Chinese Revolution eliminated drug addiction as it had become a major problem in black and brown inner cities in the United States by the time of the 1960s.[2]

The Chinese were also becoming major players in world politics. The rising strength and prestige of the People's Republic of China derived from both its support of anticolonial and national liberation movements, especially in Africa, and its leading position in the Third World for its opposition to "superpower hegemony"—to the United States which it boldly denounced as a "paper tiger" and to the then Soviet Union which it trashed as "social-imperialist: socialism in words, imperialism in deeds." To those with a racial consciousness in the late 1960s and early 1970s, it appeared that China was the nonwhite giant with a glorious ancient history and the most un-European culture standing up to the mighty forces of the white West. This racial analysis of world geopolitics was probably best stated by Malcolm X, who in the early 1960s favorably commented about the Chinese development of nuclear weaponry when the U.S. mainstream opined fear and anxiety about the nuclear club now including a Third World power.

The Chinese experience with Western imperialism and racism was also popularized in many martial arts movies. Such historical themes included the Opium Wars, the unfair treaties, discrimination such as Western zones with signs that proclaimed "No Dogs or Chinese Allowed," and even the experiences of exploited and oppressed Chinese sojourners in America. This was a major trope in the TV series *Kung Fu* that began in 1972 about the story of a Shaolin priest, played in scotch-taped "oriental" style by white actor David Carradine, who as a political refugee is hiding out and wandering the U.S. wild west, often getting into fights with racist whites.

Another important response by black and brown male youth to the images of Asian fighters is the reliance of Asian martial arts not on modern technology such as firearms and weapons of mass destruction but on physical skills, mental attitude, spiritual fortitude, loyalty, and strategy, all developed from years of training from long-standing traditions and taught via unorthodox and creatively folksy ways as depicted in these fictionalized movies. Such an example is the pupil carrying water buckets with both arms fully extended up long flights of stairs over and over again while a very much aged and diminutive "master/teacher" watches and disciplines the student for any minor infraction or slacking, as shown in a scene from one of the 1970s "kung fu cinema classics," *The Master Killer* (also known as *The 38 Chambers of Death*). This fascination with discipline and mastery of physical skill joined with an overarching philosophical tradition and doctrine underscored the black-brown urban pop cultural perception and understanding of the success of Third World guerrilla movements: reliance on indigenous methods and traditions, unwavering dedication to fight against a superpower Goliath, defending the weak and oppressed and thereby winning their support, and finding ways to defeat a far superior enemy through innovation and attrition such as striking in an elusive, unpredictable, and unfamiliar manner.

The 1960s and early 1970s was a period in American society of heightened social consciousness. In the oppressed-nationality communities in the United States emerged what I term "Third World consciousness," an anti-imperialist solidarity among "peoples of color" that identified with their brothers and sisters in their ancestral homelands who were often fighting for national liberation or independence against the Western powers, but that also represented a solidarity across national, racial, and ethnic lines. This "Third World consciousness" took political expression in Third World alliances and coalitions, both on college campuses and across communities. The struggle for a department of ethnic studies at San Francisco State University in 1968–1969 was led by a coalition called the Third World Liberation Front, an alliance of the Black Student Union, the Asian Student Union, the MECHA (a Chicano student group), and others. During this period, the receptivity for unity between oppressed nationalities was at its highest, spearheaded by radical and revolutionary organizations such as the Black Panther Party, the Brown Berets, the Young Lords, the Red Guard Party, I Wor Kuen, and the American Indian Movement. This heightened consciousness embraced a knowledge and understanding of the common oppression faced by "racially oppressed" peoples, of the parallels and connections between genocide, annexation, enslavement, conscripted labor, forced relocation, removal, and mass exodus from homelands onto poisoned and pitiable reservations, internment camps, and the like. This consciousness and concrete manifestation of solidarity and common struggle, identification, and collaboration embodied in Third World consciousness were precursors to today's co-opted and sanitized academic, government, and corporate "multiculturalism" or the reformist Democratic Party politics of Jesse Jackson's Rainbow Coalition, all of which emphasize token diversity without challenging U.S. imperialism.

While very few formal alliances and collaborations were able to sustain themselves beyond the heat of direct struggles or endure as the U.S. left and revolutionary movements subsided, a legacy was established in both radical cultural and political projects, as well as in parts of popular urban culture, with possibly martial arts and hip-hop being the most significant and self-sustaining. The latter has, of course, become mainstream and therefore depoliticized and co-opted as hip-hop is exploited from Madison Avenue ads to Hollywood movies to all facets of fashion and popular youth marketing. The commercialization and mainstreaming of the martial arts has been slower but is in full speed now with the Jackie Chan/ Chris Tucker *Rush Hour* franchise (with its TV imitation of the Sammo Hong/Arsenio Hall team-up in the short-lived CBS series *Martial Law*). We notice the marked differences between the generation of the early 1970s and today's AfroAsian pop cultural teams. Today's cinematic blacks aren't militant, on the run from the law, who speak lines like "Ghettos are the same around the world: they stink!" Rather, they are minstrel jive-shucking squeaky-voiced cops who are more interested in chasing tail than fighting for the liberation of their oppressed communities. Today's cinematic Asians, likewise, use their martial arts for the police state as, for example, cops, international spies, government secret agents, and elite covert operators instead of championing powerless workers against greedy capitalists, as the Bruce Lee character Tang does in the film *Return of the Dragon*. They are not righteous martial artists who take on domestic Asian despots and quislings like Bruce Lee, who goes after the villain Han in *Enter the Dragon,* and they do not fight imperialists and their Chinese compradors, as does Bruce Lee in *Fists of Fury* when Japanese imperialists collude with Chinese sell-outs and assassinate a patriotic Chinese martial arts master.

Enter the Dragon broke all box office records as the most popular and commercially successful action movie of all times worldwide.[3] The film particularly succeeded in Southeast Asian and Asia/Pacific markets where youth flocked in massive numbers to movie theaters.[4] *Enter the Dragon* was a Touchstone popular film that heavily affected American youth audiences, especially black, brown, and yellow urban youth. Several melodramatic, but emotionally evocative scenes have given the film signature status as a cult classic, with special political resonance for oppressed nationality audiences. Few in the United States had seen Asian females as strong fighters. Asian martial arts actress Angela Mao played Bruce Lee's sister in the film. In one scene, she roundly fights off a gang of ruffians who intend to rape her, led by the drug lord Han's principal bodyguard, the white

O'Hara. We know that O'Hara is "tough, ruthless, as one would expect of Han's personal bodyguard." Angela Mao's scene occurs as a flashback told to Lee. As told to him, when his sister is finally cornered, she commits suicide by stabbing herself with broken glass rather than be raped. When he learns how his sister died, we see Bruce Lee, as present time resumes in the film, crying for the first time ever. Later in the film, Lee and O'Hara are selected to spar in Han's martial arts tournament. Lee is at first very reluctant at hearing his name called as the next contestant. But when he sees it is O'Hara who is his opponent, Lee's face turns to icy resolve. Lee gives O'Hara the customary bow of respect. The self-confident and haughty O'Hara does not reciprocate but, instead, smashes a board in Lee's face as a gesture of arrogant scorn. Third World viewers cannot but notice the racist implications of O'Hara's effrontery. Lee's response to O'Hara is chilling and riveting: "Boards don't hit back." The emotional power of this moment on screen resonated profoundly with anyone who had experienced racist bullying. In three lightning flurries, Lee beats O'Hara. Unable to accept his loss, O'Hara goes berserk and, against the order of his boss, Han, engages Lee in a no-rules all-out street fight. Lee shows his Ali-esque élan and buffets the flailing O'Hara. In desperation, O'Hara breaks two bottles, and the parallel to the glass used by Lee's sister in her suicide is unmistakable. Lee finally kills O'Hara. Even Han must accept the consequences of O'Hara's disgrace and disobedience. The entire crowd is stunned. No one expected the unknown Lee to have been able to so easily end the life of the feared and dreaded O'Hara.

The final emblematically powerful moment in *Enter the Dragon* is Lee's simple declaration to Han in their climatic fight, "You have offended my family and you have offended the Shaolin Temple." One of my collaborator-colleague-friends, Ruth Margraff, in her research on the *wuxia* tradition of Chinese heroic epic literature and drama, noted that the Chinese values and conception of "hero" and "heroism" is markedly different from the Western, bourgeois "hero." The latter, typified in Hollywood films by the Dirty Harry character played by Clint Eastwood, tells his villains, "Make my day" as he aims and shoots his Magnum 47. Western heroes fight for self-gain, mostly as professionals paid to get the bad guys, whether employed by the police (in the case of Dirty Harry), the military, or the government or as private investigators. Typically, the *wuxia* or Asian martial hero fights not for self-gain but for principles such as honor, family, school, or community; archetypically in stories about revenge and revolution; or against unjust and oppressive despots and regimes. Lee is not a paid, professional agent or law enforcement officer but simply a martial artist who is committed to the honor of his temple, as Han was a renegade monk who violated everything the Shaolin Temple stood for, and to his family, as Han's men were the cause of his sister's suicidal death. The warrior for justice and principle is akin to the Third World guerrillas who fight not for salary but for liberation, never considering any self-gain or employment.

The resurgence in Hong Kong historical martial arts period film epics in the late 1980s and early 1990s produced a number of films that resonated with fans from the 1970s, as well as a new, younger contemporary urban audience with the reintroduction of the Wong Fei-hung hero (most famously played by Jet Li, but also done by Jackie Chan) in the popular *Once upon a Time in China* series directed by Tsui Hark. Hark had spent his formative filmmaking years in the United States, working with a then-self-described "guerrilla" media group in New York's Chinatown called Asian Cinevision and being part of the team that made the documentary *From Spikes to Spindles* about the struggles of Chinese workers from the days of building the Transcontinental Railroad to today's garment factory workers. Indeed, the story line in the first *Once . . .* film is based on hero Wong taking on the kidnapping and smuggling of Chinese men who are "shanghaied" for the coolie trade. Wong Fei-hung teams up with nationalist leader Sun Yat-sen in the second film. In all of the films, Western colonial designs on China are apparent. Wong Fei-hung is a people's hero, as is another popular character, the Iron Monkey, a village Robin Hood martial artist who fights domestic corruption and aids the poor and sick and who is depicted in the film *Iron Monkey* in the early 1990s.

However, this latest Hong Kong martial arts renaissance in films was cut short by the crash in the Asian stock market of the mid-1990s that nearly wiped out the Hong Kong commercial film industry. While Jet Li rose as a martial arts film superstar, he in no way reflected the same sociocultural and sociopolitical dynamism of Bruce Lee. Jet Li's heroes did not symbolize the struggle with Western white power or against imperialism and its collaborators. For example, in some of the *Once . . .* films, the villains are agitators against foreigners, such as the Boxer rebels and secret societies. A generation ago, however, the Boxers and secret societies were lionized as anti-imperialist heroes; one Asian American revolutionary group even adopted the name of the Boxers, I Wor Kuen: the Society for the Harmonious Righteous Fist. The political tenor of the times had changed between the era of the late 1960s/early 1970s and today. The once beacon of Third World national liberation struggle had been crushed or co-opted by neocolonialism and imperialist global machinations as right-wing and Fascist local leaders supplanted, assassinated, and imprisoned nationalists and leftists. On the international scene, there were no more Asian peasant guerrillas dressed in black pajamas kicking the ass of U.S. imperialism.

By the mid-1990s, Hollywood had caught on to the Asian action film-making techniques as a way to reinvigorate the tired and predictable American action movie and television genre, and with its mighty financial dominance, it had bought and appropriated much of the Asian talent and techniques. Hong Kong stunt teams, for example, were employed in television shows such as *Hercules* and *Xena*. Today, American movies are more frequently hiring Hong Kong action directors and buying their film-making stylizations. Asian action cinema has become another Third World resource at the disposal of First World filmmaking. *Crouching Tiger Hidden Dragon* proved that nonmartial artists could be employed to do all the choreography and special stunt effects that were once done by authentic martial artists slaving away in the Hong Kong film plantations.

The aesthetics and forms of Asian martial arts as depicted in the movies of the classic kung fu cinema era of the 1970s also contained many important tropes and parallels to African diaspora forms and traditions. A common trope in the Asian martial arts films was the need to combine unusual, uncommon, and disparate styles and techniques to innovate a new fighting form to defeat an all-powerful enemy who possesses the entire conventional fighting canon. Thus, new canons and styles are birthed in the need to create new combat skills. There is also the trope of the conflict and discord between traditionalists ("old school") and iconoclasts ("new school"), of which Bruce Lee epitomized and personified the latter with his *jeet kune do* hybridized system of combining Chinese martial arts and street fighting. Lee was a revolutionary Asian American innovator, a martial arts genius who combined acting and martial artistry, emblazing his own idiosyncratic and emblematic stylizations (from his cat sounds, to his facial and bodily gestures, etc.) and challenging and breaking traditions with bold defiance that some in the "old school" perceived as arrogance.

In addition, Lee was also transgressive for teaching Chinese martial arts to non-Chinese, including blacks; one famous student of Lee's was basketball's great Kareem Abdul-Jabbar. Lee took much heat and criticism for doing this from older, more conservative Chinese martial artists. Lee was the Asian American martial arts equivalent to a great "jazz" innovator like John Coltrane. Both Lee and Coltrane had been schooled "in the tradition" of their respective art forms, and both challenged and eventually broke with their respective traditions in order to innovate a "new" identity and expression that contained extended improvisation and that incorporated disparate formic influences. As discussed by Hafez Modirzadeh, Coltrane sought Asian musical concepts to infuse into African American musical aesthetics.[5] Bruce Lee incorporated black and brown street-fighting techniques as well as the famous footwork of Muhammad Ali, saying that his ultimate goal was to innovate a fighting style that was simultaneously all and no styles. Both geniuses wanted to liberate themselves from the boundaries of form and attain a completely intuitive approach to improvisation.

The many published volumes of Bruce Lee's philosophical notes and musings confirm his view that mastery was the attainment of intuitive, improvisational expression: "form without form" and such dialectical and paradoxical aphorisms as "the art of fighting without fighting." Unlike a lot of the "fortune cookie" fake oriental philosophizing in white Western renditions of Asian martial arts, which is most notable and repugnant in the *Kung Fu* television series, Lee's philosophizing was grounded in his studies of Daoism (he was a philosophy major at the University of California at Los Angeles) and, I would hypothesize, in the influence of African American cultural aesthetics. Such influences included the stylizations and ethos of African American boxer Muhammad Ali, who as a fighter expressed potent African American aesthetic characteristics such as the trickster method of the "rope-a-dope" ploy that defeated the juggernaught George Foreman; his lightning-fast witticisms by, for example, doing "the dozens" or "wolfing" against his opponents as part of psychologically undermining them and winning a war of propaganda for popular support; and his unorthodox boxing techniques, such as his unpredictable and evasive footwork. I also contend that, with the immense rise of the black liberation movement and its impact on American society and culture, Bruce Lee was influenced by black music, which was so prevalent and influential as part of the zeitgeist in the 1960s and early 1970s. In addition, Lee counted among his closest friends the great basketball star, Kareem Abdul-Jabbar, a known fan of jazz. Even the black movie character Williams in the film *Enter the Dragon* is seen relaxing to such hip sounds as Herbie Hancock. The concept of "soul" clearly is embodied in Bruce Lee, his "coolness" in the face of threat and danger, yet his explosive fighting ferocity and feline-like physical grace, along with the elegance of a master musician blowing his solo constantly adaptive, free-flowing and creative.

The fascination with Hong Kong martial arts films in U.S. innercity communities is the stuff of urban legend. On Saturday afternoons, a local New York City television station, Channel 5, played back-to-back "karate" movies. The term "karate" is a cultural misnomer, confusing and confounding all Asian martial arts with the specific Japanese fighting form of karate. The emerging hip-hop artists of the South Bronx and other urban communities adopted kung fu references such as Grandmaster and Wu Tang Clan. But more than taking on kung fu titles and sobriquets, these hip-hop artists aspired to the commitment, dedication, righteous integrity, and level of competitive excellence and mastery of form and craft that they identified with the martial arts. They also identified with the perceived fraternal culture of the martial arts world filled with loyal clans and rival schools of styles. Hip-hop challenges often take on the qualities of a martial arts tournament. Hip-hop "crews" are stylized after martial arts "schools."

The 1970s brown and black audiences also greatly appreciated the raw, no special effects but highly skilled fight choreography and grueling authenticity of these very low-budget films during a period when very few movie-making tricks and expensive gimmickry were used. Brown and black fans of Hong Kong martial arts films were also aware of the semi-slave-like contracts and conditions under which their favorite actors worked with the likes of the Shaw Brothers film company, a plantation that churned out historical period martial arts action dramas. This was unapologetic low-brow culture made by performers who did it for relatively meager pay for mass entertainment. However, the attraction was not the dialogue or writing but the virtuous fight choreography and martial arts performances, along with perhaps the peppering of infectious slapstick humor. Regarded as "culturally inferior" by Eurocentric high-brow art elites, Third World peoples have been able to find great talent and make art from the bowels of the low-brow. Bruce Lee became an even greater legend with his untimely death. As speculation abounded that he was perhaps murdered for bucking the Hong Kong film mafia with his assertion for artistic and financial independence, the mythos of Bruce Lee escalated. Whether true or not, such a mythos made him also a martyr among street-tough black and brown youth who relished an anti-hero figure.

Because most of the 1970s Shaw Brothers–made martial arts movies were historical period stories, they drew on and mythologized much of the *wuxia* tradition of Chinese heroic literature and drama, and, as a consequence, they popularized certain themes and story lines that were antiestablishment, anticolonialist, and anti-imperialist. Many of the martial characters were antigovernment rebels. In the case of stories set in the nineteenth and twentieth centuries, the heroes fought corrupt collaborators with foreign imperialists such as the Japanese. These stories were replete with martyrs, rebels and revolutionaries, women warriors, dissidents, and populist fighters who defended the poor, oppressed, and bullied. Such stories and settings with their defiantly courageous antiestablishment heroes resonated well with the burgeoning anti-imperialist consciousness in early 1970s black and brown urban ghettos. The gestural codes and symbols used by the secret societies were adopted by black and brown "crews," who integrated them into their graffiti, greetings, and group identifiers and emblems. Much of today's hip-hop subcultural stylizations are direct outgrowths of this influence. The connection between hip-hop and the brown-black interest in Asian martial arts closely reflects the latter's influence on and inspiration for the former. Unfortunately, the recent reverse influence of hip-hop on Asian martial arts movies is imbecilic comedic relief and patently stereotypic minstrelsy.

As the martial arts becomes an increasing area of interest to scholars and academics, hopefully more complete histories and studies of how Asian martial arts were introduced to the United States and their adaptations and developments will be discussed. While it is generally known that karate and Japanese combat forms came to the United States in post–World War II times via the U.S. military and security forces stationed in Japan, the Chinese martial arts have never received such official interest or support. Some speculate that the Chinese martial arts came to the United States as early as with the first large wave of Chinese immigrants during the nineteenth century. During the period of the Taiping Rebellions in China in the mid-1800s and the massive importation of Chinese labor to the west, Chinese martial artists were perhaps political dissidents fleeing imperial persecution, or former bodyguards without employment during China's economic crises, a theory that comes from black martial arts teacher George Crayton Jr. To be sure, black martial artist Ron Wheeler cites that the practice of Chinese martial arts remained covert and concealed from non-Chinese for much of the first century of the history of the Chinese in America.[6] Yet, by the 1970s, Bruce Lee and the wave of

Hong Kong films had popularized interest among non-Asians, and especially among blacks and browns, so much so that a few Chinese martial arts teachers began to take on non-Asian students. Wheeler's article is an excellent beginning in tracing the rise of Chinese martial arts among African Americans.

Much of what black and brown youth syncretized and incorporated were perceptions and interpretations from these movies and pop cultural renditions of Asian martial arts. However, those black and brown youth who proceeded into a more serious and significant immersion into the world of Asian martial arts and actually became martial artists would become the harbingers of a unique but important AfroAsian connectivity.

During the two and a half month tour of *Voice of the Dragon* in the United States, I had many discussions with the martial artists I was touring with and listened to the many arguments between them about the origins and historical developments of varying martial arts. Particularly engaging and interesting were discussions I had with Earl Weathers Jr., an African American talent in kung fu. What was perplexing to him were my politics of revolutionary socialism, support for the Chinese socialist revolution and Chairman Mao—my anticapitalist values joined with my interest in martial arts. After all, most of the martial arts schools in U.S. Chinatowns are very conservative and allied with the local community reactionaries such as the Kuomintang Nationalist Party, the conservative family and business and merchant associations, and the Christian YMCA and YWCA programs. I explained to him that because of racist exclusion of Chinese immigration for almost a century and the McCarthy era red-hunts and terrorizing against Communists in the Chinese community during the early 1950s, the conservatives and reactionaries were propped up heavily while the leftists were attacked and repressed. This was abetted by the fact that the socialist Chinese government had campaigned to suppress martial arts, replacing it eventually in the 1960s with state-sponsored *wuxu* as a national sport. The secret societies, by the twentieth century, especially after the Republican Revolution of 1912, had deteriorated into a reactionary force as the social base for the tongs and criminal cartels and warlords vying for economic and territorial control over a weak, decrepit, and decentralized China wrecked from generations of upheaval, corruption, and instability. Martial artists had degenerated into thugs, hired muscle for criminal gangs, mercenary militia, and triads.

In overseas Chinese communities, including U.S. Chinatowns, the martial arts schools received financial support and recognition from the merchants who hired them for security, collection of owed monies, and the perfunctory lion dance New Year celebrations and other community events. In my perspective, as I explained to Earl, the martial arts world had lost its revolutionary heroic tradition. Today's teachers, even from the People's Republic of China, are very acquisitive. There are no more real Shaolin monks who live a life of pure asceticism, which includes material denial and a vow of poverty, and who champion the rights of the poor and oppressed. Today's Shaolin Temple is a money-making tourist site no different from Western theme parks, prostituting kung fu in meaningless spectacle displays for tourists and in touring as so-called Shaolin Warriors. Many kung fu masters have come to the West as kung fu entrepreneurs. In my view, a real martial artist is committed to a way of life of helping the poor and powerless and standing up against the rich and the powerful. I told him that I knew of no such martial artist today, only of people who do martial arts either as a business, to teach exercise and self-defense or as entertainment. The handful that are working with me, I said to him, may have the potential to be "artists who do martial arts" but until they become revolutionaries and fighters of the people, will they simply be "martial artists." Earl continues to ponder what I said.

While the martial arts may not further anti-imperialist politics, it has undeniably promoted one of the strongest links of AfroAsian connectivity. In all the years of activity and work in AfroAsian connections, I have found sincere and serious interest in Asian and Asian American culture and history only among two types of African Americans: black martial artists and black radical activist-intellectuals.[7]

The black female presence in martial arts is still negligible. While Brazilian *capoeira* has attracted many black and brown male and female students and performers, and is a genre unto itself, black females have not been as drawn to practicing Chinese martial arts, though there are some black and brown women in karate and Tae kwon do (a Korean form). While all martial arts demand discipline, subservience to master teachers, and even toleration of subordination and near-abusive training, perhaps females were less inclined to venture into Chinatown ghettos regularly during the 1970s. Today, almost all martial arts schools have some females, though at the championship level, women, of any race or ethnicity, are still a rarity.

Filipino and Pacific Islander/Southeast Asian fighting styles as *kali, silat,* and other forms have also attracted brown and black followings. They deserve greater discussion and discourse in another essay by someone more qualified than I.

Curiously, the 1970s cult following of martial arts films had less influence on yellow (Asian/Pacific Islander American) youth. The Asian Movement was in its heyday, and one of its important thrusts was to oppose stereotyped media images. I remember I wrote a poem "In Memory of Bruce Lee" that conveyed the stance shared by many radical Asian male militants during that time toward the iconic image of Bruce Lee. While we welcomed the fact that Lee was not the conventional servile, desexualized, passive, geekish stereotyped image of Asian males, he nonetheless was part of another kind of stereotype that reduced Asian males to mindless martial arts maniacs. Strong and athletic Asian American males would be called "Bruce" often by black and brown followers of martial arts movies, but such an appellation was only a short distance from being called "chink" or "gook" or "Hop Sing" or "waiter/busboy." As a tall, well-built teenager I was so frequently asked the question "Do you know martial arts?" that I answered this blatantly stereotyped-influenced inquiry in a poem entitled "Third World Understanding":

> All Asians know martial arts like all niggers
> know how to sing and dance.
> Can you dig it?

As-salaam Alaikum.

It was not until much later in life that a black Cherokee friend of mine, Daystarr, struggled with me to embrace the martial arts as part of my heritage that needed to be reclaimed and revolutionized instead of reacted to for the stereotyped dilutions and mis-imaging that had been done.[8] I then proceeded to reject modern dance as a performance movement idiom in my staged productions and to use authentic martial arts as my movement aesthetic and real martial artists and as my stage performers. I also realized that by doing so, I strengthened my work in creating a "popular avant garde" as the martial arts had powerful appeal to youth in general, but especially with black and brown audiences. The legends and stories of the *wuxia* tradition are fertile and ripe for politicization and evoke truly fantastical theatrical possibilities. In the hands of skilled, imaginative, and radical writers, such as the above-mentioned Ruth Margraff, these stories, settings, and characters offer epic, complex, and penetrating dramas with a fresh and volatile mix of realism and metarealism infused with radical political allegory. This kind of stuff will kick the butt of modern dance and the stiff, square, and sterile white self-referential avant garde that pretends to be apolitical in a world that is white and self-indulgent as a function of its own class and racial privileges. It is hoped that today's black and brown martial artists could be so politicized as to understand that in the era of imperialism, the way of the warrior is to be a fighter for people's liberation, for social justice, and to devote oneself to ending exploitation, oppression, and social and environmental degradation.

In creating my large-scale performance works, I have made a commitment to use Chinese martial arts as my primary movement idiom instead of dance forms. I want martial arts to have a particular appeal to urban youth, and especially to oppressed nationality communities, to foster both greater AfroAsian connectivity and consciousness but also to use this popular medium to carry the above-described politics of anti-imperialism and for revolutionary struggle. I have thus far created three major martial arts works: (1) MONKEY, aka *Journey beyond the West: The New Adventures of MONKEY*; (2) VOICE OF THE DRAGON, an epic trilogy consisting of *Once upon a Time in Chinese America . . . The Martial Arts Epic* (Part I), *Shaolin Secret Stories* (Part II), and the yet-to-be-created *Dragon V. Eagle,* aka *Enter: The White Barbarians* (Part III); and (3) *The Black Panther Suite: All Power to the People!* The projects employ a large cast of martial artists, many of whom are African American, Caribbean American, and Puerto Rican American. The first two use the fantasy action adventure genre as a popular vehicle, offering and allowing the medium of the martial arts to promote radical and revolutionary politics.

My latest and third martial arts/music/multimedia performance work is *The Black Panther Suite: All Power to the People!,* which features three martial arts: two black male performers versed in Brazilian *capoiera*, stick and knife fighting of Pacific Islander and Southeast Asian forms, and a *Puertorriquena* trained in Japanese karate. The martial arts symbolize the militant self-defense position of the Black Panthers and the black liberation struggle and the need for organized preparation for revolutionary struggle, especially from the physical attacks of the state, which was so apparent from FBI and police assaults and attacks on the Panthers. Through my work, I hope to politicize the martial arts as a performing art and to build on the anti-imperialist identification and AfroAsian connectivity that emerged during the height of the late 1960s and early 1970s cultural and political movements for liberation.

NOTES

In a slightly different version, my essay is also part of the collection *Afro/Asia: Revolutionary Political and Cultural Connections between African- and Asian-Americans,* ed. Fred Ho and Bill V. Mullen (Durham: Duke University Press, forthcoming).

1. Bruce Lee explained to his mother his explicit intentions toward the white opponents in making the film, *The Return of the Dragon*: "Mom, I'm an Oriental person; therefore, I have to defeat all the whites in the film." Cited in Bruce Thomas, *Bruce Lee: Fighting Spirit* (Berkeley, CA: Frong, 1994), 146.

2. Fred Houn, Interview of Max Roach, *Unity* [a newspaper; the political organ of the defunct League of Revolutionary Struggle, Marxist-Leninist], 12 September 1980, 12.

3. The film has to date grossed over $150 million worldwide, and at the time of its initial release in 1973 set the box office gross of any film from Asia. Available at http://www.jadedragon.com/archives/mafilms (retrieved 10 July 2005).

4. Scholar Vijay Prashad was one among many South Asians during that time who was affected by Lee and *Enter the Dragon*. Vijay Prashad, *Everybody Was Kung Fu Fighting: Afro-Asian Connections and the Myth of Cultural Purity* (Boston, MA: Beacon Press, 2001), 126.

5. Hafez Modirzadeh, "Spiraling Chinese Cyclic Theory and Modal Jazz Practice across Millenia: Proposed Sources and New Perceptions for John Coltrane's Late Musical Conceptions," *Journal of Music in China* 2.2 (Fall 2000): 235–264.

6. Ron Wheeler and David Kaufman, "Is Kung Fu Racist?," in *Afro/Asia: Revolutionary Political and Cultural Connections between African- and Asian-Americans,* ed. Fred Ho and Bill V. Mullen (Durham: Duke University Press, forthcoming).

7. See Robin D. G. Kelley and Betsy Esch, "Black Like Mao: Red China and Black Revolution," *Souls* 1.4 (Fall 1999): 6–41.

8. A sector of the Asian American left during the 1970s did take up martial arts as part of their preparation for revolutionary struggle, as accounted to me by Alex Hing, a former founding member of the Red Guard Party in San Francisco's Chinatown, and as told to me by veteran activist-dancer/choreopher Peggy Choy (whose family has a long history of activism in Hawaii) in her accounts about Asian American left activists in Hawaii.

Afterword
Toward a Black Pacific

Gary Y. Okihiro

"AfroAsian" articulations, as shown in this anthology, undermine the prevailing black/white binary of racializations in the United States. The racial
formation necessitates that intervention. But there are other binaries at
work in the United States' social, not racial, formation. These include the
diasporic binaries of Europe and America,[1] Africa and America, Asia and
America; the bipolar gendering and sexualizing of geographies as in Orientalism; and the distinctions of "native" and "alien." Further, frequently
overlooked in considerations of "Asians" and "Asia" is the Pacific, which
often and mistakenly stands in place of or in reference to Asia, especially
East Asia. Even as Latina/os and Native Americans must be included in
any consideration of the United States' racial formation because of their
distinctions and hence imperative (in truth, "racial triangulation" is a partial rendition of the United States' racial formation), examinations of U.S.
history and Asian or African America must include the Atlantic and the
Pacific and America and the world. I find gestures in all of those directions
in the chapters of this path-breaking collection and propose that they, in
their fullness, constitute the promising future of "AfroAsian studies" as
styled by this book's editors.

Atlantic/Pacific

The American species, a long-standing and persistent idea holds, was
grafted in the "new world" from European ("old") stock. A version of that
Eurocentrism maintains that America was the western terminus of an
Atlantic civilization that embraced Europe's "cultural hearths" and their

diasporas. Columbus's first landing in 1492 in his search for Asia constitutes the beginning of this Atlantic civilization as conceived. His "discovery," although unclear to him to his death, fixed America onto European
maps that located its islands and eastern shores by binding grids of longi-
tude and latitude. Eventually, with the global spread of Europeans and
their disciplines, those coordinates would delineate and encompass the
entire world.

Paul Gilroy takes on that Eurocentrism in his *The Black Atlantic*. In
truth, Gilroy tells us, the book arose from his experience trying to per-
suade students that history and the life of the mind held significance for
their circumscribed interests and pursuits. "I worked hard to punctuate
the flow of the Europe-centered material with observations from the dissonant contributions of black writers to the Enlightenment and counter-
Enlightenment concerns," he remembered of those early morning sociology lectures and his attempts to find readings that would expand his students' horizons:

> *The Black Atlantic* developed from my uneven attempts to show these stu-
> dents that the experience of black people were part of the abstract moder-
> nity they found so puzzling and to produce as evidence some of the things
> that black intellectuals had said—sometimes as defenders of the West,
> sometimes as its sharpest critics—about their sense of embeddedness in the
> modern world.[2]

In his influential intervention, Gilroy describes a Black Atlantic that was
not specifically African, American, Caribbean, or British but was all of those
simultaneously, transcendent of nation, race, and ethnicity and emphati-
cally and mutably mixed and hybrid.

Gilroy's unit of study, in truth, is the old Atlantic world and its pedigree
of the American system, Atlantic civilization, and Eurocentrism.[3] Africans
within that universe become "embedded" within European modernity, and
racialization is more complicated by hybridity, but its constituent parts
remain in essence black and white. Slighted are Native Americans who
preceded and were overwritten by Atlantic civilization, Latina/os who embodied hybridity, and Asians who, like Africans, were transported to America and became thereby "embedded" in the "Black Atlantic."

America is surely a part of the Atlantic world and the Black Atlantic,
but it is also a "cultural hearth" of a Pacific civilization that, like its Atlantic counterpart, was a system of flows of capital, labor, and culture that

produced transnational and hybrid identities, as well as their counter-claims for homogeneity, nationalism, and racial purity. In that sense, I'd like to suggest that the United States is an island surrounded by lands north and south, but also oceans, east and west. And as an island, unlike the imagined, hegemonic insularity of American exceptionalism and con-tinentalism, the United States must be viewed properly as a center with its own integrity but also as a periphery and a fluid space of movements and engagements that resist closure and inevitable or final outcomes.

All of the essays in this book embark on a liberating crossing "beyond the traditional black/white binary," as pointed out by the editors. Addition-ally, racial formations, although grounded in space and time, have never been fully constrained by national boundaries and have always found out-lets across borders, geographic and social fences notwithstanding. Those structures, we know, of binary relations whether of race or nation or gen-der, sexuality, and class, for that matter, form hierarchies of the self and other, the empowered and those separated from power. And hence the consequential intervention of ideas such as those contained in this collec-tion of interstitial identities and even inscriptions that rupture the hege-monic binaries that privilege and impoverish.

In my contribution to this book, I'd like to venture into territory refer-enced but not detailed by several of the contributors to this volume on "AfroAsian" encounters, the Black Pacific. This detour into "the imperial and colonial zones," in Paul Gilroy's words, away from the centers and toward the margins, reveals the workings of empire not only on colonial subjects but also and reciprocally on the colonizers in the return, like spi-ders in the bananas, of the empire. In my consideration of the Black Pacific, I reflect on Oceania's islands, not the Pacific's continental rim, and its inhabitants, Pacific Islanders and Hawaiians, not the "Asians" who are a sub-ject of this collection's study. The quest to widen the purview of our schol-arship across racializations, nations, and fields as articulated by *AfroAsian Encounters* inspires and animates this move toward a Black Pacific.

The temptation is to think about the Pacific like the Atlantic, as a wa-tery crossing between solid, continental landmasses. Apt is the metaphor of a ship, as pointed out by Paul Gilroy, "a living, micro-cultural, micro-political system in motion." Ships, Gilroy explained, shift attention from the shore to the middle passage and the circulation of peoples, ideas, and cultures.[4] In the Pacific, images come to mind of Filipino and Chinese seamen on board Spanish galleons beginning in 1565 plying the trade be-tween Manila and Acapulco, and of Hawaiian sailors who, during the

1830s, comprised the majority of the crews on U.S. ships that carried animal furs from the Pacific Northwest to Canton, China.[5]

But the Pacific is not a negative space between Asia and the United States or the hole in a doughnut, the breakfast food of champions and a tasty trope for the Pacific's rim. Writing of that absence, Samoan novelist and university professor Albert Wendt rejected the "fatal impact theory" of colonial literature that pronounced the death of native cultures with the arrival of the Europeans. "We and our cultures have survived and adapted when we were expected to die, vanish, under the influence of supposedly stronger superior cultures and their technologies," he wrote:

> Our story of the Pacific is that of marvelous endurance, survival and dynamic adaptation, despite enormous suffering under colonialism in some of our countries. We have survived through our own efforts and ingenuity. We have indigenised much that was colonial or foreign to suit ourselves, creating new blends and forms.[6]

Imagine the Pacific as Oceania or the "sea of islands" as reconceived by Wendt and the Tongan writer Epeli Hau'ofa. Instead of a vast and empty ocean dotted by tiny bits of land and reefs as represented by European maps, a sea of islands conjures "a large world in which peoples and cultures moved and mingled, unhindered by boundaries of the kind erected much later by imperial powers," wrote Hau'ofa of Oceania's peoples:[7]

> Oceania is vast, Oceania is expanding, Oceania is hospitable and generous, Oceania is humanity rising from the depths of brine and regions of fire deeper still, Oceania is us. We are the sea, we are the ocean, we must wake up to this ancient truth and together use it to overturn all hegemonic views that aim ultimately to confine us again, physically and psychologically, in the tiny spaces that we have resisted accepting as our sole appointed places, and from which we have recently liberated ourselves. We must not allow anyone to belittle us again, and take away our freedom.[8]

Having left the bounded Atlantic for the expansive Pacific, and with the focus on the sea of islands and not on the crossing, in this, my brief rendition of a "Black Pacific," I expand on three intersections between Pacific Islanders and African Americans. The first involves labor; the second, education; and the third, popular culture. Like the encounter of African and Asian bodies in the Atlantic systems of labor and exchange, European settlers in America "recruited" Pacific Islanders for their plantations in the "New World." The laborers augmented the workforce of Indians and Africans, and their procurement shared features of the African slave trade. In a return of empire, an education designed to colonize Hawaiians in the torrid zone was transplanted in the soil of the temperate zone to choke the aspirations of African Americans following the end of slavery. Hawaiian music constituted another kind of return that initially captured and then was assimilated by "American" music. Those matrices of empire, involving capital and labor, ideology, and culture, map the locations and relations of power and therewith the possibilities for creating, within the interstices, liberating solidarities.

Labor

Agricultural production was the foundation of Peru's economy, and its exports were mainly grown on large plantations of sugar, cotton, olives, grapes, and grains along the country's coastal valleys. After 1854 when slavery was abolished, Peru faced a labor crisis that the formerly enslaved Africans and American Indians could not ease. Between 1849 and 1856, Chinese coolies, or bonded labor, were imported on overcrowded ships, often modeled on African slave ships and called "floating hells," and were sold in Callao to the highest bidder. At least one-third of the coolies died during the transpacific passage because of overcrowding and insufficient food,[9] and once in Peru, a historian noted, the Chinese status was "essentially that of slaves."[10] Despite the odious nature of the traffic, Peru's Congress authorized in 1861 the importation of "Asiatic colonists," a thinly disguised euphemism for "coolies," to cultivate the country's coastal estates. It was under this law that Pacific Islanders came to labor and perish in Peru.

The first ship, the *Adelante,* sailed from Callao in 1862 and returned about three months later with a cargo of 253 Polynesian (Tongarevan) recruits. The sponsors reaped a profit of $40,000 (or a 400 percent return) after selling the men for $200, women for $150, and boys for $100. The ship's design set the standard for others that followed: a hold of three compartments separated by iron bars; hatches with iron gratings over them to prevent escapes; two swivel guns to sweep the deck; muskets, revolvers, and knives in abundance; and extra crew members to guard the hatches day and night. The *Adelante*'s success prompted speculation and a rush on Polynesian labor recruitment, and ships fitted out for the African slave and Chinese coolie trades joined the Peruvian recruiting fleet.

While the initial shipment of Polynesians was accomplished with the cooperation of the British missionaries who labored among them, subsequent recruitments were carried out as armed raids that killed and captured islanders and marched them bound hand and foot to the waiting ships. The devastation was as enormous as the profits were high. Population losses on the islands from raids, deaths, and disease introduced by the invaders ranged from 24 percent on Pukapuka to 79 percent on Nukulaelae. Easter Island, with an estimated population of 4,126 in 1862, lost 1,386 to labor raids and about 1,000 to disease, and thus suffered a 58 percent population decrease. Meanwhile, the brig *Bella Margarita* realized the sum of $46,000 on a single, two-month voyage.[11]

One of the captives, Niuean Taole, described the process called "blackbirding":

> The people of Tokelau were captured in great numbers, more than those that were taken from Niué, and there were some women amongst them. Many of the unsuspecting islanders were made captives on board, when they came expecting to trade. Some of them broke loose in the struggle and leaped overboard. . . . The armed boat crews pursued them, and they were seized and hauled inboard; those that resisted were shot or were killed with cutlasses. . . . As the men and women were brought on board they were thrust down the ladder into the hold to join the Niué people, and then the ships sailed away eastward with the hundreds of captives.[12]

Peru's involvement in the Polynesian traffic ended by 1864, but the effects of that trade transformed many island communities. Perhaps most dramatic was the effect on Easter Island. According to a study:

> The old social order of Easter Island was entirely destroyed in 1862 when Peruvian slave traders kidnapped a large part of the population. They took to the guano islands on the Peruvian coast, not only the king with many members of his family, but a considerable number of learned men (*maori*). This catastrophe, disrupting the traditional mode of living, created a state of anarchy and confusion. But the events of the years that followed were even more disastrous. Epidemics of smallpox, introduced by a few kid-

napped men who returned to their island, decimated the population and struck the last blow to native culture.[13]

One of those who managed to escape Peru was the Niuean, Taole, son of a chief. He was found working at the Callao wharves by Hawaiian seamen on a U.S. whaling ship that had docked there. The Hawaiians convinced the American captain to help Taole, and they dressed him in sailor's clothes and smuggled him on board under the watchful eye of his guards. The ship immediately set sail and managed to escape despite pursuit by a Peruvian government vessel. Taole stayed in Hawai'i for several years before eventually returning home to Niué.[14]

In truth, the Atlantic is never far from the Pacific. That whaling ship, manned by Hawaiian sailors that saved Taole on Peru's coast surely must have originated from the U.S. Northeast. Yankee ships from home ports like Boston and Salem, New Haven and New York, wintered in Hawaiian waters, took on provisions and goods, and enticed Hawaiians to work as sailors on the highways that took them from the islands to British Columbia and Peru back to Hawai'i and on to Canton. From China, they sailed westward into the Indian Ocean, around South Africa's Cape, and across the Atlantic to the U.S. Northeast. Hawaiians, marooned in New York City and Boston and New Haven, were found by religious societies who conceived of the idea of a Hawaiian mission for the glory of god and mammon.

So westward those missionaries went to save the "savage" and benighted race. On October 15, 1819, at the Park Street Church in Boston, the first company of seven missionaries and their wives and children, along with three "natives" of Hawai'i, were formed into a "Church of Christ" and commissioned to go forth to convert the heathens of the Sandwich Islands. "So great was the interest in this missionary enterprise of the Orthodox New England Church," wrote the historian Samuel Eliot Morison, "that over five hundred persons received Holy Communion at a farewell service the following Sabbath."[15] On Saturday morning, October 23, the final farewell took place at Boston's Long Wharf, and after a prayer, speech, and song, the "Church of Christ" took their leave and boarded the brig *Thaddeus,* which weighed anchor and headed out for the open sea.

Among the fifth company of missionaries were the Reverend Richard Armstrong and his wife, Clarissa Chapman, who arrived in Honolulu on May 17, 1832, after an ocean voyage of 173 days.[16] Decades later, on the occasion of her eightieth birthday, Clarissa Chapman Armstrong would recall her early mission days in Hawai'i and the Marquesas as "a life amongst the heathens with the privilege of uplifting dark, degraded hu-manity," or the "children of nature, with no knowledge of civiliza-tion whatever and given over to animal lusts and selfish degradation."[17] A ma-ture Samuel Chapman praised his mother: "It is wonderful how much you have gone through; you have taught a noble lesson to your children. You have helped me and have been in my work in a mar-velous way."[18]

Growing up in Hawai'i, young Samuel played and went to school with his fellow mission children, and he readily distinguished himself and his white friends from the "darkies" like the Hawaiians to whom his parents ministered and his family's Chinese servant, Ah-Kam, "a typical China-man" with a habit for stealing, he wrote.[19] And less charitably, Samuel be-moaned the Chinese as "rat-eaters" and "these sly 'pigtails'" who come to "our Paradise" to despoil it, seeing Hawai'i as merely a place "to grind out money for their gambling . . . and their aged parents. Is the China-man capable of piety?" he pondered.[20] His father, the Reverend Richard Armstrong, described the Hawaiian objects of his affection:

The females are in great need of improvement. Their habits, conversation and mode of living are filthy. They are ignorant and lazy, lack everything like modesty, and hardly know how to do anything. Of course, the mothers being such creatures, you may judge what the children are. In multitudes of cases the pigs are as well taken care of as the children and are nearly as decent and cleanly.[21]

Years later and laboring to uplift another dark and benighted race in the U.S. South, Samuel Chapman Armstrong would fondly recollect his mission days in Hawai'i and conflate in his mind Hawaiians with African Americans and his life's work with that of his parents:

Sometimes, when I stand outside a Negro church, I get precisely the effect of a Hawaiian congregation, the same fullness and heartiness and occa-sional exquisite voices, and am instantly transplanted ten thousand miles away, to the great Kawaiahao church where Father used to preach to 2500 people, who swarmed in on foot and horseback, from shore, and valley and mountain, for miles around. Outside, it was like an encampment, inside it was a sea of dusky faces.[22]

Armstrong was not alone in that coupling of Hawaiians with African Americans. As members of a darker race, they served in the same military units during the Civil War. Armstrong wrote about Kealoha, a private in the 41st Regiment U.S. colored troops, and Kaiwi, a private in the 28th Regiment U.S. colored troops. "Yesterday, as my orderly was holding my horse," he wrote in 1865, "I asked him where he was from. He said he was from Hawaii! He proved to be a full-blood Hawaiian, by the name of Kealoha, who came from the Islands last year."[23] Kealoha and Kaiwi were unexceptional. Armstrong, writing of Hawaiians serving in the Union Army, remarked:

> I found several of them among the Negro regiments. During the bombardment of Fort Harrison, north of the James River, while commanding a support brigade, I heard my Hawaiian name, Kamuela, called from a color-guard, and looking down saw a grinning Kanaka, a corporal, who had recognized me—as cool as a cucumber. Another turned up as a headquarter orderly—holding my horse. I read, in an account of the naval land attack on Fort Fisher, that among the first seamen to volunteer for the deadly work were two Hawaiian sailors. They are all good soldiers; like the Negro, they are noble under leadership, often wonderful in emergencies.[24]

Both Hawai'i and the military figured prominently in the founding of the Hampton Normal and Agricultural Institute by Samuel Chapman Armstrong in 1868. "These schools over which my father as Minister of Education [of the Hawaiian kingdom] had for fifteen years a general oversight, suggested the plan of the Hampton School," he testified. And, "The negro and the Polynesian have many striking similarities. Of both it is true that not mere ignorance, but deficiency of character is the chief difficulty, and that to build up character is the true objective point in education." Further, "morality and industry generally go together. Especially in the weak tropical races, idleness, like ignorance, breeds vice."[25] Labor corrects those character deficiencies that disable the "weak tropical races," and the instilling of correct habits, sired by military regimentation, were the form and object of education. "The average Negro student needs a regime which shall control the twenty-four hours of each day; thus only can the old ideas and ways be pushed out and new ones take their place," Armstrong stated. "The formation of good habits is fundamental in our work. . . . the Negro pupil, like the Negro soldier, is readily transformed under wise control into remarkable tidiness and good conduct generally."[26]

We, of course, know the influence of this brand of education that deferred dreams of full freedom and equality for the life of the hand and not
the life of the mind.[27] As Armstrong put it, "The temporal salvation of the
colored race for some time to come is to be won out of the ground. Skilful
agriculturists and mechanics are needed rather than poets and orators."
And, "Too much is expected of mere book-knowledge; too much is expected of one generation. The real upward movement, the leveling up, not
of persons but of people, will be, as in all history, almost imperceptible,
to be measured only by long periods."[28] A grateful Hampton graduate,
Booker T. Washington, eulogized his great teacher: "My race in this country can never cease to be grateful to General Armstrong for all that he did
for my people and for American civilization. We always felt that many of
the ideas and much of the inspiration he used to such good effect in this
country, he got in Hawaii."[29]

Ideology

Pacific Islander and African American relations in music are as deep as
they remain largely unexplored. I am thinking in particular about the
resistances posed by Hawaiians and African Americans in popular culture
to the crude caricatures of them as "weak tropical races"—idle, ignorant,
but happy and given to dance and song. Both African Americans and Hawaiians appropriated those representations to advance their interests and
musical careers. Of course, one's repossession is another's betrayal, and
mimicry can support even as it can erode the "original." But Hawaiian and
African American musicians worked within tight spaces or race, gender,
sexuality, and nation and their labors can be multiply construed.

The most popular music in the United States before 1925, as indicated
by record and sheet music sales, was apparently "Hawaiian" music. The
foundation of that music was laid by missionaries who taught Hawaiians
to sing Christian hymns and by Mexican cowboys who introduced the
guitar. During the 1830s, the Hawaiian King Kamehameha III recruited
Mexican vaqueros to teach Hawaiians to ride horses and rope and herd the
European-introduced wild cattle that threatened to overwhelm the islands
of Hawai'i and Maui. Joseph Kekuku, in 1885, experimented with the guitar by playing it on his lap, raising the frets, and using a steel slide to produce the glissando sound that mimicked Hawaiian falsetto singing.[30] The
sound he produced soon became a staple of Hawaiian steel guitar playing.

The 1912 hit show on Broadway, *Bird of Paradise*, and the 1915 Panama-Pacific International Exposition in San Francisco led to a boom in Hawaiian music on the landed continent, and nightclubs, theatres, and orchestras hired musicians and dancers to perform "Hawaiian" music. Tin Pan Alley joined in the craze, churning out cartoons like "Wicki Wacki Woo" and "Yaaka Hula Hickey Dula," sang by the many-faced minstrel Al Jolson in 1916 in the Broadway musical comedy, *Robinson Crusoe, Jr.* In fact, some of the earliest Hawaiian music was marketed as "coon songs" and "oriental coon songs" in the late nineteenth and early twentieth centuries.[31]

Hawaiian and African American musics bore resemblances. As pointed out by the well-known Hawaiian musician and composer, Johnny Noble, both musics drew from Christian hymns and their harmonies. Before the arrival of Europeans, Hawaiian music was limited to chants consisting of two or three pitches composed by the priests in praise of gods and kings and in remembrance of historical events. The hula originally referred to the chant and the facial and hand gestures that accompanied it. Similarly, Noble observed, jazz was essentially dance music, and in the blues, singers used their bodies and facial expressions to convey the song's message. And common to both Hawaiian music and the blues or "true jazz," Noble wrote, were

> the use of the slur (glissando or vibrato); the constant moving of the melodic line in and out of microtones; a tendency to mingle major and minor modes; and a regular beat, usually depending on drums, with stressed off-beat accents. Also, both jazz and early Hawaiian music were natural and spontaneous; both were personal and vocalized; and both affected the senses and feelings with a certain haunting quality.[32]

Noble's first hit was, appropriately, "Hula Blues."

Hawaiian and African American musics differed and diverged through innovation and commercialization, but there were also instances of convergences when Hawaiian and African American musicians made crossover appearances. Jazz's influence on Sol Hoopii, perhaps the greatest slide guitarist of his time, was profound and evident in many of his recordings, and Ben Nawahi played with greats like the New Orleans singer and stride pianist Walter "Fats" Pichon and recorded "California Blues" and "Black Boy Blues" in the 1920s and 1930s. Louis Armstrong, among others, played with Hawaiian bands and in the Hawaiian music vein, and the influential blues guitarist Sylvester Weaver merged Hawaiian with African American blues slide guitar style. Oscar "Buddy" Woods was inspired to take up the steel guitar after hearing a traveling Hawaiian troupe in his hometown, Shreveport, Louisiana, and the black bluesman, Casey Bill Weldon, the self-proclaimed "Hawaiian Guitar Wizard," showed in his recordings the smooth and sweet syncretism of blues and Hawaiian steel guitar music.[33]

Hawaiian musicians toured the United States and Europe as "colored artists," and their music and dance advanced and complemented the commerce-driven dreams of tropical paradise, gentle breezes, swaying palm trees, and moonlight on water. Evoking that exoticism, the all-girl band, the International Sweethearts of Rhythm, active from 1937 to 1949, played to white and black audiences. The band itself was a racial crossover of mixed-race (black and white), Asian, Latina, Native American, and white musicians. The *Chicago Defender* called the Sweethearts a "sensational mixed band which is composed of Race, Mexicans, Chinese, and Indian girls" who played "the savage rhythms of ancient African tom-toms, the weird beat of the Indian war dance, and the quaintness and charm of the Orient."[34] That "internationalism," of course, functioned to exclude African, Asian, Native Americans, and Latina/os from the American body, but it also destabilized dominant notions of race and its distinctions, gender and its separate spheres, and U.S. exceptionalism and its parochialism.

During the 1960s, Hawaiians inspired a cultural renaissance involving language and artistic expression that supported a political movement to regain sovereignty and human and civil rights. A U.S.-abetted revolt had seized the Hawaiian kingdom in 1893, and the United States annexed the islands in 1898 without the consent of the governed. The colonization of Hawai'i included prominently the educational work of missionaries, like Richard and Clarissa Armstrong, and its suppression of native culture and promotion of useful labor and subservience, as taught by Samuel Chapman Armstrong. The revival of language, poetry, song, and dance was in resistance to colonialism and cultural hegemony and erasures and reached into Hawaiian pasts but also into allied oppositional cultures.

Reggae made its way to Hawai'i in the 1970s, and its fusion with Hawaiian forms led to the "Jawaiian" rage of the following decades. Jamaican and Hawaiian, Jawaiian has an emphatic bass sound, includes instruments like trumpets and timpani drums, uses both English and Hawaiian lyrics, and dance or hula frequently accompany songs in live performances. Besides its appeal as a musical form, reggae's attraction included its anti-colonial, anti-imperialist, and class struggle messages, along with its transcendence and the unity of all peoples. As remembered by a Hawai'i record industry executive: "Back in the 1970s and '80s, some Hawaiian [sovereignty and cultural activists] were reggae fanatics, as well as involved in the Hawaiian movement. . . . Back then, it wasn't the rhythm alone, it was the message; the message in reggae was closer to what we felt about getting the islands back—it was the message of freedom from oppression."[35]

Rap's appearance in Hawai'i exemplified its global spread and consumption, but its particular appeal in the islands was as a culture of resistance, like reggae. The group Sudden Rush promotes itself as "the true originators of *na mele paleoleo*" or Hawaiian rap music, and they are one of the few groups in the islands who devote themselves entirely to this genre. Using English, Hawaiian, and Creole ("pidgin" English), Sudden Rush addresses issues of love of the land and anticolonialism. A local critic wrote of their music: "Blending Hawaiian chant and English lyrics with hip-hop's gritty dance beat, [Sudden Rush] creat[es] a polished, urban sound on songs that explore topical Hawaiian issues like sovereignty, drug use, and cultural pride. This is no weak imitation of black rap music, but an exciting, innovative hybrid."[36] While rapping, Sudden Rush might also be chanting poetry, the Hawaiian definition of song in which poetics can only exist through music.

Culture

In positing a "Black Pacific," we must acknowledge that there is no Pacific region as an "objective" given, as pointed out by historian and cultural critic Arif Dirlik, only "a competing set of ideational constructs that project upon a certain location on the globe the imperatives of interest, power, or vision of these historically produced relationships."[37] And yet, those discourses are not simply plural but are oppositional in relations of power, one seeking dominion and the other resisting that imposition. I have alluded in this chapter to several such oppositions: Atlantic Europe and the Black Atlantic, the Atlantic and the Pacific, the Pacific Rim and the sea of islands, and the Black Atlantic and the Black Pacific. The north Atlantic might be racialized as white, while the south Atlantic, black. The Atlantic, sighted from the U.S. shore, might mark the familiar, while the Pacific, the alien other. With the focus on the crossing, the relations between Asia and America might obscure the activities of Pacific Islanders in their Oceania. And the Black Pacific must not reproduce the white or Black Atlantic and their embeddedness in European modernity.

In this conjuring of a "Black Pacific," it is instructive to realize that studies of Samuel Chapman Armstrong and his Hampton Institute focus almost exclusively on the relations between blacks and whites.[38] Needless to say, African Americans were the principals in this "mis-education," as aptly characterized and critiqued by Carter G. Woodson.[39] But a more complete understanding of Armstrong and Hampton is gained through insights garnered from their origins in Hawai'i. After all, the idea for Hampton, Armstrong confessed, came from frolics in his "Pacific Paradise." And Hampton's story is partial and misleading without a consideration of its offshoots—besides Booker T. Washington's Tuskegee Institute, the Carlisle Indian School in Pennsylvania established by Captain Richard Henry Pratt in 1879. Like Tuskegee, Carlisle was modeled on and a direct descendant of Hampton's industrial education. Armstrong, in endorsing Pratt's plan, contrasted the experiences of African and Native Americans: "The severe discipline of slavery strengthened a weak race. Professed friendship for a strong one has weakened it. A cruel semblance of justice has done more harm than oppression could have done. The Negro is strong, the Indian weak, because the one is trained to labor and the other is not." And, "The Indian question will never be settled till you make the Indian blister his hands," he wrote. "No people ever emerged from barbarism that did not emerge through labor."[40]

In this consideration of intersections, Armstrong and Hampton must not stand in place of Hawai'i and Carlisle, nor should African American history subsume or model the pasts of Hawaiians and Native Americans. And Hawaiian history for the most part has ignored African and Native American pasts, despite the fact that Hawai'i was an intimate partner of Hampton and "Negro education" and Carlisle and "Indian education." The Hawaiian mission, Hampton Institute, and Carlisle School are distinctive and represent separate and diverse histories. And yet we know their common ground, which is seeded with paternalism in the ostensible uplift of inferior and savage races and watered generously with the gospel of white supremacy. In addition, the enslavement of Africans and native peoples and indentures of Asian and Pacific Islanders in America constitute separate and unitary histories, and Hawaiian and African American musics bear complicities with and pose resistances to cultural erasures, appropriations, and installations.

Those recognitions of divergences and convergences, as this book on "AfroAsian" encounters reveals, must inform our scholarship and politics. So, too, must the lesson of the 1955 Bandung Conference guide us, in both the spirit of "AfroAsian" unity in the global struggle against colonialism and its containment by the equally widespread and potent forces of capitalism and neocolonialism. *AfroAsian Encounters* contends that the discrete boundaries of racializations, nation-states, and geographies, tragically, have demarcated our subject matters and fields of study and have grounded our imaginations and curbed our solidarities. Human activity is much too intemperate, much too unruly to constrain by pitiful disciplines like race and area studies or borders erected by states and patrolled by nationalisms, despite the monoculturalists and unilateralists who now rule the U.S. night. Moreover, transgressions, like a "Black Pacific," can easily lure us to forsake the petty, barren lands for the vast, restless, and fecund ocean beyond.

NOTES

1. By "America," I mean the "Americas," and when I deploy the "U.S." I reference the nation. Similarly, "African, Asian, and Pacific America" encompasses America broadly, including the continents north and south, Central America, and the islands along and between the continents' edges. Hence the relevance of Peru in this discussion of African, Asian, and Pacific America.

2. Paul Gilroy, *The Black Atlantic: Modernity and Double Consciousness* (Cambridge: Harvard University Press, 1993), ix.

3. See, e.g., Michael Kraus, *The Atlantic Civilization: Eighteenth-Century Origins* (Ithaca: Cornell University Press, 1949); Ralph Davis, *The Rise of Atlantic Economies* (Ithaca: Cornell University Press, 1973); Ian K. Steele, *The English Atlantic, 1675–1740: An Exploration of Communication and Community* (New York: Oxford University Press, 1986); Herbert S. Klein, *African Slavery in Latin America and the Caribbean* (New York: Oxford University Press, 1986); Marcus Rediker, *Between the Devil and the Deep Blue Sea: Merchant Seamen, Pirates, and the Anglo-American Maritime World, 1700–1750* (Cambridge: Cambridge University Press, 1987); Philip D. Curtin, *The Rise and Fall of the Plantation Complex: Essays in Atlantic History* (Cambridge: Cambridge University Press, 1990); and Robin Blackburn, *The Making of New World Slavery: From the Baroque to the Modern, 1492–1800* (London: Verso, 1997).

4. Gilroy, *Black Atlantic*, 4. On traveling cultures, encounters, and translations, see James Clifford, *Routes: Travel and Translation in the Late Twentieth Century* (Cambridge: Harvard University Press, 1997).

5. On Pacific Islanders on European ships, see David A. Chappell, *Double Ghosts: Oceanian Voyagers on Euroamerican Ships* (Armonk: M. E. Sharpe, 1997); Richard H. Dillon, "Kanaka Colonies in California," *Pacific Historical Review* 24

(February 1955): 17–23; Janice K. Duncan, "Kanaka World Travelers and Fur Company Employees, 1785–1860," *Hawaiian Journal of History* 7 (1973): 93–111; and Tom Koppel, *Kanaka: The Untold Story of Hawaiian Pioneers in British Columbia and the Pacific Northwest* (Vancouver: Whitecap Books, 1995).

6. Albert Wendt, ed., *Nuanua: Pacific Writing in English since 1980* (Honolulu: University of Hawai'i Press, 1995), 3.

7. Albert Wendt, "Towards a New Oceania," *Mana* 1:1 (January 1976): 49–60; and Epeli Hau'ofa, "Our Sea of Islands," *Contemporary Pacific* 6:1 (Spring 1994): 153–154.

8. Hau'ofa, "Our Sea of Islands," 160.

9. Watt Stewart, *Chinese Bondage in Peru: A History of the Chinese Coolie in Peru, 1849–1874* (Durham: Duke University Press, 1951), 21–22.

10. Frederick B. Pike, *A Modern History of Peru* (London: Weidenfeld and Nicolson, 1967), 112.

11. H. E. Maude, *Slavers in Paradise: The Peruvian Slave Trade in Polynesia, 1862–1864* (Stanford: Stanford University Press, 1981), 7, 14, 15–18, 194. In all, about 3,634 Pacific Islanders were recruited for work in Peru. Ibid., 188.

12. Quoted in ibid., 72–73.

13. Alfred Metraux, "The Kings of Easter Island," *Journal of the Polynesian Society* 46 (1937): 41.

14. Maude, *Slavers in Paradise*, 180–181. Hawai'i recruited Pacific Islanders for its sugar plantations in 1877 to 1887. See J. A. Bennett, "Immigration, 'Blackbirding,' Labour Recruiting? The Hawaiian Experience, 1877–1887," *Journal of Pacific History* 11:1–2 (1976): 3–27.

15. Samuel Eliot Morison, "Boston Traders in the Hawaiian Islands, 1789–1823," *Proceedings of the Massachusetts Historical Society* 54 (October 1920): 9–10.

16. *Missionary Album: Portraits and Biographical Sketches of the American Protestant Missionaries to the Hawaiian Islands* (Honolulu: Hawaiian Mission Children's Society, 1969), 30–31, 33.

17. Clarissa Armstrong, letter addressed to her children and grandchildren, dated May 15, 1885, included in *C.C.A.: May 15, 1885, 80 Years* (Hampton: Normal School Steam Press, 1885), 29, 30.

18. Samuel Chapman, letter addressed to his mother, dated May 5, 1885, included in ibid., 21.

19. S. C. A. [Samuel Chapman Armstrong], "Reminiscences," in *Richard Armstrong: America, Hawaii* (Hampton: Normal School Steam Press, 1887), 103.

20. Samuel Chapman Armstong to "Dear Cousins," Hampton, Virginia, February 5, 1881, and May 11, 1881, in *Children of the Mission, 1830–1900* (Honolulu, Hawaiian Mission Children's Society).

21. Folder, Richard Armstrong, 1805–1860, M5, B, Ar5, Honolulu, Hawaiian Mission Children's Society.

22. S. C. A. [Samuel Chapman Armstrong], "Reminiscences," 74–75.

23. William H. D. King, "A Son of Hawaii in the Civil War: Samuel Chapman Armstrong, Brevet Brigadier General, U.S.A.," *Hawaii Guardsman* (May 1954): 2–3.

24. S. C. A. [Samuel Chapman Armstrong], "Reminiscences," 84.

25. S. C. Armstrong, "Lessons from the Hawaiian Islands," *Journal of Christian Philosophy* (January 1884): 213.

26. Samuel Chapman Armstrong, *Education for Life* (Hampton: Press of the Hampton Normal and Agricultural Institute, 1913), 40.

27. See, e.g., Donald Spivey, *Schooling for the New Slavery: Black Industrial Education, 1868–1915* (Westport: Greenwood Press, 1978); and Robert Francis Engs, *Educating the Disfranchised and Disinherited: Samuel Chapman Armstrong and Hampton Institute, 1839–1893* (Knoxville: University of Tennessee Press, 1999).

28. Armstrong, *Education for Life*, 21, 29.

29. *Dedication of the General Samuel Chapman Armstrong Memorial*, January 30, 1913, Pauahi Hall, Oahu College, B, Ar683d, Honolulu, Hawaiian Mission Children's Society.

30. On the controversy surrounding Kekuku as the originator of the Hawaiian slide guitar, see George S. Kanahele, ed., *Hawaiian Music and Musicians: An Illustrated History* (Honolulu: University Press of Hawai'i, 1979), 365–368; and Lorene Ruymar, *The Hawaiian Steel Guitar and Its Great Musicians* (Anaheim Hills: Centerstream Publishing, 1996), 16–26.

31. See, e.g., the sheet music covers for "My Honolulu Lady" (1898), "My Gal from Honolulu" (1899), and "My Bamboo Queen" (1903).

32. Gurre Ploner Noble, *Hula Blues: The Story of Johnny Noble, Hawaii, Its Music and Musicians* (Honolulu: Tongg Publishing, 1948), 46–47.

33. *Sol Hoopii: Master of the Hawaiian Guitar*, 2 vols, Rounder Records; *King Bennie Nawahi: Hawaiian String Virtuoso*, Yazoo 2055; *Hawaiian Music: Honolulu, Hollywood, Nashville, 1927–1944*, Frémeaux and Associés; and *Casey Bill: The Hawaiian Guitar Wizard, 1935–1938*, EPM, Blues Collection. See also, Al Handa, "The National Steel Guitar Part Four," July 1988, available at www.nationalguitars.com/part4.html (retrieved July 2003); and Ruymar, *Hawaiian Steel Guitar*, 51–52.

34. As quoted in Sherrie Tucker, *Swing Shift: "All-Girl" Bands of the 1940s* (Durham: Duke University Press, 2000), 183–184.

35. As quoted in Ku'ualoha Ho'omanawanui, "Yo Brah, It's Hip Hop Jawaiian Style: The Influence of Reggae and Rap on Contemporary Hawaiian Music," *Hawaii Review* 56 (Summer 2001): 153.

36. Ibid., 155.

37. Arif Dirlik, "The Asia-Pacific Idea: Reality and Representation in the Invention of a Regional Structure," *Journal of World History* 3.1 (Spring 1992): 56.

38. See, e.g., James D. Anderson, "The Hampton Model of Normal School Industrial Education, 1868–1900," in *New Perspectives in Black Educational History*, ed. Vincent P. Franklin and James D. Anderson (Boston: G. K. Hall, 1978), 61–96; and Spivey, *Schooling for the New Slavery*.

39. Carter G. Woodson, *The Mis-education of the Negro* (Washington, D.C.: Associated Publishers, 1933).

40. As quoted by Armstrong's daughter in Edith Armstrong Talbot, *Samuel Chapman Armstrong: A Biographical Study* (New York: Doubleday 1904), 214, 278.

About the Contributors

Mita Banerjee is Professor and Chair of American Studies at the University of Siegen, Germany. She is the author of *The Chutneyfication of History: Salman Rushdie, Michael Ondaatje, Bharati Mukherjee and the Postcolonial Debate* and *Race-ing the Century*. She is currently working on a postcolonial study of the American Renaissance.

Cathy Covell Waegner has been on the English faculty of the University of Siegen, Germany, since 1977. She is co-editor of *Literature on the Move: Comparing Diasporic Ethnicities in Europe and the Americas* and a member of the executive board of MESEA (Society of Multi-Ethnic Studies: Europe and the Americas).

Samir Dayal is Associate Professor of English at Bentley College, Massachusetts. He is the editor of Julia Kristeva's *Crisis of the European Subject,* Michael Gorkin and Rafiqa Othman's *Three Mothers, Three Daughters,* Lucien Gubbay's *Jews under Islam,* François Rachline's *Don Juan's Wager,* and Patricia Gherovici's *The Puerto Rican Syndrome* (forthcoming), among other books. He is Cultural Studies series editor for Other Press in New York. Currently, among other projects, he is at work on a book on colonial and postcolonial Indian subject construction and on a collection of essays entitled *Postcolonial Diasporas.*

Fred Ho is a Chinese American composer, baritone saxophonist, writer, producer, revolutionary matriarchal socialist activist, and leader of the AfroAsian Music Ensemble and the Monkey Orchestra, and co-leader of the Brooklyn Sax Quartet with David Bindman. He and co-editor Bill Mullen have collaborated on the anthology *Afro/Asia: Revolutionary Political and Cultural Connections between African Americans and Asian-Americans* (forthcoming). He and co-editor Ron Sakolsky won the 1996 American Book Award for the anthology *Sounding Off! Music as Subversion/Resistance/Revolution.* Ho's own collection of writings, *Wicked Theory/Naked Practice,* will be published in 2006.

332 About the Contributors

Lourdes López Ropero is Lecturer in the English Department at the University of Alicante, Spain, where she teaches American and postcolonial literature. She is the author of *The Anglo-Caribbean Migration Novel: Writing from the Diaspora.*

Sanda Mayzaw Lwin is Assistant Professor in the Department of English and the American Studies Program at Yale University. She is currently completing a book called *The Constitution of Asian America* that analyzes the legal and cultural formation of Asian America through literary and legal narratives of citizenship, immigration, and exclusion.

Bill V. Mullen is Professor of English and Director of American Studies at Purdue University. He is author of *Afro-Orientalism* and editor, with Cathryn Watson, of *Crossing the World Color Line: W. E. B. Du Bois's Writings on Asia.*

Gary Y. Okihiro is Professor of International and Public Affairs and Director of the Center for the Study of Ethnicity and Race at Columbia University. He is author of eight books, including, most recently, *Common Ground: Re-imagining American History* and *The Columbia Guide to Asian American History.* He received the Lifetime Achievement Award from the American Studies Association and is past president of the Association for Asian American Studies.

Vijay Prashad is Associate Professor of International Studies at Trinity College. He has published eight books, including two that were chosen by the *Village Voice* as books of the year: *Karma of Brown Folk* and *Everybody Was Kung Fu Fighting: Afro-Asian Connections and the Myth of Cultural Purity.* His most recent book is *Darker Nations: The Rise and Fall of the Third World.*

Gita Rajan was named Jane Watson Irwin Visiting Chair of Women's Studies at Hamilton College in 2004–2006. She also is Associate Professor in the English Department at Fairfield University. She is co-editor of *New Cosmopolitanisms: South Asians in the United States* and *A Cultural Studies Reader: History, Theory, Practice, English Postcoloniality? —Literatures from around the World and Postcolonial Discourse and Changing Cultural Contexts.* She is currently working on a book on South Asian public intellectuals, feminist ethics, and globalization.

Heike Raphael-Hernandez is Professor of English at the University of Maryland University College in Europe. She is editor of *Blackening Europe:*

The African American Presence and co-editor, with Dorothea Fischer-Hornung, of *Holding Their Own: Perspectives on the Multi-Ethnic Literatures of the United States.*

Greg Robinson, a native of New York City, is Associate Professor of History at l'Université du Québec à Montréal in Montreal, Canada. He is the author of *By Order of the President: FDR and the Internment of Japanese Americans* and associate editor of *The Encyclopedia of African American Culture and History* and its supplements. His current research traces postwar civil rights coalitions between African Americans and Japanese Americans.

Shannon Steen is Assistant Professor in the Department of Theater, Dance, and Performance Studies at the University of California, Berkeley, where she also serves as Affiliated Faculty for the Program in American Studies. A specialist in critical race and performance theory, she writes on the intersection of Asian and African American racial determinations. She is currently finishing her book *Racial Geometries: The Black Atlantic, the Asian/ Pacific, and American Performance.*

David W. Stowe is Director of the American Studies Program at Michigan State University and a core faculty member of the Asian Studies Center. His books include *How Sweet the Sound: Music in the Spiritual Lives of Americans* and *Swing Changes: Big Band Jazz in New Deal America.*

Cynthia Tolentino is Assistant Professor of English at the University of Oregon. She is currently completing a manuscript that examines the relationship between sociological studies of race and U.S. ethnic literatures of the 1940s and 1950s. She is a member of the editorial collective for the journal *American Studies Asia.*

Eleanor Ty is Chair of and Professor in the Department of English and Film Studies, Wilfrid Laurier University. Author of *The Politics of the Visible in Asian North American Narratives*; *Empowering the Feminine: The Narratives of Mary Robinson, Jane West, and Amelia Opie, 1796–1812*; and *Unsex'd Revolutionaries: Five Women Novelists of the 1790s*, she has edited *Memoirs of Emma Courtney* and *The Victim of Prejudice* by Mary Hays. With Donald Goellnicht, she has co-edited *Asian North American Identities beyond the Hyphen.*

Oliver Wang holds a Ph.D. in ethnic studies from the University of California at Berkeley. Since 1991, he has written extensively on Asian Americans and urban culture for both academic and trade presses. He has written extensively on music, film, and popular culture for *Vibe,* the *Village Voice,* National Public Radio, *SF Bay Guardian, LA Weekly, Wax Poetics,* and other publications. He is the editor and co-author of *Classic Material: The Hip-Hop Album Guide.*

Deborah Elizabeth Whaley is Faculty in the Africana Studies Program at the University of Arizona. Her research and teaching fields include comparative American studies, Africana studies, feminist theory, cultural studies, and popular and visual culture. Currently, she is completing a book manuscript about the cultural and public sphere work of Black sororities.

Index

Wong, Shawn, 22, 247
Woods, Oscar "Buddy," 324
Woodson, Carter G., 326
Works Progress Administration
(WPA), 174, 184n5
Wright, Richard, xii, xxi, 36, 38, 40,
47n7, 246, 261; *Black Power,* 251;
The Color Curtain, xi, xx, 251–252;
"How Bigger was Born," 37

Wu, Frank, 2, 3
Wyatt, Richard, 217, 218–219

Yellowface, 174, 181, 188–201, 202n14,
205–207, 223–237
Young, Al, 174
Young Lords, xiii, 300
Yu, Henry, 38
Yung, Judy, 41